Creating a Theatre in Your Classroom

Creating
A Theatre
In Your Classroom

Edited by
BERNIE WARREN

CAPTUS UNIVERSITY PUBLICATIONS

Creating a Theatre in Your Classroom

Canadian Cataloguing in Publication Data
Main entry under title:

Creating a theatre in your classroom

Includes bibliographical references and index.

ISBN 1-895712-54-8

1. Drama in education. I. Warren, Bernie, 1953–
PN3171.C74 1995   371.3'32   C94–932648–8

Copyright © 1995 by the editor
              and Captus Press Inc.

Back cover photo: Tory James, Windsor (Dec. 92)

0 9 8 7 6 5 4 3 2 1
Printed and bound in Canada

Table of Contents

v

4 Developing a Personal Praxis: Making Connections Between Theory and Practice

Epilogue: A Lifetime's Work in Educational Drama/Theatre

Reference Section

$\mathcal{F}$oreword/$\mathcal{F}$orward

RICHARD COURTNEY

$\mathcal{T}$ he reader of this book should be forewarned (appropriately, in a foreword) that it contains some disturbing ideas. Bernie Warren has gathered together some excellent papers, written on intriguing subjects, which make for "a really good read." But between the cracks of the framework, the discerning reader will discover some assumptions that may lead her into re-thinking some basic and fundamental notions.

For, to uncover this book's secret from the very beginning, the use of dramatic action in the learning and teaching processes has begun a 20th century educational revolution. This foreword, looking forward, expects its fruition in the next century.

The dramatic act itself is used in two ways: 1) as a role enactment, or 2) as an act of self-presentation. When we "put oneself in someone else's place," "step in someone else's shoes," and "see things from their point of view," we create a fiction — one that is meaning-giving and at the core of which lies Buber's "I and Thou." In our self-presentation we flexibly take the social roles of "parent" or "spouse," "worker" or "boss" and, thereby, we: a) dramatize ourselves in a specific context, and b) negotiate meaning with others. And make no mistake about it: **when** schooling is based on dramatic action of such kinds, education is very different from normal forms of instruction in Western schools.

$\mathcal{S}$ ince educational drama began in the early years of the century, **the implications of this idea have been experienced somewhat differently according to the context in which they occurred**. As John McLeod rightly tells us in this book, the context affects how the criteria for drama are applied, and what choices are made.

Caldwell Cook's "the play way" worked them out in practice just before and during World War I. Winifred Ward experienced them in the America of the depression and the idealistic hope of a better future. For Maisie Cobby the implications of the idea existed in a Europe about to come face to face with the horrors of fascism; and then in a Nigeria facing military totalitarianism. For Peter Slade the context was World War II and the euphoria that came after it. In the reaction from that euphoria, Brian Way rejected the "intellectualism" that he thought caused it and he returned to essences — the senses, imagination and intuition. Geraldine Brain Siks experienced the implications of the idea in an America that, because the Soviets put *sputnik* into orbit first, switched from progressivism to behaviourism in education; as a result, her first book, written in a progressive context, is sub-titled *An Art for Children,* but her *Drama With Children* is set in a world of hard-nosed "behavioural objectives." Dorothy Heathcote and Gavin Bolton experienced the implications of the idea in a Britain that, after a generation of solid drama teacher training, had many experienced drama teachers who wanted more than the pioneers could offer — and in a society divided by extreme political views.

In other words, if we disagree with one of these authors, we should not blame them for living at a different time from ourselves. We cannot say that any one authority is "better" or "worse" than another. What we can say is that by using dramatic acts they are similar, but their differences are those of context.

This can be illustrated most clearly if we look at the practices of educational drama in some non-English-speaking localities. Penina Mlama in Tanzania takes her students from the University of Dar es Salaam into the backstreets of the city where they resuscitate forgotten tribal rituals from the bush among the children, helped by their parents. Drama teachers must work with great circumspection in Moslem countries: thus Métin And takes his students from the University of Ankara into the remote villages of Turkey where they learn rituals that are as old as the Trojan horse; they then perform them in Ankara to modern Turks as a form of generalized education. In mainland China, where the government rejects all notions of "educational drama" as a school subject, paradoxically, Western university teachers of ESL through dramatic activity are welcomed with open arms — because it works! Gisèle Barret of the University of Montreal teaches *expression dramatique* (a form of multi-media creative drama participated in by the teacher) which has spread so quickly throughout francophone countries that now even the Portuguese government sends groups of students annually to study with Barret. All these teachers work in particular contexts and they treat dramatic actions in particular ways: they use drama in the framework of the circumstances in which they work.

In this book, the living context for Lynn Dalrymple is Zululand in South Africa, which is very different from, say, John McLeod's context in Melbourne, Australia. And although Alistair Martin-Smith and Belarie Hyman Zatzman both work in Ontario, schooling is the context of one and university drama is the context of the other.

That the context is a primary consideration in educational drama has considerable implications, ones that alter many typical Western educational priorities: personalized teaching with small groups of 15 maximum versus abstract teaching to classes of 25 or more; personalized assessment (or the self-assessment that Rob Watling talks of) versus comparison with a so-called norm (the iniquitous Bell-curve); individual differences versus testing across systems; student activity and research versus passive receptivity of information; independent classroom-based curricula versus a system-wide or common curriculum; competition with the self versus rivalry with others; content from local cultures versus national or regional content; the valuing of mediate knowing (drama being a medium with a unique message), together with tacit and intuitive knowing, versus objective (abstract) knowledge; work as play versus work as drudgery; freedom of student choice versus teacher direction; the multiple roles of the teacher versus the teacher as instructor, and so on.

These implications were inherent in The Play Way of 1917 if we look carefully enough. It is no wonder then, that educational drama has always been feared by number-crunchers, preordinate social scientists, and the political extremists of both left or right. This is because spontaneous drama is "democratic" in the full sense of the word: it always provides a social critique that is the students' own. Teachers who use drama (falsely) for political ends are, therefore, engaged in overkill.

*A*ll the authors in this book focus on the importance of dramatic action, but appropriately they come at the issues in their own specific ways: their particular perspectives lead to specific methods. Bert Amies, an educational drama specialist in England, and George Mager, a dance/drama specialist working with disabled people in Montreal, both use personal narrative as their methodology; but where Amies is inclusive, Mager uses specific criteria to be exclusive. In contrast, Keith Yon uses a framework of personal narrative for a comparative method of description and analysis in telling of his experiences in the famous school, Risinghill, in England, and in Montreal; with great consistency he then uses the comparative method to analyse brief case studies of drama work with a number of classes. Belarie Hyman-Zatzman uses a framework of personal narrative to analyse the curricula issues of drama departments in Canadian universities according to criteria used in those departments — "scene study," "the prompt book," etc. Finally, Lynn Dalyrmple uses the concepts of history and educational change to analyse the effect of apartheid on black educational drama in South Africa. Bernie Warren has rightly chosen papers that reflect different perspectives on, and methods of working in, educational drama.

But this raises a number of issues about perspectives and methods. When schoolchildren work in educational drama, we expect them to improvise freely within a specific structure: within one group, each child puts his or her ideas into a new whole and the result is a performance in which they all share — and which they share with others. If we are to write about educational drama — to study it, not to experience it — then we should use a similar methodology. If we choose a framework of a psychologist, say, or a sociologist, then what we write is theirs not ours — it does not focus on dramatic action but on the concepts of social science. We cannot write of dramatic action while we experience it. But the least we can do is use a similar approach to that of dramatic action.

In that case, we describe, compare or analyse from our perspective: what we see, hear, feel etc. We can then allow others to do the same from their point of view. If, at best, three of us do this, we provide the data with the triangularity so beloved of researchers; then, when we compare the results from all three, we have evolved a full comparative method that also approximates to the way players operate within educational drama action. What emerges is a genuinely **dramatic method of research.**

Try it yourself with the chapters in this book. They are so rich that it is very revealing.

*T*he metaphor of "classroom as theatre" is an intriguing one in the context of the Western world at the end of the 20th century. From the infamous Bonington Hotel meetings of January 1948, the field split into two camps: between those who advocated process (the use of spontaneous creative drama) and those who stressed the art form (theatre arts, the school play, and theatre for young audiences) — with Peter Slade on one side and George Devine on the other. Intriguingly prior to this, both creative drama and the school play were seen as two aspects of the same activity. Now, after the recession of the 1980s and the severe cutbacks in educational dram and theatre, the field has coalesced once more — but in a new context.

In the 1990s, most teachers understand that dramatic action is the focus of their work and that it has many uses and applications: formal and informal; in school classrooms or on school stages; in theatre or in therapy; in churches, youth clubs, business, administration, or in the training of astronauts. **It is in its use that drama differs.**

But "the classroom as theatre" has a double meaning: 1) the teacher as actor and the learner as audience, or vice versa; or 2) the teacher and learner as players with the rest of the world as spectators. Both a metaphor and a dramatic act have double meanings: they are ambiguous. They can mean A from one perspective or Z from another view. When I "put myself in someone else's place," I create **a double relation**: myself and another are interchangeable — we are living metaphors, one to the other. We are both metaphorized as "costumed players." To the player, one part of the metaphor is "really real" (the self) and one is "not 'really real'" (the fictional other). Yet they co-exist.

In a homologous way, the literary metaphor "the roses in her cheeks" has a prime subject ("cheeks") and a secondary subject ("roses") which, brought together in one idea, bring about a double and ambiguous meaning: we can emphasize the prime subject ("the roses **in her cheeks**") which is the normal usage, or the secondary subject ("**the roses** in her cheeks"). Both, by suggesting more than one meaning, are ambiguous — perhaps, even paradoxical.

Moreover, there are metaphorical relations in all media: drama and theatre, music and dance, painting and sculpture, language and architecture. To turn McLuhan on his head: the medium is the metaphoric message. Do the metaphors of drama (the double relations) affect our understanding of metaphors in other media? I can only guess that they do. (Perhaps this is a subject for some future dissertation?)

"The classroom as theatre" is ambiguous in a similar way: from its double meaning other meanings emerge. "All the world's a stage..." or "We are such stuff / As dreams are made on..." or "The play's the thing / In which I'll catch the conscience of a king..." It may well be, as Barbara MacKay suggests, that theatre developed from story-telling and ritual or, before that, from the ritual-myth when human origins were united in a myth (story) that was enacted (ritual). In each case, what was **done** was metaphoric and ambiguous with a plethora of meanings.

"The classroom as theatre" implies a similar degree of ambiguity, whether that be in the collective creation described by Jeffrey Goffin; the symbolic rituals used by Alistair Martin-Smith; the curriculum rituals worked with by Louise Chalmers; "the rules generated by the activity" as Cecily O'Neill says; the negative and positive classroom rituals described by Charles E. Combs; the Down's Syndrome rituals of Tina and the strategic rituals used with her by Bernie Warren and Lorelei Rogers. In all cases, the ambiguity must be accepted. As John McLeod tells us, we don't wish to know how a magician does his tricks: "The whole point about magic is that it **is** magic."

If we object to the uncertainty that results, that is the contemporary way to understand existence as Heisenberg told us. And he was merely echoing William Blake's masterly line of verse: "Contraries mutually exist." And besides, no one said drama was easy...

xi

*T*he astute reader will have discerned in the above that I have cut out of this Foreword much more than is now contained herein. This is because, although this book is so exciting in its implications that my word-processor had filled up nearly 40 pages without me realizing it, I could see that Bernie Warren would never allow me so much latitude.

So I will conclude with a personal note. I can hardly suppress my excitement about this book. It not only has contributions from scholars and practitioners from many countries, and important items at that, but the academic standard is very high — which bodes well for the future. Moreover, many of the authors are the talented young people who will be the leaders of educational drama tomorrow. With the potential they demonstrate here, who can doubt that the field will move forward in strength and commitment?

$\mathcal{P}$reface

$\mathcal{T}$ his book explores problems and concerns in the training of drama educators and in the practice of educational drama and theatre. In doing so it expands upon themes and ideas begun in its predecessor *A Theatre in Your Classroom*. However, *Creating a Theatre in Your Classroom* incorporates six new chapters covering a wide range of topics as diverse as Drama and Writing, Drama in a Multicultural Classroom, Drama in Early Childhood Education and Drama in Teacher Training. It is organised into four sections: the basic 'elements' of drama; relationships between teachers and students; forms of dramatic activity; and connections between theory and practice. It ends with an epilogue: the story of one man's work, a lifetime in educational drama/theatre.

Like its predecessor, *Creating a Theatre in Your Classroom* is based upon two premises: that teaching in general, and drama/theatre teaching in particular, is an art in which successful praxis demands an understanding and integration of both theory and practice, and of form and content; and that opportunities to engage in collegial discourse play an essential part in the development of our sense of self as teachers of educational drama/theatre and in our development of a successful personal praxis.

Unfortunately, all too many drama specialists continue to work in isolation and opportunities for such informed collegial discussions remain few and far between. This lack of opportunity for regular collegial debate (which allows for an examination of different methodologies and perspectives) is still of particular concern when one considers students in training, who are often taught by a single individual, and newly qualified drama/theatre teachers who often find themselves as the only person on a school's staff with any training in this area. These problems are especially troubling in the current financial climate where training programs in educational drama/theatre are under threat, and where schools are choosing not to hire specialist drama/theatre teachers but rather seek generalists who can "cover" when necessary.

While any book is a poor substitute for personal communication, *Creating A Theatre in Your Classroom* provides the reader with insight into how several drama/theatre educators working in many different countries (Australia, Britain, Canada, Japan, Portugal, South Africa and the United States) think and work. In each chapter the contributors share their approach to their own particular area of educational drama/theatre, thus shedding light on the relationships among drama/theatre, learning and curriculum from a variety of perspectives. So while the authors do not speak with a single voice, they do identify some of the similarities and and differences in the practice of educational drama/theatre around the world.

Above all *Creating a Theatre in Your Classroom* is intended to be accessible and informative. It is full of practical ideas and tips, lesson plans and conceptual approaches to teaching drama and theatre at all levels of education. In addition, throughout the book the authors consider the use of drama as both a subject in its own right and as a "learning medium" through which teachers can help students learn in other subjects. It is hoped that by focussing critically upon their own praxis, the contributors to *Creating a Theatre in Your Classroom* will enable the reader to consider the many ways that one can create a theatre in one's own classroom and thus help enhance and solidify the reader's own personal praxis.

Bernie Warren
Windsor, Ontario
July 1994

Acknowledgements

*F*irst and foremost, I want to thank each of the contributors for providing such detailed and insightful commentaries on their work. Individually and collectively, I believe you have contributed greatly to the body of knowledge in our field and have helped to show how much the field has grown in such a very short amount of time.

I want to thank: Kerrin Patterson who helped at various stages in the development of the original manuscript; Ron Richard, my original editorial assistant, whose keen eye and invaluable suggestions helped make that original manuscript more readable; Julie Ortynsky, my present editorial assistant, whose search for clarity and consistency aided greatly in the development of this book; all of the staff at Captus Press who helped type and collate this book; in particular I must thank Randy Hoffman for his continuing support in the development of this work, especially his seemingly unlimited patience when unforseen obstacles continually changed the deadline for its completion.

My greatest thanks are to Edna P., whose sense of humour has kept, and continues to keep, me relatively sane.

Finally, a special thank you to the late Bert Amies. My first mentor, one of the most important influences on my way of working, and a man whose guidance and wisdom is sorely missed by all who knew him well.

Section One

Getting Started: The Basic Elements of Drama Teaching

The Teacher as Performer: "The Whole World Acts the Actor"[1]

BERNIE WARREN

Introduction

In 1980 I began work with a professional dance/theatre company on an exciting project: The LUDUS Special Schools Project.[2] As part of my work I visited the 27 schools involved with the project on a regular basis. I had a difficult job. I had to try to convince the teachers that there was value in drama and dance in the special school curriculum.

Initially, I spent a lot of my time simply watching the children and how the teachers worked with them. I was trying to establish a rapport with the staff in these target schools but I was also trying to find a way to sell my "product." I was a travelling salesman trying to convince these special education teachers, only a handful of whom had any formal training in dance or drama (some had no formal training at all), that they and their children could benefit from the use of my products in their classroom.

Like all good travelling salesman I had to have a sales pitch. In the first three months I travelled to every school involved with the project and observed hundreds of lessons taught to children aged 4 to 18 with special needs. Only a few of these lessons were in dance or drama; most were 'regular' lessons in mathematics, English and so on. The teachers committed to the project had already made the necessary "leap of faith";[3] however, I was still trying to find a way to talk to uncommitted teachers about dance and drama. Slowly, a pattern began to emerge. All of the effective teachers, whatever their subject discipline, had certain things in common. They all seemed to have command not only of their subject area but also of their teaching space. In addition, they had a significant presence in the classroom, which enabled them to communicate effectively with their students. This was the first time I started to perceive all teachers as actors performing in a theatre: a theatre in their own classroom.

3

All Teachers are Performers

While the role of drama as a curriculum vehicle and medium for personal development has been discussed by many authors,[4] the nature of drama is rarely understood or even discussed in Western industrialized societies except in terms of its artefact: theatre. Yet drama, which has been described as "the human process whereby imaginative thought becomes action,"[5] is more than just a performance on a stage. It is not only, as Brian Way suggests, a rehearsal for life,[6] but also, at least for some authors, synonymous with life itself.[7] From this point of view, drama is not only part of daily existence (in which adept social performers employ the skills of dramatic interaction, albeit primarily without a conscious thought), but it is also an essential element in all successful classroom teaching .

As the legendary stage director Peter Brook has pointed out, it is actors who transform any empty space into a stage; this is as true for social life as it is for the theatre. All performances require human presence. In the theatre, actors perform on a stage which is constructed both literally and metaphorically by the hands of others. Except in the instance of improvised performance, actors read from a script developed by a playwright, interpreted by a director, from whose vision a designer physically creates a stage upon which the actor performs.

Unlike their theatrical counterparts, social actors are not totally at the mercy of external forces; they are not controlled by the whims and wishes of the playwright, director or designer. Social actors have within them the capacity to be playwright, designer and director of any given scene, and as such they have the potential to create or reshape any stage on which they are called to perform. However, they are rarely alone, and many of the other influences which help to set the scene or shape the stage are beyond their control.

"One Man in His Time Plays Many Parts"[8]

In everyday life performances are often very fast paced, with social performers being required to change roles quickly. A mother insists her child get ready for school, rushes downstairs, kisses her spouse goodbye and gets into a car containing two colleagues. On their way to work they discuss an important staff meeting scheduled for later in the day. Arriving at their work, each enters her own classroom and assumes her role as teacher just as the first group of children arrives for school.

For most of us, the change from parent to spouse/lover to work associate to teacher is both rapid and without thought. However, each of these roles has a different social expectation attached to its successful performance.

4

The Classroom is the Theatre in which the Teacher Performs

Although social actors cannot change the physical nature of the meeting place, it is their physical presence which is essential for the transformation of that setting from a geographic location to the site of a human drama; actors, in part, create the stages upon which they are required to perform. Few people realize this.

Unlike their theatrical counterparts, teachers perform on a stage which is, at least to some extent, of their own making. Irrespective of the subject, the age of the class, the time allotted or the shape and organisation of the room, as soon as teachers enter the classroom they are on stage. However, like all accomplished social actors, successful teachers know, usually intuitively, that they have the power to shape the social stage. They are not only competent at adapting to the needs of each classroom but are also able, through the use of posture and inflection, to manipulate this stage to suit their needs.

There is a Relationship Between Performers and their Audience

Teachers perform for an audience for whom they act "in loco parentis," but unlike the majority of actors, they hold a position of real power over their audience. Paradoxically, however, this power is tempered because the teacher's performance is validated by their audience, who are younger or less knowledgeable than the teacher.

Although a captive audience, the children in the classroom are able to exert a direct influence on the teacher's performance. The child is at one and the same time playing the roles of audience member, director, and writer of the "rewrites" of the script from which the teacher is performing. This gives individual children a degree of power over the adult who is teaching them. Teachers' who refuse to acknowledge these interactions often place themselves in conflict with their class, creating stress and aggravation for all concerned.

Given Circumstances Suggest Appropriate Performance Style(s)

The notion of character, place and time are crucial to theatrical performances. Stanislavsky often spoke of the given circumstances: the where, when and why of any performance. However, unlike their theatrical counterparts, social actors rarely have the same range or flexibility available to them, for no matter how much they might like to, social actors can never change their social history. The roots of any teacher's character and

5

personality will always be firmly grounded in their genetic make-up and previous environmental, cultural and social influences.

In our everyday performances we are constantly responding to unspoken factors which affect our moment to moment transactions. In naturalistic theatrical performances these factors are referred to as the subtext. They are the meanings supporting and/or contradicting the text of the play. These subtextural pieces of information are conveyed by such things as the proximity of characters one to another, an individual's body posture, the intonation of certain words to convey alternate or double meanings and so on. A teacher must be able to read and respond to these subtextural, often non-verbal clues.

Whatever its length, any social scene occurs in a specific context. This context is shaped by the physical, social and emotional factors which create it and which in turn exert an influence on the functions of the scene and the actor's performances within it. The moment to moment roles played by teachers and their students are affected, as are all social interactions, by three interrelated factors, which I have referred to elsewhere as context, function and performance.[9] It is the relationship between these mercurial factors which, in effect, shapes each and every social stage.

The function of a scene — the reasons why the teachers and students are meeting — affects their performance. This factor is usually under the control of the teacher as they change from one topic to another. Context refers to a number of sub factors which are predominantly pregiven and, for the most part, beyond the control of the participants, all of which effect influence on the stage.

Context includes such diverse factors as location, architecture, climate and time of day. An open-plan school room affects the possibility of playing noisy games, especially when the group(s) next door are working in silence on an assignment. The ability to make adjustments to a classroom's lighting and heating can be used by the teacher to affect classroom interaction.

Social variables also exert a profound effect on the context of a scene and are perhaps the strongest catalysts to influence the behaviour of children and teachers in the classroom. The historical milieu, cultural background and social status of classroom participants, as well as the moods and feelings brought to the dramatic moment by the performers, all influence classroom interactions. These different contextual aspects, in relation both one to another and to the function(s) of the scene, help to determine the performance expected at any given moment.

The ability to remember is also crucial to social performance, for memory is an essential part of all acting. The ability to read and understand the scene, to draw the correct role from memory, and then to play it in a style appropriate to the expected conventions of the day is an essential skill for social survival.

Summary

The classroom encapsulates the essence of theatre, where the fundamental elements of all art (time, space and form), are already in place, and the physical medium for expression lies in the students themselves.[10] "The theatre of the classroom" suggests that learning moments evolve from natural inquisitiveness, are played out on a stage created by the relationships between teacher and student, that teacher and students are, at different times, audience and characters within the drama, and that all of this is encouraged through the skill of the teacher who acts as playwright/director/stage manager in the intrinsically dramatic process of learning.

In the classroom teachers must be both artist and educator. They must be aware that their effectiveness relies heavily on the student's ability to trust, cooperate, and open up to thoughts and feelings, making them particularly vulnerable to unintentional abuse from the teacher and fellow students. Teachers need to bear this in mind.

Finally, an awareness of the theatrical nature of classroom interactions can help students gain a greater understanding of subject material, develop drama skills, and gain a sense of empowerment and control in their ability to make practical choices on their own.

Endnotes

1. Reputed to have been on the entrance to one of London's earliest Drury Lane Theatres.
2. The LUDUS Special project was developed with the support of The Schools Council, The Arts Council and numerous other arts and educational bodies in the U.K. The work, which was carried out in 27 special schools in the northwest of England, began in April 1980 and was completed in May 1982. The project involved over 2000 children and more than 400 teachers and their assistants. The project's primary focus was the development of non-verbal stimuli and related teaching materials for use in the special school classroom. Its secondary objective was to raise the profile of the performing arts, particularly dance, in the special school curriculum.
3. The arts go beyond words; words can never convey the essence of artistic experience. In many ways belief in the value of the arts is similar to religious faith; belief, not logical argument, is necessary in the conversion. Ultimately, just as in missionary work, a point comes where individuals have to make that leap of faith.
4. See Bolton, Gavin. *Selected Writings on Drama in Education.* Edited by David Davis & Chris Lawrence (New York: Longman, 1986); Courtney, Richard. *The Dramatic Curriculum* (New York: Drama Book Specialists, 1980); Heathcote, Dorothy. *Collected Writings on Education and Drama.* Edited by Liz Johnstone & Cecily O'Neill (London: Hutchinson, 1984); Siks, Geraldine Brain. *Drama With Children.* 2nd Edition (New York: Harper & Row, 1983); Slade, Peter. *Child Drama* (London: University of London Press, 1954); Way, Brian. *Development Through Drama* (New York: Humanities Press, 1967).
5. Richard Courtney, op. cit., p. vii.

6. Brian Way, op. cit.
7. Robert Benedetti, "Notes to an Actor", in Richard P. Brown (1972), *Actor Training: Volume I*; Marowitz (1978), *Act of Being*; Warren (1988), *Disability and Social Performance*.
8. Jaques, in "As You Like It" (Act II, scene vii, line 142), *The Riverside Shakespeare*.
9. Warren, op. cit., pp. 25–37.
10. This idea is pursued in more detail in Keith Yon's chapter, "Risinghill Revisited".

$\mathcal{M}$aking Drama $\mathcal{H}$appen

JOHN MCLEOD

I have always been a sucker for magic. Recently I saw a performance of that great modern magician, David Copperfield, in which he was sawn in half, walked through glass and escaped from a truly impossible predicament. As I marvelled at these exploits, I kept saying to myself: "How did he do that?" Of course, this was really a non-question. I didn't really want to know the answer. The whole point about magic is that it **is** magic. Mere mortals may marvel, and that is what we are meant to do. To know how it is done, for me anyway, spoils the charm.

As a student, teaching was always a little like magic. I can remember sitting enthralled while our Year 8 teacher turned a group of very unpromising students into barons and dukes to illustrate the feudal system of government, or Prof. Maxwell reciting Icelandic sagas — in Icelandic — with tears streaming down his face. I didn't understand a word, but I was moved. As a student, I did not want to see the complex ropes and pulleys which went to make up such performances, for me it was enough to simply experience the event.

In no small way, it was the power and brilliance of these teachers which made me want to make a career in education. However, being an observer of brilliance is not the same as trying to create it oneself. The question of "How did he do that?" became real. The glib answer "By magic!" wasn't enough.

Trying to take apart, analyse and understand something as complex as good teaching practice is no easy task. I found it particularly difficult in drama where there seemed to be no ready-made formulas, and where it seemed to come from the children anyway. A major dilemma in teaching drama is to balance the need to structure teacher input with the desire for spontaneity and flexibility regarding student outcomes. Rigid solutions, either in the form of step by step lesson plans or a million short exercises which could be completed by any group of children, did not really solve the problem. Rigidity tended to preclude spontaneity. The alternative, though, was equally less promising. As a very inexperienced drama teacher, I remember going into a Year 4 class and simply saying, "I thought you might like to do some drama."

The children knew by my look of expectation that they were meant to say or do something. They looked uncomfortable. I looked uncomfortable; and at last, one student said, "No thanks." I was relieved and asked them to get out their social studies projects. There was no magic in that class.

It could have been that I hadn't said the spell properly. However, I had really come to the conclusion that good classes didn't just happen, nor were they the result of slavishly following an approach or ideas which had worked for somebody else, in another time and in another place. My students were my students and I was who I was. A middle road to drama curriculum development had to be sought, and one which took into account the very specific features of my classroom, my teaching style and the children with whom I was working. The path also had to take into account my educational commitments and my understanding of what drama was all about.

For me, drama was, and still is, about students making meaning of experience through taking on a role. In drama, students look at and experience the world from different perspectives, or to use the oft quoted epithet, "by standing in somebody else's shoes." This requires them to be engaged in what the drama is about, so that they can bring their own perspective and experiences to bear on the work they are creating. Engagement, though, needs to be combined with imagination: "What would it be like if I was a spy?" or "How would I respond if they had elected me to be ruler of the land?" In this way, drama transforms ordinary experience into the extraordinary and fabulous. If you are in the business of creating a new life, the dull and everyday hardly gets a look in. A young friend's favourite play occurs when he and the family dog, Poppy, embark on a long journey in which they are confronted by many trials before they can return home, exhausted and safe. Oliver and Poppy, of course, return triumphant from the dense undergrowth of the back garden in time for lunch, but they are nevertheless heroes in their created world. Dramas are about what it is to be human; and Oliver's and Poppy's adventures could well be the search for the Holy Grail or Mozart's *Magic Flute* in later times.

The question remains: How do dramas happen? How are curriculum experiences developed for students? If curriculum is the action of what goes on in classrooms and schools, then how does this action occur. Both David Best[1] and Richard Courtney[2] have drawn attention to Ludwig Wittgenstein's idea that action is the result of choices made upon the application of criteria within a specific context. Dramas don't just happen, they are the result of choices which have been made. The choices are not made in a willy-nilly fashion. Rather, we can have a set of criteria or benchmarks, always in the back of our minds to help guide our choices, and to make sure that the choices which are made are on the right track. The interesting thing about this approach is that the criteria must always be applied in terms of the specific teaching and learning context in which we are working. Different teachers can apply the same criteria, but it is likely that different choices will be made and they will come up with different results because they are different people working in different situations.

For example, one of our criteria could be: Is the classroom environment supportive of the topic being explored? To choose the exploration of Antarctica may be very reasonable in February in Canada given the severity of the winter. However, it would probably be a silly choice in Australia given the hot and dusty nature of February here.

In making drama happen, a number of choices have to be made. The obvious one has to do with what the drama is going to be about. But there are other choices also: What type of drama will be used? Is it going to be better to do scripted work or improvisation? Tableau or dance drama? Also, the size of the group is important. Will the children work in pairs or as a whole group? What style will they work in? And, how will the classroom be set up?

In this way the drama is divided into more manageable units. Every dramatic event will be built up using common principles of construction but each building will be different. This approach to curriculum development ensures that the uniqueness of each dramatic event is preserved. It is unique because drama, as all the arts, is based in the personal experiences and shared culture of a particular group of people. Drama is very much grounded in the here and now of people's experiences and understandings.

The Focus of the Drama ☐ Drama has to be about something. This, of course, is a truism; but it can be about most things. Teachers often find the focus for the drama from myths, legends, literature, current affairs, social issues, objects, the students' own interests and stories, and abstract concepts, such as "the nature of deceit."

A major criterion for choosing the focus, is to ask whether the topic can be interpreted in human terms. Dramas are about people and issues are expressed in human terms. A Year 7 teacher decided to build the drama around an antique brooch and her opening question was, "Who do you think owned this brooch?" Immediately, the object was placed within a human context. Similarly, another teacher was working on rights and responsibilities. The students were in the role of the founders of a new community and the question posed was, "What basic rules should we have for our community?" Using the terms **we** and **our** meant that the abstractness of the focus was presented in relationship to real human experiences.

The focus must also engage the students' interests and ideas and, at least, intrigue the students so that they want to explore it further.

11

In this sense, their attention is **focused**. Working with a group of Year 2 children, a teacher had brought in an old bottle and said that an elf was caught inside. Each child was asked to listen closely and to hear what the elf was saying to them. The bottle, the elf and the special message all had the effect of engaging the children. The situation also had the possibility of further questions such as how the elf came to be caught in the bottle in the first place.

The focus should also have sufficient depth so that the students can explore it in a variety of ways and at a variety of levels. A good focus is one that has many implications. Topics which can only be explored in very literal ways tend to be exhausted quickly. Simply acting out the king's feast has limited dramatic possibilities. However, there are many more possibilities if a letter was received from a disgruntled wizard who states that some of the food may have been poisoned. How will the guests tell? Will anybody volunteer to be a taster? Is it worth trying to appease the wizard?

Organization ☐ At any given moment in a class, a choice has to be made about the sorts of groupings in which the students will be working. There are really only five broad ways of organizing a class. The students can work as individuals, in pairs, in small groups, in large groups and as a whole group. Although the students can only be involved in one of these at any given moment, a single class may be designed to have students working in different ways. For example, the beginning of the class may be a whole group warm up, then some individual work and lastly some small-group activity.

Choosing which organizational unit is most appropriate can be based on the following criteria. The social health is very important.[3] Can the students work together? How much teacher control do they need? Do they co-operate well? Do they share ideas? Their past experience is also important here. Are they used to working in one particular way? In how many different ways can they work? If a group of students, for example, are not used to co-operative learning, small group activities are likely to be less successful than, say, individual activities or whole-group work in which the teacher has a large amount of control.

Sometimes the chosen focus also demands certain ways of working and this is tied up with the learning outcomes which are desired. In one Year 5 class, each student, as a sailor on HMS Bounty wrote a log of each day's events leading up to the mutiny. By getting each student to complete this task individually meant that a personal and reflective quality was introduced into the drama.

Type of Drama ☐ There are many different types of drama which include such diverse activities as improvisation, scripted work, games, theatre for an audience, puppetry and movement. This becomes even more complex when various types combine to form a dazzling array of hybrids such as improvised theatre or street theatre using giant puppets. Many of the curriculum debates which have occurred in drama have centred around this question of type. For example, adherents to theatre have been seen as being **against** teachers pursuing, say, an improvisational or games approach. These debates have not been particularly useful. Instead of looking at the **best** type of drama, we should be looking for the most **appropriate** type, given the context in which we are working. This approach to curriculum development again stresses that a decision has to be made in terms of the particular group of students. The following criteria can help ensure that the decision is soundly based.

The type of drama should build upon and extend the dramatic repertoire of the students. Once, when I was working with a group of Year 3 students I had set up what I thought was a relatively interesting drama about some pirates and some hidden treasure. I had asked the children to work out a solution to a problem by dividing into groups. One child took me aside, and in no uncertain terms told me that he didn't do drama, he told the story while the rest of the group mimed. They, in fact, were very good at this particular approach; but I was soon to realize that this was their only way of working. However, in a comprehensive drama programme, extension is as important as consolidation, and students should gain confidence in using a wide variety of dramatic types.

Variety also means that students begin to generalize from the specific dramatic experience and begin to discern those things which are common to all dramas, regardless of type. Variation enables students to look beyond the particular type in which they are presently engaged.

The chosen type should also complement the purpose and intention of the drama. If the intention is to communicate some very specific details of information dance, drama is probably not the most appropriate. Dance drama is very good at conveying general impressions, strong emotions and wide sweeps of narrative. It is not so good at giving precise details of who said what to whom.

Lastly, the type should take into account the interests and abilities of the students. I have seen both wonderful and disastrous plays performed by students to adoring parents. The technical demands of theatre are very great and some students simply have not learned the skills required.

Style □   Style is often just left to chance. Consequently, many dramas are based on the naturalism of television soap operas regardless of the focus or type; characters are larger than life and issues are black and white. Students often find style a difficult concept to grasp, and the fact that it is open to choice, is not always appreciated. Many students want the drama to look exactly as it would in real life and their work often leaves them with a feeling of disappointment because it lacks this veracity.

There are, in fact, many different dramatic styles. These can include symbolism, epic, burlesque, melodrama and absurdism, as well as the naturalism already mentioned.

For example, a group of Year 9 students were working on the topic of "Prisoners of Life." A student was sitting at a table. There were three other empty chairs. On the table was a knife and fork. The student talked at the chairs as if they were people. Three other students stood on a single rostrum on the periphery of the scene, but considerably elevated. The student at the table began to explain that she wasn't really hungry, however, she was interrupted by the other students singing advertising jingles for food products. The first student tried to counter this with, "Thank you. But I'm really very well. Really." Gradually the jingles changed to threatening commands: "Eat your dinner or you won't be allowed out!" "I'm sick of your whining!" The students came down from the rostrum, stood behind the chairs and, as they delivered a line, moved the chairs to face away from the table. The first student was left mumbling that she was not hungry as she flipped the fork around the table with the knife. This whole drama was constructed to symbolize the students' ideas and feelings towards the topic; and the everyday act of eating dinner was so stylized as to form a new reality.

Even young children can use a variety of styles as occurred in the following drama of a group of Year 3 students. Their exaggeration and broad humour demonstrated a tacit understanding of burlesque. A small group were playing with a long length of old velvet curtain. A girl draped it around her shoulders and announced that she was the Queen and that the others better watch out because she would chop their heads off if she got angry. Another student found a ruler which became her sword. For his trouble, he was promptly knighted and then warned again that his head would be chopped off. He and his companions then proceeded to bow down and sing the praises of the Queen who walked imperiously up and down in her cloak. The whole drama was played over and over with slight variations and the action was accompanied by shrieks of laughter and delight.

The description of style like type is, to a certain extent, arbitrary. Many actual dramas combine a variety of styles and any rigid boundaries between styles are often stretched.

Another way of thinking about style is to place every drama somewhere on a continuum between comedy and tragedy. This tends to add a further dimension and depth to the former categorization. Even

14

burlesque, which is the most overtly humorous, can have tragic overtones, as can be seen in Charlie Chaplin's figure of the Tramp.

The choice of style should be directly related to the purpose of the drama and to the intentions of the students. Epic, for example tends to distance an audience rather than engage them; and if it is a high level of audience identification which is wanted, epic may not be the best choice.

Style should also help students come to terms with the artifice of drama. Style and conventions of the theatre enable students to understand the ways in which drama transforms ordinary experience into art. A group of Year 12 students were exploring the possibilities of white, neutral masks in their work on *Oedipus Rex*. This device brought home to the students that characters in drama are often both individuals and types at the same time. A Year 4 class had organized their room so that one corner sectioned off by upturned tables was the monster's cave, another corner was home, and the bit in between was the enchanted forest.

As is the case with types of drama, a criterion for the choice of style should be variety. Students should possess a wide repertoire of dramatic styles in which they can work.

Classroom Environment   □   Each classroom can be seen as a micro-environment which presents a range of possibilities for constructing a curriculum and developing drama experiences with students. The physical environment can either support the students' drama or it can have a negative effect. A large and cavernous gymnasium, for example, in which there is a marked echo, would probably work against an intimate drama about the tensions experienced by prisoners in a small and confined cell.

Dorothy Heathcote[4] finds it useful to look at the classroom environment in terms of a number of continua. These include: sound and silence, movement and stillness and light and darkness. Some Year 7 students were working on the idea of waxworks coming to life and killing their creator. They decided to develop a series of tableaux in which the only moving person was the sculptor. The second last tableau was the strangulation of the sculptor and the last one showed him as one of the exhibits in the waxworks, while the other figures looked smug. The specific combination of movement and stillness was particularly effective because it was responsive to both the purpose of the drama and the students' own intentions.

There is often the view that to do drama, there needs to be sophisticated and modern theatrical equipment such as lighting, sound systems and costumes. However, the more sophisticated the environment is, often the more fixed it is. Students do not get to change things. For example, there are many safety considerations in placing and using theatrical lighting and many schools bar students from using it. Simple lighting is often more flexible because students can easily learn how to place and safely operate the lamps.

Similarly, there are some advantages in having raked, comfortable and fixed seating around a stage; but this means that most of the drama will occur within this space. Proscenium-arch theatre may be useful for some work. However, it will not be appropriate all the time. Jerzy Grotowski's[5] concept of a **poor theatre** is useful here. The actor is paramount and the drama needs to focus on the students' own resources and not be overwhelmed by the technical aspects of theatrical presentation. I remember seeing a group of students who spent more time arguing about what colour filter to use in the lights than they did on doing the drama. The question which needs to be posed is: Does the use of the environment aid, or overwhelm the students' own efforts at making meaning through drama?

By dividing dramatic action into the dimensions of focus, organization, type, style and environment, and by seeing them as choices about which decisions have to be made, the teacher can begin to construct a curriculum and make the drama happen. The choices which are actually made will directly affect both what the students learn and the way in which they learn in drama. For example, constantly employing individual or pair work will have the effect of stressing personal reflection while missing out on the more complex skills of negotiation which are inherent in, say, large-group work.

Although general criteria have been set down, and these will inform the choices which are to be made, these criteria must be applied within the constraints of a given context.

Reading the Context

In this approach to curriculum development, the context in which the drama occurs is not just a passive and empty stage upon which the dramatic action is played. Rather the context determines how the criteria are applied and what choices are made. Therefore, for a teacher to construct a curriculum, there needs to be clear understanding of the context and the way in which it is working to define the drama.

The major feature of any teaching context, as has already been implied, is the students. Any of the criteria which have been listed have to be applied in relationship to the specific students. It is not even reasonable to apply them in terms of all six-year-olds or all fourteen-year-olds. One of the great myths of education and society in general is the homogeneity of people. In real education, structures need to be devised which accommodate and celebrate differences as well as the similarities between students. In drama, this is crucial because

16

we are dealing with a form of personal knowledge. Even the cultural knowledge of the arts is to do with what links us together as a group of people rather than simply being a group of people in some abstract way. Engagement is a major aspect of working with students in drama, and engagement relies on some knowledge of the students and some appreciation of their interests, expectations and aspirations.

Teaching drama, though, is not simply a one-way street. The process of education is an encounter between people, and the students and the teacher should become a community of learners. This means that the teacher is as much part of the context as the students. You have skills, interests and ideas which are extremely important in the whole process of making drama happen. It is useful to think about the positive qualities you bring to the drama. A close colleague of mine, for example, has a very solid background in the theatre. She has seen and read many plays, and the work which she does with students reflects both the breadth of her knowledge and the diversity of her tastes. Another teacher has a skill in the areas of visual imagery and design. His students, therefore, tend to be very conscious of the way in which physical environment and the space between people work to express meaning.

The weaknesses which the teacher brings to the drama also need to be considered. All of us are a combination of both strengths and weaknesses. I am not particularly good at thinking on my feet. Consequently, I normally have a very clear idea of what choices I will make and those which I will leave up to the students. The choices which I make are usually planned in some detail before I get into the class. I have colleagues who work in the opposite way to this. It is a matter of knowing how you best work and maximizing your strengths and not your weaknesses.

The context also includes such things as the physical environment, the time of day and the season. They will all have an effect on the drama. I know one primary teacher who refuses to do any drama on a windy day; in her words, "The students are all over the place and you never get any sense out of them!"

There is another level of context which has to do with the school in which you are teaching. The arts are sometimes regarded with suspicion in schools. They are seen as forms of recreation to be pursued after the real work of schooling is done. In these days of economic rationalism, recreational pursuits are often not afforded a high priority. Drama is also one of the newer arts and can sometimes be seen as on the periphery of the mainstream curriculum.

This, of course, is not always the case. Many schools are very supportive of both drama and the arts and have a clearly articulated rationale which ensures that all students participate in artistic experiences.

The school's perception of drama needs to be taken into account. In one school, the Year 12 students undertook a season of Tennessee Williams's one act plays. However, in another, anything written after 1900 would have the effect of generating apoplexy in the administration. In Australia, at least, drama teachers were often seen as educational radicals which led them to ignore the school context in which they were working. This did not serve drama well. Schools simply went on with their own business and tended to see drama as increasingly irrelevant.

Schools are now heavily involved in creating policies about such things as curriculum development, assessment procedures and teaching strategies. A great deal of the interesting educational debate and innovation is occurring at the school level. Drama teachers should be both cognizant and involved in the development of policies and ideas. Arts teachers, in the past, would often remove themselves from the debates by claiming that the arts were fundamentally different from other areas of the curriculum. Taking the moral high ground in this way, unfortunately, did not have the desired effect. The arts tended to get lumbered with curriculum practices which were derived from and appropriate to other areas of the curriculum. In one school I recently visited, most assessment was undertaken on the basis of written tests and essays. However, for the teacher, drama was a form of **knowledge in action**. Consequently, she felt that the students were being assessed in a way which was not compatible with the way in which drama worked.

Claiming such blanket difference does not serve drama well. There are aspects of the curriculum which are different for drama, but there are also areas which are the same. It is a matter of knowing which issues are truly significant and fighting for those within the school context.

The final level of context concerns both politics and the general community. The experience of living in the late twentieth century is one of extraordinary change. As somebody pointed out, the only thing we can be sure of is that nothing will be the way it was. As a way of dealing with this change, many governments simply create more and more policies. Every year teachers are confronted by an ever increasing pile of material which they are meant to read, digest and enact. Well, that's the theory, however, as Harry Broudy[6] put it, if you stand still long enough in education, you will ultimately be leading the parade!

Cynicism aside, the skill is to know which of the policies are the most important and which are going to last, at least for a short time. As a barometer of policy change, I tend to use friends and family who are outside education. I find them surprisingly accurate at predicting issues and trends. It is important to pick up the current trends and to discern the implications they have for your own teaching.

Many people dismiss policy development as irrelevant and too far removed from the day to day problems of teaching. This is a mistake because the decisions which are being made at the classroom level are related to the wider social and educational context. In parts of Australia at the moment, for example, we are witnessing a reassertion of central control over education. This is a very significant change from the practices of school-based decision making of the last twenty five years and it is these twenty five years which have paralleled the development and expansion of drama teaching. Consequently, the very basis of drama's success in the schools is now being undermined because many curriculum decisions are now being made outside the specific school context. Drama teaching needs to rethink a number of its practices in the light of these changes. These are local concerns, but every locality has its own issues which need to be addressed.

The context changes over time and varies from place to place. Teachers must be aware of these changes and be willing to rethink the choices which have been made. Curriculum is therefore not something which is set down and then forgotten. Curriculum is a dynamic process of making decisions which are responsive to different students and changing circumstances.

Making the Choice

In this approach to curriculum development in drama, choices have to be made, and they have to be made by the people who are directly part of the specific teaching and educational context. The choices cannot be made either systemically by ministries of education, for example, or by professional curriculum developers such as writers of books. A week by week drama programme cannot be set down and used by all teachers. A course of study which is appropriate in one situation is not transferable in its entirety to another. A change in context changes the result of the decisions which need to be made, even though the same criteria can be applied.

The question remains though: Who makes these choices? Traditionally, curriculum decision making has been the province of the teacher. They have been expected to possess an overview of the policy context, a detailed understanding of the discipline in which they are working, and sophisticated skills of assessment and evaluation so that programmes can be designed to suit the individual needs of the students. Under the present approach, these would not diminish. Teachers are very skilled people who have been trained to fulfil these tasks.

However, in my understanding of drama, which was given towards the beginning of this chapter, emphasis was placed on the students' control of the drama. Students should use drama to make sense of their lives and experiences. Placing the student at the centre of the drama experience in this way does, however, have an effect on the complementary process of curriculum development.

Making decisions about their drama is an important step in gaining confidence and control. Deciding such things as style, type and focus ensures that the drama is expressing and communicating what the students have to say. Being in control of the drama means that the students are making significant choices about that drama. A major aim of a comprehensive drama programme is to ensure that students have confidence and the skills to use drama in their own lives and outside the formal classroom context.

This is not to suggest, of course, that all decisions should be left to the students. A number of the criteria mentioned above deal with the expansion of the students' dramatic repertoire. These assume that the teacher can see possibilities of which the students are not even aware. Rather, I am suggesting that the traditional approach of the teacher making most of the curriculum decisions needs to be redressed. A more balanced approach is necessary. It was suggested above that classrooms should be seen as communities in which decisions are negotiated and choices are shared. Communities are not comprised of people who all share the same skills. They are heterogeneous groups in which individuals possess a variety of skills and strengths. It is a matter of sharing the decisions so that the various strengths of individuals are maximized. Over time, though, increasingly more decisions should be placed with the students. Control requires practice.

As teachers, we always work towards our own redundancy. A comprehensive drama programme should enable the students to work independently and make the drama happen for themselves.

Endnotes

1. David Best, *Philosophy and Human Movement* (London: George Allen and Unwin, 1978), p. 79.
2. Richard Courtney, *Re-play — Studies in Human Drama in Education* (Toronto: Ontario Institute for Studies in Education Press, 1982), p. 179.
3. Liz Johnson & Cecily O'Neill, *Dorothy Heathcote Collected Writings on Education and Drama* (London: Hutchinson, 1984), p. 93.
4. Dorothy Heathcote, "Drama," in *English in Education*, 3(3), 1969, pp. 58–63.
5. Jerzy Grotowski, *Towards a Poor Theatre* (London: Methuen, 1969).
6. Harry Broudy, "The Arts as Basic Education," in *Journal of Aesthetic Education*, 12(4); 1978: p. 21.

Section Two

Creating Learning Moments: Relationships Between Teachers and Students

Walking Backwards to the Future:
Teachers as Guides to New Worlds

CECILY O'NEILL

Teacher and Artists

Many artists are teachers, and there are those who would claim that all good teachers are also artists. Artistic creation and learning both require the deliberate setting up of conditions in which significant experiences can occur. Although it is possible to push the analogy too far, the experience of learning and an encounter with a work of art are both a process of discovery — a process that can provide a powerful sense of disclosure and illumination, of growing insight and mastery.

The teaching of any arts subject, and in particular the group process which is drama, is a cognitively sophisticated and demanding activity. It requires the exercise of imagination and sensibility, as well as an understanding of the possibilities and limitations of the artistic medium in which one is working. It demands a subtle attention to detail, nuance and implication, the ability to exploit the unpredictable in the course of the work and the confidence to shift goals where appropriate. It requires the ability to work through others and to make positive use of the creative impulses of everyone in the group.

Very few of these demands were apparent to me when I began teaching drama. The first time I heard Dorothy Heathcote speak, she said that in drama the teacher is creating "a shared learning experience." Although I thought that this was also my objective, I was unaware of the real implications of this belief for my own practice, and the demands it would make on me and on my students. Until then, my main function as a teacher had been to provide ideas for my students — ideas which allowed them to work through a number of different tasks and exercises — and to oversee their work. Although

23

it seemed that these games, trust exercises and brief improvisations could lead into drama, in practice none of them was ever allowed to develop to the point where it had a life of its own. As teacher, I was in charge of the ideas, so control of the materials of the lesson stayed firmly in my hands.

It was some time before I realised the limitations of this approach. The first difficulty was that as each lesson consumed a large number of ideas, my mind soon became blank. Handbooks, in-service courses and helpful colleagues kept me going for a while, but it became clear that these teacher-generated "ideas" belonged too firmly to the teacher, and never became materials for real aesthetic exploration.

The Classroom Climate

Keith Johnstone, a most gifted teacher and leader of improvised drama and theatre, noticed that at his workshops people frantically scribbled down the exercises he used, but few paid any attention to what he was actually doing **as a teacher**. I had the good fortune to be exposed to Johnstone's work at this time, and it was precisely his qualities as a teacher which struck me. He made it clear that it is the teacher's responsibility to manipulate the group into an appropriate frame of mind before real exploration can take place. One way of achieving this exploratory and risk-taking climate is for the teacher to accept the blame for any failures in the work. This may seem to imply an unacceptably low status for the teacher, but, as Johnstone makes clear, the teacher's status is likely to rise, since "only a very confident and experienced person would put the blame for failure on himself."[1]

When the teacher takes on this responsibility, the possibility of failure suddenly ceases to be frightening, and the normal teacher-student relationship begins to dissolve. The teacher/leader in improvised drama is not without power, but like all power it rests in responsibility. The drama teacher cannot hope to simply remain the final arbiter, the evaluator of the work of others, or the single source of knowledge in the classroom. The teacher must grow into other more complex duties.

For teachers who make improvised drama the heart of their work, their chief responsibility and the most important outcome will be the creation of a shared dramatic context — a fictional world in which ideas, events, issues and relationships can be safely explored and embodied. The first step for teachers is to empower the students, to allow them a genuine share in the proceedings. The teacher must come to value the student's ideas and contributions as much as their own. The everyday rules of the classroom must be suspended, not in order to allow anarchy, but to replace them with rules generated through the new activity — the rules of the medium in which the exploration is taking place.

It is not only a fear of losing control **physically** of the group which can deter the teacher from working in this way, but a fear that material other than that which has been officially sanctioned by the teacher or the curriculum may be accommodated in the classroom. In most school situations, the teacher exercises discrimination over the kinds of material which the students will encounter. In improvised drama, the work may begin in the curriculum, but if it becomes a "shared learning experience," the dynamic forms of participation and transformation which are at the heart of the work will resonate with the "dreams, desires, voices and Utopian longings"[2] of the students. It may be difficult for teachers to accept that there is more in the lesson than they themselves put there.

Spontaneity and Control

Watching Johnstone at work, it became clear that it was not enough to create the right climate for experiment, or to simply accept and encourage the spontaneity of the students. If I was to work effectively as a teacher and an artist, it would be necessary to tolerate my own spontaneity as well. To be spontaneous does not imply behaviour which is merely impulsive and unthinking. Spontaneity demands much more than this, involving "a quality of mind...thinking afresh, balancing impulse and restraint, and integrating imagination, reason and intuition."[3]

It also demands a generosity and freedom of spirit, in submitting to the workings of a process which is not entirely rational. It would be necessary to loosen my rational grip both on my own imagination and intuition and on the work itself.

The integrity of the work itself demands to be respected. Bruner sees the freedom to submit to the art object as one of the conditions of creativity: to be dominated by an object of one's own creation is "to be free of the defenses that keep us hidden from ourselves."[4]

We do not usually think of a performance or a piece of improvised drama as an "object," but Beckerman has no difficulty in defining theatre events as "dramatic objects." "Whatever the path to it...the performed object is realized through the medium of the living performers."[5]

What is true of the dramatic object is also true of the creative process. If it does not in some sense "take over," the process is likely to remain contrived and mechanical. A successful art object or process will develop a life of its own. As well as being shaped by the artists, it will also shape its creators. The integrity of the "dramatic object" may be difficult for the drama teacher to accept, but it will provide both motive force and guidance for the evolution of the work.

Working from Within

As I began to accept the spontaneity of the students and the autonomy of the work, I tried to work increasingly from the "inside." Influenced by the work of Gavin Bolton and Dorothy Heathcote, I took on roles within the drama. This complex strategy, however, did not yield all its secrets immediately. At first, I was merely one of the crowd, another "explorer," or "townsperson" or "bank robber." Heathcote[6] tells us that if we are functioning as extras in the drama, merely "adding to the number in the cast," we may have begun our journey, but there is still a long way to go.

It occurred to me that the teacher, working in role in the drama, could actually control the work. Still mistaking my function, I sought, by taking on a role in the drama, to acquire **more** power than I had as the teacher. Typically, the roles I chose were those which appeared to contain the greatest authority — kings or queens, prison governors, ships' captains, the leader of the explorers and so on. I thought that in role I **added** the power of these leaders to my own teacher power, and my plan was, of course, to stay firmly in control of the work. The children knew better. Kings can be replaced, prison governors killed, captains thrown overboard and leaders disobeyed. I was often "dead" or disregarded within minutes of beginning a piece of drama. The rules of the game permitted my overthrow, as the children implicitly understood, and taking part in the work implied that I, too, must obey the drama rules. I had to submit. I was forced to rethink my function and try to see **below** the surface power of the role.

Gavin Bolton, whose analyses of drama in education have done much to clarify both its nature and purpose, claims that the practice of **"teacher-in-role"** challenges our very conception of teaching. He describes the technique both as a strategy for learning and a significant principle of teaching. It uniquely inverts the assumptions underlying the traditional pedagogical context:

> The teacher in role has power but it is not of the conventional kind. It carries within it its opposite: a potential for being rendered powerless.... The power relationship between pupils and teacher within the drama is tacitly perceived as negotiable.[7]

This is what my students had "tacitly perceived" as they "killed" me, and what I had failed to understand.

As I became more confident in working in role, the opportunities it offered became clearer. These included the possibility of initiating a piece of work economically, modelling appropriate behaviours, moving the drama along, and sometimes, challenging the students from within. I could be inside the work to "attack and yield, provoke and withdraw."[8]

Although I was still struggling to understand the operation of the drama form, at least I was working with my students inside the process. For the artist, this stance is inevitable. For the teacher of the arts, it has not always been seen as a necessity. If we are to operate as artists with our students a realignment of our position is essential. We must not remain satisfied with providing what Witkin has called "the primary creative impulse," content in placing our students "under starter's orders."

Witkin believes that in teaching the arts, fundamental contradictions arise because the curriculum and instruction remain "external to the pupil's expressive acts."[9] He believes that teachers of the arts do not understand the nature of the creative process, and that this limits their role to one which merely facilitates or inhibits. He claims that when teachers do not exercise a teaching function during the ongoing creative process, their effectiveness is seriously weakened. By remaining external to the students' expressive act, the drama teacher relinquishes reflective control of the medium. The teacher needs to enter the creative process from the outset, from the very inception of the work, and control and develop the structural demands inherent in the experience. The creative act can only be disciplined from within.

In reflecting on my own practice, I discovered that I failed at first to understand how the creative process operates. Then, abandoning the position of overseer of the activities, and trying to operate from within as a co-artist with the students, I remained too often in control of the content of the drama instead of working to develop its structure. I did not grasp the true aesthetic function and responsibility of the teacher/leader.

Although improvised drama is a group process, it is no more democratic in its operation than the production of a piece of theatre. The drama teacher, working inside the creative process, may adopt something of the functions of the director, playwright, designer, stage manager and even audience in the theatre, but, because of the nature of the activity, will go beyond these purposes. Like workers in the theatre, the task for teachers who work through improvised drama is to alter at a stroke the participants' customary orientation to time and space. Their purpose is to lead their students across the threshold of an imagined world, which comes into being as they enter it.

Dramatic Worlds in the Classroom

In the classroom, the dramatic world comes into existence and is maintained by the efforts of everyone in the group, including the teacher. Almost more sharply than theatre, these fictional classroom "worlds" will exploit the tensions between illusion and reality. These illusions can only be established through the agreement of the group; the class-room possesses none of the aids to the kind of hallucinated participation which the theatre offers.

In the theatre, the limits of the dramatic world and the real world are strongly marked in both time and space. The moments in which each is dominant are clearly marked by the raising and lowering of the lights or the curtain. In the classroom, the two worlds are seen to occupy almost the same place and time. While the essential features of the dramatic worlds created in the classroom have everything in common with those created on stage for an audience, the dramatic world in the classroom is created, experienced and validated not by actors and an audience but by the participants themselves.

I believe that the most economical and dramatically effective way to lead students into a dramatic world is to take on a role in the drama, and to be absolutely clear about the function of the role. Among the most useful possibilities which become available are the following:

- asking the question which creates the "world" and designates the first task for the participants.
- narrating the circumstances in which the participants find themselves.
- creating the atmosphere of this "world" and confirming the genre to which it belongs.
- establishing the moment of change at which the participants discover themselves.
- setting up the web of relationships which defines the students' roles and attitudes.
- initiating the encounters which will clarify the students' roles and the world they inhabit.

These are just some of the prospects for action contained in the act of conscious self-presentation which is what teaching in role involves. The real purpose of using role is emphatically **not** to give a display of acting, but to invite the students to enter the fictional world, to respond actively, to begin to answer the question, to oppose or transform what is taking place. Like the audience in a theatre, the students are caught up in a complex web of contemplation, speculation, anticipation, and response, and through the agency of the **"teacher-in-role,"** the dramatic world begins to define itself.

It is worth noting that great dramatists typically waste little time on establishing the nature of the dramatic world as it has been before the play begins. It may be described to us, or we may deduce what that world was like, but we meet it at the moment of change. This moment is often marked by an arrival (Christy Mahon in *The Playboy of the Western World,* Blanche in *Streetcar named Desire),* a return (the Ghost in *Hamlet,* Hedda and later, Eilert Lovborg in *Hedda Gabler),* a question (King Lear's question to his daughters), or a message (news of Desdemona's marriage in *Othello).*

In improvised drama, we can use the same kinds of keys to the doors of the dramatic worlds we want our students to enter. Beginning a scene with an arrival will precipitate the kinds of encounter which will define the development of the drama. Refugees, for example, arriving in a new country are greeted by an apparently sympathetic official (played by the teacher) who gradually reveals the kinds of discrimination and segregation which the immigrants will face. Or perhaps space travellers reaching an unknown planet encounter an alien (again, the teacher). The refusal of this alien to accept the fact that male crew members are in positions of authority brings about a questioning of the power attached to gender roles, and leads to the creation and exploration of a society where females are dominant.[10]

Asking the right kind of question, and asking it in role, will effectively bring new worlds into being. A challenge which is hard to ignore occurs in "The Haunted House" lesson in *Drama Structures.*[11] Here, the question asked of the students by the teacher (in role as the ambiguous "Mrs. Brown") is "Would you spend one night in Darkwood House for $100?" The question drags the world into being, establishes the genre, and provides a task which, like Hamlet's task of revenge, may take a very long time to achieve.

In the past, when I used role as a way of gaining more power in the drama, I would probably have become the great king, thereby making explicit what could otherwise provide a source of ambiguity and exploration. Later, in order to avoid this, I might have joined the class as an adviser. I might have spent time establishing the details of the kind of kingdom we inhabited and the limits of our responsibilities as advisers. All these features can be made clear by asking the students the kind of questions which will reveal a great deal about the king and also define the limits of their responsibilities as his advisers.

With Grade 6 students who were working on the theme of "Africa," I introduced the dramatic world by briefly narrating the beginning of a story about a great king, who lived long ago in Africa. I asked the students to imagine that they were his advisers. In role as one of the advisers, I brought a message from the great king. He had decided that it was time to take a wife. Could we, as his trusted advisers, choose a bride for him? When the class had decided that they could undertake the assignment, several other tasks were immediately set in motion. After much discussion, beauty and cleverness were rejected as criteria in the choice of the king's bride; they carried problems with them.

Finally, we had a list of criteria including sufficient good looks, health and intelligence, resourcefulness, kindness, honesty and lack of greed.

The next problem was to determine how we could discover whether any particular girl possessed these qualities. The advisers, disguised, travelled throughout the land, pretending to seek a bride for their own sons. A number of potential candidates were tested for the required qualities by other advisers, posing as poor and hungry travellers, or people with problems, or wealthy strangers who offered temptations. Each candidate who passed these tests then had to face a further trial: she had to show her ability to help her people in times of trouble.

The greatest problem facing people in Africa, the advisers concluded, was the lack of water. The final trial took the classic form of a riddle, and the circumstances surrounding the test were both formal and ritualistic. This was the question: If each girl had just one bowl of water, and before her stood an old woman, a baby, and a cow, to which one should she give the water? Each girl chose differently, and each of the advisers had their own notion of what the correct answer should be.

After much deliberation, the advisers could reach no decision. Still in role as one of the advisers, I chose to add another element. I announced that before we chose the king's bride, it was only fair to tell the candidates something about the king. None of us had ever seen him face to face. He ruled through us, and we carried out his wishes. There were many rumours about his true appearance and nature, but no one knew the truth. Which of the candidates still wished to be considered? Three of the girls agreed to risk the encounter. As a way of completing the work, the class created three different versions of what the king actually was. One group decided that he was a magical animal, the second group that he could not speak, and, the most interesting of all, the third group agreed that he didn't actually exist. Here, the search for a wife had been, in reality, a search for someone brave, resourceful and kind who could really rule the kingdom.

This "world" had clearly much in common with fairytales and myths. Responding to the implied genre, the students evolved classic activities appropriate to this kind of world — tests, disguises, hidden identities, riddles, choices and ordeals. The actions they chose were those which dramatists and storytellers have used down the centuries.

Working with the students inside the dramatic world, my function was to provide the initial impulse, the question. I was also able to support, authenticate and enlarge their experience while respecting the organic growth of the work. I had to struggle not to dominate their explorations, and yet ensure that the world continued to evolve. I could not have known in advance the direction the drama would take or the decisions the students would make, but I had to remain watchful for opportunities to support, enrich and extend the experience.

Working in Open Possibility

Ideally, it is the **work** — the creation and maintenance of the shared dramatic fiction — which dictates the ways in which it evolves. There is a kind of aesthetic necessity which operates in the group process of drama. Any creative structure will contain unknown variables which must be accommodated. Rosenberg characterizes the artist as working in a kind of "open possibility"[12] and this accurately describes the drama teacher at work. John Dewey equates the artist to the scientist:

> Like the scientific inquirer, the artist permits the subject-matter of his perception, in connection with the problems it presents to determine the issue, instead of insisting upon its agreement with a conclusion de-cided in advance.[13]

The craftsman uses skills to achieve a predetermined end, but the artist employs skills to **discover ends through action**.

The earlier comparison between teacher and artist might seem to founder on the fact that the significant experiences which the teacher strives to produce are likely to be new to the students but not to the teacher. Although teachers may learn something as they teach, they cannot usually guide their teaching by what they themselves are learning but by what their students discover. In improvised drama, however, the significant experiences which occur are likely to be as novel to the teacher as to the students.

Although the end of the work may not be known, each new stage will impose fresh choices and decisions that could not have been fore-seen at an earlier stage. Utter watchfulness is the first necessity, an ability to respond immediately to the innumerable variables which may enforce a subtle change of plan.

Toleration of anxiety and ambiguity is also essential, as well as a willingness to take risks and court mystery, and the courage to confront disappointment and, on occasion, the possibility of failure. These qualities must pervade the drama teacher's approach to both the students and the work, since the teacher is a "human event rather than a transmission device." The teacher must, by necessity, both model and embody the very values and attitudes which are being fostered.

Drama teachers do not **own** the work, although they may have done much to create it. It has a life beyond its creators. The teacher is **servant** to the work, labouring to bring it to being, to trap the students in its confines, just as theatre workers do their audience.

The Drama Teacher as Liminal Servant

Peter McLaren, in a fascinating and provocative study, characterizes teachers as liminal servants.[14] He borrows the concept of liminality from anthropology, where it refers to a social state, often an initiation or rite of passage, in which participants lose their usual roles and status. It defines a time and space "betwixt and between" one context of meaning and action and another. In this state, literally on the threshold (the "limen" in Latin), participants are neither what they have been or what they will be. They are caught up in a process of separation, transition and transformation. Victor Turner, whose work has influenced McLaren, links this condition with playful and theatrical activities, which also belong to a time and space held apart from ordinary life.[15]

In the liminal state, people "play" with familiar elements and disarrange and de-familiarize them. Thus, they are engaging in the basic activity of all art, which according to Shklovsky, is to force us to notice, to help us to see afresh, to promote novel perspectives on the world.[16] McLaren, who values the skill of drama teachers in shaping learning experiences, regards every teacher as a potential "liminal servant" whose duty is to engage in a pedagogical surrealism which disturbs commonplace perceptions. This "de-familiarization," which he sees as a crucial element in teaching and learning, is identical to Brecht's "alienation effect."

The aim of drama teaching has been defined as a search for fresh insights and understanding, for new kinds of "knowing," rather than the pursuit of technical skills or the acquisition of knowledge **about** the activity. If this is so, the drama teacher is perhaps the best example of the liminal servant at work.

Working in role, the teacher can lead the students across the threshold into the imagined world of drama, a place of separation and transformation, where the rules and relationship of classroom life are suspended. In this dramatic world, students are free to alter their status, adopt different roles and responsibilities, play with elements of reality, and explore alternate existences. When the dramatic world takes hold, acquiring a life of its own, all the participants will return across the threshold changed in some way. If we can imagine alternative realities, then it is possible to bring them into existence.

Peter Brook claims that the theatre director is "a guide at night who does not know the territory."[17] Yet he has no choice. He must continue to guide, learning the route as he goes. Drama teachers are also guides to new worlds, travelling with incomplete maps to the terrain, taking risks, and not knowing what lies ahead. Perhaps it is best if we imagine the guides, the liminal servants, trying to lead the way while walking backwards, so that they do not become intent on reaching a predetermined destination as quickly as possible. It is just as important for these guides to know where the travellers have come from, and the nature of the journey so far.

As teachers and students, working together to create and inhabit fictional worlds, we are making promises to each other. These promises re-enforce the value of what is taking place — we are exercising and celebrating our freedom, community and responsibility. Through our explorations of dramatic worlds in the classroom, we are putting our students in touch with their own potential so that they may appropriate the future.

Endnotes

1. Keith Johnstone, *Impro: Improvisation and the Theatre* (London: Faber and Faber, 1979), p. 29.
2. Peter McLaren, "The Liminal Servant and the Ritual Roots of Critical Pedagogy" in *Language Arts*, Feb. 1988; 65(2): p. 166.
3. Adam Blatner and Allee Blatner, *The Art of Play* (New York: Human Sciences Press, Inc., 1988), p. 23.
4. Jerome Bruner, *On Knowing: Essays for the Left Hand* (London: Atheneum Press, 1962), p. 25.
5. Bernard Beckerman, "Theatrical Perception" in *Theatre Research International*, 1979; 4(3): p. 159.
6. Liz Johnson and Cecily O'Neill, *Dorothy Heathcote: Collected Writings on Education and Drama* (London: Hutchinson, 1984).
7. Gavin Bolton, "Teacher in Role and Teacher Power." Unpublished paper, 1984.
8. Peter Brook, *The Empty Space* (Harmondsworth, England: Penguin Books, 1972), p. 122.
9. Robert Witkin, *The Intelligence of Feeling* (London: Heinemann, 1974), p. 96.
10. Cecily O'Neill and Alan lambert, *Drama Structures* (London: Hutchinson, 1982), p. 212.
11. O'Neill and Lambert, ibid., p. 166.
12. Harold Rosenberg, *The Tradition of the New* (London: Paladin, 1962), p. 42.
13. John Dewey, *Art as Experience* (London: Allen and Unwin, 1934), p. 138.
14. Peter McLaren, "The Liminal Servant and the Ritual Roots of Critical Pedagogy" in *Language Arts*, Feb. 1988; 65(2): pp. 164–179.
15. Victor Turner, *From Ritual to Theatre: The Human Seriousness of Play* (New York: Performing Arts Journal Publications, 1982), p. 114.
16. Victor Shklovsky, "Art as Technique" in *Russian Formalist Criticism*, edited by Lemon and Reis (University of Nebraska Press, 1965), p. 4.
17. Peter Brook, ibid., p. 43.

*I*nside the *M*agic *D*ustbin:
*C*reative *A*pproaches to
*U*nacceptab*f*e *B*ehaviour

BERNIE WARREN & LORELEI ROGERS

Prologue

It was early in the class, the first of a new year, and Tina,[1] an ebullient 8-year-old with Down's syndrome, was already making her presence felt. I (BW)[2] had not worked with her before, but stories about her were legion. I could see that if I didn't act soon things would quickly get out of control.

My first instinct was to tell her to sit down at a desk away from the other children. I was about to shout at her when I saw a large metal dustbin (garbage can). In it was the customary black plastic sack. I glanced again: it was empty, and therefore clean. I don't know where or why the idea came to me but in one flowing movement I swooped down and picked up Tina. I told her she had been chosen for a very special journey to the kingdom of the magic dustbin. Gently, I placed her inside the bin. Perplexed, she asked what was so magical about the "bin." I told her that its special magic helped children who were noisy to calm down. I told her that I would come back in a minute to check whether the magic had worked. For the next five minutes or so she stood in the bin watching the class. When I returned she was ready to rejoin the class.

Over the course of the next few weeks the magic dustbin became a game sometimes used by Tina to gain attention but nevertheless effective. This "technique," borne out of desperation, became an ingenious and non-authoritarian means of controlling Tina's often unpredictable behaviour in a way that she accepted and enjoyed.

Introduction

All teachers are forced at some point in their careers to deal with behaviour they find to be unacceptable. This chapter looks at how we help to construct behaviour in the classroom. It also looks at ways in

34

which that behaviour may be reframed. In particular we discuss a novel in-service project, based on drama and the arts, which aimed to make teachers more conscious of their own role in the creation of behaviour that they find unacceptable.

Initiated by Lorelei in her role as Co-ordinator of In-service Programs in the Faculty of Education at the University of Calgary, we first got together to share information and to reflect on our own practice and our extensive experience as classroom teachers. The idea that drama and the arts could be presented to, and used by, non-specialist classroom teachers as process rather than as content disciplines came out of these discussions.

The idea that drama and the other arts can be used not only as an agent for change but also to provide opportunities for individuals to reflect on their practice was to become a recurrent theme as we collaborated on the design and delivery of several different in-service courses. In all cases, these courses were designed with the intent of meeting either the perceived or articulated needs of serving non-specialist teachers. This chapter focuses specifically on the first of these courses, *Creative approaches to channelling unacceptable behaviour.*

Initial Design

> "...for us knowing is an experience. Action and knowledge are united in the actor, and our account of knowing is therefore, of the actor with her personal narrative, intentions and passions."[3]

As Connelly and Clandinin have pointed out, the practical knowledge of teachers and students is complex because it embodies in a history, in the moment and in the act, all modes of knowing aimed at the particular event that is called forth in the teaching and learning act.[4] It seemed to us that a perennial and perplexing issue for classroom teachers is the issue of classroom management. Teachers are always looking for a key, a twist, a variation on current practice to deal more effectively with the discipline and management problems that arise in every classroom from time to time. They are generally interested in new ideas in this area as they search for ways to make their classrooms positive, effective learning environments. We came to believe that if we could successfully present the idea that there were alternative ways of viewing, understanding and modifying behaviour we could make a real contribution to the everyday needs of practising teachers.

The design of the first course was heavily influenced by the predetermined guidelines used for all courses offered through the in-service program. This meant that courses were to be 20 hours long, involve some form of academic assignment, and be offered on a pass/fail basis. Additional regulations required that all participants be certified teachers.

What we wanted to achieve with the course was to present to teachers alternative ways of ordering daily experience in their classrooms. More precisely, we wanted to focus on discipline and classroom management issues and alternative ways of seeing and dealing with them. Lorelei suggested that we use Joyce and Showers' model[5] to design the first course. Their model had five essential steps: the study of a theoretical base; demonstration by persons relatively expert; practice in protected conditions; coaching and companionship; and figuring out optimal uses. As most of this is an integral part of drama education, and particularly developmental drama, this seemed an appropriate model to build on. Ultimately, we wanted to engage teachers in the discovery and mastery of creative approaches to unacceptable behaviours, and to present the arts and drama as vehicles and processes for accomplishing this.

Theoretical Perspective

The course, *Creative approaches to channelling unacceptable behaviour*, was first offered at a residential school for emotionally disturbed children over two weekends in March 1984. Designed as both a practical introduction to the creative arts and a process by which to help in the development of reflective practice by teachers, the course emphasized the beneficial effects of artistic activity in the reframing and redirecting of students' classroom behaviour. Consequently, although both were referred to during the course, the primary focus was not so much on teaching a subject or on moving curriculum moments forward, but rather on highlighting the value of the arts in encouraging individual development, both by teachers taking the course and by their students.

The course was based on two underlying suppositions: that the process of teaching is inherently dramatic, and that no behaviour is in and of itself "bad." We made use of the notion that behaviour is influenced by both its **function** — the reasons why the act is undertaken, and its **context** — where and when the behaviour occurs. We suggested that the relationships between function, context and behaviour (performance) determine whether the behaviour is either appropriate or not.

We also asked the participants to consider that much of a child's inappropriate performance may be as a result of being unable to "read" context and/or function; this will often lead to inappropriate behaviours being chosen. For children from socially deprived backgrounds with few suitable role models the necessary behaviour may simply be out of their range of responses. We reminded participants that almost all human behaviour occurs for a reason and many children's behaviours, despite being viewed by some adults as aberrant, may be defense or survival strategies for that child. Consequently, the emphasis throughout was not on the removal of behaviours; rather we emphasised ways that would help teachers reframe behaviours.

We suggested from the start that deviation from normal expectations can be devastating. Whatever their reason(s), children exhibiting unacceptable behaviours need to be helped to understand what is expected of them and, where necessary, be given opportunity to practise these behaviours in a supportive and non-threatening environment. However, it is important to remember that a "deviant" is created not by what they do but by how we react to it. The behaviour itself is not "deviant"; it only takes on that character in relation to other persons and their responses.

Appropriate behaviour is, to a large part, socially and culturally determined. In special situations (e.g., schools and youth protection facilities), this is doubly true. In these environments teachers and other professionals replace parents in determining what constitutes appropriate behaviour, and while views may differ, teachers tend to influence and reinforce each other's views of a particular child. This labelling often tends to create a vicious circle, with some children getting a bad name as a behaviour problem early on. This label sticks throughout the child's school career. To put this another way, teachers, by determining when a child's behaviour is inappropriate, often transform it into a problem needing discipline. Viewed this way, teachers hold the key to both the creation of, and the potential solutions to, behaviour "problem(s)."

We believe it is much easier to prevent a behaviour from being perceived as a problem than it is to correct it after it has been "labelled." Consequently, a major thrust of the course was to help teachers reframe their own responses to behaviour, to try to find ways that they can be more relaxed and, as a result, less likely to construe unacceptable behaviours as being a problem. We wanted them to think through why they deem the behaviour unacceptable (particularly effective when working in small groups of peers who act as moderating influences) and to try to find creative ways of dealing with the problem — ones that avoid setting them up as an authority figure.

Creative Approaches: A Rationale

As most of the participants had little or no background in any of the arts, a basic rationale was needed. We emphasized the artistic process, diverting participants' attention from this society's fixation on artifacts. The emphasis throughout was on the notion that, contrary to many of the participants' initial beliefs, artistic experience was accessible to everyone. However, we also pointed out that engagement in artistic activity is a personal pursuit, one that must be undertaken by the individual (i.e., it cannot be done to them). We also emphasized that the arts make extensive use of symbol and metaphor and are predominantly non-linear. Consequently, particularly in the initial stages of artistic exploration, there are no right or wrong answers. Taking away a notion of right and wrong reduces the possibility for failure and as a result may help lead to small successes. Given that many modern day problems result from feelings of alienation and anomy or from lacking an outlet for personal self-expression, the arts provide a means of empowerment and expression which can help counter these malaises. Above all, we emphasised that, by engaging in artistic pursuits, any behaviour can become purposeful, and even unacceptable behaviour (e.g., anger) can be put to good use.

We also discussed how artistic activities can be used to aid concentration, build co-operation, develop communication skills, constructive self-expression and physical control, promote relaxation and creatively redirect energies previously viewed as destructive or unacceptable. Also, by helping teachers feel more relaxed, these activities can help prevent them from transforming student behaviours into problems.

Course Content

Course activities were chosen to show how to redirect youthful energies, often manifested within the classroom as unwanted or uncontrollable behaviours, shaping them to useful and creative purposes. Wherever possible, course content was developed in response to the specific identified needs of the group, but material (games, techniques, ideas etc.) was always chosen to illustrate "praxis" — the coming together of theory and practice.

Much of the course was given over to providing teachers with tools that they might use in shifting behaviour from inappropriate to appropriate by directing/coaching/assisting students to correctly read context and by modelling and discussing appropriate performances. For example, there are times when it is acceptable to be noisy and boisterous and others when it is necessary to be quiet. By creating, discussing and modelling each setting and behaviour with students, the teacher advances the ability of students to understand the context of situations of each sort.

One evening a group of teachers was engaged in an exercise which examined the notion of appropriate and inappropriate "noise." To do this they were going through a variety of esteem-enhancing name games. Some of the activities called for quiet attentiveness, others encouraged laughter and joking. Some required a single speaker at a time while others encouraged the participants to speak simultaneously.

At a particularly raucous moment an administrator of the school in which the course was being held walked past the open door. The teachers were oblivious to his presence as they laughed and talked but I (LR) saw his frown of censure. In a flash of insight I realized that his performance was "inappropriate" because he was unaware of the context in which the activity was occurring. This served as confirmation and reinforcement of the shaping thesis that all of us, not just our students, can behave inappropriately if we have not correctly understood the context and function of an incident.

We would also suggest that planning a noisy activity as a relief for students bursting with energy and restlessness may have a positive effect, especially if used prior to settling down to a serious activity demanding full concentration. From this perspective, five minutes of planned appropriate "noise" could serve as a productive period in the day. This, then, becomes another possible role of the teacher — as planner of various contexts which allow children to practise appropriate performances in protected environments.

Specific Examples

During the course, a wealth of activities[6] were presented to the teachers. Below are examples, one from each of four areas covered in the course:

i) AREA: *controlling non-verbal vocabulary*
    ACTIVITY: *"People to People"*

> This simple anatomical game focuses an individual's attention on individual body parts. Group works in pairs. There is one person, "it," who calls anatomical commands (e.g., hand to hand). Pairs respond by placing the identified body parts together. At any time "it" may call "people to people," at which point individuals find a new partner. This normally leaves a new person calling commands.

Every physical task can be broken down into movement phrases and sequences. All individuals have a unique "movement signature" which affects the way they work at any physical task. In addition, all individuals have a "movement memory" (i.e., the ability to remember movement sequences). Both movement memory and movement signature are affected by an individual's awareness of their body parts (i.e., arms, legs etc.), and how those parts work. This in turn can affect coordination and success at many physical tasks. At a very basic level, an inability to comprehend and control how the body works will often "conspire" to frustrate or retard the assimilation and understanding of new movement phrases and therefore the learning of **any** new task.

39

ii) AREA: *channelling anger*
   ACTIVITY: *"Consonant Karate"*

Individual makes "knife-hand" as in a " karate chop." A deep breath is inhaled and then exhaled forcefully, accompanied by the sound of consonants (e.g., c, t, d, f, v, b. May also use the sound sh). As this occurs the individual cleaves the air with her hands and stamps her feet. This can be worked into a rhythmic tribal dance by standing the group in two lines facing one another a good distance apart. The group moves together and apart stamping and exhaling consonants. Care must be taken to emphasize that this is a "non-contact" dance. It is also important to establish that only the letters are to be exhaled. It is especially important to establish "control" signals and your own level of comfort before beginning the exercise.

There is some suggestion that stamping releases endorphins and has a calming effect.[7] This leads to the observation that "controlled temper tantrums" may have a beneficial effect on angry or aggressive individuals. As all "swear" words demand explosive exhalation of the consonant for their maximum effectiveness, (e.g., f-ck, sh-t, d-mn etc.), this can be an extremely valuable exercise with adolescents who have a limited and unacceptably vulgar vocabulary.

iii) AREA: *gaining insight into emotion*
    ACTIVITY: *"Emotional Tableaux"*

This is a non-verbal activity undertaken in pairs. Each group creates a tableau depicting a particular image. After a few minutes, taking turns, one tableau is copied by all the other pairs. The original pair goes around making sure that the tableau is exact, by physically correcting any inexactitudes. After a moment or two of holding the tableau, the rest of the group tells the original pair how they felt and what they thought the tableau represented. Finally, the original pair shares with the group what their tableau meant to them. This process carries on until all of the group has had a chance to lead.

Often it is very difficult to put feelings and emotions into words. This becomes increasingly difficult when the experience is both powerful and immediate (i.e., the experience is being lived through in the present tense). Exercises such as "Emotional Tableaux" may not be able to translate feeling into language exactly but they can give a sense of an individual's emotional state and lead to insight.

iv) AREA: *relaxation and release*
    ACTIVITY: *"Draw your Mad"*

Working in pairs, individuals take turns to express what makes them angry, sad, happy etc., using soft chalk pastels and strong cartridge paper [Bristol board]. One person chooses a colour and applies it to the paper while talking to their partner, beginning a typical sentence "it really makes me angry when...", and then providing an example (i.e., "It really makes me angry when I see an animal being hit").

To truly represent "anger" on paper requires a great deal of energy being focused through the stick of colour and it is not unusual for someone in this state to tear the paper as they "paint." Anyone watching this activity becomes aware of how anger can be physically displaced through colour and form using these art materials. More importantly the individual has a record of that feeling and can respond to it after the "picture" is finished. The ensuing discussion between creator and teacher often leads to moments of insight for the individual, and in skilled hands, this activity can be a valuable "therapeutic tool" for the human service professional — teacher, doctor, counsellor etc. — working with them. In general terms, working with simple visual arts materials (e.g., soft pastels, large sheets of bond or Mayfair paper etc.), with soft music playing in the background, can be very therapeutic.

Assignments

The courses were designed to enable participants to take away activities that they can try with their own students. The results of these explorations could then be brought back to the class for discussion and feedback from the group and the instructor. To encourage reflective practice, a journal assignment and school-based observations between sessions were designed to encourage teachers to step back, reflect on their practice, and then bring these reflections back to the group for discussion.

One activity was to create a thumbnail sketch of a particular behaviour that was deemed unacceptable. We used a list of basic questions about the child and his behaviour to build up what we referred to as a thumbnail sketch.[8] This was conducted in the week between classes. Using another series of basic questions,[9] these sketches were then used in small group discussions to help participants review, reframe and redirect behaviours of children presented to the group.

The assigned journal had two parts. The first was to be a record keeping of activities and games used throughout the class time. This would provide the teacher with a set of instructions for tested

41

experienced activities that could be used with their students either during the period of the course or at a later date.

The second part of the journal was for more personal reflections. Participants were encouraged to record their own reactions to the ideas and activities presented during the course and thoughts that had been triggered by discussions. They were also asked to commit to paper, plans that they had for changes in the ordering of daily classroom experiences for themselves and their students.

Discussion

From the very beginning, we tried to create within the course a sense of "communitas" — a coming together and sharing with an emphasis on the personal knowledge and strengths of the participants. However, the more the course was taught, the more the emphasis was placed on peer-directed learning through the sharing of experience and knowledge with others.

The course aimed throughout to help teachers lay aside preconceptions. In particular we were trying to lay aside the image of the arts only as disciplines, so that teachers could experience them as processes or vehicles for understanding themselves and shaping appropriate responses. Throughout the course, teaching was referred to as an art form, not a science that could be reduced to formulas and equations, and the "artistry" of the teacher was discussed using a theatrical metaphor, "the theatre of the classroom."[10] In doing this we hoped to enable teachers to realize they were not on "foreign soil." We wanted to help them realize that the "artistry" they already possessed could be used in a way that might prevent the creation of behaviour problems.

As the courses developed, the journal assignment, often mandatory for university drama courses, took on particular significance to the development of informed praxis. As the journal took on more significance within the class — shifting from simply being an assignment to being the seminal assignment in the course — an interesting parallel was occurring in education generally: the growing realization that reflective practice is essential to success within the classroom. For more than 10 years, Heathcote had been arguing that, to be successful, teachers must come to terms with who they are, not what facts they know, suggesting that "knowing what's irrelevant is the most important thing in teaching."[11] It was through these journals that the teachers taking these courses started to become aware of who they were and what was irrelevant in their teaching.

As more courses were offered, and feedback started to be received from teachers, the format used for delivering the courses was subjected to experimentation. New courses were offered at the university as well as in school and community settings within Calgary and in outlying rural areas. The number of contact hours were varied and rules restricting admission only to practising teachers were relaxed. Child care workers, social workers, nurses, psychologists, school administrators and classroom aides all, at one time or another, became participants in one or more of these courses. Each experiment led to a change in the design of the courses, a development which not only affected the form and content of the arts-based courses themselves, but also exerted an influence on the design and delivery of other courses offered by the in-service program.

It would be reasonable to suggest that the courses were not the only things that changed. We also experienced changes as a result of both the variations in the format and from the insights provided by teachers through their journals and in-class discussion. As a result, we reached a more articulate understanding of the teaching/learning continuum and were able to explore more deeply the idea of the classroom as theatre.

In placing behaviour within the perspective that it is labelled as "bad" not by the person engaging in it, but rather by their society (i.e., behaviour is judged against specific social norms), we implicitly asked teachers to take the moral shadings away from student behaviour and set them in the realm of coachable performance. This opened up new vistas. It enabled them to see the misbehaving child as literally that — a child who is missing the appropriate behaviour because of an inability to read the situation, or because of a lack of experience in producing the necessary result. In this light, "bad" behaviour is transformed, becoming a problem with possible remedies and thus offering the teacher and their students new hope.

Epilogue

Finally, let us return to Tina. Despite her often unacceptable behaviour, much of the problem was constructed by the adults around her. She had poor communication skills and a low frustration level. She knew that by behaving badly she could get attention. The magic dustbin did not in any way solve these problems. What it did do was, at those times when a "time out" was needed, prevent an authoritarian struggle, a tactic which often got her more infuriated. The magic was that being placed in a magic spot seemed to help Tina calm down.

What is more, unlike some of my colleagues, my level of stress in working with her was relatively low; the game element of my intervention meant that I never got into a "knock 'em down, drag 'em out" power struggle with her. Removing myself from the role of "policeman," I was able to work on providing her with a stimulating environment in which she could learn. Over the course of our working

43

together she spent less and less time in the magic bin[12] and more and more time being a productive member of the class.

Endnotes

1. Not her real name.
2. Where "I" is used in the text the initials BW or LR will be used to denote which of us is "speaking."
3. Connelly and Clandinin, in *Learning and Teaching the Ways of Knowing*, (Eighty-fourth yearbook of the NSSE part II), edited by Eisner (Chicago: University of Chicago Press, 1985).
4. Ibid.
5. Joyce, B & Showers, B. (1982), "The Coaching of Teaching" in *Educational Leadership*, October 1982: pp. 4–10.
6. For details of activities used in these courses see Amies, H.T., Warren, B., & Watling, R. *Social Drama* (London: John Clare, 1986); Warren, B. & Dunne, T. *Drama Games* (North York, Ontario: Captus Press, 1989); and Warren, B., (ed.) *Using the Creative Arts in Therapy* (Cambridge, MA: Brookline Books, & London: Croom Helm, 1984).
7. This stems from research carried out in the early 1960s on African tribal stamping dances. Our source was personal conversations with Marion Lindkvist, Director of Sesame and a leading pioneer in the development of dramatherapy in England.
8. Questions used to form thumbnail sketches of unacceptable behaviour:

    Personal characteristics:
    a) Name/Age/Gender
    b) Height/Weight/Distinguishing physical features
    c) What is the student's overall disposition? Is there anything distinguishing about their movement signature?
    d) How many are there in the family unit (i.e., number of brothers or sisters, rank in the family [i.e., youngest, oldest etc.])?
    e) What is known about parental management style?
    f) Have there been complaints about behaviour of any siblings?
    g) Has the individual recently experienced a move, death or divorce in the family?

    Details of the student's behaviour:
    a) Describe behaviour deemed unacceptable.
    b) Why do you find behaviour unacceptable?
    c) What is your typical response to the behaviour? What effect does this have?
    d) Describe where and when it most usually occurs.
    e) Is this behaviour context specific (e.g., only occurs on Mondays)?
    f) Is this behaviour function specific (e.g., only occurs when asked to read out loud)?

9. Questions and actions used to help reframe behaviour:

    a) Other than this specific behaviour, is there anything to suggest:
    • a physical/endocrinal/physiological/neurological problem?

- a learning disability?
- a cry for help (e.g., childhood sexual abuse/family problems)?
- family bereavement?

b) Do my colleagues have similar/different problems with this child? If so, how can we help each other:
- find positive uses for behaviour?
- find explanations for its survival value?
- find ways to restructure context(s) in which behaviour occurs?
- find ways to make "learning" and our interactions more positive?

c) Can I change the child's behaviour and/or my expectations?

d) What role am I playing? Is it this role that causes conflict? If so, is there any way that I can change this?

e) Is there any way that I can view this behaviour positively? Can I re-direct this behaviour without drawing attention to it? (i.e., Can I place it in a context which does not force me to play the role of authoritarian or angry parent?)

f) Can I find ways to allow the child to review their behaviour and take responsibility for their own actions?

10. See "The Teacher as Performer" in this volume.
11. Heathcote, D. *Three Looms Waiting*, (film) (London: BBC, Omnibus, 1972).
12. From the first class on, I always made sure that there was a clean and empty plastic sack in the bin for these classes.

*U*nacceptable *A*pproaches to *Creative Behaviour*

CHARLES E. COMBS

ntoine de Saint-Exupery begins his book, *The Little Prince,* with the story of his "career" as an artist. He tells of being so impressed with the image of a boa constrictor swallowing its prey whole that he drew a picture which he considered to be very scary: a boa constrictor digesting an elephant. When he showed his masterpiece to grown-ups, however, they usually replied, "Why should anyone be frightened by a hat?" Because the grown-ups were unable to understand his first drawing, he made a second — a sectional view showing the boa constrictor with the elephant inside. He then writes:

> The grown-ups' response, this time, was to advise me to lay aside my drawings of boa constrictors, whether from the inside or the outside, and devote myself instead to geography, history, arithmetic and grammar. That is why, at the age of six, I gave up what might have been a magnificent career as a painter. I had been disheartened by the failure of my Drawing Number One and my Drawing Number Two. Grown-ups never understand anything by themselves, and it is tiresome for children to be always and forever explaining things to them.[1]

I was stimulated to write this piece by a conversation I had with Bernie Warren, where we were discussing his courses on "creative approaches to unacceptable behaviour." It occurred to me (while playing with the phrase) that all too often I've seen or heard of teachers taking unacceptable approaches to creative behaviour, for whatever reasons they may have had. Intuitively, I knew there was something important to explore in the notion of "unacceptable approaches to creative behaviour."

46

Upon reflection, I believe the significance of this lies in examining our "inner cores" as teachers. That is, what has drawn us to the vocation? I come to this point from a lot of thinking about what has drawn me to teaching — and to teaching theatre and drama, specifically. I've talked to a lot of theatre professionals, educators, and students, and I believe a commonality is that we all have our own particular "broken wings" (as Dorothy Heathcote calls it) when it comes to our personal need to work in the extraordinarily expressive medium of theatre/drama. Generalist teachers, too, should reflect deeply on just why they were drawn to their profession — one which has at its heart the qualities of giving, sharing, loving and drawing out.

The notion of drawing out students is particularly important, since it is literally the meaning of "education" — the process of educing. Drawing out implies openness: that is, vulnerability on the part of both the teacher and the student. If the teacher is authoritarian, guarded, aloof, or insecure, then the student is not liable to be open, receptive, secure, malleable — amenable to being "drawn out." In a word (or so) the essence of the teacher/student relationship (like the parent/child one) should be honesty and trust which is based in love and respect.

I am sure you remember your favourite teacher; I'm also sure you remember your least favourite. Also, I'll bet you have some wonderfully strong memories of your school days — the high points of your elementary and high school education. If you're like so many others of us, I have a hunch that your fondest memories are connected with the arts, crafts, social activities or athletics, rather than with the traditional subjects. Certainly, though, many of us have highs and lows associated with the traditional subjects also, where we may recall "acing" a test or winning a spelling or math contest, and these experiences, too, may linger vividly in our memories. Why is that? Probably because you had an emotional investment in your work or play — not just an intellectual one.

Of course, when you're wrapped up in what you're doing, you may be vulnerable. That is, you are liable to experience higher highs and lower lows than you would if you were playing it safe by remaining aloof, noncommittal, or emotionally insulated. If you think back to the highs and lows of your school experiences, you may discover those that made you feel good about yourself, as well as those where you felt victimized, injured, rejected, ignored, manipulated or unjustly treated. When you experienced a "high" you were approved or accepted — that is, your self-esteem was enhanced by others' actions towards you or by your own knowledge of your self-worth or the worth of your work. On the other hand, when you experienced a "low" your self-esteem was undermined, either by a teacher or by peers.

This suggests that a provocative model may be used to examine the teaching process, one in which teaching may be compared to parenting and the notion of psychological maltreatment may be used to inform our consciousness regarding our behaviour. First of all, I'd like to talk about psychological maltreatment. I'll give some definitions and some descriptions, then I will try to connect it (through the use of anecdotes) to unacceptable approaches to creative behaviour. Finally, I will come back to some thoughts on acceptable approaches to creative behaviour — as well as ways to elicit and encourage it.

C hild abuse can fall into three major categories: physical, sexual, and psychological. It is assumed that any well-functioning teacher does not physically or sexually abuse her students. Similarly, the average teacher does not emotionally batter, neglect or abuse his pupils. However, I think we all can remember instances where we felt victimized by teachers who either inadvertently or purposely hurt our feelings deeply. Moreover, I'll bet that if we are honest with ourselves, we can recall instances where we snapped at a student or in some other way "put them down" just because we were "having a bad day." Therefore, I think it is important that we examine psychological abuse in order to see how it may relate to inappropriate reactions by teachers in the classroom.

James Garbarino, Edna Guttmann and Janis Seeley, in their book, *The Psychologically Battered Child,* choose to bypass the distinction between emotional abuse and neglect (the one being "active" and the other "passive"), calling the entire area psychological maltreatment. They note:

> The definitions of emotional abuse include verbal or emotional assault, close confinement and threatened harm. The definitions of emotional neglect include inadequate nurturance/affection, knowingly permitting maladaptive behaviour (for example delinquency) and other refusal to provide essential care.[2]

They go on to note that behaviour may be considered to be psychologically abusive when "it conveys a culture-specific message of rejection or impairs a socially relevant psychological process, such as the development of a coherent positive self-concept."[3]

According to Gertrude Morrow, in her book, *The Compassionate School,* the most prevalent form of abuse is psychological. She notes that educators particularly, should be concerned about psychological abuse because it "impairs a child's ability to develop a sense of competence and self-worth, without which normal social and emotional development do not occur."[4] She goes on to note that psychological abuse takes three forms: emotional neglect, emotional abuse and verbal abuse. She defines emotional neglect as the failure to give children emotional nurturance, thereby causing them to have no trust in themselves, to feel empty inside, to feel unloved and unlovable. Emotional abuse, she notes, is more subtle and complex than emotional neglect, and consists of the "use of intimidation, manipulation, blame and punishments within a power relationship to accomplish an adult's goals for a child."[5] As a result of emotional abuse the child may suffer one or more of the following: burdensome guilt, shame and humiliation, extreme embarrassment, overwhelming anxiety or crippling fear. Verbal abuse destroys the child's sense of self and integrity. It is a barrage of derogatory and demeaning labels which make the child feel rejected, unlovable and bad, and which the child internalizes as a part of his or her self-image. It is a way adults use words as weapons to express their anger and disappointment toward a child.[6]

Clearly, the notion of self-concept, self-esteem, ego strength or social competence are central to the healthy development of the person, and should constitute a significant aspect of the goal of education. Because psychological maltreatment undermines specifically the sense of self, it is important to see how it does so. Garbarino, et al. define psychological maltreatment as "a concerted attack by an adult on a child's development of self and social competence, a pattern of psychically destructive behaviour."[7] Parenthetically, it should be noted that the authors reiterate that psychological maltreatment consists of patterns of abusive behaviour by adults. As educators who may occasionally be guilty of "unacceptable approaches to creative behaviour," I think it is important to note that we are usually talking of instances of abusive or neglectful behaviour rather than patterns. However, even these instances can be painful.

According to Garbarino, psychological maltreatment takes five forms:

1) **Rejecting**: the adult refuses to acknowledge the child's worth and the legitimacy of the child's needs.
2) **Isolating**: the adult cuts the child off from normal social experiences, prevents the child from forming friendships and makes the child believe that she is alone in the world.
3) **Terrorizing**: the adult verbally assaults the child, creates a climate of fear, bullies and frightens the child, and makes the child believe that the world is capricious and hostile.
4) **Ignoring**: the adult deprives the child of essential stimulation and responsiveness, stifling emotional growth and intellectual development.

5) **Corrupting**: the adult "mis-socializes" the child, stimulates the child to engage in destructive antisocial behaviour, reinforces that deviance and makes the child unfit for normal social experience.[8]

Subsequently, the authors specify the behaviours that constitute maltreatment in each of the major developmental stages of life and for each category.[9] They also deal with degrees of severity for maltreatment, noting that it may be mild, moderate or severe. For our purposes we will just look at the categories of school age (5–11 years) and adolescence (11–18 years).

Rejecting ☐ generally involves behaviours which make the child feel abandoned or unloved. School-age children may be made to feel negative about their self-concept because their accomplishments are belittled, they are scapegoated or they are labeled with such names as "dummy" or "monster." In adolescence the young person is not encouraged to develop his social role toward more autonomy or self-determination. Thus, the maltreating parent may "infantilize" the adolescent by treating him like a young child; they may subject the young person to verbal humiliation and excessive criticism; or they may expel the youth from the family.

Isolating ☐ is generally seen in cases where the parents deprive the child from having normal social relations. It may range from failure to provide occasions for normal social interaction, to the active thwarting of all efforts by the child to make contact with others. In school-age children this may be manifested in parents removing the child from such social relationships with peers as inviting friends to the home or playing with other children. Adolescents are prevented from participating in such activities as joining clubs, after-school programs and sports, and are often punished for engaging in normal social activities such as dating. Further, they may be withdrawn from school to perform household tasks such as caring for siblings.

Terrorizing ☐ usually involves threats to the child which suggest imminent but vague punishment, or which intentionally stimulate intense fear by creating a threatening atmosphere in which the child or young person is punished for failing to achieve unreasonable expectations set for her. School-age children may be placed in no-win situations where they are subject to inconsistent demands by parents or where the "rules of the game" are constantly changed, thereby placing them in the position to be constantly criticized because they have no chance to successfully meet expectations. Adolescents are subject to threats of public humiliation through the revelation of embarrassing events or characteristics, and may be ridiculed in public.

Ignoring ☐ involves parents who are so preoccupied with themselves that they are psychologically unavailable to the child and are unable to respond to the child's needs. The behaviours may range from a lack of sustained attention to blatant silent treatment. This lack of access to parents is "passive" and is an aspect of neglect rather than the more abusive and "active" behaviour of rejection. School-age hildren may feel unprotected by parents who fail to intervene when the child feels threatened by family members or peers. Adolescents may be shut off by their parents who refuse to discuss the young person's problems and activities, or they may be displaced as objects of affection by parents who focus on other relationships or interests.

Corrupting ☐ generally refers to the mis-socialization of the child by her parents. It involves the reinforcement of antisocial and deviant behaviour patterns in such areas as aggression, sexuality or substance abuse, thereby making the child unfit for normal social experience. It may range from the parents conveying the impression that they encourage the child's unsuitable behaviour to the active encouragement and reinforcement of such behaviour. With school-age children the parent may reward the child for precocious aggressive behaviour, drug use and sexual activity, and may expose the child to pornography or involve the child sexually with adults. The adolescent may be more actively encouraged in deviant behaviour, with the parent involving the young person in prostitution, drug trafficking, and violence.

*N*ow, the question to ask is, how can this knowledge of psychological maltreatment be applied to teaching, specifically to teaching in the arts? First of all, however, I'd like to illustrate maltreatment through the use of some anecdotes I've gathered. Some are from my own background, but others are from students and colleagues. Significantly, many of these students are in-service teachers who are in their 30s or 40s; thus, their stories from their childhood assume greater importance, I think, since it is apparent that they are still affected by their maltreatment even after many years.

For the sake of my argument I have translated some of the definitions of psychological maltreatment to the arena of education. Within that frame of reference one may see that not all forms of abuse or neglect seem to be common. In fact, for two categories I have not included any actual instances of maltreatment; however, I have kept these sections in for the sake of continuity and have described some potential forms of maltreatment.

1) Rejecting ☐ The teacher belittles the accomplishments of the child, scapegoats the child, labels the child with demeaning names, humiliates or excessively criticizes the young person.

The art teacher at the school where I teach told my class that they would not use glue or paint because "they were not capable" of handling these things.

* * * *

My little sister's pre-school teacher told her that she would not hang up her picture of a squirrel because there were no such things as purple squirrels. Donna came home crying, got out her bottle of Pal Vitamins, and said, "See, there really are purple squirrels."

* * * *

When I was in Grade 7 I was to introduce a play. At rehearsal the director said if I was to stand on the stage to read, then I must wear a long skirt to cover my knees since they were not very pretty because they are double jointed and bend backwards. I was so embarrassed I did not do the introduction. As a matter of fact, I never got on a stage again.

* * * *

A third grader's mother told me that her son had written a play that had a role for every member of his school class — a very important point since his teacher couldn't find a play with the right number of characters. His teacher said she liked it, then asked him where he found the play. When he said he'd written it himself, she asked what book he'd taken it from. When he said it wasn't from a book, but it was something he'd created, she said she wouldn't use it because "if it wasn't from a book it wouldn't be any good."

2) Isolating ☐ The teacher cuts the child off from normal social experiences of the class, prevents the child from forming friendships, or from participating in school activities.

While I did not find any anecdotes clearly reflecting this attitude, I can recall instances where teachers have isolated (or didn't include) certain students — whether it was because they were "troublemakers," for other "disciplinary" reasons, because they weren't bright, or because they just didn't like them. Perhaps the following anecdote comes closest insofar as the needs of the child in question are clearly neglected and he is made to feel an "outsider" in his classroom.

> In my first teaching job in rural upstate New York I was given the opportunity to do a musical with the elementary chorus, Grades 5–6, 120 singers. I had regular bi-weekly rehearsals with the whole group, but I received permission from the principal to work with the eight leads separately. At one of the early special rehearsals all the leads except one boy were there, so I decided that I'd go to get him. I walked into his Grade 6 class, and he was working at remedial things on the board. I went to the teacher and quietly asked if he might be excused, and as I was walking to the doorway with him, she said loudly, "Oh yes! Take him with you! He can't do anything in here — maybe he can sing!" All my words of comfort as we walked down the hall to the music room, I fear did not do much to restore his wounded self-image.

3) Terrorizing ☐ The teacher verbally assaults the child, creates a climate of fear, bullies and frightens the child, sets unreasonable tasks, arbitrarily changes the rules or expectations, or publicly embarrasses or ridicules the child.

> A rare but devastatingly crushing moment in my school experiences occurred in Grade 3. One day during Social Studies the teacher was explaining something at the chalkboard. I was not paying the closest attention, reading in my book instead. All of a sudden she turned around, glared at me, and shouted, "Why don't you join the Foreign Legion?" After a moment she regained her composure and continued with the lesson. I was so stunned and shocked all I could do was blush, freeze up and feel mortified. It took me months to get up the courage to ask my mother what the Foreign Legion was and why my teacher may have wanted me to join it.

* * * *

> I have a memory back from my fifth grade year, the time of year for the Grade 5 camping trip. We were

53

all very enthused about the whole idea, and to make things even more exciting the teacher announced that we were having a camp folder design contest. My mind raced in all directions. What would I put on it? There were so many exciting things to do, why not put all of them on my folder?! I would win for sure; no one would have that idea. I began work immediately, drawing each and every one of my ideas. I filled the folder. And as most kids do, I labeled each thing so there would be no mistake about what they were.

And then it happened. I turned to the person next to me and asked them how to spell the last thing on my list. As I was asking, the teacher saw me and immediately flew over to me and began screaming. When I told her why I had been talking, she became furious! She told me that under no circumstances were we allowed to talk when working, and she took my almost-complete, prize-winning folder and tore it up. She told me that it was awful and it was cluttered with too many things. Why couldn't I be more like Corina who had a single flower placed neatly in the middle of her folder (and who incidently won the contest). I was given a new folder which I was not allowed to decorate — a folder that was left blank along with my heart and my enthusiasm for being creative. I'll never forget that moment. I had had faith in that folder, and now I was confused. Was my artwork really junk? Was I letting my imagination go too much? Should I always be conservative and draw a single flower? I wrestled with that confusion for a long time, and even though I am an artist and an art teacher today, many times I wonder deep down — "is my work any good? Or, was my teacher right?"

* * * *

When I was in the fifth grade and learning fractions, I was so interested that I did "extra" homework. When I turned it in, my teacher tore it up in front of the whole class, saying: "If I wanted you to do extra work, I would have asked you for it." That was it for math!

4) Ignoring ☐   The teacher is insensitive to the needs of the child, perhaps because of preoccupation. The teacher may subject the child to silent treatment, or be unavailable when the child feels threatened. The child feels unprotected, unloved, and unworthy.

> I was about eight years old and was spending the summer at playground — a town-sponsored programme that keeps children busy with arts and crafts and games during the summer months. I remember that I loved to draw and was always in the arts and crafts room with crayons and paints doing what I loved to do — draw. I was probably the youngest in the room that day, for I remember walking in and feeling intimidated by the older children. I did go in though because I wanted to draw. I sat and drew a beautiful picture — the Peanuts character sleeping on his dog house. It was Snoopy. I thought it was the finest piece of art work I had ever created. Then one of the older kids came over to see it. She was immediately overcome with laughter and soon the other children had joined in. I had misspelled "Snoopy" as "Snoppy" on the top of my paper, and the other children were hysterical with laughter over this detail. This was one of the most humiliating experiences of my life — and nobody did anything to help me.

5) Corrupting ☐ The teacher may encourage anti-social behaviour in such areas as physical aggression, intimidation, manipulation, cheating, ethical "shortcuts" etc. Examples could occur in science, theatre, athletics, journalism and other areas where an unethical or maltreating teacher could suggest that "the end justifies the means."

Again, I did not find anecdotes that specifically reflected corrupting behaviour on the part of a teacher, but I think we are all aware of coaches who ask their student athletes to intentionally injure an opposing player, or who urge them to "win at any price." Further, I'm sure there are instances where teachers may not question where or how students have obtained certain things — like props (in the case of theatre) or information (in journalism).

Significantly, Garbarino, et al. differentiate between emotional maltreatment and emotionally challenging situations. They write:

> pychological abuse attacks character and self; neglect fails to nourish character and self in important ways. Challenge, when it occurs in the context of supportive

relationships, can induce the growth of character and an enhanced sense of self.[10]

To this I might add that in the classroom the notion of "challenge" can slip over into the area of abuse or neglect if teachers do not constantly monitor their feelings and behaviour toward each and every student. We have seen in the earlier anecdotes just how easy it is for a teacher who is "having a bad day" to inflict scars on sensitive and creative students — and it is apparent how lasting these scars are.

Felicitously, drama in the classroom provides the "context of supportive relationships" which Garbarino et al. suggest is necessary to enable "challenge" to contribute to personal/social/emotional growth. Advocates propose that the child, through experience in drama, may grow in several important areas of personal and interactional development: self confidence, self esteem, the art of creative and co-operative problem solving, communication skills, the ability to empathize with the thoughts and feelings of others, the ability to express and understand emotionally distressing states of mind, the ability to co-operate socially, the ability to internalize the laws or norms of social interaction, critical thinking ability, and participation in the aesthetically valued process inherent in the creation of improvisational drama.

I believe that drama should be based on certain fundamental attitudes and behaviours: trust, support, co-operation, concentration, control, and agreement to pretend. Once these are accepted as the "rules of the game" in the classroom, then drama (in its infinite variations) can be used to explore and examine the complex emotional and social lives of the students through the processes of playing, questioning, problem solving, decision making, reflective analysis, and critical evaluation. In short, the students who are emotionally and intellectually open and engaged are amenable to being "drawn out" — educated.

Drama activities may range from very simple exercises and games to complex dramatizations of a near-theatrical nature, and its participants may range from preschoolers to adults. A primary difference between drama and theatre art is that drama is not practised for the purpose of audience entertainment. Rather, it exists for the appreciation of its participants. The activities pursued in drama span a continuum which has at one pole exercises and games, and at the other, non-scripted (but prepared) scenes complete with character development and the dramatic elements of conflict, crisis, focus and resolution. Drama employs theatre techniques, skills, attitudes, and devices, yet the product of the participants' labours is not crystallized into a finished artistic product. Rather, the phenomenon of the artistic process is the overriding concern of all involved. This aesthetically valued process of dramatic construction and interpretation is equally important to other life skills which may be developed through drama, since it contributes to what might be called "dramatic literacy."

Perhaps the greatest difference between theatre and drama lies in the essential component of reflection. While audience members of a theatrical production may be moved to great feelings and thoughts, they seldom are provided the formal opportunity to reflect on the nature of their reactions to the work of art. Rather, if there is reflection, it is of an informal nature, occurring by chance. In drama, however, the participants are guided through a discussion regarding their thoughts and feelings on the construction, consequences, and implications of the drama which they have just created and performed.

While drama is different from theatre, it should also be differentiated from children's spontaneous play and from simple imitation, for it is neither the one nor the other; it partakes of elements of both. It should be understood that while spontaneous play is the child's natural medium for mastering their physical, social, and emotional environment, it is pursued at the whim and pace of the child. Also, while imitation may provide a means for duplicating (and perhaps identifying with) another's actions, it is tied to the simple act of copying without necessarily understanding, and thus could be perceived of as learning only at a very elementary level.

In drama, a problem-solving focus (whether the child's own problems or fictional ones) is given to the children's collective play, thereby giving purpose to the act of imitation: specifically, the purpose of creating an objectively rendered and socially accessible "played reality." Thus, the form which the child's play takes in drama is ordered and governed by the problem to be solved in drama, external reality, and the child's internal (intellectual/emotional) reality, as well as by the attitudes and procedures intrinsic to the practice of drama.

Dorothy Heathcote in her film, *Three Looms Waiting*, calls drama "a real man in a mess."[11] If this is so, then the problem which is posed to the children in drama should be a personal/social/emotional/moral one rather than only a physical one which may be resolved intellectually or materially. Thus, the emphasis is placed on human feelings, thoughts, actions, and reactions rather than upon mechanical ingenuity as would be the case were the problem a merely technical one.

This idea is compatible with my theoretical and practical approach to drama, since I believe we only learn when we are challenged — especially within the context of supportive relationships. In my teaching I follow the paradigm of "experience/analysis/synthesis." That is, I present my students with imaginary problems to solve, allow them to work through the problem, then encourage them to "make sense" of the solution, and finally help them integrate their thinking into their existing world view. This model is based on my work with the learning theories of Jean Piaget, who believed that we construct an operational picture of the world (in its physical, social, and emotional complexity) through an interactive process where we continuously adapt to an ever-changing "reality" by taking in new information (which may disrupt our existing scheme of things) and subsequently change our world view to fit the new stimuli.

By presenting opportunities for my students to actively explore what might be called "problem areas" and subsequently to structure their thinking (and even their feelings) I believe I am giving them the chance to become "dramatically literate" — to participate in the essence of theatre/drama. This in turn will allow them to participate more fully and easily in the essence of life. After all, the point and purpose of the arts in education is to free the human spirit, to allow the child to be emotionally expressive so they can share in the human experience to the fullest. If the spirit is shut down, closed off, stunted, then teachers are doing perhaps the greatest disservice of all.

In sum, dramatic literacy is developed by participating in the processes of theatre/drama while developing and honing the requisite skills and attitudes, among which is the ability to open up, to trust, to be emotionally vulnerable. And perhaps this is the most difficult to nurture, since the teacher has to share these qualities. If, as a teacher, you don't, then you run the risk of practising "unacceptable approaches to creative behaviour."

Now, I don't want to leave the readers with the fear that they will invariably permanently scar their students' emotions or stifle their creativity if they aren't perpetually sensitive and aware. It's just that teachers have to constantly monitor their feelings and expressions just as parents do when they are raising their children. It's my hope that this article will help bring to consciousness the harm that an injudicious comment may cause, and that it will suggest a way for both the teacher and the students to practice emotional and aesthetic education. I even have a happy anecdote to illustrate my point and to close this chapter:

In the eighth grade we were supposed to write a poem based on the first two lines given to us by Sister Mary P.:

It's Spring, it's Spring
The birds are on the wing.

We knew that we were expected to express the appropriate sentiments about faith and religion — probably ending up with a poem that went:

58

And in this holy season
We all God's praises sing.

Well, when Mike F. read his poem we all held our breath at his sacrilege! He wrote:

It's Spring, it's Spring;
The birds are on the wing.
Absurd, absurd;
The wings are on the bird!

We waited for him to get zapped, but when the teacher smiled, then laughed, we all released our joy together.

Obviously this was important to me — and I think it's the right approach to creative behaviour.

Endnotes

1. Antione de Saint-Exupery. *The Little Prince*. Trans. by Katherine Woods (New York: Reynal & Hitchcock, 1943), pp. 7–8.
2. James Garbarino, Edna Guttman & Janice Wilson Seeley. *The Psychologically Battered Child* (Jossey-Bass, San Francisco. 1986), pp. 4–5.
3. Ibid., pp. 5–6.
4. Gertrude Morrow. *The Compassionate School* (Englewood Cliffs, N.J.: Prentice-Hall, Inc., 1987), p. 113.
5. Ibid., p. 126.
6. Ibid., pp. 120–21.
7. Garbarino et al, p. 8.
8. Ibid., p. 8.
9. Ibid., pp. 22–9.
10. Ibid., p. 20.
11. Dorothy Heathcote, in *Three Looms Waiting*, a BBC *Omnibus* programme (Ipswich, England: Concord Films).

Acknowledgments

Janna Aldrich, Beth Ann Chase, Robert Colby, Ellen Comiskey, Dianne Dunion, Regina Gilvey, Caron Goyette, Carleen Graff, Maria Macri, Janet Makar, Marge Ryan, Jean Sherman, Robert Swift, Karen VanBlarcom.

I Love You, Alicia Alonzo:
From Institution to
Integration

GEORGE C. MAGER

I was in love with Alicia Alonzo. During my teen years and as a young hopeful dancer, I had seen the beautiful prima ballerina perform. She had that fire, that passion, that Latin seductiveness I had never seen on a dance stage before. And I fell hopelessly in love as only a dramatic adolescent can. When I learned that she was legally blind and that audiences were not supposed to know, my passion increased; I wanted to be her helper, her caring other, in short — her seeing-eye dog. How pure and elevated I felt, for my feelings could now be translated into adolescent idealistic thoughts.

But she didn't need me, didn't even know I existed. She was a great artist concerned with all those things of technique and interpretation and those things still unlabelled which make one the "great artist." She certainly did not need my undying love, nor my pitying concern which would undoubtedly only hinder her.

In the years to come, as I worked with disabled and handicapped persons, what I unknowingly learned from my loving Alicia Alonzo became my personal law: "audiences should never know." And as I developed, the law became addended: "audiences should never know, or if they do know, should never care." The disability is not the art and should never stand in the way of the art.

In the Spring of 1988, the Secretary of State of Canada, upon the advice of Rick Hansen, hosted an Access Awareness Conference in Ottawa. Its purpose was to encourage the integration of persons with a disability into the mainstream of Canadian society. As part of its programme, a gala performance was held at the National Arts Center featuring talented artists from across Canada. Many of these artists were disabled. The Canadian Broadcasting Company taped the performance and it was aired nationally as "A Very Special Gala."

At the time, I was directing the Mackay Theater of the Deaf and Mackay Center Stage — a troupe of wheelchair dancers. As our contribution to the Gala, we combined the two groups, added a few non-disabled dancers and performed a dance piece — dance for dance's sake. Our purpose was merely to dance, to enjoy music, and to find creative expression through our interpretation of that music.

If there was a secondary purpose to our dancing, it was thrust upon us. People questioned "Why do you use dance? Is this some form of therapy?" We could only respond that everyone who wishes, has the right to dance, and if they dance well, they have the right to perform for others. There was the Alicia Alonzo Law: we must perform so well that audiences might momentarily forget the disabilities and see only the dance.

Much theatre we currently see performed by persons who are disabled strives to make social statements, tries to educate audiences about inequities towards "the disabled" in our society. Undoubtedly, this would appear to be a necessary step towards integrating persons who are disabled into the mainstream of society. However, if disabled persons are to be an integral part of our society, we must arrive at the point where our focus is on individuals and not their disabilities. There must be a distinction made between the wheelchair and the person who sits in it. And we must always maintain our artistic standards, never accepting poor art to excuse disabled persons. To do so would be a disservice to the art and the artists, disabled or not.

The Mackay Center Stage

A number of years ago, I had taken several professional dancers to perform for students at the Mackay Center in Montreal, Quebec. The Mackay Center is an institution once labelled "for deaf and crippled children." At the time I was Artist-in-Residence with the Adirondack Dance Theater at the State University of New York in Plattsburgh, N.Y. The Adirondack Dance Theater had asked me to choreograph a ballet to be presented in elementary schools based on the classic children's story *The Little Engine That Could*. I had been agonizing over how to conceptualize a locomotive that would not be trite. During our presentation at the Mackay Center, I found my answer. Children were effortlessly racing all about the gymnasium in electric wheelchairs. They were so adept at manoeuvring, starting rapidly, stopping instantaneously and swirling about in arcs and circles, that the wheelchairs seemed an extension of their bodies. As I watched from afar, I could almost describe individuals just from the way each person used his wheelchair. Their personalities ranged from the somewhat docile to the near hyperkinetic.

And I knew I had my unique train.

The teachers suggested I might do well to utilize the services of an entire class of young men who suffered from Duchenne Muscular Dystrophy, a degenerative neuromuscular disease which ultimately renders individuals totally dependent on others for care. In fact, these young people only had minimal finger control of the joy sticks which stopped, started, and were the steering devices for the wheelchairs.

When I first went to speak to these young men (Duchenne Muscular Dystrophy is primarily a disease of men) about performing in a ballet, they kept heads down and barely offered audible responses. I repeated my request, telling them that I had little knowledge of choreographing for wheelchair-bound persons and that this would be a learning experience for me as well. Still they did not respond. I became annoyed at their reluctance to speak and to accept or reject my offer. I told them that I needed an answer immediately, but that I wanted them to know that our working together would be conditional: if they were not good, I would not let them perform. Every head raised and they told me that they would be willing to try.

And I learned again. Disabled persons do not want to perform to be seen as oddities, nor do they want to be allowed to perform merely because they are disabled. They, as all people, want to be seen as competent in what they do. They agreed to work with me because I had promised that I would only let them perform if they were good. And they were good. If there were problems with the production, it was certainly not because of the wheelchair dancers; rather, the deficiencies were evident in the choreography. My inexperience in working with wheelchairs in movement became very obvious to me. I was limited in my ability to note the capabilities of wheelchair dancers. Despite our very positive reviews, I was displeased with my own performance as choreographer.

I spoke with their teacher about my feelings of inadequacy. She helped to lead me in the right direction when she suggested that I should go observe them in a game of wheelchair hockey.

Again, I learned.

These young men played hockey with the same aggressiveness and intensity that one noted from NHL players. They rammed their chairs into others; they hollered and swore at each other; in short, they were no longer the passive young people I had been working with for the past two months. Their passivity was engendered by my attitude towards them. Unwittingly, I focused too much on their disabilities and limited their potentialities. I was being too careful, too controlled. I had limited their, and my, creativity. We eventually went on to create many dances and theatre pieces together and to tour throughout much of Canada and the U.S. We developed to the point where they would select a piece of music they liked and asked if we could choreograph a dance to it. Our creations began by their organic movement responses to the music so that themes could be developed. Choreography became a collaborative effort, with me acting more and more as critical audience. They were dancing, and being applauded by audiences and were no longer the introverted, heads-down people I had originally met. I recall sitting in the audience during one of the performances of Mackay Center Stage and my concentration was interrupted by the sounds of crying coming from a father of one of the young men. He was seated directly behind me. I put my hand on his arm and he leaned forward to whisper in my ear: "I never imagined I would be sitting in an audience applauding my son performing on a stage. And more important, my son never thought that he would be applauded for performing on a stage."

The experience of dancing and performing had a profound effect on these young men, as well as on me. Their teachers, family and friends remarked that they had become different people, confident and more focused on their own abilities. In effect, there was a therapeutic aspect to what we had been doing. But that was not our focus. We worked to create together; any therapeutic effects were as a result of striving for excellence in our artistic endeavors. Eventually, three of these young men established themselves in an independent living program. They have their own apartment, employ their own attendants, and are enrolled in colleges and universities in Montreal.

The Mackay Theater of the Deaf

Given that the institution I was involved with housed both physically disabled and hearing impaired persons, it was only natural that I become involved with the creation of a theatre of the deaf. The director of the institution was a hearing person who had been raised by deaf parents. He was fluent in American Sign Language and felt strongly that training in theatre techniques would enhance language acquisition skills among the deaf students. He encouraged me to develop a program.

At the same time, I met with a degree of opposition from a number of teachers of the deaf (there was actually a split among the professionals) who felt that music and dance were part of the hearing world and should not be imposed upon the deaf. As a novice in the field, I felt that the only people who could enlighten me were the students themselves. The theatre course was therefore set as an extracurricular activity which students could elect, or not, to be involved in. Actually, given that students were generally bussed directly home after school, participation in the programme would complicate matters sufficiently so that only those really wanting to be involved would do so. Many of the participants would have to be travel trained, so that they could take public transportation home for the first time in their lives. Commitment to this programme would be needed, given the obstacles. The turnout for tryouts on the first day were very excellent. So many students turned out that I had to change production plans to accommodate them all — for no one would be turned away. My question was answered (and continued to be for the next several years) that dance, music, and theatre experiences were wanted by these hearing-impaired persons.

Contemporary medicine and science have advanced so that few individuals today are completely deaf. Still, among the group I worked with, a significant number of students fell into the category of profoundly hearing impaired. Some of the students could hear the music only slightly with their hearing aids, others could not. My greatest concern was that I could not communicate in sign language. The director of the institution allayed my fears, suggesting that theatre people should certainly be able to communicate non-verbally. And he was right. Communication was never a problem. Some students were able to read lips and, when necessary, would sign to others for me. For the most part, I found that my own theatricality — my rather histrionic personality — communicated things well to the students. I also discovered that deaf students have to make themselves understood to so many people who cannot sign, that they have become very adept at mime.

They made themselves understood to me very well.

Much has been written about teaching rhythm to persons who are deaf. I have never found that to be a problem. Rhythm is probably an inherent thing. Students were able to pick up rhythms from me, either by observing me dance, or by dancing with me. I found that once rhythms were learned, the deaf dancers adhered to them tenaciously. This produced some comical moments for all of us. There had been occasions when a record would skip, thus changing tempo. The deaf students would continue dancing, perfectly, to the previous tempo. If hearing dancers were performing with them the result was truly humorous.

There is such a beauty to sign language that we would frequently use signing as a basis for movement. This would, of course, not be readily recognized by audiences; however, the effect upon young dancers who are deaf is significant. First, they developed a pride in realizing that there is beauty to their language. They have been stared at in public places so often, that to see their signing as a basis for dance movement gave them new insight into the value of their language. Second, novice dancers, hearing impaired or not, frequently benefit from the use of language to clarify movement. It takes many years of dancing before movement becomes a language of its own. We are a verbal society and, in fact, tend to respect people who minimize their expressive behavior when communicating with others. Therefore, the use of verbal language (sign language) to clarify movement for beginning dancers can be helpful. Third, sign language is movement itself. To take signs, which one normally does with one's hands, and do them with one's whole body, produced some beautiful movement experiences for the group.

Concluding Thoughts

Persons who are physically disabled and people who are hearing impaired have taught me much about creativity. It is important to see the richnesses in individuals and not focus on their deficits. It is so easy to fall into the trap of not seeing the distinction between the wheelchair and the person sitting in it. Once one understands the difference, one is free to give eminence to the wheelchair on stage, at times, or to the person. The wheelchair can be a tool which the person sitting in it uses to express, to create. I have also learned not to be afraid of working with disabled persons. If movements I choreograph are too difficult, or uncomfortable for individuals, they will tell me. I rely on the developing artists who are disabled to inform me of what best suits their capabilities. I have become fearless in making requests for movement, because not to do so would be condescending. I have learned that all artists have abilities and limitations: therefore, I no longer see one group of people as less capable than another. Rather, my creativity must be to engender creativity in those with whom I work.

I have moved from working in institutions for the disabled and currently work only in integrated settings. This decision on my part is based on ethical and philosophical considerations. I am wed to the notion of integration. Bernie Warren and I have developed a theatre company called 50/50 which offers the opportunity for disabled and non-disabled performers to work together in mutually supportive and creative ways. We continue to learn much from this experience.

Section Three

Creating a Theatre in Your Classroom: The Many Forms of Dramatic Activity

You Can't Get There from Here:
Working with a Set Drama Curriculum

LOUISE CHALMERS

*T*wo weeks until the end of term. I must find a way to end our dramas on the Berlin Wall and teen suicide, a way to pull together a collection of monologues which deal with a range of themes from prejudice, Sir Lancelot's bravery, the trials of baby-sitting and what everyone has begun to refer to as "Sarah's Boot of Hatred" speech.

For me, this is the exciting part of teaching drama, for it is now that I feel I am teaching. The students involved in the role dramas are committed to developing a character, understanding how circumstances are going to dictate the actions of their characters and moving the drama forward. The students who are working with the monologues have already chosen characters who fascinate them and are ready to bring them to life, to put them into a presentation format which will entail their looking at each others' work to spot similarities in themes, attitudes and personalities. My knowledge of dramatic form and dramatic tension will be useful. We are all involved in an act of creation.

When I first started teaching drama, I had a much different approach to planning and structuring the classes. My primary concern was to determine what I was going to teach and how I would evaluate what the students had learned. When I looked to theatre as a definition of drama, I would plan activities which explained or experimented with the following:

1) the actor's craft — interpretation of text through speech and movement;
2) the playwright's craft — communicating ideas, conflict, setting and relationships; or
3) a combination of both.

69

When I wanted to emphasize group co-operation, we played games. The lessons had four basic phases: 1) the introduction; 2) the experimenting, playing or "teaching"; 3) the working, planning or "learning"; and 4) the presentation and evaluation. As the teacher, I planned and led the sequence of activities, organized the groups, checked for involvement, suggested ideas, encouraged participation, disciplined student behaviour, and evaluated the final product. The students were expected to engage themselves enthusiastically in the activities and present what it was they learned.

When, in the mid-eighties, I started reading about Dorothy Heathcote's work, I was surprised by her totally different approach to planning to teach drama. She planned what to make "a play about," rather than what aspect of drama to teach. She would draw on her knowledge of dramatic structure to develop the drama so that its meaning could be clarified. She would choose a drama that had role possibilities for everyone. She would plan what role she would take in the drama to best focus the dramatic problem, to manage the group interaction and to provoke thinking and involvement. I started to teach in a much different way.

I began to feel more satisfaction with my drama classes. We seemed to be genuinely engaged in creating drama, in really learning "in," "about" and "from" dramatic language. Ironically, I became less able to specify my course content and to create objective evaluation criteria. The only valid representation of student learning with which I was comfortable was their own work. I found myself at odds with the provincial curriculum I was hired to teach. I have no patience for organizing learning in a hierarchical arrangement of behavioural objectives. I know from practice that there is no real learning unless there is personal participation on the part of the learner, and that when I prepare to teach I am looking for ways to involve my students. I wanted to find proof that real learning doesn't necessarily occur as a result of:

1) following carefully-set-out procedures based on the notion that knowledge is an increasingly complex synthesis of component and simpler ideas;
2) studying elements of the subject does not necessarily result in an understanding of the whole subject; and
3) the teacher playing the role of the expert who knows the subject and can evaluate how much the student has learned about the subject.

I decided to conduct a study. My goal was to analyse and compare the learning that occurred in a drama lesson when two different teaching strategies were used. In the first, the objectives, activities and methods of evaluation would be predetermined by the teacher in conformity with a set curriculum. In the second, the method for exploring

70

a dramatic situation would be agreed upon and entered into by the teacher and students without prespecifying the nature and sequence of the action or the outcome. I persuaded a friend to allow me to conduct this experiment with his Grade 9 class of 14–16-year-olds. He would videotape the proceedings. The students and I agreed to keep journals. Instead of assessing how much students learned, either through a test or presentation, I decided to look at three aspects of the classroom experience as indicators of student learning:

1) The Atmosphere in the Room, Enjoyment and Group Dynamic

Group Dynamic □ This is an important factor because of the social nature of drama education. Students work within the framework of the class whether they are working in small groups, one whole group or individually. An open and judgment-free atmosphere will allow the greatest range of experimentation and hypothesizing about truths of human nature.

2) Level of Contribution and Commitment

Commitment □ The Morgan Saxton Taxonomy[1] of personal engagement was used as a guide to judge student contribution and commitment. This scale uses the following definitions:

> INTEREST: we have used this term rather than "attending" because developmental psychologists consider that interest is an emotion in its own right, and one of the earliest to appear.
>
> ENGAGING: being involved in the task.
>
> COMMITTING: the development of a sense of responsibility towards the task.
>
> INTERNALIZING: the recognition of the relationship of the task to the self, revealed as a "change of understanding."
>
> INTERPRETING: the need to communicate that understanding.
>
> EVALUATING: the willingness to put that understanding to the test.

3) Quality of Student Response and Reflection

Reflection □ Student behaviours were observed and journals were read and analysed to see if their classroom experience did lead to new understandings. I assumed that very careful analysis of the actions and thoughts of the individuals involved in the classroom experience would provide insight into how students learn.

Description of Lessons

LESSON 1

In this lesson, students were expected to develop their skills of vocal sound production and to realize the dramatic use and effectiveness of sound.[2] As the teacher, I explained the purposes of the exercises, and the expectations I had of student performances.

I began the lesson by asking the students to focus their eyes on an imaginary object and vocally reproduce a sound they associated with that object, such as seeing a plane land. Simultaneous activity freed the individual student to experiment without fear of being watched. In the next exercise, the students were asked to close their eyes and collectively attempt to recreate the sounds they associated with a specific place (e.g. the peaceful forest). The activity introduced them to the notion of the emotional quality of sound.

The activities which followed allowed the students to experiment with the various dimensions of sound and introduced them to the vocabulary describing sound: volume, pitch, tempo, melody, rhythm, harmony, cacophony and effect of silence. The final test of achievement was based on an improvisation where the class was divided into two groups. Group One arranged Group Two (eyes closed) into a tableau, and then communicated to them where they were, by recreating sounds they associated with that place. Once the "frozen" individuals realized who and where they were, they were to "come alive" and complete the improvisation in any way they wished. In this way, Group One could test how successful they were at communicating and establishing an atmosphere of sound.

LESSON 2

The objective of this particular lesson was to develop collectively a spy drama in which the human dimensions of power, status and deception would be explored.[3] The topic was chosen by me, but presented to the class as open ended.

The lesson began by dividing the class into two groups. One group would be passengers travelling on Canadian passports through Russia to China. They were to fill out a standard passport application which would establish some basic background for the roles they would play in the drama. For the purposes of the drama, we decided to draw straws to determine who the spy would be. Members of the other group were government agents. I approached them in role as their supervisor, telling them we had reason to suspect one of the passengers travelling on the Siberian Express was a spy. Their first mission was to decide what tactics they would use to find the spy and then to find him. If they had any questions or suspects, they were to see me.

All of us then engaged in a period of dramatic playing in which guards and interrogators questioned the passengers. This went on until I stepped out of role and asked each of the groups that had formed to continue their scene in front of the class. In this way, the whole class could discover what was happening, and information about and techniques for dealing with the situation could be shared. I could check to see if real characterization and understanding of the drama were occurring.

Having observed that the students were "showing" rather than "being" their characters, and therefore not developing any real drama, I needed to find some way to show them that spying was not a game, but a grave international crisis that had serious consequences for the spy. In role as a spokesperson for the Russian government, with two student volunteers assuming expertise as a train engineer and a travel agent, we addressed the conference of the Canadian press and attempted to allay any fears about halting the train in Siberian Russia. The improvisation demanded that everyone assume "the mantle of the expert." Press members were charged with the professional responsibility of determining and reporting the truth about the halted train. The role necessitated their questioning, probing and listening to the information provided by the government officials who had to come up with plausible explanations for the train delay.

Initially, the questions were silly and superficial, intended to focus on details of the mechanical breakdown — perhaps to trick their classmate who assumed the mantle of the train engineer. Gradually, however, the questions began to deepen. Queries about political relations between Canada and Russia, and the presence of military guards aboard the train, increased the tension in the conference as the reporters began to suspect a cover-up. The scene lasted a full 60 minutes and by half way through, every hand was up — all the "reporters" were anxious to clarify the issue. The government officials terminated the press conference amid shouts and accusations of a cover-up.

The students were then asked to resume their original roles. In role as the train conductor, I informed them that my government, concerned for their well-being, was providing them with telephones to make a one-minute phone call to anyone they chose to explain the predicament in which they now found themselves. The guards, without prompting, distributed phones, explained how they worked and became very solicitous of the passengers' welfare. After a period of playing with the situation, we heard the phone calls. Students demonstrated a firm grasp of their characters and the situation. The added tension of having to make the call in one minute produced some very powerful monologues.

It was now time to focus on the dilemma of the drama. Up to this point, the guards had done quite a bit of questioning, but had not reported a suspect to me. Their characters tended to be stereotyped as bad guys, complete with bad Russian accents. Talk had become a way of **not** dealing with the issue. The class was then divided into groups composed of a guard and two passengers. Working in mime, the student playing the guard was to accuse the others of anything, as long as it was not related to the drama. The others were to figure out what they were being accused of and improvise the scene non-verbally. When tension was running high, and people were gesticulating wildly, I stopped the improvisation and returned to the drama. As their supervisor, I told the guards/interrogators that it was absolutely imperative for them to find the spy. International attention was focused on us. I could delay the train no longer. Intense questioning followed. Language was very precise. The "silly" Russians disappeared.

After several minutes, I, in the role of the government official, stopped the drama and announced to the whole group that the train had not been halted because of a mechanical difficulty. It had been stopped because there was a spy on the train. The passengers would now stand up one by one, and my guards would tell me if they were suspicious characters. Three were isolated from the others and, after some deliberation, one character was correctly accused of spying. I then told the spy that I would spare him his life if he would tell me who, amongst my guards, was his informant. This sudden turn of events heightened the tension of the drama. A single student was charged with the responsibility of making a decision, and yet it was a significant event for everyone in the room. The guards, who were the suspects, were anticipating and mentally rehearsing a defence against a possible accusation. The passengers who identified with the spy urged him to pursue his own freedom and to point an accusing finger at one of the guards. The spy himself, encouraged by the concern of the others, took the time to think, and eventually decided to personally accept all the responsibility. It was a big decision and one he did not take lightly. The drama ended when he decided to die rather than reveal his sources.

Findings and Observations

LESSON 1
I.   Atmosphere in the room, enjoyment and group dynamic
     a) Teacher's Observation
         There was a general spirit of co-operation in the room and most everyone made an attempt to participate. The teacher participated in the initial activities which had the effect of encouraging

74

the students to attempt the activity, even if they could not completely abandon themselves to it.

Students found vocal exploration (range, volume and pitch) a new and somewhat bizarre experience, and were at different times, and to varying degrees, self-conscious. There was a great deal of giggling. Two girls were conspicuous by their lack of enthusiasm and chose to absent themselves from some of the activities. There was a collective self-consciousness and resistance to participating, particularly noticeable when I asked the class to re-form the groups in which they had been the day before. In a ploy to delay the next activity, they pretended they had forgotten.

The one moment of pure enjoyment came when one group completely let loose and extended the range of their experimentation (i.e., the extremes of loudness and softness, cacophony and harmony, and staccato and legato) in becoming an "orchestra." They were not as daring in the presentation of their experiment to the class. Very little came out of the other groups.

The students enjoyed sculpting each other into tableaux, but mostly because they delighted at having their friends compromised — awaking to find themselves in a humiliating position.

I found myself constantly explaining to the class why they were doing the activity, what they should be focusing on, giving and answering questions about instructions, asking for responses to the activity, and in the absence of a student response, supplying my own. It came as no surprise when I analysed the video, that I had talked for 60 per cent of the time. Only 40 per cent of the time was spent on dramatic activity.

b) **Students' Journals**
Many of the students referred to the embarrassment they felt at doing the activities, and their struggle to get involved. Individuals felt the scorn or judgement of their peers, but were challenged to complete the activities. The following excerpt from one journal is typical: "At first I found it embarrassing, but then I got used to it."

One student mentioned the sense of pride and accomplishment that resulted from his making an important contribution to the collective creation: "I felt I was important in the laboratory because there were certain sounds I made that helped it sound like a lab."

75

II. Level of contribution and commitment

a) Teacher's Observation

Using the Morgan Saxton Taxonomy, the students following this lesson achieved the first two and last levels of personal engagement. They were interested enough to get involved in the task, and they were willing to put their understanding of "voice atmospheres" to the test by doing an improvisation with their peers.

Their participation did not demand any personal commitment from them other than fulfilling the wishes of the teacher. They demonstrated what they had learned by doing the improvisation — they did not want to talk about it. It was done. It did not excite them to do more, to talk or to begin a personally-significant project.

Certain individuals became quite keen about some of the activities, but it was more in an atmosphere of fun than learning. Contribution and commitment increased in activities that were closer to their own experience.

b) Students' Observations

The students found it difficult to get involved in an activity so far removed from their everyday experience and were easily distracted. Gradually they became more involved.

"At first I didn't say a thing. There weren't many people participating in the noise in the forest; therefore, neither did I."

* * * *

"Even though I was waiting and also had my eyes closed, I knew what I was doing and I felt 'in character' most of the time. Yet when we started to continue the sounds and actions, I felt even more 'in character' — a monkey."

* * * *

"In the improvisations, it was weird but fun acting like animals. It really sounded like a zoo."

* * * *

"When I realized why we were doing what we were doing, I enjoyed myself."

* * * *

76

"There were moments I was not aware of the teacher because I was being someone or something else."

III. Quality of student response and reflection

a) Teacher's Observation

There were two occasions when the whole class produced quality and enjoyable work: sleepwalking and experimenting with spontaneous sound and silence. Both of these were collective activities where the focus was not on any individual. They had to listen to each other's input and add to it. There was energy and sensitivity.

Oral reflection was nil, partly out of politeness, and partly because of the negative atmosphere. It was definitely "not cool" to get involved in such bizarre goings-on. When asked what they thought they had learned, students replied using the exact words of the behavioural objective: "To create an atmosphere using vocal sounds." The activities produced no reason to analyse or extend their experimentation with the medium. They saw their success in terms of having completed the activity, not in terms of an inspirational source or awakening.

b) Students' Observations

The students strove to find the positive in the experience. Their journals indicated a sensitivity and awareness their actions did not.

"I found it interesting to use my voice in different ways to create different environments. I never realized all the words which describe sound."

* * * *

"It was good for a change to do things with sound. Sometimes you learn things you never knew before."

* * * *

"I felt I was being creative."

LESSON 2

I. Atmosphere in the room, enjoyment and group dynamic

a) Teacher's Observation

The room was charged with an excitement about getting involved in the drama. It was something new the students were trying. The newness of the situation inspired rather than intimidated them. The activity was purposeful and focused.

77

There was occasional giggling, but this time it arose not out of self-consciousness, but out of excitement at seeing others getting involved. The students actively strove to suppress their own giggling so that they could reimmerse themselves in the drama. There was plenty of evidence of self-discipline.

The group dynamic was very healthy. The stress was on the collective, not on individuals. There was no fear of ridicule, for the emphasis was not on individual achievement, but on the single focus of the drama — to find the spy. Very little time was spent giving instructions (they were given in role as part of the drama) — the collective energy moved the drama forward. There were interruptions to focus the drama, but they were always active and related; the purpose did not have to be explained, but was obvious to the students.

The two students who were most reticent in the previous lesson were very active in this one. There were occasions when individual students took strong initiatives and became leaders in the drama, not to show off, but to focus the drama. They had an idea that was important to share, a contribution to make that would affect the whole drama. They were able to assume the focus quite naturally because it was within the context of the drama.

b) **Students' Observations**

There was a general positive response to the idea of working collaboratively with the teacher.

"She was an interrogator, not a teacher. She was my enemy. It was her against me."

* * * *

"Lots of the time it was more fun having a teacher who taught me as well as acted with me."

* * * *

"The teacher didn't talk as much in this lesson."

The students commented on the positive atmosphere generated by the collective action of the class.

"I found it weird that the class really participated 'together.' There were so many questions asked and I thought nobody would have the guts to ask any. It was fun."

78

* * * *

"I participated because it made me feel important."

* * * *

"I always like to participate, but sometimes I haven't the guts. I participated a lot in the train ride to China. What I liked was that everyone was involved. The whole class was included in the scene which made it easier to bring out my own character."

II. Level of contribution and commitment
a) Teacher's Observation
Using the Morgan Saxton Taxonomy, the students achieved the first three levels of personal engagement. They were interested in what they were doing, involved and committed to their role and the role drama. Some obviously reached the fourth stage when they were asked to consider whether they would endanger another to protect their own. The role drama ended with one student saying, "I have the front-page story." He was still identifying with his role as reporter and was clearly shocked at the turn of events and the death of the double agent who turned herself in. He, one might say, had reached the interpreting stage. The fact that the class did not reach the evaluating stage was a result of a lack of time and teacher direction.

The nature of role-playing demands interest and commitment. Without it, nothing can occur or continue. Once students clearly realized they had the power to make the lesson interesting, that their contributions were necessary and that they were learning from each other, the role drama went as far as they could take it.

When I spoke to the two girls who were so negative about the first lesson and why they had reversed their attitudes in the second, they said that the presence of the story, a context, made it much easier to get involved. They could be a character they could motivate and understand. Creating sound for its own sake seemed silly and too abstract.

b) Students' Observations
Most student journals reflected a real identification with their role and commitment with the drama:

79

"At one point something struck me. I just said what I felt, which was quite hard at the moment because I was quite upset."

* * * *

"When we supposedly had a telephone, I felt good about that part. It made me realize how frightened and partly angry I was at the situation."

* * * *

"I felt I had really sunk into my character when I was brought to the conference room, probably because that is when I was really pressed by them and had to come back with really good answers."

* * * *

"I was a spy. I was havoc. I was interrogated every second. They didn't even let me talk to Aunt Margaret who was telling me a burning story. When the train stopped, paranoia walked in. I was scared and acted too quick."

* * * *

"The teacher was in control, but we ourselves basically took over with our own characters."

* * * *

"I really felt that I was in the train scene. It was realistic."

III. Quality of student response and reflection
a) Teacher's Observation
There were two occasions when there was deep-level thinking about the dramatic situation: first, during the press conference; and second, while the spy decided whether to betray his source. Over the course of the three days, most of the students identified more deeply with their characters and were able to express that identification, if one viewed it from the outside, with some quite powerful performances. Ironically, the careful and precise use of language, which was the purpose of the exercise, did not come until the students had experienced trying to communicate without words.

80

b) **Students' Observations**

Most students were able to draw parallels between the drama and their everyday lives.

"I realized that by acting someone else, it can make you feel better. It's really exciting to become someone else for a short while, then come back to your own personality."

* * * *

"I created a whole new human being and history."

* * * *

"I felt it was a real-life dilemma that may or may not happen."

* * * *

"When I was talking on the phone, my character became more clear to me and I understood what I had to do, and did it. The person I played came out and did my part."

Conclusion

Michael Polanyi's theory of tacit knowing states that there are two aspects of knowing: the focal and the subsidiary. We come to know the focal, the comprehensive entity, by dwelling on the particulars, the subsidiary.[4] Developing a drama about discovering a spy was always the focus of Lesson II, the "comprehensive entity." By taking a role in the drama, the students dwelt on the particulars, the subsidiary. Knowing "what" to say and "how" to say it were not treated as separate acts. It was assumed that the students would know how to say something because they realized what it was they wanted to say while dwelling in the dramatic context. The drama clarified what they knew; the collective drama activity and the "**teacher-in-role**" modeled how it should be said. The lesson transformed the students' inchoate observations and experiences into personal understanding by giving it linguistic and expressive shape through the framework of the drama. In effect, the students "created meaning" from their participation in dramatic activity by integrating their personal experiences with the artistic and social experiences framed by the drama class.

They were excited by the experience of privately realizing something and simultaneously testing that realization in a larger context, of creating something by their contribution to the drama and watching

81

the effects of their contribution to the development of the drama. They experienced being both viewer and performer, of being both actor and playwright.

In Lesson I, the students practised elements of dramatic language in isolation from the drama. There was no focal aspect for the "knowing." Students were asked to recall, reproduce and imitate sounds they had previously heard. The personal experience the initial activities recalled were objective perceptions and observations, not necessarily embedded in any personally-significant context. The subsequent activities required students to make sounds without understanding their aesthetic power. Since no meaningful context had been established, it was entirely possible, and evident in this case, that the required performances were executed without using the imagination, without transforming the recalled perception into anything new and without using the imagination to transform sound into art. The students operated outside of a dramatic context. They were students studying the "art" of theatre. They produced sounds for no reason. There was no drama to which to transfer their skills. Their journals indicate that if we had done a zoo story, for instance, in which there had been a reason to make zoo sounds, their work would have been of a far superior quality.

Polanyi states that the focal and subsidiary are not linked of their own accord, but by the person, that there is no meaning without the personal participation of the knower.

> Nothing that is said, written or printed can ever mean anything in itself; for it is only a person who utters something — or who listens to it or reads it — who can mean something by it.[5]

This study shows evidence of this willing engagement. The students totally immersed themselves in the spy drama. Seeing the drama unfold, and watching their friends manipulate the drama by playing a role, inspired them to get involved. It was absorbing work to forge roles for themselves. Their journals spoke of how "talk emerged from their mouths" because their experience in the drama was so real. They wanted to be involved and took control of their own behaviours, so that they could continue to participate. Their motivation in doing so was not to satisfy or impress the teacher, but to "create drama." This was the most impressive factor. They were pleased with their learning: "I can create a whole new person," "I have the front page story," "It's good to be another character." Some were even able to criticize their work — "I acted too quickly" — and nobody waited for the teacher to deliver the final mark.

The activities of Lesson I did not engage the students; they embarrassed them. Their journals indicated how hard they worked at blocking out their anxiety about appearing ridiculous. It was interesting how fascinated they were by sound and how the class, in the way that it was structured, was not the place to explore the fascination. The focus was on the individual student to be a good "sound" artist creating interesting effects. The quality work came when their work was collaborative.

The greatest participation of the learner was not in the preplanned activities, but in the thwarting of them, as evidenced in their wasting time, deliberately being silly and pretending to forget things. In the absence of a dramatic context, the students created their own.

Polanyi also sees learning as an apprenticeship, a relationship in which the child learns from the practitioner. For example, he says:

> Speech is learned by intelligent imitation of the adult. Each word must be noted in a number of contexts until its meaning is roughly grasped; it must then be read in books and used for some time in speech and writing under guidance of the example of adults in order that its most important shades of meaning be mastered.[6]

The function of the teacher in the voice lesson was to deliver the set curriculum and evaluate individual student achievement. I was not involved in the creative process prescribed by the lesson. I was the outside expert who could offer help and suggestions, and ultimately assess the worth of the students' work. The students resented the difference in status. I was constantly being asked why I was asking them to do things. They deliberately resisted doing things well. It was when I also chose to do the activity that the resistance to it decreased.

In the spy drama, the teacher took the same risks as the students, working alongside with them, focusing and questioning in role. Students modelled their work on the teachers and even risked taking control of the drama.

Summary

It would be easy to conclude from this study that real learning, in the sense of creating personal meaning, does not necessarily occur as a result of following set procedures replicating the creative process, or by studying elements of a subject in isolation. The limitations in the scope of the study itself challenge the validity of this conclusion. The reactions of only one group of students were analysed. Only one lesson from the entire programme of study was taught. Neither lesson was a perfect execution of its description. However, the significant contrast in experience between the two lessons, and the powerful responses of the students, indicate that learning in drama occurs when 1) the classroom experience is embedded in a dramatic context; 2) student input is vital to the development of the lesson; and 3) the teacher is a practitioner of drama.

Oh yes. My mind has wandered many times as I have struggled to write this chapter. I think I've figured out how to end the term. I found a good book on teen suicide which may save our work from becoming too maudlin by providing us with a few hard facts and true-life stories. We're going to have to decide whether the story of the Berlin Wall is a story about "the death of an ideal" or about "freedom at last." The monologues present a larger challenge for reasons too complicated to go into here. But I think we have to go for the crazy and just present a wonderful pastiche of unlikely characters, a celebration, no doubt, of the class from which they arise.

Endnotes

1. Norah Morgan and Juliana Saxton. *Teaching Drama* (London: Hutchinson Education, 1987).
2. Gouvernement du Quebec. *Curriculum Guide, Secondary School Drama*, 1986.
3. Cecily O'Neill, Alan Lambert, Rosemary Linnell, & Janet Warr-Wood (eds.). *Drama Guidelines* (London: Heinemann Education Books in association with London Drama, 1987).
4. Michael Polanyi and Harry Prosch. *Meaning* (Chicago: The University of Chicago Press, 1975).
5. Michael Polyani. *The Study of Man* (Chicago: The University of Chicago Press, 1972).
6. Michael Polanyi. *Science, Faith and Society* (Chicago: The University of Chicago Press, 1964).

Starting Drama from Small Dramatic Moments: From Play to Drama to Play

YURIKO KOBAYASHI

Introduction

Play is the most powerful learning medium in Early Childhood Education. While children play freely most of the time in national and public kindergartens,[1] teachers in Early Childhood Education need to understand, stimulate and encourage children to play more, for play is "the child's way of thinking, proving, relaxing, working, daring, testing, creating and absorbing."[2] Children, and their teachers, can learn many things through playing.

Play is also dramatic for it involves "the mental act of imaginative transformation."[3] Recently, I have been trying to find a way to connect drama to the child's natural play. Through sharing my teaching experiences with three- to four-year-old children,[4] I hope to clarify the way I link play to drama and drama to play.

In this chapter I will focus on one series of "playings" based on Snow White which lasted for about two months. Many things happened during that period. It is impossible to write about all of them. So I have chosen eight sessions which were not formally planned, but happened through spontaneous play, and in which I developed the activities along with the children. First I will describe each session, and then discuss ideas for teachers that arise from each of them. In addition, I will try to give some ideas, points and suggestions for play and drama with small children.

Moment 1

Miki was a four-year-old girl who loved dramatic play. One day she came to me and said, "I am Snow White!" So I immediately picked up an imaginary apple, held it out before her and said, "Why don't you

85

have this apple?" She shouted, "There is no apple!" So, I drew an apple, painted it, cut it out and asked her again, "Would you like to have this apple? It is delicious. Eat!" Dissatisfied, she responded, "Too thin!" Anyway, she took it from me and pretended to eat an apple. But she seemed not to be fully satisfied with the apple which I made.

OBSERVATIONS AND IDEAS FOR THE TEACHER

It is important for the teacher in Early Childhood Education to observe children's playing in daily life, catch the small dramatic moment and develop it with the children. They have their own images which they develop spontaneously as they play. Therefore, the teacher should not pull them into a drama which you imagine and create, but you should adapt yourself to their images. However, it is not always easy to discover their images and play with them. When you feel you do not fit in with them, you should try another approach or activity. If you do not find the right moment all day long, you do not need to be disappointed about it. You might find it the next day. You just need to keep trying; first try something, and then something else. The right moment will come sooner or later if you keep seeking it. This process gives you some ideas and ways to find the right moment.

Moment 2

I realized that Miki was not satisfied with the apple which was made of thin paper. I made a new apple which was three-dimensional. I stuffed a red plastic bag with red paper and tied it up with brown elastic tape. I thought other girls might want to play with apples. So I made a few apples before children came to school. I also prepared all the materials for making apples for children and put them on the work table.

When the children came to school, I was making apples. Some children came up to me and asked, "What are you making?" and began to make apples with me. We made a lot of apples and put them in a basket. I thought that the children could use them for playing *Snow White*.

OBSERVATIONS AND IDEAS FOR THE TEACHER

It is useful for the teacher to make various objects to use in drama. This experience and process will help you to develop your ideas and images. Also, it helps you develop the skills and confidence to make props.

It is difficult to create something with nothing. Making the same apples will not harm children's imagination and creativity. "To imitate, 'to hold the mirror up to nature' requires, after all, a complex operation beginning with the child's selective observation of the world around and within himself, melding into the absorption of this data, a recombining and interpreting of it and a reproduction of some new arrangement of it."[5] I think the props of the apples stimulated the children to develop their imagination and the drama activity. I made a lot of "half-way apples," because I observed they really wanted to complete the apples by themselves. I think it is extremely important for the children to have the experience and sense of accomplishment through playing repeatedly.

Play gives the children time and space to repeat the same thing as much as they like. Through these experiences the children can acquire confidence. So they play more.

Moment 3

Miki, Noriko (four-year-old girl), Yuka (four-year-old girl) and I played one scene in *Snow White*: the old woman giving the poisoned apples. The three girls were Snow Whites and I was the bad old woman who was the Queen. We played it over and over again. Then two other girls came and watched us. So I held out the apple in front of them. But they were too shy to play with us. They seemed to need to watch us for a little while.

The next day, four of us (Miki, Yuka, Noriko and I) played the same scene. Noriko suddenly said, "When Snow White eats the poisoned apple, she should die!" I responded, "I see, how to die? Noriko, please show us." Falling down on the ground, she said, "This way!" I said to Miki and Yuka, "Snow White dies when she eats the poisoned apple. You see?" Miki nodded. Yuka said, "I see. O.K.!" I said, "Let's do it again?" We added the new scene which Noriko created. We played the same scene again and again.

OBSERVATIONS AND IDEAS FOR THE TEACHER

Objects like the apples are important in dramatic play. The apples were important props in this activity. The children stimulated their imagination by the apples which they could touch. Also they could get, hold and throw them. They seemed to feel much more reality in the scene because of the apples. A child's make-believe world makes use of available objects: a doll is a baby, leaves and mud are food, a wooden panel is a door etc. Once a girl puts on an apron, she becomes Mother. Once she puts on a long dress, she becomes a princess. Objects and costumes stimulate the children to play and sustain playing.

It is not necessary to start at the beginning of the story in *Snow White*. Children can start in the middle of the story. It is important to start the small dramatic moment which a child imagines and creates.

Children repeat the same thing over and over again until they are satisfied or bored with it. But each repetition is not the same. There is something different or new. The teacher should give children time and space to do the same thing freely with a warm and supportive atmosphere. To create such an atmosphere, the teacher must first listen to the child's words everyday and become interested in them. This curiosity will give you the power to create a warm atmosphere.

If the children are too shy to do drama, the teacher should give them enough time and space to watch it. When you feel the right moment, ask these shy children to play with you. This is important. They might join you, say "No!" or run away. But you do not need to feel disappointment or failure. You can try some other time with some other way. Each child is different. It is important for you to notice these differences and any gaps between the children and you. Each teacher is different, too. There are so many ways for you to ask them to do drama. You should figure out your own way to stimulate the children to play through trial and error. In this process, you will understand the children and play more.

Moment 4

While we had been doing dramatic play, I realized that most children in the class did not know the whole story of Snow White. So I read the picture book of Snow White at our meeting time. The story was long, so some children got tired of listening to the story, but the girls who had been playing listened to it carefully. They seemed eager to know the whole story.

OBSERVATIONS AND IDEAS FOR THE TEACHER

There are many ways to start a drama activity. The teacher can start by reading a book for the children and dramatize it with them. If you are good at telling a story, you can use the story to start drama activity. If you are good at singing a song, you can start from a song. If a child brings a thing: a shell, an acorn, a leaf or a toy, you can start from it. You can start drama from anything in which the children and you are interested.

This time I started with the child's image and words — "I am Snow White!" — in her natural play and developed it in play with the children.

I read the picture book for them to know the plot of Snow White. The children do not need to dramatize the whole story of Snow White exactly. But I felt that it was the time for them to know the plot of the story. This instinct is sometimes right, but sometimes wrong. The important thing is to observe the child's play carefully and keep trying to stimulate it. Then you can catch the right moment or perceive it. You should trust your instincts. At the same time, you have to sharpen and polish all your senses.

Another important thing for the teacher is to study the materials which will be used in playing and drama. There are many books of *Snow White*. If you already know of several, you can choose one of them which will be suitable for the children to play and do a drama activity.

Some stories are easy to dramatize, but some are difficult. It is useful for you to have several favourite stories to dramatize with the children.

Moment 5

The children seemed to understand the plot of *Snow White*. So I added a new scene: the queen is looking at the mirror before the poisoned apple scene. After the children left the school, I made the frame of the mirror with cardboard and aluminium foil.

The moment when Noriko came up to me the next morning, I picked up the mirror frame and said, "Dear mirror, dear mirror! Who is the most beautiful in the world?" She immediately became the mirror, faced me through the frame of the mirror and said in the role of the mirror, "That is you, the Queen." She changed her voice as soon as she became the mirror. I responded, "Well, I would like to hear it again. Dear mirror, dear mirror! Who is the most beautiful in the world?" She said, "That is Snow White!" I responded, "What did you say? Snow White? Oh, how dear, no!" I did not tell her what she should say, but she picked up the line in the scene. Other children came up and watched us. Noriko and I had an audience, so we repeated the same scene several times.

OBSERVATIONS AND IDEAS FOR THE TEACHER

Drama is basically "an improvisational, non-exhibitional, process-oriented"[6] activity. The teacher follows the children and develops drama along with the children. The main role of the teacher is to observe the children's needs and help the children to express them. Once they feel safe to express themselves, they will give you lots of ideas. Then you pick up their ideas and develop them in drama.

It is important for the teacher to observe children not only during a drama activity, but also during the children's daily life at school. Through careful observation, you will find the cue, which is the small dramatic moment to play with them naturally and spontaneously. Once the children give you the licence to play with them, they will give you more cues. You will find the joy to play with them not as a teacher, but as their playmate. You will understand the children, play, and drama more by playing with the children. After this experience, you "can provide the environment which stimulates and allows the child's full development"[7] through playing. It is fun and a joy to play with the children naturally and honestly.

Moment 6

Several girls had been doing dramatic play of *Snow White* with me for about a month. Some boys began to show interest in our dramatic play, but I did not ask them to play with us, because they seemed to be hesitant about joining us. But they kept watching us, so I brought a bucket, took the part of the queen in the secret place and began to stir imaginary poisoned soup with a ladle in front of them. I tasted the special poisoned soup and said, "Well, this soup needs a little more something. Oh, I get it! Let's put in my snot." I pretended to pick my nose and flip it into the soup. The boys shouted with laughter, "Yech!" or "Gross!" I asked them, "Put something in. I need much more poison." Toshiki (three-year-old boy) sat on the bucket, made the sound of passing wind and pretended to have a bowel movement. Kenicki (four-year-old boy) pretended to throw up loudly in it. The other boys laughed. They each took turns putting other things in the bucket. All the boys around us did it without hesitation. I stirred the soup again, tasted it and said, "Well done! Let's dip apples!" I dipped them and put them in the basket.

OBSERVATIONS AND IDEAS FOR THE TEACHER

Play is voluntary. The teacher does not need to force the children to play together. They need the time to watch and observe what other children do in play. Watching itself is part of playing. When the time comes, they start playing naturally, spontaneously. It is important for the teacher to give the children enough time and space. They will sense this and understand that the teacher gives them the choice to join in play whenever they want. But if they do not want to play, they can watch others playing as long as they want. At the same time, the teacher should let the children know that she knows they are watching the playing, but she does not force them to do something. Children gain freedom when they begin to play with other children.

The boys had been saying vulgar words in their daily life at school: shit, pee, puke and so on. They needed to use them in a framework. That is why I asked them to use them in the drama activity. They enjoyed this scene because they could say these words as much as they liked. They did the drama activity almost everyday, but only this scene. After these activities, they still used these words in daily life for a long time, but gradually they were bored with saying them. They did not say them by the end of the school year. Play and drama have the potential to provide catharsis. You better believe it. Adults are restrained from many things by common sense, custom, taboo and manners. It is hard for the teacher to accept things that go against socially-accepted ideas. But the children can do anything they want in their playing. Also, they can learn social custom and manners through playing. You do not need to worry too much about the vulgar language. If you give them the accepted way to use the words, they will realize by themselves that it is not right to use them in real life.

Moment 7

I thought it was time to play the whole story of *Snow White*. I and another teacher led the drama activity based on it. I took the part of Queen and the other teacher was the narrator and Huntsman. We started the at beginning. The scenes which the children and I had been doing for several weeks were played by them. The scene of Huntsman was a new scene for them, so the teacher became one of the huntsmen and led the children who wanted to play it. The children gave us new ideas in the activities.

In the scene of making poisoned apples, I held out the pot to the children and asked them to add something different. When a child added the same thing as another child, I asked him to choose something different.

At the end I implied that the Queen died because of jealousy. She fell down on the floor. The children watched some scenes, performed some of them, and experienced the whole story.

OBSERVATIONS AND IDEAS FOR THE TEACHER

The children had repeated several scenes before this drama activity. They already had several different experiences and were interested in it. It was a long session, but the children's attention was held for over 30 minutes.

It is important for the teacher to know what children are curious about. You have to analyse where the curiosity comes from and why they feel curious. I knew several children in my class were strongly interested in the drama activity of *Snow White* because of the repeated experiences. You can plan a drama activity after the children have played with its elements and materials, but play is always first.

I showed the children the last scene. The Queen became angry with Snow White's beauty, was jealous of her and fell down on the floor. I think the children could sense the Queen's death and this strong emotion. Children will experience death and many different kinds of feelings and emotions sooner or later in their lives. The teacher should not hide or sugar-coat these things. We have to show them to the children truthfully in and through play and drama. The children can rehearse feelings and emotions in play and drama.

Moment 8

After an activity Haruna (a four-year-old girl) and Kanaho (a four-year-old girl) played *Snow White* with puppets.

Haruna seemed to be impressed by the mirror scene. She said to the mirror, in anger, "How dare you! Say it again! Who is the most beautiful in the world?"

Noriko and Yuka wore white dresses and pretended to be beautiful princesses. Noriko asked the teacher, "Which princess do you want to get married to? Me?" Yuka said, "No! Me!" Noriko said, "I am kinder than she." Yuka said, "No! I am kinder than you. And I am beautiful too." Yuka said, "No!" Then the teacher who was the prince said, "I don't like princesses who always argue." Suddenly they hugged each other and pretended to be very good friends. Next day Noriko and Yuka pretended to be princesses again, and shouted while falling down on the ground, "Help me! Help me!" Nobody came, but they repeated to do the same thing all day long. They seemed to be impressed by the last scene of the Queen's falling down.

One day Miki said to me, "I asked Mom to read the book of *Snow White*. I love it." Her mother told me, "At home, she is Snow White everyday."

OBSERVATIONS AND IDEAS FOR THE TEACHER

The children did not play the scenes of *Snow White* with me any more. They played by themselves using ideas from the sessions. Haruna and Kanaho projected emotions into the puppets.

Noriko and Yuka became the princess instead of Snow White and used the baskets and the apples in their own make-believe story. They used the idea of competition for beauty and the action of falling down.

The children picked up the ideas and actions which they needed or wanted to use in their own playing. I think the series of *Snow White*'s drama activities made the child's natural play richer and deeper.

Summary

"Play is the thing"[8] in Early Childhood Education. Drama is "rooted in the natural dramatic playing of childhood".[9] Drama should start from a small dramatic moment in the child's play. The role of the teacher is to observe children and their playing, to sense/feel the small dramatic moment in it, and develop it along with the children's needs and curiosity. Then drama should be fed back into the child's natural dramatic play. The child's natural dramatic play should be deeper and richer through the drama activities which are led by the teacher. The most important role of the teacher is to sustain and stimulate the children to play more by themselves. Play is most important in Early Childhood Education, and the most powerful learning medium for both the children and the teacher.

Endnotes

1. In Japan there are two main types of schools in Early Childhood Education. The nursery school and the day care center (which are under the control of the Ministry of Public Health and Welfare), and the kindergarten which is under the Ministry of Education. The Outline of Kindergarten Education enforced by the Ministry of Education since 1989 emphasizes child's play. It suggests that, "Teachers should teach children through playing." So the children come to kindergarten and start playing until lunch. They start playing again until the meeting time, when teacher and children meet together for about 15–30 minutes. Sometimes the teacher tells a story or performs a short puppet play. After the meeting they go home.

    Most kindergartens have some sort of a performing day once a year. So teachers often do "drama" with the children before this special day. Some teachers do "drama" regularly. This depends on each kindergarten and teacher. However, they do not call it "drama", but rather they call it "drama-play" which is similar to child drama or creative drama. But the problem is that most teachers do not have enough training and knowledge of drama and theatre.

    The Ministry of Education does not ask the colleges to offer a course in drama, creative drama or child drama for the student to be certified as a kindergarten teacher. Very few programs in Early Childhood Education have a course in Creative Drama. The name "Drama" is not normally used in an Early Childhood Education programme in Japan. Some programmes have a course in "Children's Theatre" where instructors teach a sort of drama, creative drama or child drama. Students of Early Childhood Education do not have to study drama, but they have to study child's play which includes dramatic play/make-believe. I include a course in child drama in my programme.

2. Peter Slade, *An Introduction to Child Drama* 7th impression, London: Hodder and Atoughton, 1976, p. 1.

3. Virginia Glasgow Koste, *Dramatic Play in Childhood: Rehearsal for Life* New Orleans: Anchorage Press, 1978, p. 6.

4. In the kindergarten where I taught, there were 20 children, ages three–four, and one teacher per class.

5. Koste, p. 19.

6. Helane S. Rosenberg, *Creative Drama and Imagination: Transforming Ideas into Action* New York: Holt, Rinehart and Winston, 1987, p. 4.

7. Koste, p. 148.

8. Koste, p. 2.

9. Koste, p. xi

In the Beginning:
Storytelling in Drama

BARBARA MACKAY

During more than a quarter of a century of working in drama in education, I have come to know that when people come into a classroom space to participate in drama and theatre for the first time, they are apprehensive and self-conscious. It is only preschool children and those in kindergarten who seem to feel no concern about the prospect of participating in dramatic play. As they move on in their schooling, however, they encounter the serious work of learning to read, which changes their world forever. They now have a daily awareness of making mistakes, for either one can recognize and speak written words, or one cannot. There is no blessed ambiguity here, no freely-imaginative flow, no possibility of compromise or negotiation, no way of resaying or reinterpreting the words with bold and unique new colours and meanings (this is only charming and quotable in the preschool years or much later, by poets). In short, there is a meeting or confrontation with something immutable — the law of the printed word. School becomes imbued with a sense of the need to adhere to the structures of external knowledge in order to ensure success. It becomes a place where the possibility of failure is ever present.

Thus, when children (or adolescents or adults) enter the world of classroom drama and theatre, they bring questions from their educational and cultural pasts, beginning not so much with "What do I expect from this?" as "What does this expect from me? What do I have to know about this before I can master it? What must I do to do well? How sympathetic will the teacher be if I get it wrong? What about the others? How much do they know? Will I have to stand up and perform in front of them when I have no idea what to do? Will I be made to look a fool?"

Because people who are feeling worried and awkward cannot learn happily and well, my own teaching goals have been devoted to lessening these tensions. To try to accomplish this, I have sought ways to integrate the self's pleasure, and a renewed sense of its own abilities with those features of drama/theatre which have been developing over long vistas of time and history. Therefore, I have needed to reflect not only on the dynamics of learning, but also on the quintessence of theatre, now and in the past.

Certainly, for the beginning student, the meaning of theatre, is "acting in front of others." This concept is a source of anxiety for them, but it is also a true, if somewhat simplified, description of what happens in the theatre. Theatre is largely accepted and understood as "the thing seen," as the action of human beings performing predetermined stories and interactions as if they were occurring in reality. David Coles refers to the "as if" and to the immediacy of theatre in The Theatrical Event.[1] He suggests that it is only in theatre and the performance of ritual that "imaginative events take on for the moment the presence of physical events and physical events take on for a moment the perfection of imaginative events." His reference to ritual is apt, since it is one of the deepest roots of theatre and has much in common with theatre, including a special space for the action, known boundaries for the completion of the action, heightened language and a knowledge by the participants that imaginative truth is being experienced as present truth.

Another ancient source of theatre is storytelling. In what follows I want to suggest that, in the same way that theatre is understood to have developed from traditions of storytelling and ritual, so might classroom drama begin in rituals of storytelling, most especially when told by the students themselves.

We hear from Bruce Chatwin in The Songlines[2] that the primal cry of humanity is I AM, and in The Way of the Storyteller,[3] Ruth Sawyer tells us that storytelling grows out of "the primal urge to give tongue to what has been seen, heard and experienced." She reminds us that very young children often give direct expression to their experiences by continual storymaking in singsong, their bodies undulating to the rhythm of their musings. So too in early Greek theatre did the chorus chant reflections on the great events of its protagonist. So too does my two-year-old granddaughter sing her great events where she is the protagonist:

> I'm in my room with my toys
> There's a bird outside
> Mommy is downstairs
> Mommy is downstairs
> I'm going to the park.

In her discussion of storytelling, Ruth Sawyer provides a lovely chant-story from a four-year-old:

Winter is gone
I am out with my red engine
It is full of electricity
It makes the headlights shine
Today I planted my prune pits
Tomorrow day they will grow
The world is full of sunshine
It is on my engine
It is on my planted prune pits
I can feel it shining on my stomach
Mother and I will pick the prunes
And I will eat them for supper.[4]

As with early childhood, early theatre was storytelling in poetic form. Throughout the Middle Ages, in the absence of permanent theatres, a tradition of travelling troubadours, minstrels, bards and balladeers existed across Europe and Asia. They were found, for example, in gypsy encampments, Norse seaports, in the mountain villages of Aragon and among the tribes of Israel. In Spain, they were called *juglares de boca* — jugglers of the mouth.

If we could return to ancient Ireland, we would see no playhouses and no plays as we know them. Rather, there were travelling poets who roamed the countryside, visiting kings and chieftains and carrying bells to announce their coming. They recited genealogies of kings and created lore about mountains, streams, caves and other natural features of the countryside. (Early Irish poetry is known as *dindschenchas* which means "place-lore"). They often entertained with musical accompaniment — harps, pipes, drums and bones. Their purpose was no different from theatre, as we have come to know it: to entertain, to provoke laughter, to enthrall, to quicken the spirit, to tell about hitherto unknown worlds, to mourn the passing of heroes, to probe human frailty, to celebrate victories and to explore the mysteries of being. The tales told to hushed listeners at great fairs and private houses were filled with journeying and merriment, romance and warnings, blood and betrayal and struggle and triumph. They are said to have originated within the tradition of funeral games and the mourning of the dead.

It has long seemed to me that, whereas times may alter, patterns remain. There is, for example, the film *The Raggedy Rawney* which, though made in 1987, has many of the qualities of old tales. It is about travelling gypsies. Its form is picaresque, which is frequently defined as "the adventures of rogues." (The archaic meaning of rogue is "idle vagrant" and vagrant is "wanderer, stroller — as in player or musician.") In the film, the gypsies are moving through a countryside in wartime, some in old trucks, others in horse-drawn caravans. They are not only trying to stay out of harm's way generally, but they are trying to protect the young men in their families from marauding soldiers seeking conscripts. The raggedy rawney of the title is a young soldier, terror-stricken by his encounters with death, who joins the travellers disguised as a madwoman. What struck me anew while watching the film was the great power of story when large and universal themes are told or enacted. The story includes not only the adventures of a soldier on the run, but old curses, a drowning, new and old love, a gentle simpleton, an aborted child and a joyous wedding — all in the shadow of great fear of death. The centre-piece of the film harkens back to the very source of narrative with the enactment of a ritual funeral, including the burning of the corpse and an enormous keening song of mourning without words, holding the community together against the dark.

The profound narrative instinct, developed I believe in response to the great passages of life, has many representations and elaborations, from liturgical drama, commedia dell'arte, grand opera, cabaret, environmental theatre and movies to rock videos. Many young children still have the good fortune of experiencing narrative at its source, of having tales read to them where the reader becomes a lost child, animal, ogre, witch or all in one. Though the reality of the poet in the open air or on a raised dias in a long and narrow banqueting hall of wood and stone, telling tales and playing all the parts, has all but disappeared, the archetype, nonetheless, remains both in our childhood experiences and in our cultural history. Thus I am able to revive it in the classroom.

I often tell stories: some of my own favourites like *Rapunzel*, or an abridged version of *The Tale of Two Cities*, *Hansel and Gretel* or *The Happy Prince*. Or, to younger children, I tell "made-up" stories, developed spontaneously with input from them. I will begin by asking "What do you want the story to be about? Who or what should be in it? What are their names....?" One of my favourites developed in this way concerns a one-legged man called Charlie and his companion, a one-legged dog called Jamwater, who finally find their lost limbs encased in gold on the wall of a witch's cave at the bottom of the sea. Charlie and Jamwater have many adventures, including being captured from their treehouse, deep in the woods, by drunken hunters. But all ends happily. The name "Jamwater" delights the children.

More frequently, I design classes in such a way that people tell their own stories. These are shorter and less elaborate than tales; they might be described as scenes rather than acts or a whole play because, developmentally, students in the beginning of drama work cannot sustain the invention of a long story. Sometimes I suggest that a story be told about "what I dreamed" or "what I remember about the first time I went swimming." At other times, I encourage stories from the

97

imagination. At all times, I concentrate on talk, ensure that people's narrative is respected, and focus on the story that is there (no matter what), rather than commenting on what is "missing" or what "should be" in it. I move groups developmentally, from telling their tales, to telling them with the addition of sound and movement, to their full performance.

I like to let the content flow from simple principles: with content specific to the age, experience, goals and interests of the group, and to my own mood as well as the group mood. The principles are these:

1) Drama process needs boundaries so the participants feel secure. However there should be freedom of expression within the boundaries. In my own work, this includes a ritual of sitting in a circle to begin and end the drama period, talking and ensuring that people listen to whomever is speaking. It also includes the development of an understanding that the group does not argue with, or "critique," the content of individual's comments, stories and other creative work. I find this works best by modelling — that is, I am an active listener myself.

2) As with all drama processes, storymaking needs to be planned developmentally. It is never enough to say: "Now go away and make up a story and come back in 15 minutes and tell it to us." The imagination is not stimulated that way, and the results are liable to be cliché-ridden and embarrassing. And if a group is working together to develop a story without adequate guidelines or preparation, then frequently there is argument about content; the task of creating a work of the imagination is superceded by a need to compete with other people's ideas.

3) I have observed that there are fewer tensions about developing ideas when individuals are given adequate time to explore their own responses to the guidelines or stimulus of the day. Therefore, no matter the starting point and instructions for a storymaking process, I always begin with the personal (i.e., "what is your own response to this?"), and I ensure that the response can be expressed in some way, often by asking the participants to write freely on pieces of paper.

4) The principle of adequate preparation time includes the element of private exploration without the need to instantly perform. Therefore, when I ask for personal initial responses, be it free writing, singing, moving, painting or thinking, I ask that individual responses take place all at the same time, so that there is a kind of privacy in the group setting. Individuals soon become accustomed to ignoring the others at this particular stage of the process.

98

5) When the storymaking process has been designed to culminate in a group story, there will be less tension and controversy when elements of each person's personal responses are creatively incorporated into the whole. Therefore, guidelines for the group process always include specific instructions about joining ideas already developed by each individual in the group.

In the beginning stages, I have found it useful to ask groups to introduce themselves by simply telling the story of their names. So the ritual form begins. We sit in a circle. I start: "My name is Barbara Elizabeth Fletcher MacKay. I am called Barbara because of my mother and father, Elizabeth after Princess Elizabeth, and Fletcher, which means arrow-maker, from the days when names were assigned according to the work we did. MacKay is Scots, and means son of Kay. There are many spellings...." Each person talks in turn. Everyone listens. There is an easy pleasure in hearing the range of style, story and background that individuals inevitably bring to the telling of their tale. People tend to relax into the telling because there is nothing special required — no flights of the imagination, nothing beyond I AM. And who can argue with the story?

I find that although the imagination needs to be stimulated before storymaking can progress, it is not very difficult to find the stimulant. (I once worked with a group for a whole day's storymaking on the subject of **door**.) It needs only to be of interest to you and the students, and as leader, you need to be sensitive to the building of the responses so that there is a rich sharing at the end. For example, I often use music or objects to stir the imagination for storymaking. The process can take 30 minutes to an hour:

1) **A piece of music**
   Relax. Listen to the music (or move to it). What images emerge? What thoughts and feelings? Write them down in a freely — flowing way — don't worry about spelling and grammar right now. Look at what you've written. Underline your favourite phrases. Now share them with someone else. Make a poem together, or make a story together using two elements from each person's writing. Share it with the group by reading it aloud in turn, or moving to it, or adding sound to it.

2) **An object**
   Find an object that you like (in the park, playground, desk or school bag). What if the object were a person or a creature? How old is it? What kind of person or creature would it be? (example, flower: colourful, going a bit to seed, bends with the wind). If it were singing a song, what would it be? (All hum the different

songs together). What's its name? It has just come home from a journey; tell its story or bring it to two other persons/creatures/objects and make introductions. Or join with two others and make up a story about the three. Act out the story like a puppet play.

Other stimulants for storymaking that I have used include blown-up slides of human actions such as a policeman taking away a prisoner, someone huddled under a tree someone waving goodbye. Sometimes I place objects, stuffed toys or dolls across a room with the instructions that a journey (to music) will be made to recover them.

I also use face painting to stimulate spontaneous storymaking. Students are provided with individual mirrors, and water-based clown paints and coloured make-up sticks are available. They are encouraged to paint their faces in any way they wish, and then to tell a story into a tape recorder about the character that has emerged in the mask. Then I take the tapes home and transcribe them, typing them cleanly so that it looks like "real" text. Sometimes I read them aloud as stories for the group, giving every poetic nuance, and feeding them back as genuine literature. The students are delighted by this. Here, as always, I am struck by the degree of attention that they can bring to others' creative work. Overall, I have found that once the rituals of storymaking have been established, students become almost enraptured, not only by the process of their own imaginations, but by those around them. One of the things that seems to intrigue them most is the variety of responses to the same stimulus.

It is not always the case that storymaking in the classroom is instantly harmonious and successful. I have known times, particularly with young adolescents, when sitting quietly in a circle listening to others' storymaking efforts is all but impossible for them. They want to hide, to disappear into fits of giggles or into small groups to share private jokes and languages. They fear exposure and embarrassment; they fear looking different from the others; they fear looking as if they are trying too hard to please. So I begin with active games like freeze tag and play fighting, where energies can be both used and contained. And at this stage I have found it useful not to ask them for stories, but to provide one for them, and preferably one that can give them opportunities for movement and action within the safety of the group.

Once, for example, I worked in an all-boys school and the story that the 11-, 12- and 13-year-olds loved to play was derived from *The Lord of the Flies*. I would begin by telling a story about boys at school (like them). An atomic bomb was about to drop. They must prepare themselves quickly to leave on an airplane where they would be taken to safety on a tropical island. Time only for one letter home and permission was given to take a favourite object. I would then lead them through the action. A knock on the door with a message. Preparation. Letters (this done quickly by pretending to write, all talking aloud). The chairs in the room became an airplane. A landing. Then (as in Golding's version), the boys were on their own. I might ask them to sit down and tell me what happened next, though more often I would stand aside and watch them take the story forward in action. Many times as they improvised the rest of the tale, finding food, water and shelter, there would inevitably be a quarrel about leadership. (As few of them had read *The Lord of the Flies*, it was intriguing to observe the parallels.) Playing these archetypes of fear, adapting, struggle and seeking survival, seemed always to relax them for many drama lessons to come. It was a kind of initiation — for me and for them — whose source seemed to be the primitive tradition of young boys becoming men at puberty by going into the wilderness.

Another story that I found useful for this age group was initially a more surprising one. *The Lord of the Flies* story is full of predictably appealing high adventure, but by chance I discovered that preteen and teenaged children like to play a story based once again on the theme of making a new world in the wilderness, but of quite a different character. This is a movement story that I created for university students in drama in education, and one I imagined that very active preadolescents would find too interior, simple and unadventurous. The story is designed to be told and then acted out by the group in mime to a prepared background soundtrack of music to suit the action:

Once upon a time there was a dark grey planet in a dark grey corner of the universe and the planet was covered with dark grey specks of dust. The dark grey planet had been there for eons and it had never seen the sunlight. If you could look at this planet you could not know that within every speck of dust on it there was the dream of a colour, there was a colour-yet-to-be. (You are that speck of dust. What dream of a colour is in you?)

One day there was an astonishing thing, a kind of electricity in the air, an unknown movement. And then a few rays of sunshine appeared. The sun rose in the sky. The specks of dust trembled, breathed deeply, felt colour growing inside. They grew, they stood, they moved, they walked, leaving footsteps of colour. Colour flowed from their hands and fingers. As they moved they saw dark grey trees and gardens and rivers and animals. So they coloured their world. And they came together and built houses and tents. And just as they

101

were finishing their shelters, rain came, but they were safe inside. And the colours did not wash away.

Around this time I was invited to a school for five sessions with forty 11- and 12-year-olds to demonstrate "how to do drama." The children had no idea who I was and the first two sessions were frantically unproductive. (I now believe that part of the problem was my own anxiety about needing to perform.) "Well, why not," I thought, "I'll try the colour story; things can't get much worse. They might like the music." The music combined electronic sounds — Simon and Garfunkle's *I'd rather be a sparrow than a tree*, Anne Murray's *Hey! it's nice to be with you* and *Singin' in the Rain* by Gene Kelly. It worked. In fact, in the final two sessions, "doing the colour story" was like a favourite bedtime story: "again, please again." When I reflect upon it, birth and freedom of choice and creation are of course large and universal, and therefore appealing, ideas. However, "great themes" were not in my mind at the time. It is counterproductive to be too consciously archetypal, yet one discovers over and over again that storymaking will inevitably contain the archetypes, albeit in an infinite and absorbing variety of specific details. I have seen and heard thousands of original stories in classroom drama; many have been **about** the same themes, but I've never seen or heard the same story twice. It's been a continuous pleasure.

I want to finish on the theme of infinite variety and with a caveat: I advise not burdening yourself with worries about whether or not the stories produced by students are "good" stories. It's less inhibiting for you and for them to simply find procedures and boundaries and then to just let them flow. Surprising things can happen, beyond the boundaries of predetermined standards of quality. Eventually, by so-called objective criteria, some of the stories may be very good indeed, and eventually storymaking will become theatre making. However, the purpose should remain with the values of enjoying talk and image for their own sake, holding the group together, "against the dark." Once students are comfortable with the process of storymaking and with their own imagery, then moving ahead into greater complexity of form, style and learning seems not only to happen naturally, but with more richness, confidence and an altogether deeper sense of the power and beauty of theatre.

Endnotes

1. Coles, David, *The Theatrical Event* (Connecticut: Wesleyan University Press, 1975).
2. Chatwin, Bruce, *The Songlines* (Middlesex: Penguin Books, 1988).
3. Sawyer, Ruth, *The Way of the Storyteller* (Middlesex: Penguin Books, 1970).
4. Ibid., p. 48.

$\mathcal{A}$ Script for Written Performance: Learning About Writing Through Drama

SHIELA ROBBIE

Introduction

It was the challenge of forming an English department in the new Arts Faculty of the Universidade do Algarve in Southern Portugal (a dramatic experience in itself — and I do not just mean chaotic) that led to my use of educational drama and subsequent research in drama and writing. My students were all Portuguese and training to be English teachers — enthusiastic, lively and orally competent, but distinctly lacking in writing skills. The Portuguese are a very emotional, demonstrative and giving people. On the whole, they are outgoing, extremely sincere and lend themselves easily to drama. Unfortunately, for most students, language learning had, up to that point, been based upon skills training, proficiency being deemed as the ability to complete exercises with the least number of errors, and learning seen as the ability to pass tests. Thus, there was a definite need to unite life outside the classroom, with that within it. The students were willing (if somewhat sceptical) and the teacher was willing. Little did either realize how things would change — in more ways than one.

After a year of experimentation, a full-scale research project was formed and is still underway. The research results have been spectacular, beyond even my dreams. It is parts of these, with relation to drama and writing, that I would like to share with you. Whether you are teaching EFL (English as a Foreign Language), native speakers, adults or children, I would urge you to consider experimenting with some of the ideas that follow. The place from which we speak plays an important role in determining what we say, so I would ask you, for the moment, to look at things from the perspective of an EFL teacher, and then consider how my experience could be put to use in your own classroom.

Reaching Out Through Drama

"The world we have made as a result of the level of thinking we have done thus far, creates problems we cannot solve at the same level of thinking at which we created them."

— *Albert Einstein*

Upon receipt of the first writing assignment from my students, it was plainly evident why it was that they regarded writing with trepidation and loathing. They had become trapped within the sentence at the expense of the text. Writing was not about meaning or making meaning, and had become restricted to editing skills. Composition writing had become the stringing together of sentences in the quest for linguistic accuracy, resulting in a text where the content was totally incongruous to the intellectual capacity of the student. The EFL writing classroom had been concentrating on the "EFL" part of writing, to the detriment of basically everything else related to the learning experience. It was ironic that English was classified under "Linguas Vivas" (Living Languages), whereas it had been treated as an abstract system — an editorial activity and not a human one. The students needed to be taught to select words not from the dictionary, but from the context of life.[1] Drama was one of the things that facilitated that move forward.

Behind this view of learning is the Bakhtinian doctrine that we get ourselves from others, namely:

The way in which I create myself is by means of a quest: I go out to the other in order to come back with a self. I "live into" an other's consciousness; I see the world through that other's eyes. But I must never completely melt with that version of things, for the more successfully I do so, the more I will fall prey to the limitations of the other's horizon.[2]

At the heart of dramatic meaning-making is, in effect, a search for a script for new thinking and learning, what Bolton calls "an invitation to participate in the existential present,"[3] a journey into new and familiar settings, and for the teacher of writing, this has exciting implications.

Dare to be Different

Introducing drama to a group of students, most of whom have never been to the theatre and none of whom have had drama at school, can be quite a shock to their system (not to mention that of the teacher or the institution in question). **And** it is all the more powerful as they have so much to discover and they discover it for themselves, individually and collectively. As students reading an M.A. in English and as future EFL teachers, my students had specific goals. It was obvious that a change in methodology was necessary and that it had to be negotiated. The students had to be willing to try something different, not just suspend their disbelief of the fictional world, but to be willing to place their trust within me as their teacher, in whose hands their learning lay for the rest of that academic year.

I would urge any teacher who meets with resistance from their students at the introduction of drama into their classroom, to persevere. I found that many of the students who were most sceptical, were those who made tremendous strides forward.

I was lucky in that anything "to do with drama" was considered a little crazy, so I could get away with a lot. Students walking into the refectory donning silver paper and large bows were "oh — just Sheila's pupils." Being English helped, as we are considered rather eccentric. So for those with innovative thoughts for foreign countries — remember, you need to be persistent and convinced in what you are doing. Dare to be different.

Elaborating the Script

INITIAL CONSIDERATIONS

No class is the same and every teacher has different talents. As regards drama in the classroom, my experience has been to follow instinct and to stick initially to that with which I feel happy, and then experiment as both the group and the teacher become more innovative. The more the whole group is willing to step outside the boundaries of experience, the greater their experience becomes. When they do so, the students' knowledge of how spoken, written and drama texts work or fail in differing situations, and their knowledge of the power structures evident in the world at large grows. That is where the magic lies.

I have used a combination of improvisation and forum theatre[4] to explore themes initially chosen by me, and more latterly by the students themselves. EFL textbooks are often organized thematically, and drama sessions can be based around the themes of the book or one special subject that is causing difficulty, depending upon the students' needs.

It is important that the drama belongs to the students — that it is their drama, negotiated, developed and explored by them. Only then are the texts which emerge produced socially and with conviction. One set of first-year students asked me to do a workshop on the theme of drugs, after a local incident, when drug smugglers were caught by the marine police while bringing drugs by sea from Morocco.

The drugs were dumped overboard. This resulted in packages floating ashore and a mad dash by those on the beach to seize what they could. This fired the students' enthusiasm which was reinforced when, while scuba-diving, my instructor and I found part of one of the abandoned packages.

Any theme can be developed; it is the teacher's job to find how best to do so. To deal with the drugs problem as a real-life problem was too close to home for these students. Instead they went back into an imaginary world where Delta X, the drug that made all your wishes come true, had found its way back onto the black market after having been banned by the government. Thus a real problem was dealt with in a fictional world, raising questions of values and the dangers and consequences of taking drugs, while also investigating the lives of those who relied on the production of drugs for their existence. The experience worked on many more levels of meaning and significance than, for example, investigating what occurs when parents find out that their son is taking drugs. The commitment to this particular drama workshop was noteworthy, and Einstein, who invented the drug "Delta X," still lives on today.

The art of the teacher lies in resisting the temptation to dictate which route is to be taken in the drama. By not losing sight of the language being used, surreptitiously heightening the language (by intervening in role, or introducing written material to be emulated or replied to) or ensuring that opportunities for the specific type of writing she wishes to emerge as a result of the drama, are furthered. Indeed I have found that my role as "teacher of writing" has not been to create opportunities for writing — they have appeared by themselves, whether solicited or not — but to select which opportunities would best further the aims of the workshop in question.

Time being limited, there is always a need to strike a balance between writing during the drama, in role and writing after the drama. Something I found particularly useful was to use the workshop during subsequent writing classes, and all writing assignments between workshops were related to the drama that had taken place that day, or as a direct result of the workshop. Writing thus ceased to become a lifeless, mechanical act and became either essential for the furthering of the drama or future dramas, as well as being an opportunity to try out new ideas or styles, within a protective framework. Later this developed into reflective writing or more abstract, discursive compositions. The "blank page" no longer became a problem.

I quote from student journals:

> When writing my composition I realized that my words
> kind of flowed, I was writing more fluently.

* * * *

Sometimes it's difficult to write. When we have an opinion, we can write about it, or we can always read something in a magazine or newspaper, and then we can write about it. But when we make or create the situation ourselves, we want to write about it. It's easier and more interesting because it happened and our imagination created it. It really seems easier to write.

* * * *

What I find most difficult in essays is to start writing them. Sometimes I don't know what I should write. I can't find ideas. Drama helps me because by remembering, I can imagine something more vivid. I'll explain: in dramas we live in a large variety of moments by acting, and in essays we live with words as we write them on the paper. It's easier when we have already lived these moments. We write the kind of essays where you put all your mind, and by the end you feel that you have really done something. You wrote down on paper feelings, emotion; you expressed them to others. Yes, it helps a great deal.

To my colleague who took me to one side the day of a workshop and asked me gently: "Isn't this a bit childish for university students?" I would suggest she asks the students.

Plotting the Connection

Let me take you briefly through one of the initial drama sessions with second-year university students at the above mentioned university to give you an insight into the processes at work. This is by no means a lesson plan for reproduction; its aim is to give you a taste of the nature of the drama/writing event within context, with the intention of facilitating your response to the issues raised thereafter.

THE SIBYL[5]

The Way In — Building the Context   □   The ground rules were laid down, one being "no Portuguese." The drama commenced with myself in role as narrator. I read out a scroll which told the familiar story of the Greek Sibyl, who presented the nine scrolls of knowledge to King Tarquin, and offered to exchange them for that which he most valued. The king told her the price was too high, so the Sibyl burnt three of the scrolls. She then repeated her offer, this time the six scrolls for the thing he most valued. Once again he refused, and she burnt three more scrolls. The offer was repeated once more, and at this point, the scroll was illegible. The narrator needed her audience to help her discover what this story told them about the land and its people.

I must point out here that the aim was not to re-enact the narrative, although as a teacher of writing I had in the back of my mind to make the students eventually write the contents of the scrolls. They were allowed to choose their own focus. I have found that with students not used to drama, an extract or story is often an effective "way in" to drama, as it gives them ideas to work on. The reading of the scroll was also used here to set the **register and tone**[6] of the language to follow, and to use the visual image of an elaborate scroll that had been partly destroyed by fire to draw the students into the story.

To give them confidence, I asked them to step outside the drama to recapitulate the story, and it emerged that they were interested in the importance of the gods to the kingdom. Enthusiastic about being able to move about in the classroom in groups, they were then encouraged to recreate statues or monuments using their bodies and any objects in the room. I should mention here that the class consisted of 35 students in total — quite a lot of students to keep occupied at the same time. Each monument was then given an inscription by the students — in English or Latin — and each group had to explain the significance of their statue and who or what it symbolized. (I also brought in a marble slab with a Latin inscription on it, prepared in conjunction with their Latin tutor in the hope that they would become interested in the statues in the story). It was amazing how quickly the students' imaginative powers came into play, and different gods of the earth, fire, air and sea were found side by side with symbolic representations of the struggle of forces in the kingdom. This led to the elaboration of a model and a map of the kingdom, once they had come to a consensus on what it was like. Belief in their own kingdom was thus created. These parts of the drama where written and spoken language are not that evident are extremely important, since, as we all know, there is no point in going forth unless there is belief in what is happening by all parties.

Making Sense of their Story □ The ritual of the court scene where the scrolls were presented was shown as a still image (tableau), and via **thought tracking**[7], the impressions, hopes, fears and roles of those present were touched upon. The students were then asked to form a circle and step outside the drama to discuss what had happened. This raised several questions leading to class discussion of the land, its people and their attitudes to its rulers. Later on in the drama the students returned to the still image, and further thought tracking took place, when their understanding of the kingdom had deepened.

Discussion of the kingdom and short improvised scenes were used to discern what the worries and problems of the people were, and why it was that they needed the Sibyl at all. To discover what it was that the king would most value, these students decided to visit him in order to find out what he was like, and how he felt about his role. A selfish, cruel and confident character emerged.

A visit to the king provides innumerable opportunities for writing. However the teacher has to be guided by a) what it is that the students want; b) time; and c) the aims of the workshop.

One option, had there been more time, would have been for groups to construct an artefact somewhere in the palace, which was important to the King, containing objects and pieces of writing, clues as to what he was like (e.g. the manuscript of a page of a journal, a letter from a counsellor etc).

If the aim of the meeting had been to persuade him to address a question to the Sibyl, the question would need to be formulated and a scroll written stating the subjects' case and how the question would be addressed to the Sibyl. (This is very important — an unsuitably worded question usually produced little in terms of an answer.) For example, several groups could formulate questions and the best two could be presented.

The students in question here decided for more serious tactics. First, they wanted to **hot seat**[8] the king and ask him some direct questions. This they did extremely effectively. Then, through improvised scenes worked out in groups subsequently performed to the class as a whole, they explored different things taking place in the kingdom which included a discussion between the king and his counsellors, and a secret meeting of people plotting against the king and his latest tax laws. This in turn led to a visit to the Sibyl for help. Once each group had presented their scene to their peers, conclusions were drawn.

Creating their Kingdom ☐ Charred manuscripts and old artefacts were suddenly produced by the "**teacher-in-role**" as students formed groups of archaeologists whose task was to discover whether or not the artefacts belonged to the lost kingdom, and to present a report to a meeting of the archaeological society.

The manuscripts had been prepared previously and included such diverse things as a biblical extract, part of a speech from Julius Caesar, a poem in Middle English and part of an old chronicle. Care had been taken to write them on parchment in old script and to make certain parts were illegible.

Needless to say, these sufficed for subsequent lessons on their content and style, discussion of their real origin and inevitably, **discourse analysis**.[9]

The drama provided the stimulus for both a written and verbal report, which had to be produced at an archaeological meeting in the register adequate for the occasion. Work upon the manuscripts took place in English and was extremely assiduous. It had become important for the students to find out about the kingdom, since no one supported the king, and the conclusions of one group were often questioned by another until a consensus was reached.

These reports, subsequent to the drama, served as a basis for work on the writing of reports, which in turn led to further written work on opinions, persuasion and argument. In this respect, the teacher has to further her aims as regards writing.

Subsequent improvisation work in groups and as a whole entailed another visit to the Sibyl, correct presentation of the peasants' problems and their request that she visit the king. The Sibyl ("**teacher-in-role**') made this as difficult for the pupils as possible. The re-enactment of the Sibyl's visit to the king (interrupted by "**teacher-in-role**" as chronicler reading a scroll speaking of unrest and complaints about the king), including the actual burning of the scrolls (in a cake tin), led the king to renounce the thing he most valued — his throne.

Drawing matters to a Conclusion □   Finally, sitting in a circle, a sheet of paper was passed around, and each student wrote the most important thing that would be written on the scrolls which contained the knowledge to rule the kingdom. These were then read aloud, in a ritualistic manner.

FURTHER WRITING

I always give the students a written assignment subsequent to the drama. Initially these were chosen by me. As the students became accustomed to the drama, they were full of ideas about what to write, and these would be discussed and a choice of two or three decided upon. This class wrote a page of King Tarquin's diary the day before the Sibyl's visit with the last three scrolls.

In a later lesson, time had moved on, and the scrolls had become very important. They were always consulted in times of trouble and danger. Three titles were found for the scrolls, and short extracts were written.

The compiling of the scrolls involved lengthy negotiation and almost armed combat! Headings were agreed upon for various sections, and individual contributions were made and then evaluated by peer groups. It was amazing to watch these students, who had completely forgotten that they were working in a foreign language, and writer's block was certainly the last thing on their mind. Such dedication and motivation had not been witnessed before, and it was unnecessary to stress the importance of register and tone as well as content. The students worked as if their lives depended upon it. It was as if the concrete, the abstract and the symbolic worlds had become fused with the real world. Drama has often been described as the bridge between the abstract and the real world. Here was an example.

Diaries were written of how people's lives had changed as a result of the scrolls. Other writing involved the elaboration of "The Daily Chronicle," a newspaper showing how the news would have been presented had there been newspapers at that time. The newspaper was in minute detail, not just including the front page story and editorial, but news of taxes, reforms. and advertisements for things as diverse as plots of land and chastity belts!

Further discussion and compositions explored what else it was that the king could have given up to get the three scrolls. Subsequent writing led to the theme of values and justice, and whether the king was right to make a decision without consulting his people. Questions about intentions, motivation and consequences of taking certain decisions and actions, came to the fore, as did speculation as to how the drama could have been different and how that would have changed the story.

The writing tasks given were therefore at first "in role" and used to further the drama situation or to help create its context. Later, writing led initially to reflective, and subsequently to more abstract, thinking upon the values and social implications arising from the drama. These were compared with life in the present. The students' reactions in role were contrasted with how they thought that they would have reacted as themselves. Care was taken to develop the chance to write in different genres, and this enabled discussion of how a serious newspaper, a tabloid or a magazine would report the story today, compared with how the royal chronicler and a historian would have reported it at the time in question.

Scenes developed further to the workshop included interviews of eyewitnesses of the ceremony — from the counsellors and the guards, the palace cleaners peeking through the curtains, to old people reminiscing about what had happened. Oral stories were then compared to written stories, and thus differences between speech and writing explored.

Once the context and the main subject had been formed and belief created, the possibilities for writing were endless.

Finally the students were presented with the outcome of the original myth which was compared to their own.

The Nature of the Written Text

A SOCIAL TEXT

It is important for a foreign language learner, and indeed any writer, to learn the language system. What the drama process evidences is that it also important for the student to learn how to make use of it, not just to communicate, but to be conscious of the need to adjust to the audience and set the boundaries of the text socially rather than linguistically.[10] Meaning is constantly negotiated through the drama, among the participants, and that meaning becomes encapsulated in the text. Writing is no longer "practice," but a genuine need to communicate, explore and interpret. Here is a short taste of one of the student's work, writing as King Tarquin:

> Today, for the second time the Sibyl, from the Great Cave, came to see me, and again fear and terror entered my soul.
> My power seems powerless; my throne is only another seat, my people do not respect me, but I am the King, I am their leader, I alone should give orders...
> ...Oh Gods! why have you abandoned me? Please come and enlighten my spirit with your wisdom.

Not only the tone and register, but the choice of vocabulary and sentence structure have been chosen carefully for both meaning and effect. This is something that is evident in all texts resulting from drama, and I use "all" consciously. The dedication and involvement of the student are evidenced in the more adventurous use of language and attention to detail.

With their concern for, and involvement with, the people and events in the drama, the students learn to draw upon capacities they are unaware they possess, in order to explore the possibilities of writing. It is at once a profoundly personal and profoundly social experience.

Some students, as they gain confidence in a protected time and space and learn that every contribution is welcome, surprise even themselves when they find out of what they are capable. Take the example of a bright student who was struggling with his written English, convinced he would never progress. Here is part of a text produced shortly prior to the Sibyl drama-workshop described above:

> Most of the times, when we are passing hours doing nothing we start thinking and facing real truth, the reality, what has happened with us, the things we have done and the good and bad times we spend on the past, and the good and bad that will come on a near future. This poem is from one of my periods of reflection , trying to face reality. It's untitled...

During the workshop he untypically took an active part and found to his surprise that he could work with his peers rather than sit silently alone. As the drama session began to unfold, so did his ability. As Bruner has pointed out, sentences need to make contact with the learner's muscles, the student learns a language by using it over and over again, and as situations become more demanding, so his proficiency in using the language grows.

Let me share with you an extract of the student's diary written as King Tarquin:

26th of April, 116 (year of God)

Dear diary,

Today I faced one of the most difficult episodes of my life, therefore I should have no other means than to confess myself.

I was laid down on my bed when a strange face appeared to me, I noticed that the sky was all covered by clouds. The image spoke to me with a smooth voice. I didn't understand but my body frozed immediately. The only thing that came up to my mind was that I was facing the dark side, the evil side of darkness. I called my Guards, my Counsellors and nobody answered me, I was really frightened.

The image remained for a few moments, I have no idea how long, staring at me and she whispered: "Keep doing your job and soon you'll join our side...

It is impossible to do the text justice within the space of this chapter. Differences between one text and another are evident at first reading. Analysis of the text from a linguistic and social semiotic perspective[11] does show considerable development as regards language ability, style, content and register. Indeed, as I shall explain later, much of my research has led to me using these ways of looking at text in the quest to understand the drama/writing process.

The Imagination

One of the most striking factors in the texts arising from or within drama sessions is the use of the imagination, the working of a fiction within a fiction. In the same way as meaning was negotiated between the students, each came away with their own view of that meaning, their own interests, and wove them into another fiction while remaining faithful to that created in the classroom.

One student in a drama on time travel, writing of the president of the United States sentenced to death, says:

John Taylor, the man sitting in the defendent chair, flowing into a deep hipnotic sleep through his most profound thoughts. Mind doesn't establish a real fronteer, it's a doorway where love, hate, fear, cinism, compassion, braveness, warmth, responsibility and a whole universe of responses all levitate.

The putting of imagination into words is always a tricky business, especially when in a foreign language, and does not always work the way the writer had intended.

We have cold sweats, our teeth shake as well as our legs...

* * * *

It isn't right when we are educated with such love and then we hop away from home, like a stupid horse.

* * * *

I think that the idea of making a brochure about Time Travel Incorporated is great. It pulls our imagination off. When I like a subject my mind starts working right away, but if I dislike it I crash into a "deep coma" that keeps me still in a frozen ice-cube.

* * * *

The first workshop was like a thunderstruck.

By drawing upon the imagination in the drama process, everyone has a chance of making meanings within meanings. Most drama teachers have used the theme of emigration in their dramas. I developed the theme with my first-year students, as many of their parents had emigrated and then returned to Portugal. The drama commenced with a trunk in the centre which I had filled with artefacts wrapped in brown paper. In turn, each student ceremoniously unwrapped their artefact and decided why it had been taken on the journey of the owner of the trunk. To avoid each person having to stand up at the beginning of the drama without any preparation, they were allowed to write down the reasons for taking it, and then each in turn walked into the centre of the circle and talk about their artefact. My favourite was regarding a set of antique forks. It was the forks who spoke:

We are 12 forks and we belonged to Queen Elizabeth. We were stolen by a pirate during a trip to Scotland. Please help us. We want to go home. This pirate has been using us; he has rotten teeth and doesn't even wash us. We have been locked in this trunk and we are seasick. Please, please send us home.

The idea of using the family heirloom to build belief had been borrowed from an idea of Jonothan Neelands,[12] and it is uncanny how some of his students also spoke as the heirloom itself: "We are worn with honour and dignity. We are kept with pride...." Students all over the world can connect with drama, and as this shows, sometimes in the same way.

In my drama session, the students were then given a brown paper package which was passed around them as they sat in a circle. They were asked to imagine what it was that they would take with them, as imaginary characters who were emigrating, and who could only take one thing with them. It was to everyone's surprise when the most unwilling and often disruptive male pupil stood up and said, "This is my wedding dress...." The engagement of this pupil led to an extremely productive drama session. By including any disruptive pupils or those considered outsiders within the process of the drama, a bond was created that continued outside the classroom. In one particular case I had a class which was always divided in two. Half of the students sat on one side of the room, half on the other. Their first taste of drama involved a television chat show. I was incredulous when I found them all sitting at a table in the refectory an hour after class, passing around a chocolate bar and playing their own version of the game in Portuguese. The sharing and creating of knowledge as a group led to increased empathy, to an awareness and acceptance of others and to their solidarity as a class.

Evoking Meaning through the Senses

Just as the senses and spectra are used to create atmosphere within the drama, they are referred to again and again in the texts produced. As Terry Threadgold excellently puts it, we are dealing with "a semiotic chain of events,[13] enacted on and through bodies, in which meanings are made now in one media now in another then superimposed upon and embedded within one another."[14] There is a marked increase in the references to the senses in the texts which result from drama. When the senses and the imagination are drawn together, the results are quite spectacular, the grammatical contribution only forming part of a complex whole:

I looked up at the clear blue sky. Not a cloud in sight. Mid-December and the temperatures were soaring. Soon, and in a matter of minutes, that clear blue would turn grey and the usual daily thundershower would pour down, leaving the smell of wet earth in the air and warm vapours rising from the torrid tar. Children on their way home from school rushed to take off their shoes and socks and walked through the puddles. They treaded on the mat of freshly-fallen jacaranda blossoms. The picture pulled at the strings of my heart and I recalled the words of a famous writer: "You can take people out of Africa but you can't take Africa out of people...

It is this sense of feeling and identification with that which is written about that makes the texts so different. The words have become "peopled" in a Bakhtinian sense.[15] Drama is not a bridge to the abstract, as the language produced is far from abstract; it is more than a system. It is to do with social reality, with relationships, feelings, purposes, past histories, cultural attitudes, with what it is to be human. That is why it is not a "waste of time" to let the students engage properly with the situation before any oral or written tasks are given. It is through taking part in the experience that many of the meanings are made and differing viewpoints explored.

A Semiotic Perspective

Whether it be gesture, sound, imagery or any other form of semiology[16] that can be used in the drama process, each and every one influences the texts produced. As Gunther Kress points out:

> Discourse is a site where meaning plays between participants in a semiotic exchange, whether this is speech or dialogue, comic or film, ritual or game.[17]

Space does not permit me to develop this topic as I would like. On a very basic level, let me draw the teacher's attention to how a symbol can help the students enter the drama more readily. I remember a student sitting in the middle of the circle in role as the cleaning lady Miriam in the drama on old age. She seemed to be searching for words in the panic of what to say and how to say it. I handed her a feather duster which she clutched fiercely and said, totally in role: "Master Robert was too much of a gentleman to do such a thing." An object had helped her identify with the role and access the register, without any prompting from the teacher. It was she herself that elevated the language of her peers.

The written texts generated by a drama are a mixture of sign systems that interlink to provide particular meaning of that drama experience for the individual writer. Let me give you the example of a text written by a first year student after a drama workshop on old age and loneliness. The drama session was particularly moving, ending with a Heathcote-type coffin where Miriam lay, and to which the son who had left her to die alone and rejected, came to pay his last respects. Many of the students shed real tears and entered role completely. A student wrote to me afterwards thus:

> The final scene was so moving, tears were in my eyes.
> It was such a special moment! Thank you. God bless
> you.

The writing assignment subsequent to the drama was to write the letter that Robert, the son, never sent to his mother.

The student in question started her letter where the drama had begun, in the old lady's garden. She evokes a vivid picture of her sitting with marigolds on her lap, using her senses to create atmosphere:

> I see you in the garden.
> Balancing back and forward in the old rocking chair, which I have no memory from whom have you inherited it; with Marigolds in your lap.
> Now, you are in the warm kitchen; I can still feel the marvelous apple perfume in the air; the Marigolds were left in the large rectangular wooden table, waiting for the hands, that will gently place them in a beautiful jar...

She then builds her own personal fiction, changing the name of the old lady slightly to fit in with her fiction:

> Dear Mary, those flowers were named after you; and I haven't seen one for twelve years.
> Do you still put them in the center of the table, mother? Perhaps not. Julie told me you prefer roses or gardenias, now!

The symbol of the marigolds is used to explore the feelings expressed. For example:

> I know why; marigolds make you remember...when I
> was a little boy, I used to pick them up, just to make
> you angry, but also to make you smile; because inno-
> cently with a brat voice I would say:
>
> — She loves me, she loves me not, she LOVES me!

There had been no marigolds in the class drama. The only flowers
had been those described initially in the old lady's garden, and those
that someone laid on her coffin at the end. The student has created
her own signifier which she interweaves at the end with one from
the drama session itself.

> Don't say it's too late, forget the snake...bring the Mari-
> golds with you, Mary.

The drama session had begun with a piece of string which had become
a snake in an old lady's garden, providing the lead into the theme
of old age and loneliness.

It would take a whole book to deal with the nature of the semiotic
processes in drama.[18] I would, however, like to make salient the fact
that these processes tie the drama and writing processes together in
such a way that they are inextricable. Indeed it becomes undesirable
to try to untangle them, since it is in their interweaving that unpredicted
particular and special meanings are made. In one of the student's own
words:

> I think we got to know what drama really is in fact:
> a chance to play with words and give action to several
> moments of life even like death. By the end I believe
> that everybody cried or felt very touched.

Visual Representations

Another feature of the texts that is exciting is the use that the students
make of the visual.

> I also enjoyed more doing a piece of writing about an
> imaginary world and an imaginary character because
> I had the chance of creating things as I saw them in
> my mind.

As students write, they often open their piece with visual imagery,
whether related to the drama or their own cultural and social histories:

Millions of names written in gravestones reminded me
of that fatidic day, the one I killed who loved and believed me.

Visual imagery provides a link between the real and the fictional
worlds that co-exist in what Bolton calls "metaxis":[19]

Two words of obedience — Yes Mum. When you're
three years old the world seems just a big round thing,
like is shown in the children's channel, that only has
your house and your cousin's houses in it.

As recent work by Gunther Kress and Van Leeuwen has shown
it is vital to take into the account the visual semiotic when analysing
a text. I was amazed at how much use the students made of the visual
in their work, especially in the newspaper articles that were produced.
The layout of text and pictures and/or drawings, and the choice of
size and type of graphic representation, are extremely important to
the overall meaning of the text, and some very powerful messages
were conveyed.

In texts written with relation to drama, attention was paid to small
detail that had been unknown before drama was introduced into the
classroom. For example, when a text was typed, there was explicit use
of typeface. In the letter using the marigolds image for example, the
typeface that is closest to longhand was used, so that it looked like
a letter. In an examination where the task was to write a magazine
article to attract attention, the student drew an aeroplane pulling a
banner with the title of the article on, to explicitly draw attention to
it. This is yet another way in which culture forms part of the text that
is produced.

A Notion of Performance

As studies of the semiotics of theatre and drama have shown, a dramatic performance is composed of several messages from several
agents, simultaneously embracing differing signs and sign systems.
Hence there are various levels of performance upon which the constructed fictions operate.

The notion of text as a performance limited socially, in space and
time, is extremely relevant to the drama classroom. Let me give you
just one example:

During the drama on emigration, one group had 10 minutes to
devise a "parting scene" and present it to the class. An extremely powerful scene emerged. This group were exploring the nature of the
experience of a Jewish lady who was going to Germany to find out

if her son was alive. The students had adopted as their props a big family bible, some chairs, a trunk, and had made themselves skull caps to symbolize the fact that they were Jews.

The scene started with a still image. To the right, a male student stood on the chair with the open Bible. To the left, the lady was shown taking leave of her family who were seated and weeping. Suddenly the boy started to sing softly in English a song with the chorus: "It's just so hard to say goodbye." As he sang, the others started to move, and he lowered his voice so that we could hear what was being said, but did not stop singing. The action was timed so perfectly that the final words of the scene to the left of the stage were: "It's just so hard to say goodbye," said at the same time as the last line of the chorus of the song being sung.

The scene was extremely evocative and shows the multimodality of text. The visual interacted with sound, silence, movement, stillness, song and dialogue. Particular sign systems were in interaction with persons, with bodies in space and time. The way the drama was produced was evidenced by the performance. It was produced collaboratively and it needed the whole group to make it work, what Wagner would call "distilled human experience" The students were drawing upon their personal knowledge, perhaps of the Jews leaving Portugal, of films they had seen on video such as *Mousegames*, in order to distance the theme of emigration from themselves. The choice of the music was not to do with oppression, but with the Portuguese sense of *saudade* or longing, sadness and sentiment, upon which their traditional *fado* songs are hinged. As their ability to manipulate the art form grew, so did their ability to use their bodies to speak more than one language at the same time. Their sensibility to language, culture and history induced meanings found through social interaction profoundly unique to the group that had created them.

This scene prompted a student to write, unbidden, of her own personal experience:

> The Jewish departure scene has moved me to tears, it
> has really touched my heart! So, I have decided to write
> about my two most distressing departures...

Each text provides a different subtext for each student.

It is moments like this that drama is made of. The example also exemplifies the problems involved in describing what is taking place, the need for a **metalanguage**[20] which provides a feel of the whole human event, formed of multiple meanings which in turn lead to different readings by different individuals. Drama in the classroom is in essence the construction of a text generating other texts. Each individual reading provides in turn a different piece of writing which also contains various meanings, a dramatic performance in itself. Writing during or after a drama is not just about taking part in a drama session and exploring cultural and social events. It is much more than that. It involves a balance between the individual and the intersubjective perspectives, between performance and the social semiotic. It deals with utterances, words and texts in personal and social histories. And as Gunther Kress points out:

> It is only in the discovery and description of the whole system and its interconnection with other systems that the meaning of any social activity can be fully understood.[21]

Each text procreated by the drama is different and is composed of more than the language in which it is written, a careful construction of both identification and detachment. **Students do not leave the classroom, take off their "drama hat" and put on their "writing hat." They take their "drama hat" with them.** The text that results is the product of negotiated meaning in chosen situations, with a view to the exploration of a specific topic. Each writer selects and organizes for themselves the experience that they have been through. The texts are socially produced in a joint act of discovery, but the individual person and their personal interests and response to the drama, in relation to their own particular place in both the real and fictional worlds, are also central to their interpretation. It was Ausubel that pointed out that meaningfully-learned material is retained longer than something learned by rote, and these sessions have certainly proved that, as did the exam results at the end of term.

Throughout the drama, both consciously and unconsciously, the students clarify their thoughts and select new information and viewpoints to take on board. At a pedagogic level, this leads to greater richness in content in the essays produced. In what other type of classroom is the range of language practice so diverse, where the student is required to question, speculate, clarify, argue a case, address a problem, report, evaluate, criticize, respond, announce, listen, get information, select, examine, authorize, clarify, direct, inform, focus direction or attention, design, alter, argue, demand, instruct, interpret, justify, predict, assess, recommend, reflect and act? I could go on.... And moreover, the social, historical and cultural environment necessary for the exploration of the implications of language use is provided in context, without bearing the consequences of the real world at large. This is doubly important to my students who are studying a foreign language in an institution that does not, as yet, send its students abroad to study for a year, as is the norm in the U.K. Having been a language student myself, I know that the real test of whether you have learned a language is when you arrive in the foreign country and have to fend for yourself. I vividly remember asking for a packet of worms instead of a packet of peas (guisantes/gusanos).

At another level, a whole range of power structures are at work in the students' search to discover their own voice, and they learn how to use, manipulate and challenge those structures. Confidence in writing is reflected in that voice and particular expressions of meaning. The students' attention to genre and form, written, dramatic and visual has been very specific, in itself another kind of performance.

The concept of Bakhtinian voice is central to my reading of the texts in the sense that students, socially positioned within one culture, draw upon different values, different voices in differing cultures and upon cultural and social histories. Both the verbal and the non-verbal experiences form part of the texts which refer back to the fictive and creative voices. The drama process is a special way of exploring differing experiences, the dialectic of power and control, through activity. It provides the site of interaction of word, body and mind, evidencing the nature of the experience for the writer and reconciling it with his knowledge of the world.

While exploring the interactions of the various strands of meaning which evolve, one of the aspects of the texts in which I have become interested is the transformational power of dramatic art and of the writing act itself. The students learn through transformations on various levels. The male student who sang at the departure scene started off the drama session by playing the class comedian and refusing to get into role. That is a transformation on one level. The Miriam text took the paper flowers laid on the coffin and turned them into a powerful metaphor. This is yet another level. By plotting linguistic transformations through both written and dramatic texts, patterns are beginning to emerge. Transformation in drama can include metaphor and myth, while it can also include parody, inversion and disruptive narrative.[22] It can also lead to ideological transformations.

The importance for the teacher is two-fold: (1) to find out how the students learn through these transformations which are initiated in the mind, the mind in interaction with others, embodied in the drama and then both consciously and unconsciously related to real life; (2) to discuss the significance of the specific transformations which emerge in this powerful process. Indeed the drama theorist has a transformational job on her hands: to build upon the work of theorists within the field and related fields and transform them into one which allows for the importance of the system while preserving personhood. She is working with a script where the process as well as the product is important. Discourse in drama is produced by the social agent within a social space. Furthermore, a total and unified understanding involves the interconnectedness of writing with mental and cognitive processes. Here, Vygotsky's[23] work on the use of gesture and symbolism in play, the relationship between language and development, and his zone of proximal development[24], aids our interpretation.

Implication

If drama and writing are seen as components in a learning process, where texts are generated and transformed, and if the student is seen to learn through language as well as about language, drama is more than a motivational stimulus, more than a teaching tool. It is about working with and within the art form and with different types of language in particular situations. Thus, any explanation of the drama/ writing process necessitates seeking an understanding of how the pupils have grown both socially and linguistically, and requires language to be seen as part of social behaviour. My aim in teaching writing is practice, not perfection. Only by developing the knowledge of how to use language will the student be able to use it in the real world. The drama process encompasses all kinds of language, verbal and non-verbal, combining high mental activity with physical activity. Students work with experience on both emotional and intellectual planes, in order to respond to, and engage with, both the fictional and the real world.

Educational drama centres around intersubjective meaning, the social semiotic and performance. My research is evidencing the nature of the text that is produced and the learning processes involved. In sharing part of it here with you, as a practitioner, I wish to encourage teachers of writing to bring this creative and exhilarating experience into their classroom. As a researcher, I wish to make salient the need to investigate, describe and theorize further the essence, potential and significance of educational drama. In the foreign language classroom there is a need to move beyond the communicative bandwagon, to deal with the changing needs of students in today's society, by drawing upon contemporary practice in other disciplines. Drama can facilitate the journey, for, in the words of a first-year student:

> Drama is a revolution. A sweet new and very interesting revolution. We are free to play with our imagination , to share our deeper feelings, express our thoughts. Drama is a fresh awakening.

Endnotes

1. V.N. Voloscinov, *Marxism and the Philosphy of Language* (Cambridge, Mass.: Harvard University Press, 1973), p. 192.
2. Clark and Holquist, *Mikhail Bakhtin* (Cambridge, Mass.: 1984), p. 78. Mikhail Bakhtin, a Soviet Scholar, advocated a sociocultural approach to language and human mental functioning. His work dealt with the psychology of language, cognitive development and educational practice. Bakhtin claimed that the "word is half someone else's," that voice is social and does not exist in isolation.
3. G. Bolton, *New Perspectives on Classroom Drama* (Simon & Schuster Education, 1992), p. 33.
4. A small group enact a situation while the rest of the class observe. Both actors and observers can stop the action at any time if they feel it could be done better in a different manner, or if matters are not proceeding as best planned. Those observing can step in and substitute those acting.
5. This workshop was developed from an idea of Sue Hubbert's Head of Drama at the Institute of Education, University of London.
6. *Register* relates text to its context. Register often means the speech variety used by a particular group of people usually sharing the same occupation or interest. A particular register often distinguishes itself from other registers, by using words or phrases in a particular way and sometimes by special grammatical constructions. *Tone* refers to the variations in a person's speech or writing. In the drama session, by adopting a particular type of language, the teacher leads the students to unconsciously adopt the same style. By intervening in role or by the introducing written texts as artefacts, the teacher can set an example of the style of language to be used.
7. Revealing publicly the private thoughts/reactions of the students in role at specific moments in the actions. See J. Neelands, *Structuring Drama Work* (Cambridge: Cambridge University Press, 1992), p. 54.
8. A group working as themselves have the opportunity to question a player who remains in character. See J. Neelands, op. cit., p. 28.
9. Analysis of spoken and written language whereby language is seen as larger meaningful units than the sentence, such as paragraphs, texts conversations. Discourse analysis is concerned with the making and remaking of meaning within any spoken or written exchange.
10. G. Kress, *Learning to Write* (London: Routledge & Kegan Paul, 1993), p. 36.
11. A linguistic perspective takes into account the structure, function and meaning systems of the particular or language variety used by the author. A social semiotic perspective is concerned with the relationships between language and social structure. It considers that meaning is related to human experience and is socially constructed.
12. J. Neelands, D. Booth and S. Ziegler, *Writing in Imagined Contexts: Research into Drama-influenced Writing* (Toronto: Toronto Board of Education, 1993) No. 202.
13. A series of events involving different sign systems working individually and simultaneously to produce meaning.
14. Terry Threadgold, in "Performing Genre: Violence, the Making of Protected Subjects, and the Discourses of Critical Literacy and Radical Pedagogy" *Changing English*, Vol. 1., No. 1 (London: Institute of Education, 1992).

15. See M. Bakhtin *Speech Genres and Other Essays* (Austin: Univ. of Texas Press, 1986).
16. The study of the process of production and reproduction of signs and sign systems.
17. See G.R. Kress and R. Hodge, *Social Semiotics* (Cambridge: Polity Press, 1991), p. 182.
18. See E. Aston and S. Savona, *Theatre as Sign-System* (London: Routledge, 1991); K. Elam, *The Semiotics of Theatre and Drama* (London: Routledge, 1991); and M. Esslin, *The Field of Drama* (London: Methuen, 1987).
19. A dual perception of the world. There is one world in which the participants agree to "make believe" and there is the fictious world of the drama.
20. The need for an all-embracing way of linking all the processes at work, a language in which to describe the complex signs and systems at work.
21. G.R. Kress *Linguistic Processes in Socio-cultural Practice* (Geelong: Deakin University Press, 1985), p. 67.
22. Drama texts, both written and spoken, can at any point change or challenge the narrative of what has gone before. Thus, like society itself, it is characterized by conflict as well as harmony.
23. See L. Vygotsky in Cole, M. et al. (eds.), *Mind in Society* (Cambridge, Mass.: MIT Press, 1978); L. Vygotsky, *Thought and Language* (Cambridge, Mass.: MIT Press, 1962).
24. In Vygotsky's terms "the area of ability for which one's previous achievements have prepared one, but which awaits assisted performance for its realization." Thus in his view, the teacher/student or student/peer interaction is necessary for the student to achieve that which he or she is fully capable of.

Acknowledgement

This chapter is dedicated to Ole Larsen, for his inspiration, criticism and unfailing support.

Using Video Cameras in the Classroom

ROB WATLING

*D*uring the Dark Ages in Europe it was only the privileged few who could read and write. Most of them were clerics in the Church and they were consequently part of the most powerful and influential communications network the world had ever seen. The non-literate cultural traditions that had survived for so long were squashed beneath the power of the new ways of recording, processing and transmitting the beliefs, history, knowledge and wisdom of a continent.

The invention of the printing press was supremely important for this communications monopoly, yet it proved to be a two-edged sword. For while its simplicity and availability provided a way of producing vast numbers of bibles, tracts and documents, it also opened up the possibility for the wide-scale distribution of alternative ideas and cultural expression. The struggle for universal literacy in the ensuing centuries has not been easy, and there are many parts of the world where it is only just beginning. Even in the so-called "developed world", there are pockets of illiteracy which are a glaring indictment on the efficacy of our educational system.

Now that the audiovisual media are the most important means of expressing and circulating the ideas and values of our culture, we should be making sure that we teach our children to handle the new languages. If we are to defy the resurgence of the "communications monopoly," our children need to be able to read **and write** the products of the new technologies. The importance of being able to write as well as read these products cannot be overestimated. Can you imagine what an outcry there would be if a literate society such as our own were to deny its children the chance to write in their lessons? "You may read this book, but you may not write one of your own. You may watch me write on the blackboard, but you may not copy it down yourself. The written word is excellent for teaching, but is completely inappropriate for learning. Anyway, it is far too complicated for the young mind to encompass." There would be many angry parents. "But you must teach it! Writing is a vital skill in a literate society," they would shout. "Many parts of our culture are transmitted through the written word. To be able to write is to be able to communicate thought, knowledge and feelings to others in the society." "Don't worry," the teachers would reply, "We are teaching your children to read. That is far more important. They can study the works of great men and women, to entertain themselves and broaden their minds. And if they come up with anything of any real value, there are always professional writers who can put their ideas down on paper for them." The suggestion is risible. And yet that is largely what has happened in the latest stage of the Communications Revolution.

In the average school these days you will find several television sets. Some are used to watch broadcast programmes for schools. Others are connected to video recorders to watch material at more appropriate times. Yet others are connected to computer terminals. But what is going on? If we return to the reading/writing analogy, the children can be said to be reading the texts presented to them by the television. They are faced with a language (albeit an audiovisual one) consisting of signs and codes which have particular meanings. The children's task, in watching the television, is to look and listen to the signs, decipher the codes and make sense of the language using their own knowledge and skills.

This can rightly be called a type of reading and needs to be considered as such if we are to appreciate what is really happening. But this isn't difficult, people might argue. Anyone can watch television. Certainly my two-year-old son can watch television and make a great deal of sense of it in a way that my five-month-old daughter has yet to learn. He can recognize many of the representations he sees on it. ("There's a horse." "That's a car.") and that they differ from each other ("There's another horse." "That car's broken."). He can follow simple stories and make judgements about what he sees ("Man goes in a house." "Go away nasty Woman."). He also knows enough about their construction to say "All gone now" when the credits come up at the end of a programme. And he already knows that Tom should not fight Jerry, but it is alright for Jerry to fight Tom. These skills of reading images and constructing meaning from them are becoming gradually more sophisticated, just as is his ability to read books, though he can not yet recognize individual letters or words on the page. When the time comes, I shall also teach them both to "write" these audiovisual languages by encouraging them to make their own media products. I would love to see them record their own voices on tape, to take photographs with still and moving cameras and to manipulate and play around with the meanings they produce. What does a tape sound like if played back slowly or quickly? Why does that picture look so frightening? Can you make it look a happier picture? How do you know that's the same woman? What can you tell me about the cat on the mat? And just as I want to work in a partnership with their teachers in developing their skills in other areas, I will hope to find schools using audiovisual equipment in a developed and sophisticated way. Not simply as an aid to **teaching**, but as part of **learning**. Not simply to present material to them in a new way, but to let them create their own meanings. Not simply for audiovisual reading, but for audiovisual writing, too. This chapter explores the importance of these new audiovisual skills, looks at their functions within the classroom, their role across the curriculum and presents some practical suggestions for how you might start to do this sort of work in your own school or at home. It can be done. It needs to be done. You can do it.

This chapter describes some pioneering work in this field which was carried out in Wales in 1988–9. It draws on my own, admittedly rough, structure of three uses for video cameras in the classroom and describes in more detail some more-developed classroom practice. It concludes with some thoughts on the wider relevance of this type of work and the major considerations I advocate for people wishing to explore it to its full potential.

Three Functions for Video Cameras in the Classroom

I have used video cameras with children from three years old to mature students in Higher Education, and while the age, aptitude and the application of the group may change, there are only three main ways in which the camera can be used: recording and archiving, observation and assessment, and practical Media Education.[1] I shall be discussing these in turn and, while I shall devote more time to the third option, I do not want to suggest that it is somehow superior. While it is more complicated to operate successfully, and is often more rewarding for the class, it is not necessarily more important for your work. Equally, I do not wish to suggest that these categories are mutually exclusive. A project which sets out to be a record of something within the school may be used later for assessment. Similarly, a piece of creative video making may revolve around an archiving exercise. As in all aspects of education, these techniques are not an end in themselves. They are offered as ways in which you can achieve other curricular goals. In particular, as I shall explain, these techniques are suitable for the development of language, self-expression, confidence, group-work and technological competence. They can also offer a better understanding of subjects from maths to French, physics to art, geography to dance. They are a form of communication, and have a role to play in the transmission of ideas from one person or group to another.

RECORDING AND ARCHIVING

There are any number of occasions within the school year which are worthy of recording and archiving. Some are more obvious than others: the school play, Sports Day, the last day of term, parties, celebrations, special visits by classes to places of interest and so on. There are plenty of other subjects and events also worth recording: the unusual science project, the "mundane" work in the middle of term, the "small" achievements of the special unit, the spontaneous successes of the third-year drama group, the day the rain came down so hard the buses were all late, the one time when Class 4 managed to get down to work at the same time and so on. Let us look more closely at some of these and see how the school would need to be ready to make the recordings.

Special Events ☐ All the major events in a school's history are ripe for simple documentary recording. A single camera and probably an extension microphone will get perfectly adequate results provided you follow a few basic guidelines. Always prepare the documentary as much as you can. Write out a description of the tape (however brief) which will act as the script for the team who will operate the equipment. This may just be a few simple guidelines about the order of things to be recorded, or it may be a full-scale storyboard, looking a bit like a comic strip, with a separate picture and description of each shot. For example:

Shot 1: The class getting onto the bus at school and passing the school gates.

Shot 2: The class singing in the bus on the way to the Farm Museum. Voice-over of teacher explaining where they are going and why.

Shot 3: Children getting off bus and paying at the kiosk.

Shot 4: Children studying map of farm. And so on.

The main advantage of this is that it makes sure that everything gets recorded on the day of the trip. It also encourages the programme makers to think ahead and to decide to include things like interviews with people they meet, shots of the preparations and follow-up work. It also introduces a discipline into the whole programme-making process which makes it more organized and more likely to do the job it is designed for. If possible, send the team on a rehearsal visit. This is much easier if the recording is being made in or near the school, but any camera and sound rehearsal will improve the chances of good recordings. There is less likelihood of turning up with the wrong number of leads, trying to record in impossible conditions or trying to tape an interview in an unsuitable room. It may also be a chance to get some extra material which can be used in editing the finished tape (shots of place names, outside shots before the snow starts, preparations for the visit etc.). Make sure that the recording is an integral part of the event if possible, use children as part or all of the crew. The student can certainly be involved in the editorial process, helping to suggest what should be included, left out or emphasized. Make sure they are aware of what is going on, ask their advice, use their skills. Not only will this give novel suggestions for the recording, it will introduce them to the process of video making, and make them feel they are involved in the programme. They will feel that the programme belongs to them, rather than merely being about them. And I promise that their stake in its success will benefit them and the finished product. Pay as much attention to sound as to picture. This is true for all recordings, of course, but there is a tendency to rely too heavily on the camera's own microphone, which is usually only good enough for general sound recording. An investment in one or two extra microphones and a specific person to operate them will make the world of difference.

Other Recordings ☐ If you are going to use the camera to record more everyday events around the school, the camera will need to be readily accessed and there should be plenty of people available who are capable of operating it. Don't hide the camera in the cupboard; it can't record anything in there. The more the camera is out and about in the school, the more the children will accept its presence, and the more likely it is to be ready when you need it. Train the children to use it; there is actually very little that can be done to modern equipment that will damage it. Don't drop it, force it, point it at bright lights, expose it to extremes of temperature or get it wet. It is very unlikely that children will damage it by pressing the buttons in the wrong order, and they are probably more adept at handling the technology than you are. They can quickly learn the basics of video production, and be ready to pick up the camera at a moment's notice to record their own work, the unexpected event, the funny moment. Finally, there is little point in making these recordings if they are never to be seen. Decide from the start where the tapes will be kept and for how long. Who will know about their existence? Will they be catalogued? Who will be allowed to see them at school or to borrow them for viewing at home? Will you arrange special screenings for children, parents, friends and the authorities? Will people be allowed to make copies for their own use? Are there any ethical questions involved about who should see tapes of children in certain circumstances? If you think through these questions, you will be far more likely to produce tapes which are worth keeping, and to have an active video archive which is properly integrated into the life of the school and its members.

OBSERVATION AND ASSESSMENT

Any record, as I have said, needs to be used if it is to be of any value. One of the most fruitful uses of a video record is as a diagnostic tool. Some simple examples might show you its potential:

The Drama Lesson ☐ The seven-year-olds were acting out a scene from the Greek myths and needed to represent the sea. The teacher asked them to lie on the hall floor in lines and to roll backwards and forwards like waves while Jason's ship passed between them. Several sessions of practice had come and gone, and the children were still moving in all directions, making completely different movements, and managing to upset the Argos, drown Jason and ruin the Golden Fleece. Eventually, the teacher videotaped the entire shambles and used the tape to explain to the children exactly what was needed, and where they were going wrong. At last the idea clicked, and Jason and his Argonauts could reach the safe haven of the school stage.

The Science Experiment ☐ A group of 13-year-olds had been asked to build bridges capable of withstanding certain loads. Using different materials and techniques, they then tested their constructions to breaking point. The experiments were carefully videotaped to make absolutely sure of the weight they could bear and the length of time they could withstand certain pressures. Each bridge was recorded with an introduction and commentary from its designers, who could use the tape to discover the precise strengths and weaknesses of their work. The tape was also available for other classes doing similar projects.

The Social Skills Session ☐ The group of teachers had been given an apparently simple task to complete, but had almost come to blows by the time they had finished. They had become unusually caught up in the intricacies of the puzzle, and one man in particular had clearly been infuriated by the obstinacy of one of his colleagues (who was, in fact, correct in her analysis of the problem). The discussion afterwards centred on their disagreement. "I really resented it when you told me to shut up," she said. "I didn't say that," he objected, but the tape proved him wrong. In fact he learned a lot from the exercise about the way he might react in certain circumstances at school, and the videotape helped him identify some areas of his behaviour he might wish to address. "It's no wonder your Deputy Head ignores you," said one of the participants. "If you treated me like that, I'd ignore you too."

The Art Therapy Workshop ☐ Emma is physically- and mentally-handicapped and has virtually lost the use of her right hand. Elspeth, a potter, had been working at the school for six months as an artist in residence, and had done a lot of work with Emma to try and develop activities which would encourage her to use both hands on the clay. One of the sessions that I happened to be videotaping worked unusually well (perhaps Emma was even showing off to the camera), and towards the end she gradually brought her right hand more and more into use until it was firmly pressing on a large chunk of clay. The tape was available for Emma's teachers, parents and physiotherapist to see her success and to examine how Elspeth had gently encouraged her towards it.

The Child Development Unit ☐ A two-year-old boy had been identified as slow to develop, and in some of the tests, he was reluctant or unable to play creatively despite the encouragement of his mother. However, when he was left in a room with his three-year-old sister, a video camera showed how he was willing and able to build towers, play with the dolls and generally interact quite well. The child psychologist was now able to concentrate on the relationship between the boy and his mother, rather than on the child's development.

The Reception Class ☐ A four-year-old was frequently in tears as his mother left him at school each day, and was sometimes tired and irritable by the end of the day. Only a short video made by the teacher could convince his parents that he was busy, lively and generally very happy in the classroom — when they weren't looking!

Self-assessment ☐ One teacher I knew had serious discipline problems with two eight-year-old boys in her class. When we talked about the use of video cameras within the classroom, she was delighted at the thought of being able to make random recordings to show their parents just how dreadful they were. After some discussion, however, I persuaded her that this was not necessarily the most appropriate use of the camera. If the boys knew what was going on, they might alter their behaviour, either by being "good" when the camera was on, or by acting up for its benefit. If they didn't know about the exercise, it could easily be seen as unethical. Instead, the teacher decided to use the recordings to analyse **her own** actions in the class, and to see if she could discover what role her reactions to the boys may have in determining their misbehaviour.

PRACTICAL MEDIA EDUCATION

As I have already pointed out I believe the full potential of the video camera can only really be achieved when it is in the hands of the children themselves. However, this is only so if they (and the staff) are suitably experienced and supported, and if the proposed use is fully integrated into the curriculum. When I first started this sort of work in a residential special school, the children would constantly ask to mime their favourite pop songs to the camera which I operated. There was some tradition of this within the school and, to be fair, it was quite fun, but there was rarely anything very significant going on, and I felt that an opportunity was being lost. Here were groups of underachieving children showing some rare levels of enthusiasm, a pile of equipment capable of who-knew-what and a member of the staff with time to arrange as I saw fit. I spoke with a member of the care team who had some technical audiovisual expertise, and we started a practical video making course for beginners.

Using the more basic equipment, we taught them the rudiments of electricity, how video cameras work and how to control them. We then went on to the simple ways of making programmes (storyboards, short adverts, simple dramas) and rehearsed some short sequences using a simple vision mixer. Eventually the call came again to do some miming. Fine, we said, but this time the recording had to be properly planned, designed, rehearsed and finished to agreed specifications. This rarely happened, of course, partly because of the children's low levels of patience, and partly because we all got carried away with the fun and excitement of it all. At least the whole exercise was less superficial and the children were developing real skills in media theory and technology, and also in working together as a team. They needed to communicate ideas to each other, consider various possible courses of action and come to collective decisions, use new languages with confidence and try to achieve goals they were setting themselves. When they felt more confident, we went on to other forms of programme, such as interviews with members of the public on subjects ranging from "What does your family do at Christmas?" to "What do you think about drugs among young people?" or recording role reversals between social workers and children. They also produced a public service tape to show the other children the need to learn to swim, and simulated job interviews for school leavers.

Looking back, I think we probably moved too far too fast with these children, and I have discovered since that more can be achieved by making simple tapes well, than by trying complicated forms and getting only half-satisfactory results. For example, I suggest to teachers that are new to the video camera and are trying to integrate it into their classes for the first time, that they should not point the camera at the children for at least half a term. I know this might sound like a contradiction to the sort of practice I have been outlining so far, but I have found it to be a very valuable preparation for more-developed projects. I have been very lucky that I have usually been able to work with small groups of six or less. For the teacher with 30 children, however, there are few more effective ways of introducing complete chaos into the classroom than letting them see themselves misbehave on video. We know from our own experience that if we see something to do with our own lives on the television, the radio or even in a still photograph, we do not look or listen properly. We concentrate instead on the way we look, the things we hate about ourselves, the silly things we didn't mean to say, the funny expression on Aunt Margaret's face or the bit where Uncle Peter bumps his head. The same is true in the classroom, and if you expect a serious response to a tape before you have developed a serious understanding of the medium, you will probably fail.

This is not to say that valuable work cannot be done in the early stages. Far from it. Let us take the simple example of a group of nine- or 10-year-olds exposed to video for the first time within a history lesson. The subject is "The Road to Civil War." The children are going to study the root causes of the conflict, its development and major protagonists, the decisions that were made, the alternatives available and the final outcome of the saga. All the elements of the project are to be illustrated on a giant wall map (the road), and key moments marked by crossroads, turning points, obstacles etc. As the map is completed, the teacher suggests that they make a video of their work. Each time an illustration is ready for the map, it is placed in front of a video camera pointed safely at the wall, ready focused and fastened safely to the tripod. The children adjust the picture and operate the camera for their own work. When the whole map is complete, extra shots of the map are taken — important areas, interesting developments, extra features, material from books and elsewhere — and the whole series is then copied onto another tape in an order which can be decided on by the children. They then write and record a commentary which is easy to do with an extension microphone plugged into the camera or any video recorder. In the process, they will have not only completed an interesting history project, but will have had the chance to appreciate picture selection, sequencing, framing, imaging, representation, scripting and planning, as well as the technical operation of the equipment. They will also have made a thoroughly respectable tape, under carefully controlled conditions, to which everyone in the class has contributed, and of which they can all be proud.

One of the main reasons for the success of projects like these is that they do not stand on their own, but have clear roles within a lesson. In particular, such an exercise can help fix the main points of a project in the children's minds as they organize and construct a clear explanation of their work for the benefit of an audience. It was one of the main aims of "Media Across the Curriculum" to ensure that our practical media work was properly integrated into other areas of the curriculum, and that video recordings were not just made for the sake of it. The final three portraits of projects we supported in Media Across the Curriculum will illustrate how we did this in practice.

Media Across the Curriculum

In 1988 West Glamorgan county council (in Wales) took the unusual step of ensuring all its schools had access to a VHS camcorder. They also put VHS editing suites at three strategic locations around the county to assist with post production. What they failed to do, however, was to allocate sufficient staff to support teachers in the operation and use of the equipment. While they were able to handle introductory training sessions in button pushing, there was no one with any experience of Media Education who could support schools in their work, to help them develop good practice, encourage the use of the equipment in all areas of the curriculum or even act as a sounding board for ideas. At the time I was working for the West Glamorgan Video and Film Workshop, a small group of local people trying to promote the use of film, video, photography and television among all areas of the local community, in both the English and Welsh. We managed to attract support from the county council and the Welsh Arts Council for a one-year pilot project to encourage the development of this equipment's use within schools. A local videotape manufacturer provided us with some free stock. Simultaneously, the Department of Education was finishing its plans for the national curriculum, through which it meant to ensure consistent teaching practice throughout the country and recognized levels of attainment by all children at all stages of their education. Although their plans had immense shortcomings (many of which took time to identify, and are still being tackled through constant reworkings of the national curiculum guidelines), they did, for the first time, recognize a role for Media Education within the curriculum. Our brief was clear: to promote the use of the camcorders in all areas of the curriculum, laying particular emphasis on their potential for the development of skills within the guidelines for English and Welsh. Two of us worked part time on the project and we developed a five-strand operation:

1) A series of in-service training courses for teachers on the practical and theoretical aspects of Media Education.
2) A programme of work in two schools (one English and one Welsh) to develop examples of good practice.
3) The establishment of a resource library containing books, teaching packs, videotapes and a small amount of ancillary equipment for use by schools.
4) Occasional events on special subjects.
5) Links with other centres offering similar services.

Most of our efforts went into the first two of these strands, and after a year, we believed we had made significant contributions to the development of good Media Education practice within the county. While we did find time to work in other areas, video had an understandable emphasis placed upon it by the need to train teachers in the use of the new equipment.

Portrait 1: Oystermouth Primary School,
Mumbles, Swansea ☐ The 10- and 11-year-olds at this small seaside school had been working for a long time on an oral history project with a small community theatre company. They had been conducting interviews with local residents who could remember the Second World War, then doing follow-up work on the themes and ideas back at school. This had involved creative writing, further investigations, collecting artifacts and memorabilia and artwork, and eventually improvising re-enactments of the stories they had been told. These were then performed to audiences of parents, friends and to local residents, including the original interviewees. We were asked to help with the video recording of one of these performances, but decided instead to offer something they could integrate into the rest of the children's work. I took a small group of children, three girls and three boys, and taught them how to use the video camera which was based at the school. They learned the simple principles of its operation (setting up, using the tripod, white balance, zoom, focus, framing the picture, lighting, sound and so on), and then the importance of good preproduction. They chose one of the reconstructions from their repertoire and wrote an outline script for it. It was the story of a local resident, now retired, who remembered being in church on the day that Britain declared war on Germany in 1939. The service had been interrupted by a policeman who gave a message to the vicar about Chamberlain's ultimatum to Hitler. The children decided to record the scene in the actual church and to preface it with an interview with the woman who had told them the story. They also decided to add a "postscript" of an old woman sitting by a radio listening to Chamberlain's historic radio broadcast to the nation. It took about four weeks to prepare and record, and the children edited it themselves over another two weeks. It was well received and even won special comment at a young people's film and video festival. More importantly, it had involved the children in an exercise which had introduced them to the theories and practice of video production, while augmenting the aims of the original project. It was a great deal more valuable to all concerned than a simple recording of one of their performances.

Portrait 2: Ysgol Gymraeg Lonlas ☐ Many requests for help in recording school events provide the project opportunities to do more developed work. One such request came from this Welsh language school, the oldest Welsh school in the county, about to celebrate its 40th anniversary. Again, rather than simply help them with their video recordings of the celebration, we encouraged them to accept a cross-curricular project with one of their classes. Sian, our Welsh language worker, began by getting the children to produce "sun pictures" (negative images of objects created by placing the object on a piece of photographic paper and exposing it to sunlight). Far removed from the video project, it was designed as a first step in helping the children understand that images do not just happen, but are the result of deliberate actions or people with something to say or show. Sian then went on to do some simple exercises with other images (mostly photographs) exploring the ways that we make sense of them, and how our "readings" match up to the original intentions of the person who made the image for us, to look at **how** we can tell that the little girl is sad. How has the photographer made sure that we don't think she is happy?

When the school was opened in 1949, it was not widely supported by the local community. Indeed, the whole issue of Welsh language education was far more controversial then, than it is today, for there is virtually no opposition to a recent proposal for a new Welsh school. Sian explored this with the children by asking how the supposedly-neutral media agencies might have discussed the prospect of their school's opening, and how that might compare with the coverage of contemporary preparations for the new school. She asked, for example, what sorts of pictures might be used, who might be interviewed, what sorts of questions they would be asked, in what language they would be allowed to speak to the community and how their views would be presented to the public. She also did a practical exercise with the video camera to see how they could portray the school in its best and worst lights by selection of images and commentary. By this stage, she was beginning to get the children to understand that the practical and intellectual choices they were about to make in the production of their video would have significant effects on the type of messages it could contain. As they went on to make the recordings and edit them, they were doing so in a far more informed way, getting more out of it than just another tape about another school anniversary.

Portrait 3: Waunceirch Primary School □   Meanwhile I was working for one afternoon a week in a school which, for a change, did not have any major expectations about the kinds of tapes I would make with the students. Rather, I was given a free hand to develop the use of the camera (and other aspects of media education) alongside the teacher's project work on "Breakfast," which was her topic for the term. All her work centred on this theme. Geography was studying where our food comes from and the types of transport used to get it to our homes. History looked at the way this meal has changed over the centuries. Maths looked at the packaging — its weight, volume, shape, size etc. Science looked at vitamins and nutrition. I decided to look at cereal packets with the class, first as media products themselves, then as the subject of detailed attention by advertisers.

We began by looking at the packets and discovering how similar and different they all were in their shape, size, colours, design and so on. In the next session, I wanted them to begin to understand that the appearance of the packets was not accidental, but the result of deliberate choices by the designers — that they were "constructions." Our task was going to be to "deconstruct" the packets and their appearances. I began this by asking them how many pieces of cardboard they would need to make a cereal box. Most thought six pieces were required, based on their knowledge that the packets were cuboid. Others thought eight, because they knew that each end had two flaps you could open. Eventually each group opened out a pack to discover that it was made of one carefully cut piece of cardboard printed on one side only, but with the words and pictures printed at various angles so that they would be the "right way up" when the box was put together. This was quite a surprise for some of them, and I pointed out that if we looked closer at the packet, we could continue to find out more about the way it was "put together." We pasted the opened-out boxes onto card and started to look closely at what was printed on them. The cereal name was obviously there (10 or more times on some packets) along with pictures of the product, always in a bowl with milk and a spoon. There were descriptions of the product — "Crunchy whole wheat flakes," "Tasty golden flakes of corn" — and more prosaic lists of ingredients — "Maize. sugar, salt, malt, vitamins." There were signs to tell us weight, price, nutritional content, manufacturer's address and so on. There were also large areas of the packets devoted to things which had very little to do with the cereal at all. These included free gifts, special offers, ads for other products, graphics, illustrations, markings to help the printing and cutting processes and, in some cases, areas of block colour print.

The next stage was to "deconstruct" a television commercial for a breakfast cereal. I showed each group the same commercial and asked them to describe what they had seen. I then showed it to them again, and again, and again, each time asking them for more detail about the sound and pictures that made up the commercial. I reminded them that the more they had looked at the cereal packets, the more they had noticed, and that the same was proving to be true about the television ads. They discovered, for example, that the commercial was made up of 19 discreet shots in 30 seconds, and that each shot could be studied closely for what it showed the audience about the product, what the accompanying sound track told us and how the ad also gave us certain impressions about the product and what it would be like to eat it. Gradually, they built up a collection of very sophisticated "readings" of the commercial and some fascinating understandings of what the advertisers were trying to persuade us to believe. Later the class teacher helped the children to draw sketches of each of the 19 shots and to write captions for them using the words from the soundtrack. The best of these were then redrawn in colour and pasted onto large cards, thus recreating the original storyboard for the commercial. I explained that the original advertisers would have produced something very similar during the production process. In the next session, the children recorded the pictures onto video using the school's camcorder, and I then copied these onto another tape, synchronizing the pictures with the original soundtrack. (Only a lack of time prevented the children from doing this themselves). The finished tape, along with the drawings and packets, was shown in a school assembly. In the meantime, I had contacted the advertising agency who had designed the campaign, and they sent us a copy of their original rough storyboard. The children were obviously delighted with this and wrote back to the company with a copy of their video.

It was in many ways a simple exercise, but one which was designed to bring some basic elements of Media Education into the classroom. By the end of it, the children had been introduced to the notions that media products are "constructed" — not accidental — that they "speak" to us in certain ways which we can understand and analyse, and that we have an active role to play in producing meanings when we see and hear these products. They also learned some practical media skills through the exercise, and were encouraged to share some of their discoveries with others in the school through their presentation and the possibilities for future work. Since that time, the class teacher has integrated the video camera into more of the children's lessons, and they are currently completing a short documentary about their next project which is all about pigeons. They recorded some of their general work, reproduced science experiments in front of the camera, collected some shots of a pigeon loft and explained what they know about the birds diet, feathers rings and so on. I also ran a training day for the rest of the staff in an effort to encourage them to start using the camcorder.

The principle advice I gave them, as I do anyone coming new to this type of work, is to think small. It is too easy to get over ambitious when the camera comes out of the cupboard, and to try and copy the techniques and values of broadcast television. It is far, far more important to decide what you want the camera to do for you in your lessons and to devise simple ways of achieving those ends satisfactorily.

POSTSCRIPT

Since completing the work in Wales, I have been involved in a number of educational media projects, and am currently conducting research into the future of practical media work in British education. I am now more convinced than ever that good media work (like any creative activity in education, and particularly subjects like drama and art) is never an end in itself. Its strength lies in its ability to offer opportunities for teachers and students to improve their practice, their lives, their culture or the position of people around them. These changes do not have to be extreme. Even the smallest move in the "right" direction needs to be applauded in the times we live, and anything which addresses our humanity is to be welcomed.

In adopting this position, I recognize a debt to radical educators such as Michael Apple, Shirley Grundy and particularly, to Paulo Freire and those who have built on his work in the light of recent developments in social and political theory. Freire believes that to be human is to name the world, and by doing so, to change it, and that our vocation is to do this in the joint causes of love, humanity and liberation. These might sound like lofty ideals for the classroom, but those of us who work in the creative arts must hear an echo of his appeal, paraphrased by Peter McLaren:

> The task of the critical educator is to provide the conditions for individuals to acquire a language that will enable them to reflect upon and shape their own experiences, and in certain instances, transform such experiences in the interest of a larger project of social responsibility (McLaren and Silva, 1993, p. 49).

In order to do this well, I believe we should constantly be attempting to do a number of things in our work. If these sound somehow philosophical or obscure in comparison with the practical activities I have outlined above, I do not apologize, for I think we need to consider the basis of our work quite deeply if we are ever to improve it. I would suggest six closely-linked ambitions:

1) *To explore flexible solutions to specific curricular issues.*
We have seen some of this potential in the work I have outlined above. Media Education in Britain is not always exploited as a cross-curricular activity, since it is still battling to develop its own base within the school. The continuing drive towards a prescriptive curriculum strengthens, rather than undermines, the isolation of specific subject areas. Most good books on media work suggest this, and the important

question is whether it can become cross-curricular without losing sight of my second point.

2) *To encourage critical engagement with media texts.*
The acquisition of media literacy should always include the development of critical autonomy. By this I mean that good teachers will help their students to a considered understanding of the assumptions and issues that lie behind the production, distribution and use of media products. This is a vital skill for people who wish to engage fully in a modern society which constructs so much of its culture through the audio visual media.

3) *To encourage critical engagement with other issues.*
Our students' knowledge and experience are vital components of their education, and so is their ability to reflect upon and challenge that knowledge and experience. We need to encourage them to explore the assumptions behind the beliefs and values they encounter, so that they can begin to construct their own world from a position of strength. In turn they must learn to explore and challenge these new positions, constantly refining and challenging the world and their place in it. Creative work demands this particularly, for if we are to tackle the elements of our lives we see as burdensome, or to celebrate the areas we see as worthy, we need to do so with ever-sharper vision.

4) *To develop group work.*
The most creative media work is never done by an individual. It is conceived, produced or distributed among groups of people who all contribute to its achievement. Groups who work together need to decide on common goals, to plan their activities collaboratively, to have a firm idea of who the material is for, how it will be shown and what difference they want it to make when people have seen it. This usually means that they want their audience to know, feel, think, question or do something that they didn't beforehand. The clearer they are about this at each stage of their work, the more likely they are to succeed. This is as true when they are making a record of their school field trip, as when they are using a camera to explore what it means to be young in today's world.

5) *To contribute to changes in education.*
Implicit in most of what I have written is a criticism of dominant teaching practice. I believe that all teaching, but particularly that in the creative arts, has a responsibility to examine and where necessary, change the conventions of education.

6) *To avoid cultural reproduction and encourage new cultural production which is relevant to the needs and social positions of everyone involved.*
Group and social skills, self-expression, critical reflection and so on are admirable goals, but they should not be seen as valuable in themselves. The faculties we help our students to develop must be of relevance to them within and beyond the classroom. We will not be able to do this unless we encourage them to move away from simply replicating the culture in which they are embedded, and towards the creation of new ways of talking to each other about the things that concern them.

Educators need to reclaim the right to contribute to society on their own terms and the terms of their students, and it is not only in Britain that there are concerted moves to restrict teachers' rights to work in this principled way. It will fall to those of us who work in the creative arts to ensure that we keep making opportunities for the work outlined above and in the other chapters of this book. No one is likely to make those opportunities for us.

Endnote

1. Media Education, the development of children's critical and creative approach to the media, needs to be seen as distinct from Media Studies which in Britain is a separate subject with its own syllabus. The same distinction might be made between the need to develop literacy (in a broad sense) in the teaching of all subjects, while retaining literature as a separate area of study.

*I*nterplay:
Integrating Arts in the Classroom

ALISTAIR MARTIN-SMITH

Preface

In order to frame this chapter for the reader, I wish to identify the context in which our initial explorations in integrating the arts took place. First of all, the drama described in this chapter occurred during the summer of 1987 and represents my first efforts as a drama teacher working with artists to discover whether integrating the arts in a class room setting was an effective way of learning.

From the successes and failures of that first summer, we continued to work together with many of the same children for a second summer. While the focus in the first year was integrating the arts, the native theme was chosen by the children after participating in a drama based on Paul Goble's *The Iron Horse*. We started with the children's own conception of native people — understandably stereotypical at first. By introducing them to other picture books written and illustrated by Paul Goble (*The Gift of the Sacred Dog* and *Buffalo Woman*), we hoped to deepen their understanding of native issues and values. What emerged was that the children began to share some of the native people's concerns: they began to see themselves as guardians of the land, responsible for the well-being of the environment.

During the second year of Interplay, we made an actual journey with the children to Ste-Marie-Among-The-Hurons, where we listened to a native storyteller recount Ojibway legends. Inviting a native Canadian to be our resource person was an important follow up for those children who had been introduced to native values during the first year of Interplay. The native oral tradition of storytelling echoed the children's own concerns about the environment which they voiced during the first summer. As the children transformed their stereotyped ideas through explorations in drama and other artforms, their understanding of native issues deepened.[1]

A Rationale for Integrating the Arts

Richard Courtney states: "To create art is to state one's personal identity..."[2] If a child has a particular image, thought or feeling to express, then he should be able to choose the best form in which to express it. Much as a visual artist can choose to draw, paint or sculpt, the developing child should be able to choose whether to dance, sing or enact.

I believe that the obstacles which prevent adults from discovering a connection among different art forms do not exist in the same sense for children. In developmental drama, the creative imagination can flow freely from one art form to another, given the necessary encouragement and motivation.

Each of the arts has a unique symbol system which the child learns to manipulate as they practise that art.[3] In drama, the teacher can set up a context which concentrates the developmental process of the child. By integrating other expressive arts in this process, the teacher provides more opportunities for symbolic play, which is essential to cognitive, affective, moral and aesthetic development.

This chapter contains a description of Interplay, a pilot arts programme for junior children (Grades 4–6), which examines a technique for integrating the expressive art forms of drama, visual art, dance, music and writing.

Many educators have asked the question, "Why should we integrate the arts?" Perhaps it is more useful to ask why schools have accepted a separation of the arts in the pedagogy of arts education. Elizabeth Kelly offers a plausible explanation of why we may have overlooked this approach in dramatic art:

> Curriculum drama is a continually evolving, unabashedly eclectic method of teaching. The fact that theatre/drama techniques involve many aspects of the other arts works both with and against its full recognition as an art form. Used as a process for learning, it naturally co-ordinates the other arts, but as a result of this complexity, it is frequently shunned as an impure art, and its true potential for learning is left unrecognized.[4]

I believe that the potential drama has for integrating other art forms is also unrecognized. This is due to the difficulty of attempting to unravel the complexity of the dramatic moment, but also because we do not fully understand how drama is able to integrate other art forms. Before describing the research which leads me to favour the practice of integrating the arts, it is useful to examine two historical precedents, Plato and Hesiod.

Plato's attitude to the arts reminds us that experience in the arts lays the foundation for the child's education. In the *Ion* he says:

> ...Shall we begin then with the acknowledgement that education is first given us through Apollo and the Muses [for] he who is well-educated will be able to sing and dance well.[5]

We rarely think of singing and dancing as criteria for being an educated person. Simply because Hesiod wrote that the Muses were the source of divine inspiration, does not mean that we can accept it as fact. Now that education is becoming more responsive to the child's needs, we need to know more about how the Muses were involved in the process of inspiration.

Theogony asserts that knowledge of the universe comes directly from the gods through the medium of the nine daughters of Zeus and Mnemosyne. The Muses are described by Hesiod as descending from Mount Helikon, "their bodies hidden in dense air..." They are invisible; their anthropomorphic bodies veiled in mist, serving only as a visual aid to memory. Similarly, their song is a musical aid to memory: "through the darkness of the night/they pass in lovely song."[6] As Mnemosene's daughters inspired Hesiod's poem, integrating the arts helps to create mnemonic devices in the child's mind to fix oral language so it is available during reflection.

An Holistic Approach to the Development of Literacy

Working to integrate the arts helps to bridge the gap between image and word. It allows the child to choose to express in images thoughts which are too difficult to express in words:

> Moods very often need to be expressed through paint and sound as well as through words and movement. The creative media should be seen as complementary and interdependent, rather than isolated one from the other.[7]

This approach is not new in the world of therapy, where children who have lived through traumatic incidents are encouraged to draw what they are unable to tell. The children draw pictures and then are encouraged to tell stories about their drawings:

> Drawing is an active self-expression. You have the child go over the trauma, moving from actions such as a drawing, to words so that in the retelling the child achieves some emotional distance from the event...[8]

Children must be encouraged to develop and strengthen their images in order to give clarity to their vague thoughts. They can readily express themselves to their peers in drama, where a shared fictional context, tone of voice, facial expression and gesture help them to make meaning. These words and images can be further strengthened through music, poetry or dance. This endows them with rhythm, so they can be fixed in the child's memory.

The way in which drama functions to create meaning can be contrasted with meaning-making in writing. In monologue, the meaning has already been forged by the writer, whereas in dialogue the meaning is not in the words themselves, but belongs to the interaction between the speakers. Bakhtin says that meaning in dialogue is not contained by the spoken words:

> There is no reason for saying that meaning belongs to the word as such. In essence, meaning belongs to a word in its position between speakers...; meaning is realized only in the process of active, responsive understanding...[9]

Dialogue, which is constantly determined by the child's moment to moment interaction with the listener, does not have the permanency of writing. It is, of course, this quality of writing which allows us to have a representation of human thoughts which we can return to and reflect upon.

When the arts work together to create such mnemonic devices, children can engage more easily in writing. Since their words become tied to the rhythms of music or dance, the result is often "an indestructible nugget of language."[10] Brian Way notes this connection between the use of sound in drama and language learning:

> The use of sound is connected not only with movement, not only with the stimulation of ideas for stories and character, not only with mood and atmosphere...it is also concerned with, indeed deeply interwoven with, speech.[11]

When children attempt to engage in an art form, often their imagination does not immediately flow. However, when they engage in a dramatic context, they are stimulated by the layering of sound, visual images and speech. One student wrote in her journal what she planned to do that day in drama:

> I have nothing really in mind, and am just going to see what happens because I have to get started before my imagination knows where it wants to go.

K. is developing an awareness of the liminal phase of mental readiness necessary to engage her own creative process. After the drama, she comments:

> It's amazing the way all these ideas and thoughts come to mind while I'm in the drama.

Like the Muses, the arts should not be separated from one another, but allowed to function as different pathways in a holistic approach to literacy. When the child is allowed to play with images in a fictional context, drama, dance, music, visual art and writing will work together powerfully, fixing those images in the child's mind. As the Muses appeared to Hesiod dancing and singing, the child's images "...are not objects, but are movements or processual rhythms, which **operate as structural dynamics in interplay.**"[12]

This rhythmic interplay of images in the child's mind has implications for the arts curriculum. As Sue Jennings points out:

> It is impossible to separate drama from art and music, even though the tendency of our schools and colleges is to provide training in a specific category.[13]

These ideas concerning the theory behind integrating the arts were not immediately apparent, but were formed only after several summers of working with children.

Planning an Integrated Arts Programme

Our research into the potential for integrating the arts in the classroom was named, appropriately, "Interplay." Our team consisted of myself as drama leader, visual artist Maya Ishiura and writing coach Mimi Mekler.

The research began with a general question: can children discover a way to integrate the arts in a summer arts enrichment programme that encourages them to explore their imagination playfully? Before starting to work with the children, we had no definite idea of what would be of interest to them. At one stage in our planning, we thought that we would stage a medieval fair with jugglers and dancers. But rather than impose a predetermined structure, we decided to design the programme around a theme. As we learned more about the children, they would let us know what was important to them, and the structure of Interplay would emerge.

In July, 1987, we held our first half-day summer school for 42 junior students (Grades 4–6), sponsored by the York Region Board of Education. Our reason for choosing the nine- to 12-year-old group was that they already had experience doing drama in the classroom. They had also, by this time, developed some ability in visual art, music and writing.

The theme of the summer programme was to be the hero journey. We felt that by exploring heroes, we would encourage the children to develop confidence by extending their sense of self. According to Joseph Campbell, the hero journey, whether of Odysseus or of the shaman, involves three phases: 1) separation, 2) initiation, and 3) return.[14] Once we had decided on a theme, our questions became more specific. Could children embark on an imaginary hero journey? If so, could we map their journey through their expression in drama, their drawings and paintings and their written stories?

We originally thought that the children's heroes would be figures prominent in the media with whom they could identify, like Rick Hansen and Terry Fox. We also examined what we considered were significant influences on children's culture, like Barbie and the Rockers, and Transformers. But the children's heroes did not turn out to be characters they admired; their heroes were themselves. They created their hero from a projection of their own inner qualities, rather than from an identification with an exterior figure. During Interplay, the children became engaged in an imaginary inner odyssey toward self-expression, mediated by the arts.

Week I: The Journey Begins

On the first day of Interplay, we focused on getting to know the children by playing name games, discussing the daily schedule and modelling the routines we expected them to follow. We used a circle formation for a daily checkin and checkout so that each child's voice would be heard. These sessions, during which the children were seated on a carpeted floor, lasted about 15 minutes, and gave each child equal opportunity to voice feelings and ideas from the day's events.

An important feature of the child's day was the snack. Each morning after recess, the children ate a snack provided by two of the children. Snack provided an occasion for social talk, and was an important step in the bonding process.

We also made provision for two high-school students who tutored the children, scribing for them in their daily diaries when necessary, and taking a leadership role in the drama. At every opportunity we sought to establish trust between the Interplay leaders and the children. This practice was essential to the success of the programme.

At first we thought that by allowing the children to interact with guest artists in drama, storytelling, dance and music, they would develop a repertoire of skills in the arts. With our theme of the hero journey in mind, we asked storyteller Bob Barton to tell us a journey tale. After the story, we encouraged the children to respond in whichever art form they felt most comfortable. The children's art incorporated our journey theme, but in terms of our planning, we felt lost because no direction had yet emerged.

Some of the students chose to respond to the telling of the folk-tale in visual arts. The children's assumptions about each art form's potential became clear. The story had been about Timba, an African princess who goes on a long journey to remedy the sufferings of her village. The students asked many questions about the appearance of the villainous serpent king, but none of them hesitated to depict Timba as if she were a Princess Diana look-alike. Automatically, they pictured her as having blonde hair with a western-style gown and diamond tiara. Most of the children were unable to integrate the African context of the story into their portraits of Timba. However, some pupils succeeded in incorporating the African context in their depiction of the journey. By imagining the journey as if they were Timba, it was easier for those children to access images from within the African context of the story.

As in their visual art response, the children had definite preconceptions of the purpose of a dramatic response to the Timba story. For example, N. wrote in her daily diary under "What I plan to do":

> I think I'll try drama. I hope we can do some games
> like "Kings court" or "the hula hoop" game, or "mur-
> der wink."

Even by the end of the day she had modified her idea. During checkout she wrote:

> Well I went to drama and I found that the little skits
> were fun and I enjoyed them.

This still seemed to be a long way from the potential David Booth believes drama has for bringing children together:

> Drama allows children as a whole group to sit around
> the tribal fire and conjure up shadows, voices and

events dreamed into reality or long gone. The children are able to weave a collaborative web through shared responses, inventing new metaphors, learning through analogy, reworking past myths into new realities. By "joining in," they are storying with their own voices, experiencing the sounds and joys of language. It is a human process full of talk and life.[15]

During the first week, we realized that we did not understand how to integrate the arts. What we were doing might be called multiple arts. We continued the process of allowing the children to choose in which discipline they would enjoy working, until we realized that their choices were influenced more by peer pressure than by an inner urge to express themselves in a particular art form. We tried regulating their choices with an elaborate system of library cards and pockets, which we called the Choice Board. It was still not what we had hoped for, and yet was probably a necessary stage in our process.

During that week, the children began the "Me Project." We wanted them to share a common vocabulary so they could recognize and share their emerging emotions and intuitions. We did not know what a powerful effect the project would have on the children's process until weeks later when we saw what powerful and original artwork the children produced. Discovering what it meant to express a feeling in visual art, writing and drama helped the children choose which art provided the best form for their feelings.

Beginning with their silhouettes, they painted the "Me Inside," known affectionately as "Guts," within the outline of their bodies (see Figures 1 and 2). Within another silhouette they wrote in their feelings. One child's stomach growled "hungry," another's fist said "angry." During the same week they painted the "Me everybody sees," depicting themselves in their everyday clothes. Finally, in week three, they painted "Identities" or the "Projected Me," as their Indian characters revealing inner qualities discovered in the dramas. The children were working on life-sized silhouettes on brown mural paper, so they were literally standing in front of themselves, working on themselves. Working on that scale demanded a kind of dance which externalized inner qualities — the children imagined themselves in various poses, such as Great Hunter, straining to pull his bow taut; Mountain Lion, with claws extended; or Thunder Wolf, caught in the middle of a leap. As well, there was the dance of the painter — the stretching and bending as the student attempted to paint the figure, along with the sweeping movements of the arm holding the brush, thus linking ideas with a physical commitment to the work.

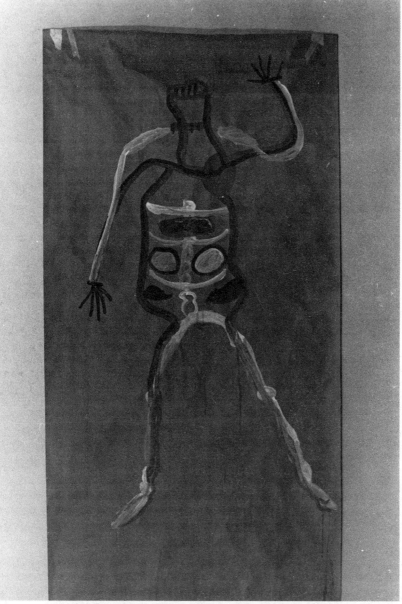

Figure 1:   A child's "Me inside" painting, showing how the inner organs are arranged within the silhouette. Rather than painting her heart, this child created a "special feeling" organ in the centre of her body.

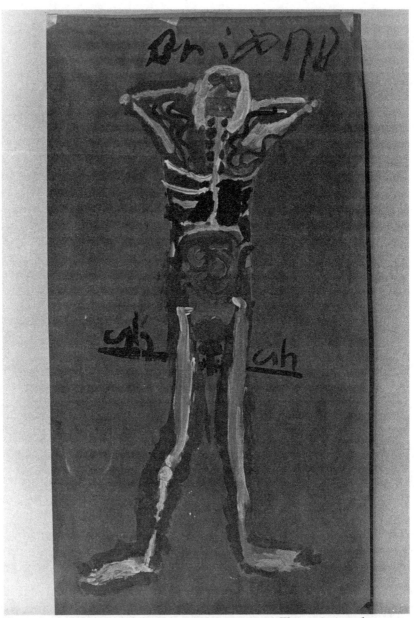

Figure 2: Another child's "Me inside" painting. This painting shows an understanding of the complex layering of systems in the body. The skeleton, the circulatory system and the digestive organs are all carefully painted within the silhouette.

In drama, we worked with the silhouettes from the outside in, reversing the process begun in visual arts. We tried to identify the inner feeling from the external physical position portrayed in the silhouette. As K. describes in her diary, we used the device of the shadow:

> In drama today we broke up into groups of two: one person was the person, the other the shadow. We had to make up a situation where the person was saying something, and the shadow was saying what the person was really thinking inside. I think it was a really good idea.

The physical doubling provided by the shadow may have helped the child later on to be present in the fictional context of the drama and alternately, to be aware of the physical reality of the gymnasium. However, there is another kind of doubling which mirrors this physical doubling. It involves the way the metaphoric intelligence of the brain responds to the fictional context in drama.[16] What Courtney calls "doubling" refers to this inner process:

> Such doubling is...inherent in the way imaginings are created. To think of the "as if" alternately (but seemingly simultaneously) leads us to actual and fictional actions. By comparing the actual and fictional, we reach the truth for us.[17]

David Booth explains how inner "doubling" works to enhance language development:

> Although the child is in a make-believe situation in story and in drama, the real world continues to exist, and the learning that occurs for that child lies in the negotiation of meanings — symbolic and actual — taking place in both modes.[18]

By the end of the first week, we learned that finding the right context was the key to integrating the arts. If we could create a "make-believe situation," doubling would occur, and the child would begin to negotiate meaning through the frame of the drama. It was not until the second week of the programme that we recognized that doubling was actually happening. One student wrote in her journal:

> Today I plan to continue our drama. It has become like a second life to me and each day I come here I live it.

Week II: Finding the Context

The breakthrough came for us in our second week of the programme when we bused the children to the Faculty of Education, University of Toronto to work with David Booth, our guest artist in drama. In that echoing gym, there were as many teachers as there were children, and we all wondered what could be accomplished with so many.

Undaunted, Professor Booth started us on a journey of discovery by sharing with us the story of *The Iron Horse* by Paul Goble. He recounted how the Plains Indians lost entire herds of buffalo to white hunters who were unaware of their vital importance to native people. To them, the shooting of herds of buffalo from the windows of trains was mere sport. Booth modelled the Indians' dilemma for the children in role:

> Nobody knows this but us. Nobody knows who knows but us. And we know where the buffalo are, and we have them hidden. Unfortunately, the hunters want our buffalo. Why would they want our buffalos, that we've got hidden? They might want meat. If they were [white] train hunters it wouldn't be meat, but there might be another tribe that wants meat, and that's exactly who this group of adults is. They're another tribe of Indians on the prairies. Their buffalo have all been killed by the white hunters and they want others to start their stock with, [but] if we give up our hundred, we will not have enough to start our stock of buffalo...[19]

We identified with the buffalo after an initial session of role-play in which the 80 adults and children worked together in role as buffalo. In that sweltering heat, with the drama drowned out from time to time by the sounds of dump trucks from the street construction outside, you really sensed the power drama has to unite. At the first sign of danger, the buffalo stampeded, only to be "killed" by the sound of the rifle, symbolized by Booth rapping percussively on a tambourine and pointing to the victims.

We then divided into two Indian tribes: The tribe who had lost their buffalo (the adults) and the tribe whose buffalo were kept hidden (the children). In the drama, the former had to convince the latter to share their buffalo. However, if the tribe of children agreed to share, their own herd would soon be depleted and all their buffalo lost. In her journal, I. comments on the dilemma:

> I think that we should not trust the other tribe and not help them because when it was the buffalo hunting

season the other tribe did not hunt for food but we did. Now they want us to give them our food. Yet if we have enough food we will help them out. The reason I think we can't help them because we don't have enough buffallo's for both our tribes. If that is the question — which tribe would survive I think it would be the tribe that set out hunting for Buffallo's before winter season. It was also hard to see the other tribe die but if we could help them we would. Although if we hunt other things and join forces we could hunt more and faster.

In spite of the heat, the children concentrated and focused, arguing eloquently for their tribe's needs; but by the end of the drama that day, no solution had been found. We were given the task of resolving the dilemma by the end of the week on our own. Having a time limitation helped us to focus on the problem and not be diverted to other issues, such as punishing the white hunters. We did not foresee that the buffalo drama we did that day would capture the children's imaginations for the rest of the summer. The buffalo drama was never neatly resolved; it became an ongoing negotiation or never-ending story:

It's fun adding ideas, which always come flowing into my imagination when we start the buffalo drama every day. I think the buffalo drama is wonderful, because it's not all set up for you; you have to make up things as you go along.

Likewise, playwright Sam Shepard says his stories are never ending. Once the creative process begins, the next moment evolves from the preceding one. To give the story an "ending" interrupts the flow of the imagination.

There's always something false about an ending to me. There's an obligation involved, and yet at the same time it feels false. It continues — there isn't any ending. "The End." I wonder who came up with "The End."[20]

That day the children made a physical and emotional commitment to the buffalo drama and the hero journey had begun. After two weeks of Interplay, we learned that it was drama which provided a context powerful enough for integrating the arts. Drama became the centre of a circle around which work in all the other art forms found its place. The children sat in a circle in the classroom everyday and also in the drama during the rituals, mirroring the Indian's sacred circle. We rarely think about the effect sitting in desks in rows has on the child's developing mind, but one wonders what effect sitting in a circle had on their ability to work together as a group, discovering the process of integrating the arts.

In the journal writing, we asked the children to reflect on the events which had taken place in the drama, and to imagine future events. In our responses to their writing, we tried to mirror their ideas and their possible consequences. In her diary, N. wrote:

> I feel that our tribe should keep our buffalo because their tribe has horses, corn and other foods. Anyway if we are to give our buffalo away what will we have for next year. We will be the tribe to die. We worked for our buffalo and we need to keep our buffalo for us. I gave some dinner to them for some were sick and dying! But I don't know they might have their own buffalo. I don't know, do you?

In the Comments column, Mimi wrote back:

> Do you think that giving just one meal to the starving is enough? When I give that kind of charity, I sometimes feel guilty that I haven't done more.

Each day the student's journal was divided into three sections, each with a different purpose: the child was asked to record "What I plan to do" and to sum up at the end of the day "What I did." "Ideas in Progress" followed with a blank page for drawing. Each page had a space for comments by instructors, parents or peers. The journal enabled the Interplay instructors to follow the child's attitudes and movement from one art form to another. The child was empowered with the opportunity of choosing their focus for each day, evaluating their personal performance and of commenting on the group work.

We wanted the students to share in the planning of the drama by telling us what they wanted to happen next. We encouraged shared planning by scheduling weekly conferences. The instructors charted the students' written ideas for consideration by the entire group. N. comments on the results of these brainstorming sessions:

> I thought the ideas we wrote down about the journey really got everyone thinking and imagining!

We encouraged the children to find their own way of integrating their written ideas within the drama. Many children found means of incorporating their strong beliefs in ways which were not immediately evident, but which strengthened the belief of the group when shared. For instance, K. wrote frankly in her journal:

> Right now I really think this is a dead-end situation. The best thing I can think of is to wait until more buffalo were born, and we could spare a few, and then trade them for crops... Our tribe had managed somehow to gather 100 buffalo, if they had not, it wasn't our fault. Still, I could not bear to watch them dying. I was one of the women who shared my food...

Every child's opinion was respected, even if it was not shared by the group as a whole. C.'s view was unequivocal: "Let the other tribe die." Another child, reflecting her identification with the situation, responded more sympathetically:

> Sometimes I find it hard to trust the other tribe, but I'm realizing that if there is no trust, than there's no solution.

Listening to the other children's points of view helped the entire group to respond with empathy to the suffering of the other tribe.

Week III: From Bashful Brena to Mystical Crow

By the third week, the tribe was divided into smaller groups, and each of these "families" had its own identity. There were the Women with the Secret of the Buffalo, the only ones who knew where the buffalo were kept; the Mapmakers, who guided the tribe on their journey; the Scouts, always on the lookout for signs of danger; the Wisewomen, guarding the knowledge of the tribe; and the Hunters, providing food and protection.

With the help of Susan Green, guest artist in movement, each family developed its own unique dance. One of the Interplay instructors or tutors joined each of the families to help the group develop its dance. Mimi's group — The Women with the Secret of the Buffalo — benefitted from her experience in theatrical movement. Their dance evolved in the drama into a colourful evocation of their powers — always moving, evasive like their secrets, flinging into the air a multitude of rainbow-coloured scarves. The dance ended with a ritual involving the invocation of the buffalo spirit.

During the negotiation phase of the drama, the children did not always agree with our ideas:

Teacher (in role as leader of the adult tribe): Have you a decision for us?

C. (in role as leader of the children's tribe): But we can't. We cannot lend you any of our buffalo because we don't have enough for ourselves but we are very willing to share with you our knowledge on, um, healing your sick, and our hunters will help yours to find other animals like deer and bear and duck and all kinds of other things, you know, pheasants and...and we're also willing to co-operate with you so both tribes will be happy even if you don't have buffalo.

Teacher (in mock rage): Ungrateful people...

C. (persuasively): How can we take food out of our own children's mouths. I mean, we also are a tribe that needs for our children (chorus of agreement).[21]

After a long period of negotiation, the children's tribal leaders were persuaded to accompany the members of the adult tribe who, though they had no buffalo themselves, knew of a place where the tribe's buffalo might be safely hidden. S. wrote in her journal about that day's drama journey describing her "heroic" struggle against the elements:

> I like to imagine so much that I imagine about the Journey like it's sad. First we were going over a river because there's no bridge so we go over rocks. Then we go through slime although there is insects like the fever bug, the fire bug, and the blood bug. They were all suck[ed] into the slime, but we were not hurt a bit. Then we go over 3 mountains then we go over another river. Then we set our camp there.

The children enjoyed crawling and climbing over the imagined landscape created using a pathway of gym mats, benches laid end to end, crunchy paper, stair units and tunnels. More than enjoyment, however, the journey created opportunities for dramatic play, as K. recorded in her journal:

> I really had lots of fun today during "The Journey." I pretended I had a baby, and everytime I had to go through a tunnel, or over something, or something hard, I would pass my baby to Julie in front of me, and she would give it to me when I got through.

In addition to co-operating with the other children in problem solving during the journey, the drama provided opportunities for each student's struggle for identity. K. could afford to try out different ways of behaving to see what the consequences might be. Working in the arts helped the children to realize that we constantly edit our self-expression, selecting what is most appropriate to be shared.

The pressure of the dramatic context helped the children to focus on the immediate problem to be solved. Occasionally some members of the group lacked focus in the drama, and had difficulty maintaining their belief. When that occurred, those who believed strongly in the dramatic fiction drew the others in by sharing their own belief (see Figure 3). K. wrote about her own frustration with some students and shared it during checkin the next morning:

> I didn't help make the teepee, because my baby was sick. I went to the people who had said earlier that they specialized in medicine but they just goofed off, and didn't seem to care. I wish they would be more involved in the drama.

Due to the children's interest in the ongoing drama, their imagination began to extend beyond the classroom. The children started to bring in cherished possessions that they thought might contribute to our store of knowledge about the Indians — a skin drum, a necklace of bear claws, a pamphlet on the bison. We were excited when two children from the Women with the Secret of the Buffalo family returned from recess carrying branches entwined with wildflowers to help lead the buffalo to the new hiding place. They explained that as they travelled, the smell of the flowers and grass would help "to remind them of the land they leave behind." The other members of that family group soon made their own wands and used them in their rituals. The children's acceptance of their creative act within the context of the drama boosted the girls' self-confidence. Since they possessed a skill which was highly valued by the others, they became more popular among their peers.

Drama encouraged the children to view their peers from new perspectives and to see different aspects of their personalities, giving them new access to one another and altering their social hierarchy.

As we started on our dramatic journey together to find the secret place, several problems were introduced spontaneously by the children. Those carrying babies were exhausted or sick from travelling through difficult terrain. As night fell, the two tribes became lost in the woods trying to find a good spot to set up camp. Later, they realized they were on the right track when some Scouts found several birch-bark scrolls, which had been hidden in the "forest" before the drama journey began. Much discussion ensued as to the authenticity of the scrolls.

Figure 3: The author in role as a Scout, having sighted a wild animal, shares his find with a Hunter. The child is completely focussed on the task at hand. He has been drawn into the drama, and his strong belief will enable others to believe as well.

Some children wondered if it was a trap to make them leave the safety of the woods. As K. wrote in her diary:

> ...the other tribe could have written them, and could be waiting for us on the other side of the forest...for the letter said that they might not return to their country. Perhaps the white men wrote it, but I doubt that they would know of our journey unless they had spies, but that's possible. Or, as someone said, Maya's father could have written them.

With the children's growing commitment to the drama, the urgency to solve the problems which faced the tribe was shared by all. In this charged atmosphere, it seemed as if children had tapped an understanding and knowledge of human suffering which was archetypal.[22] One of the scrolls found was inscribed with these words:

> Everywhere the crying, the death wail. I felt the coming end. All for which we had suffered lost![23]

The suffering which the children (in role as Indians) endured at this point in the drama suggests that they were experiencing Campbell's second phase of the hero journey: "the initiation."

The instructors involved in the drama were able to suggest possible solutions to the dilemma of what to do next. Maya, in role as a member of the adult tribe, claimed that she had journeyed there as a child. She remembered some landmarks she had seen — a river, a dark thick forest, an open plain. When pressed for specific details by the tribe of children, she said her memory was clouded by a fever, but recalled a great waterfall at the end of the journey.

The next day, questioned further by the group of Mapmakers, Maya recalled enough details so that they could paint a large map to guide the tribe on its journey. The map helped to fix their experience in their minds, and provided a common basis for a discussion of the way ahead. The waterfall became a common image: a goal toward which all could journey together. As instructor, Maya was careful not to be too specific, just adding enough detail to hint that there would be further challenges ahead to overcome. As visual artist, she was also able to help them choose the best medium in which to make the colourful map.

Becoming lost in the forest was not the only test of group cohesion which helped unite the tribe during the "initiation" phase of the buffalo drama. When the hardships of sickness and starvation became too great to bear, there was always death. One hunter thoughtlessly killed a sacred crow and angered the ancestors. When a baby died, the Wise

Women attempted to summon the spirits of the ancestors and ask them if the tribe would survive their ordeal or perish.

A ritual dance was created to invoke the spirits of the Eagle and Bear to lead the starving tribe to food, and to take them safely out of the forest. The making of the map cheered them by indicating there was a way out of the forest. The group learned a folk-song to help them feel brave when surrounded by darkness.

To survive the hardships of the journey, the children had to find heroic qualities within to aid the tribe in its survival. After the journey, they were ready to name these qualities. We modelled the process of how Indians received their name, not at birth, but as young children, after they had revealed their true character. In role, the children wrote boastful name stories to explain how they had received their names as a gift from the ancestors. Finally, the children chose an Indian name, according to an inner quality they felt they possessed. They were asked to write their name stories in their diaries to explain the choice they made.

B. incorporated the incident of the death of the crow into her name story. By associating her gift of intuition with the sacred animal, her Indian identity takes on heroic proportion:

> If there were no more buffalos my tribe would die. How could we stop this from happening? As I was thinking a crow suddenly appeared. Right away I could tell that it wasn't just an ordinary crow. Suddenly I heard deep voice say "Don't worry. You won't run out of buffalos. 25 of the buffalos will become pregnant tomorrow." Then before I could say anything the crow flew away. I went to tell the chief but the chief didn't believe me. The next day 25 of the buffalos did become pregnant and our worries were over. From that day on people came to me with their problems so that I could ask the crow for advice. After that all the Indians called me the "mystical messenger." But later I changed my name to Mystical Crow.

A.'s Indian identity also displays heroic characteristics by challenging the authority of the tribal chief to save others from danger:

> Long ago the oldest and wisest Indians would tell stories to his tribe, about different events and adventures in Indian History. Sometimes even about their ancestors from long ago. Now my tribe's oldest man still tell tales and stories to the tribe. Well one night in are

incampment when we were telling stories a strange feeling came of over me. I felt hot. I felt like something was going to happen like a fire. A forest fire. I told the cheif. He denied the fact of the fire. After I herd people screaming Fire! Fire! I was right. I walked near to where the fire began and in a flash the fire disapered. I had found out I had some power from one of my ancestors. And so I was named after him: Flashing Fire.

The next stage in Interplay involved exploring these chosen identities in visual art. First, the children painted their Indian identity within and extending beyond their own action-silhouette as the final step of the "Me Project." This involved a process of extending the child's self-image to include her character, imagining it as an extension of the self.

As their stories enlarged their inner qualities to heroic stature, so their projected identities became larger than life. Huge wings sprouted, capes with strange symbols swirled and flames crackled like auras. One child, who in the early stages of our work had described herself as Bashful Brena, was suddenly transformed into Mystical Crow (see Figures 4 and 5).

These character paintings became the basis for the children's costume design. The basic costume for each child was an over-sized white cotton T-shirt, with the options of a cape or skirt formed from a semi-circular piece of canvas. The children painted on their designs using tempera paint mixed with an acrylic additive to render them colourfast. Accessories were left up to each child to add later. They added elaborate details like fur, feathers and textured applique work, made from crêpe paper, paint and glue. Children also brought materials from home and took their costumes home during the weekend to work on them. During this exercise, the instructors stressed that the effect of the costumes was to help the audience imagine what the children already had.

During the negotiations, while the children were in costume, some began to use a heightened level of language in role, reflecting their growing ability to select and use words to argue convincingly:

How can we take food out of our own children's mouths? I mean, we also are a tribe that needs for our children.

This skill in argument is an example of how the child's Indian identity, projected through the visual art of the costume, contributed to the children's belief in the dramatic moment.

Figure 4:   Mystical Crow's identity painting. She has already begun to project herself into her Indian identity by incorporating her own clothing into the design.

Figure 5: Thunder Wolf's Indian identity projects not only the attitude of fierceness so valued by his family of Hunters, but also his ability, represented by the extended claws.

By the end of the third week, drama, visual art and writing were working together to mirror the imagination of the child in the fictional reality of the buffalo drama.

Week IV: The Buffalo Drama in Performance

As our performance date drew near, new problems arose. Whenever a particular form was imposed on the children, they resisted it. They seemed to know intuitively the difference between an event which moved the drama forward and one which did not. The buffalo dance, for example, did not work because there was no need for it. It had been choreographed with the students as a ritual beginning to the performance. The family group dances, such as the dance of the Women With the Secret of the Buffalo, represented the Indian's mystery and power during the drama, as did the Hunters' dance, which exalted their prowess in stalking and killing animals.

The students did not understand at first what the performance meant. Until that point, they had been improvising the dialogue. Did performance mean that they would have to repeat word for word incidents which had been improvised during the process? One student inquired in her journal:

> Today I thought that the journey was very good. I want to know, are we going to say what we said before or are we going to make it up as we go along?

Even though the instructors stressed that each moment would be different, the children demonstrated a strong desire to recreate what had occurred spontaneously the day before in the classroom. What the children had convincingly mimed during the process, they had difficulty believing when they tried to repeat it for performance, knowing that an audience would be present. N. wrote:

> I loved what we did. It was very real to me and I tried to believe in what I was doing but tomorrow I'm definitely bring[ing] my own baby. (See Figure 6)

Even though N.'s belief in the baby was strong, she was not convinced an audience could share that belief. Many of the girls shared this fear, as Maya observed in her notes:

> Today we had a problem. The girls brought in a multitude of plastic dolls.... I attempted to recreate her success of yesterday — the moving incident when out of the blue, she volunteered that her [baby] sister had

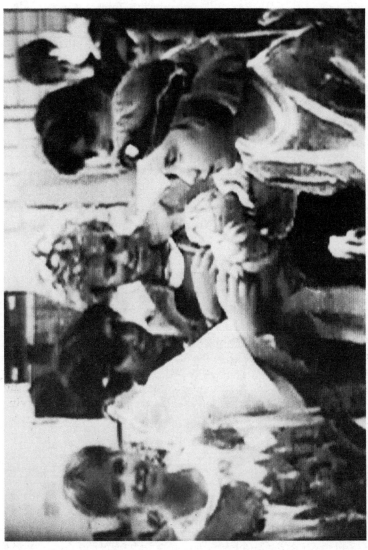

Figure 6: During the journey, three of the participants are distracted by the crying of their doll. In the same moment, another child (right foreground) is focussed on the negotiations between the leaders of the two tribes.

died on the journey... Today, the very real plastic baby in its white bonnet seemed silly... I sat near her and heard her trying to coerce the others to recreate the sick and dying of...yesterday's drama.

In performance, with an audience present, this moving incident dissolved into self-conscious giggles. The children's reaction encouraged us to consider the relationship between process and performance.

As part of the process toward conscious, articulate thought, drama is not intended to be shared with an audience in its unfinished form. Like writing, drama can be subjected to an editing process so that what is enacted is refined to make the meaning clear for a particular audience. Presenting drama to an audience before it has been edited may even have a negative effect on the child's developing self-confidence, since the child may be ridiculed by his peers for presenting something not understood. On the other hand, standing up to ridicule may strengthen a child's self-image.

On the last day of Interplay, I. wrote about the difficulty of communicating what she had experienced during Interplay to her peers:

From the minute I walked into interplay I knew I liked it a lot. I didn't know why, I just did. Well the days passed in interplay and I loved it. But as all good things do, the days passed too too quickly and it was the last weekend of interplay. One of my school friends called and asked if I could play. Another of my school friends was there. I decided to go. It would be nice to see them again. When I got there all they wanted to do was dance and talk about boys. When I told them about interplay they laughed and said it was babyish. It was there that I found out what I loved about camp. You can imagine and no one says it's babyish. And that's what's so special about interplay!

By the morning of the first performance, which we staged for the other students at summer school, the stage was set. We decided to use only one half of the gymnasium, and to play on the gym floor in the round, seating the audience on mats and benches along the walls. We also used the apron of the stage at one end of the gym to provide another level for the children to explore during the journey. Most of these decisions were made so that the children's voices would not be lost in the enormous space. To provide atmosphere, we hung all the children's identity paintings on the walls around the playing and audience areas, which gave the effect of a multitude of animal spirits "watching" the drama unfold.

We had a minimal number of props and set pieces, which were more symbolic than realistic. Each family's teepee was constructed by the children from cardboard refrigerator boxes (donated by an appliance firm), decorated by each group with an identifying banner. The waterfall, through which the tribe disappears at the end of the journey, was represented by clear plastic shower curtains cut into strips and hung on a piece of wooden dowelling between two boxes. We used no special lighting, only the fluorescent fixtures already present in the gym.

For the final presentation of the buffalo drama, we decided to invite the children's parents to participate in the performance, in role as adult buffalo. Most were a little nervous at first, but when one or two parents volunteered, the rest soon followed. When the children entered the space in role as Indians and found their parents already in role as buffalo, they were a bit surprised. They soon joined them, grazing on the prairie grasses, every so often casting wary glances about, looking for the first sign of danger. When the "shooting" started, the adults instinctively formed a protective circle around their "calves," but one by one the buffalo were picked off by rifle fire until none were left. The floor of the gymnasium was strewn with bodies; only the white hunter remained (see Figure 7).

It was a very strong moment. The parents were given an emotional perspective on the children's work which no amount of skillful narrative could have provided. To the drama teacher it was using frame within a frame; to the children it was discovering a way to share the emotional power of the original problem with their parents.

Another strong moment in performance involved one child who was scapegoated by the tribe. In drama, children can project negative feelings onto a character who is protected by the role he plays. B., who had difficulty focusing during the drama, was singled out during the invocation of the ancestors. He was the Hunter who had killed the sacred crow. When the ritual failed to invoke the spirits of the Bear and Eagle, the Wise Women blamed his character, Black Panther, insisting he had not closed his eyes during the ceremony. Black Panther's punishment was mitigated by the fact that he was a member of the valued Hunter family. After he was dragged into the centre of the circle, the Women passed their staffs harmlessly over his head and the ritual began again, this time with his co-operation.

Having passed through the initiations of hunger, sickness and death, the tribe headed off toward the waterfall with a renewed sense of purpose. With a map to guide them, they felt secure they would find a place where the buffalo would be safe. What awaited them beyond the waterfall was unknown; perhaps yet another challenge in their never-ending journey.

Figure 7: The "shooting" of the buffalo by the white hunter. The two who are left standing will soon be "shot" as well, joining the others on the ground.

Summary

In Interplay, the need to move from one art form to another came from within the context of the buffalo drama. Drawing the map became necessary when the children became lost in the woods; the character identity stories arose from the need to identify and record the heroic contributions the children made to the tribe.

By integrating the arts, the child has the opportunity to use words spontaneously to find personal meaning in a specific context. By moving from medium to medium, they have the opportunity to compare and contrast the different symbolic meanings offered by each art form. As Vygotsky has pointed out, meaning is created by moving back and forth between the word (or image) and the child's experience and feeling.[24] Comparing the symbolic meanings offered by different art forms gave the children access to a network of interconnected meaning.[25]

In Interplay, the children became conscious of the interconnectedness between events in the drama and their thoughts and feelings. By developing and sharing the child's personal meaning in action and in writing, Interplay provided an articulate bridge from the child's predominantly oral culture to their literate expression.

The story of the buffalo and the theme of the hero journey provided a rich fictional context which was explored through the media of drama, visual art, dance and writing. In Interplay, we demonstrated that the arts were stronger together than any one of them would have been on its own. Drama provided a contextual centre for the children around which all the other art forms found their place. It is the essential ingredient which makes an holistic approach to language development work. As Courtney says:

> Drama is the kernel of all of the arts...[since] the primal act is the generic origin of all artistic media.[26]

Integrating the arts provides a context for many different kinds of learning, and allows children to perceive their artistic product as one stage in an evolving process, rather than as the final goal. One child's final journal entry uses poetic language to sum up her experience in Interplay that summer:

> There once existed two tribes in saddened times,
> Of when the white men committed demeaningful crimes.
> Although the buffalo were treasured by some,
> Others cried out in hunger while left with none.
> There was this time when both tribes met,
> They decided to join in brotherhood but they still held

the buffalo's secret.
They soon departed on a journey,
On one woman's trusted story,
The journey lasted days and nights as the bright moon
shone it's sparkling lights.
The journey was never-ending, as we are now still look-
ing for it's ending.[27]

Endnotes

1. As we were so close to the process ourselves, we sought an outside opinion
from Cedric Isaac, a native artist from Walpole Island, Ontario:

     The Interplay programme is good because non-native children's
     eyes are opened to native spirituality. They realize that what they
     see on T.V. is not always the truth. It's important because our
     next world starts with the children. Doing plays like this provides
     glimpses into the truth about native people. The arts dig down
     deep into people's spiritual values which are hidden in the soul
     where we can't always reach. That's why I say that art is medicine
     for the soul.

     If you wish to plan your own drama based on native issues, resource
     people can be contacted and curriculum materials obtained through the
     Canadian Alliance in Solidarity with Native Peoples (CASNP, PO Box 574,
     Stn. P, Toronto, Ontario, M5S 2T1). Several teachers have shared their
     experiences planning for native studies units in the April 1991 issue of
     OPSTF News (Ontario Public School Teachers' Federation News, 1260 Bay St.,
     Toronto, Ontario, M5R 2B7).
2. Richard Courtney, Re-Play: Studies of Human Drama in Education (Toronto:
O.I.S.E. Press, 1982), p. 157.
3. Howard Gardner, "Shifting the special from the shared," in S. Madeja
(ed.) Arts and aesthetics: An agenda for the future (St. Louis, MI: CEMREL
Inc., 1977), pp. 272–273. Gardner believes that future arts education research should focus on the child's use of symbols: "Our wager is that
the crucial character of artistic knowledge and education will most clearly
emerge if the arts are seen as a symbol-using endeavour, calling for certain
kinds of cognitive skills."
4. Elizabeth Flory Kelly, "Curriculum drama," in Nellie McCaslin (ed.), Children and drama (New York: Longman Inc., 1981), p. 92.
5. Plato, "Laws," in A.D. Lindsay (trans.) Dialogues (London: Dent, 1935).
6. C.J. Rowe, in Essential Hesiod, (C.J. Rowe, trans.) (Bristol: Bristol Classical
Press, 1978), p. 41.
7. Sue Jennings, Remedial Drama (London: Adam & Charles Black, 1978), p. 9.
8. Dr. Spencer Eth, in an interview with Daniel Goleman, "Treating Trauma,"
in New York Times Education Life, Jan. 7, 1990, p. 40.
9. M.M. Bakhtin, Speech Genres and Other Late Essays, V.W. McGee (trans.)
(Austin: University of Texas Press, 1986), p. 232.
10. Ivan Illich and Barry Sanders, A.B.C.: The Alphabetization of the Popular Mind
(New York: Vintage Books, 1989), pp. 5–6.
11. Brian Way, Development Through Drama (London: Longman Group, Ltd.
1967), p. 88.

12. Richard Courtney, *Play, drama and thought* (4th edition, revised) (Toronto: Simon and Pierre, 1989), p. 177.
13. Sue Jennings, op. cit., p. 9.
14. Joseph Campbell, *Myths to live by* (New York: Bantam Books, 1972), p. 209.
15. David Booth, *Drama Words* (Toronto: Toronto Board of Education, 1987), p. 96.
16. Howard Gardner, *Frames of mind* (New York: Basic Books), 1984, p. 292. According to Gardner, when the child becomes a symbol user, he finds it easy "to note similarities among different forms within or across sensory modalities and to capture these in words (or other symbols); to make unusual combinations of words, or colours, or dance movements, and to gain pleasure in doing so."
17. Richard Courtney, op. cit., 1989, p. 176.
18. David Booth, op. cit., p. 57.
19. David Booth, quoted in the video *Interplay*, (38 min.) (Toronto: Interplay Arts Associates and John Baumann Film and Video, 1988).
20. Sam Shepard, interviewed by Ross Wetzsteon, "Unknown territory," *Village Voice*, Dec. 10, 1985, pp. 55–56.
21. Quoted from the video *Interplay*.
22. As our drama unfolded, it seemed to parallel the tragic retreat of Chief Joseph, who in 1877 led the Nez Perce tribe on a heroic journey to escape persecution from the U.S. Army.
23. Chief Joseph, in William Allard, "Chief Joseph," in *National Geographic*, 151, 3, March, 1977, p. 428.
24. L.S. Vygotsky, *Thought and language* (New York: Wiley, 1962), p. 152.
25. Howard Gardner, op. cit., 1983, pp. 309–11. Gardner calls this network of symbolic meaning "channels of symbolization — means of codifying information that have evolved within a given culture and are now furnished directly to the younger learner." While Gardner notes the appearance of a "literal-minded" phase when children are inducted into the symbolic systems of our society, I interpret this to be a result of a literal-minded educational system. In Interplay, children displayed a remarkable ability to explore and play with the "channel of symbolization" offered by the Indian culture of our drama. Drama appears to be effective in co-ordinating individual intelligences.
26. Richard Courtney, op. cit., 1982, p. 67.
27. In the buffalo drama, the children were preoccupied with solving the problem of finding a safe place to hide the buffalo from the white men. The issue of when and how they would return was put out of mind so they could commit their energies to the journey itself. The final phase of the hero journey, "the return," could be explored as a sequel to the buffalo drama. Like Chief Joseph, "we intended to go peaceably to the buffalo country, and leave the question of returning to our country to be settled afterward." *National Geographic*, v. 151, n. 3, p. 423.

Acknowledgements

The programme upon which this chapter is based was funded jointly by the Ontario Ministry of Education, under its grants to Summer Enrichment Programmes, and the York Region Board of Education. I am grateful to York Region's Language Arts and drama consultant, Susanne Barclay and area superintendent Jerry Diakiw for their support; to guest artists Bob Barton, David Booth and Susan Green for their inspiration; to Maya Ishiura and Mimi Mekler, both members of the Interplay team; and to Richard Courtney for the quest.

Photographic credits: Tory James (photography), John Baumann (video) and Wayne Tousignant (video frame grab).

The Emotion in a Motion: Using Basic Aspects of Laban's Movement Theory to Explore and Develop Characterizations with Senior High-School Drama Students

SANDRA KATZ & TERRENCE SLATER

"An actor can represent character and circumstance if he knows enough about their inherent effort characteristics."

— *Rudolf Laban*

"It teaches me not to be afraid to look silly."
— *a drama student after completing the Laban work*

Students come to a drama program for a variety of reasons, but mostly for a different kind of educational experience. Initially, what they want and what we, as educators, want them to learn, don't always merge. We repeatedly hear them ask, "When are we going to do plays?" In response we attempt to explain that the delay is based on our belief that they need to develop their basic skills both physically and vocally before endeavouring the complexities of script work...or (in their own words) real acting!

What we know about our students' work is based on our combined years of observation in the classroom, and we have drawn these significant conclusions:

a) students confuse stage acting with acting for television and film.

b) students develop characters which are imitations of media stereotypes; a wealth of characters from life and literature remain
   unexplored.
c) students become paralysed by text; they find it difficult to grasp
   the dynamics of language (i.e., the movement or flow in dialogue).
d) students have difficulty stretching themselves beyond their own
   personal centres — both emotionally and physically.

It would be inappropriate and even dangerous for us to accuse
any one particular, current television situation comedy or drama of
destroying the imaginative development of drama students. In fact,
there may be certain aspects of contemporary television acting which
could be (for drama teaching purposes) considered quite beneficial.

Our goal for this chapter is to provide a new structure and a useful
language for the drama teacher and student. What we hope to provide
is a simpler, more efficient and quicker method for developing characters
and exploring ways of expressing characters from text/dramatic literature.

The following series of exercises and explorations using Laban theory and his eight working actions was attempted with a semestered
class of 19 Grade 11 drama students in the fall of 1993. Portions of
these exercises were also used in previous semesters in other senior
drama classes, as well as in two professional development workshops
for Ontario drama teachers.

In the pilot Grade 11 class, all but one student had a minimum of
one previous drama credit. As with most high-school drama classes, levels
of ability, maturity, commitment and willingness to explore new methods
and techniques varied from total enthusiasm to active scepticism to virtual
indifference to what was going on. In order to maximize learning opportunities, two other units (on trust building and group dynamics) were
covered before embarking on the Laban work.

As any high-school drama teacher will attest, teenagers tend to
be extremely self-conscious of their image and are most reluctant to
risk looking "silly." Some members of this particular group of students
had shown a remarkable willingness to share quite intimate details
of their lives with each other in earlier work; this indicated that they
were potentially very open and ripe to overcome the kind of embarrassment and loss of face involved in extreme physicalization and
movement away from one's own physical centre.

The sequence of the exercises which we describe below was carefully
considered in the development of the Laban unit. Each lesson was executed
as a mini-unit in a class period of 75 minutes, or over a few days. The
duration depended on how readily students responded to the experimentation with Laban's work; any teacher could modify the sequence to fit
her particular school time frames and student response. There should be

176

a strong level of openness, trust and concentration established in the class-room before the exercises are undertaken.

Our initial objective was to establish clearly the relationship between movement and emotion; that is, any movement is capable of stimulating and creating an emotional response consciously or unconsciously in the performer of the movement. The preliminary work focused on simulating the movement of robots.[1] This was designed to get students involved in their bodies and by way of contrast, to introduce in the next class the theme of how movement can express emotion and how, in turn, movement can create emotion. When this series of very basic robotic and mechanistic movements was completed, their feedback revealed feelings of loneliness, fear and alienation, even though they were together in their familiar surroundings of the drama room. They had not been allowed to smile and were in effect, devoid of emotion or expressing emotion. Their feelings of alienation were a natural response to the very unnatural way in which they were moving and relating to each other.

After reviewing the implications of the previous activity by listing the emotions aroused by the mechanistic movements, we emphasized the real relationship between movement and emotion. Students understood and accepted this idea based on their involvement. We then sought to explore the ability of bodily expression to convey emotion.

We played a "guessing game" which we have subsequently dubbed, *Guess the Emotion*. We compiled a list of emotions which we printed on slips of paper. A student was asked to leave the room. The rest of the group selected a slip and were asked to move about the room physicalizing that emotion, i.e., rage, joy, fear, disappointment and shock. The student returned to the room and was given three chances to guess the emotion being expressed by the group.

This game was successful and students became very involved. After we had done approximately 10 different emotions, we asked the students to respond to the following questions: Which emotions were easiest to express? To decipher? Which were the most difficult? Was there a particular aspect in the body movement of an emotion which revealed the emotion or was it the complete attitude of the body?

At first glance, this game might seem very elementary, especially for senior drama students who have already explored bodily expression in creating tableaux or dance/movement pieces. As well, we found in this game that students often used stereotypical gestures to express a particular emotion. However, the game's usefulness was apparent by the fact that students were challenged in attempting to identify the emotion: a surprising number took all three guesses or couldn't identify the emotion. This led us to realize that we were assisting students in isolating and reconnecting body movement and emotion.

Introducing Laban's Eight Working Actions Through Simulated Physicalizations

Having established in the students' minds the very clear relationship between movement and the expression of emotions, we were ready to proceed into the core of Laban's work. To begin, we asked students to move around the room at their own pace and to consider how the tempo of their particular movement could be described: i.e., was it slow or fast? Were they moving in a straight line or in no particular direction varying it randomly? How were they feeling as they moved?

We then asked the students to create each of the following eight movements using the scenarios described below:

Laban Action	Scenario
Slashing	You are lost in a lush rain-forest jungle with much undergrowth; you are attempting to hack your way out of it with a machete or knife.
Punching	You are terribly thirsty and have only one coin; the machine eats your money and fails to deliver your can of pop: you want your money back. What do you do to the machine to try to recover it?
Pressing	You are moving into a new home or apartment and are attempting to push a huge, heavy box of books into a corner.
Wringing	You have an important job interview tomorrow and have finished washing out your only decent shirt or blouse; you are trying to have it dry by tomorrow morning.
Dabbing	You are a painter who is preparing a painting for a major exhibition; you are putting finishing touches on your most important painting.
Flicking	You are on a picnic; two or three very annoying and very persistent mosquitoes are continuing to buzz close to your face; how do you get rid of them without actually killing them (you are a pacifist)?
Floating	You are in love and have just asked your beloved an important question, to which she has responded with the answer you wanted. You are walking towards her to express your joy with a kiss; you are not in a hurry.
Gliding	You are a skater and are completing a solo finale as a member of a national skating team or the Ice Capades.

Having completed each action once, we repeated them randomly, attempting whenever possible to juxtapose extreme opposite actions. i.e., "flicking" (light, quick, flexible) with "pressing" (strong, sustained, direct) in order to highlight the extremes of the characteristics of movement according to Laban.

We asked students to describe each action in terms of weight, space, and time: i.e., did the action feel "strong" or "light"? "quick" or "sustained" (one initially could describe it as "slow" for the sake of clarity)?

Introducing Laban's Theory of Movement

THE MOTION FACTORS OF WEIGHT, SPACE, TIME, AND FLOW

The motion factors of weight, space, time and flow were introduced to the students with the following objectives in mind:

- to acquaint students with the language of Laban and introduce the basic elements of his movement theory.
- to get students to understand the concept that all movement can be broken down into the four motion factors of weight, space, time and flow.
- to teach students the specific vocabulary of Laban's eight working actions: i.e., "wringing, slashing, pressing, punching, floating, gliding, dabbing, flicking" so that these actions could be recalled and performed on demand as actions in themselves, and later so that these actions could be directly and specifically applied to text.
- to explain that that these eight actions are the result of the maximum variety of combinations; that these combinations are based on the dual nature of each of the four motion factors: i.e., weight is either "light" or "strong" (see Chart 1 on the next page) and can be combined with either a "flexible" or "direct" and "sustained" or "quick" factor. Likewise, a "strong" action can be combined with any of the same factors. This in turn leads students to understand the theory of opposites which underpins Laban's work.

We had followed the creation of the eight working actions using movement scenarios with Laban's theory in order to cement a connection between the practical and the theoretical. Students, at this point, seemed unclear about the purpose of this work. We emphasized to them that we were using Laban's theory of movement as a practical tool to explore text and character development through movement, and that its application for acting was the goal for drama students.

The motion factors of weight, space, time and flow are the four specific categories through which every movement can be analysed and, in turn, described. At this very basic level, it was helpful to view them as aspects of "energy production" of a specific movement. Each motion factor is subdivided into two opposite elements which describe the movement further.

The following definitions of the motion factors were given to the students:

ACTION: A bodily movement expressed through the motion factors of weight, space, time and flow performed for a functional purpose with a measure of conscious volition.

WEIGHT: The dynamic factor; the impact of receiving or transmitting sensory stimuli (subdivided into the elements of LIGHT and STRONG).

SPACE: The kinetic factor; the reflection of thoughtful movements in one or more planes of space (subdivided into the elements of FLEXIBLE and DIRECT).

TIME: The rhythmic factor; the intuitive perception of the relation between the past and the future (subdivided into the elements of SUSTAINED and QUICK).

FLOW: The cyclic factor; the feeling of the viscosity of movement (subdivided into the elements of FREE and BOUND).[2]

This simple chart is the key to understanding the structure of Laban's theory and his descriptive terminology.

CHART 1

Motion Factor	Elements	
WEIGHT	Light	Strong
SPACE	Flexible	Direct
TIME	Sustained	Quick
FLOW	Free	Bound

After introducing this chart, we again asked students to recall the eight scenarios. We asked them to perform those actions again. We then questioned them about each of the actions using Laban's terminology:

1. *Weight*: When you perform the action, are you using a lot of energy (strong) or very little (light)? Does the action "feel" strong or light?
2. *Space*: When you create this movement, are you or is your arm moving in space in a circular motion (flexible) or in a straight line (direct)?

3. *Time*: As you perform this movement, are you moving slowly (sustained) or quickly (quick)?

The answers to these questions, of course, are obvious and should produce a unanimous response.

Note: Although "Flow" is one of the four motion factors, it does not directly relate to the purely-physical production of the movement; instead, it may more properly be viewed as the attitude in or with which the action is performed: i.e., an action performed with "free" flow would be any action that is performed in an open, giving or extroverted way or, quite simply, "happily"; an action that is performed with "bound" flow would be any action that is performed in a closed, withdrawing or introverted way or, quite simply, "angrily." At more intricate or sophisticated levels of Laban's work, analysis and application of the "flow" factor is important. At this basic level, however, it need only be referred to as an aspect of the theory that can be overlooked at this time in order to maintain simplicity and clarity for both students and teacher.

THE EIGHT WORKING ACTIONS

We then introduced the specific Laban terminology for each of the eight actions as outlined in the following chart:

CHART 2

Action	Weight	Space	Time
PUNCHING	strong	direct	quick
PRESSING	strong	direct	sustained
SLASHING	strong	flexible	quick
WRINGING	strong	flexible	sustained
DABBING	light	direct	quick
GLIDING	light	direct	sustained
FLICKING	light	flexible	quick
FLOATING	light	flexible	sustained

As we progressed through the chart, we asked students to relate each of the eight actions to each of the movement scenarios.

After we had worked through each of the eight actions, we reviewed the entire chart to begin to see the pattern behind the structure of the eight actions. We looked at all the "strong" actions first, then moved into the "light" actions; likewise, we examined the actions in terms of the space factor and then in terms of the time factor (see below). This review also reinforced knowledge of the descriptions of each of the eight actions and enhanced students' ability to recreate the actions on demand.

CHART 3

Light Actions	Strong Actions
FLOATING (Flexible, Sustained)	WRINGING (Flexible, Sustained)
FLICKING (Flexible, Quick)	SLASHING (Flexible, Quick)
GLIDING (Direct, Sustained)	PRESSING (Direct, Sustained)
DABBING (Direct, Quick)	PUNCHING (Direct, Quick)

Sustained Actions	Quick Actions
PRESSING (Strong, Direct)	PUNCHING (Strong, Direct)
WRINGING (Strong, Flexible)	SLASHING (Strong, Flexible)
GLIDING (Light, Direct)	DABBING (Light, Direct)
FLOATING (Light, Flexible)	FLICKING (Light, Flexible)

Flexible Actions	Direct Actions
SLASHING (Strong, Quick)	PUNCHING (Strong, Quick)
WRINGING (Strong, Sustained)	PRESSING (Strong, Sustained)
FLICKING (Light, Quick)	DABBING (Light, Quick)
FLOATING (Light, Sustained)	GLIDING (Light, Sustained)

After completing the review of each of the eight actions in terms of specific motion factors, students were asked to recreate the actions repeatedly and randomly. In order to reinforce the learning and to recreate the action fully, students performed an individual action a minimum of three times rather than simply once.

Then students performed an action such as a punching (strong, direct, quick) and followed this immediately with its exact opposite: a floating action (light, flexible, sustained). Since "weight" and "time" are the two motion factors which we seem to most readily sense and, therefore, recall on demand, we first asked students to create opposite "pairings": using "strong" vs. "light" and/or "quick" vs. "sustained" actions fixed these actions firmly for students. We provided side coaching for the students encouraging them to perform each action with full energy and commitment; the full benefits of this work can only be realized by performing each with clarity and precision.

Satisfied that the students had acquired a working knowledge of all eight actions, we asked them to add an unrecognizable sound to each action. They repeated these actions in a random order as above, and then focused on pairing opposite actions with both the action and an appropriate accompanying sound.

We allowed students to stop at any point and rest. We asked them for feedback, e.g., which actions were more difficult to perform? Which were easier? Did they sense the clear difference between the actions, i.e., between a "punching" and a "floating?"

At this point we moved to "text." We gave students a simple word or phrase such as "hello" or "good morning" and asked them to deliver this using each of the eight actions. Simple words and short phrases like these can be easily performed using each of the actions. As students recreated "hello" with the various actions, we asked them to be aware of how they were "feeling" as they recreated the action. Then, we asked them to address the "hello" to an imaginary friend or acquaintance. By this point we had moved beyond the mechanistic recreation of actions for their own sake into "interpretation" of text and character exploration.

Each one of us has our own emotional and physical centres from which our personality emanates. While we express ourselves physically in a variety of ways depending on the context of any particular situation (setting, relationship, obstacle or problem at hand etc.), each of us has a usual or regular tempo of movement through and by which we express ourselves. For the actor, Laban's eight actions provide the basis for characterization and for transformation through the physicalization of energy tempi that are vastly different from our usual tempo.

We asked students to consider which of the eight actions most precisely described her movement or tempo most of the time. Students were asked to state what each believed was his usual tempo. Likewise they supplied feedback on each student's personal self-analysis. The success of this would be dependent on the openness and trust level within a given class.

In the work ahead, each student would be encouraged to explore and create characters different from the ones they normally create, and which were quite different from themselves as individuals: in short, to explore working actions or tempi that would be very different from their own usual tempo. This would involve taking some bigger risks, but the rewards to be gained from this work would also be greater.

Character Exploration Based on Working Actions

Following the outline of basic Laban theory, we then moved into a series of intentionally-fun exercises to encourage involvement and active use of the working actions for character exploration. The majority of the exercises involved whole or large-group improvisation; this provided students with a sense of safety and security as they each began to use a specific working action to create a character.

As an energizing warm-up, we allowed students to dance free-form, which was useful after the fairly rigid structure and seriousness of the previous lesson.

Then we reviewed the eight working actions by giving students their three descriptive adjectives and asking them to select the appropriate action. We asked students to recreate each of the eight actions physically. Instead of simply creating the action with the hand and/or arm, they were asked to incorporate the movement into the entire body. They then moved around the room as they created these actions. This was easier when they did the "sustained" actions, but it was important for students to also attempt this with the "quick" actions.

Sounds were added to the actions, and then these were followed by a new word or phrase. The emphasis here was on whole-body production of the action. We were ready to begin specific character exploration. We began by selecting any public setting or situation such as a shopping mall, dance club or workplace with which all students were familiar. Students were asked to list the variety of roles that exist within each setting: i.e., dance club — d.j., bouncer, bartenders, musicians, waiters, club patrons etc. Each of these roles was discussed in terms of the eight working actions, and then students had to consider the "stereotypical" perception of the role (i.e., a bouncer would most likely be seen stereotypically as a "punching" or "wringing"). Although students did not agree on every choice, we used these differing viewpoints to begin to expand the repertoire of interpretations of each of the various roles in terms of its likely stereotype.

Students selected a role within the chosen setting, and each had to explore a specific working action for that particular role. They created a "set" using tables, chairs etc. and avoided use of props. They were instructed to mime any objects required such as glasses, trays, microphones etc. Students moved into the situation as they wished and began to explore using the selected role and working action. The teachers participated "in role" with the students, and also observed students' levels of participation, commitment to a particular action and willingness to "look silly." Laban's work at this point is particularly useful if students can be encouraged to go to the extremes of energy production in creating a working action. Since this can create considerable self-consciousness for some students, we encouraged them to continue trying. We stressed that at this point everyone was exploring new and unfamiliar physical movements.

During a feedback session, students' perceptions of the exercise varied. Some students found the exercise useful in terms of physicalizing a role and using a specific working action to explain how and why it was useful for them.

We asked students to consider the following questions: How was this energy production or "tempo" different from the student's own usual "tempo?" Was it difficult to sustain this action over an extended period of time? For students who felt uncomfortable, we suggested that they try another action which might be easier to sustain.

After feedback, we created a new situation. Initially, we had created a dance club with some success, particularly for those who had chosen job-related roles. After discussion, we changed the setting to a modern-day passenger jet aircraft enroute to Australia. We clarified the variety of roles within that particular situation. The role of pilot was stereotypically viewed as a "gliding" or "pressing"; however, the student who selected this role made a conscious choice to portray the role as a "floating." Immediately this inspired others to play against conventional type, such that the cabin crew became a very unhospitable group of "wringing," "punching" and "slashing" flight attendants. The results proved hilarious and relaxed the class immensely. Student passengers chose a variety of different actions; being "strapped" into a seat clearly limited their ability to physicalize the working action using their whole body and reduced the pressure on them to perform a working action continually. The value of creating a truly "fun" exercise, however, cannot be underestimated. Indeed, the subsequent feedback led to a valuable discussion about "convention," playing against type and the ingredients of comedy.

Up until this point, students had chosen the working action that they had wanted to explore for a role that they had also chosen. In the following improvisational exercise which we dubbed, *stuck stereotypes*, we now focused more precisely on character within a specific context. Within this structure, the teacher could immediately, or would eventually, provide each student with a specific working action to perform; this would be dependent on the teacher's on-the-spot assessment of how students are responding to the work.

In groups of four, students were given the setting of either a jail or a stalled elevator from which easy exit is difficult or impossible. They had to assume the role of a stereotypical character and justify why the character would be in that particular setting. First we tried this as a regular improvisation without using any Laban actions; then using a Laban action of each student's own choosing; and finally, providing each student with a specific action chosen by the teacher.

Trying the improvisation using each of the three stages proved very useful in allowing students the opportunity to see clearly the changes that could occur in characterization and dramatic potential, once Laban's work is introduced. When we had reached the third phase and were selecting actions, we deliberately gave working actions that are "opposite" in nature — i.e., "wringing" (strong, flexible, sustained) and "dabbing" (light, direct, quick). This enhanced the level of conflict between the

185

characters considerably (see Chart 3). For example, when focusing on the weight factor, we listed all four "strong" actions and all four "light" actions on separate slips of paper and made two distinct piles; one person from each group randomly selected a working action from one pile; the other person chose one from the other pile. This provided a valuable element of random chance to the students' work; at the same time, the teacher was still able to decide from which pile a particular student would make her choice. For a student who is traditionally shy or prone to "light" tempo action in his own life, we had him choose from the "strong" pile as a way of stretching the student. As well, it was also fun to go against convention and give male students "light" actions and female students "strong" actions.

This exercise proved very successful in getting students to overcome reluctance to experiment with Laban's work. Students were still not performing for an audience, but in a smaller group they were required to participate more fully. The jail or elevator setting naturally focused attention inward on the group on a shared problem, i.e., how do we get out of this place? The teachers worked in role as police officer, jailer or elevator repairman without the right tools. The exercise ended with feedback from students.

A Brief History of Rudolf Laban

This lesson provided a very brief outline of Laban's life. Rudolf Laban was born in Bratislava, Czechoslovakia in 1879. In his childhood, he closely watched the movements of a variety of people and animals in his town. "He was interested to see how the local peasantry went about their labours and how the women managed to walk with lightness and grace as they carried heavy loads on their heads."[3] He became a dancer, and later a choreographer, director and movement analyst. In 1928 he published "Kinetographie Laban" which was his own system for recording, studying, analysing and controlling movement in dance, drama, physical education, physical therapy and anthropology. This system is also known as **Labanotation**. With the rise of Nazism in central Europe, Laban fled to England where he remained for the rest of his life, continuing his exploration and analysis of movement. He died in Weybridge, Surrey in 1958.

As we discussed Laban's work and history, an important issue arose within the class. Laban viewed the opposing elements within each motion factor as representative of either gender: i.e., male or female. Thus, he attributed all "strong" actions as being "male," and all "light" actions as female; likewise, all "direct" actions as "male," and all "flexible" actions as female; all "quick" actions as "male," and all "sustained" actions as "female"; all "bound" actions as "male," and all "free" actions as "female." Clearly, during Laban's lifetime, socio-sexual roles were much more clearly defined, reinforced and acceptable. In today's evolving society, such distinctions, of course, will be seriously questioned by anyone determined to move beyond rigid sexual definitions. This, in turn, led to a discussion of political correctness in modern society, and the fact that traditionally, theatre has relied on conventions based on the recreation and reinforcement of "types" and stereotypes. These "types" establish a recognizable and easily-comprehensible world for the audience, be it a Shakespearean tragedy or a Feydeau farce. However, the use of "types" makes it difficult to justify to students who are socially aware in a politically-correct age. We suggest that this issue does not have to become inflammatory since the majority of students already accept these "types" from their exposure to popular media (i.e., advertisements, television sitcoms, films etc.).

Improvisations

In this lesson, students worked in pairs to explore a particular working action in opposition to a very different action (see Chart 3) — all the strong (male) actions: punching, pressing, wringing, slashing vs. the light (female): floating, gliding, dabbing, flicking. Likewise, all the direct actions vs. flexible actions, and all quick actions vs. sustained. The teacher attempted to stretch each actor by giving an opposite factor to her normal tempo of movement.

The situation of going on a blind date or meeting a new room-mate was given to the class. We started with "convention" and gave males the "male" working action and females the "female" actions. Students improvised either of the two scenarios. Then, using the same scenario, students went against convention, with males using a "female" action like floating, and females, a "male" action like punching.[4] This easily made the situation comic because students were dealing with the opposite of expected physical and vocal qualities (which also stretched the students). Students were provided with the problem of meeting someone for the first time and within that situation, had no easy way of getting out. This was the first time that they were asked to apply the factors to a recognizable and true-to-life situation. Many of the students at this point wanted very much to resort to naturalism and their own usual tempo of movement. "This doesn't make sense; I feel silly" was a common response. The teacher must work to reinforce any success in experimentation with unfamiliar working actions. Teenage self-consciousness and preserving one's familiar persona is at work here. Ultimately, the laughter produced by the obvious differences between the two characters or in the non-traditional behaviour of "male" vs. "female" was essential in helping students see the value of this technique. Furthermore, the lesson itself became an important learning tool about the very essence of drama — that all drama involves conflict and opposition.

Application of Laban's Working Actions to Text and Character Building (with Assessment Criteria)

Students were asked to present each action in relationship to a minimal script (text) in order to assess their comprehension of the theory, their mastery of the working actions and their ability to perform both physical and vocal characteristics of each of the action's varying motion factors. We were not doing character exploration here as much as simple assessment of students' learning. Peer evaluation could involve later feedback in whole group discussion on students' estimation of their own success and difficulties encountered in applying the working actions to text.

Students were given a minimal script of no more than eight lines. Either a different script for each pair or the same script for the whole class could be used. A wealth of miniminal scripts exist.[5] As well, teachers can make up their own dialogue scraps:

A: Where are you going?
B: Over there.
A: It's cold.
B: I know.

Students worked in pairs and memorized the script. The teachers then asked each pair to rehearse the script using a variety of opposing working actions (i.e., punching vs. floating, pressing vs. flicking etc.) When the class was ready, each pair performed the script; students were not told in advance which specific working actions they would be using. Instead, the teachers randomly selected opposing working actions for each new pair to test their ability to perform the working actions on demand.

The chief advantage of using a minimal script in this exercise was that it provides few, if any, details about the characters and the context in which they're operating. After all students had been assessed, we used the most successfully-executed performance and asked the class to establish the names, personalities, occupations and relationship of the characters and the setting. Each pair could also choose its most successful performance and do the same. Once this had been done, students rehearsed the script using the same working actions as before. Each pair then performed its work again. We asked for feedback about the clarity of the relationship between the working action and the type of characters they were trying to portray.

Following this, we reversed the process and asked each pair to create a short eight-line script based on opposing working actions. Through this exercise, students should have been able to more fully

188

understand the clear relationship between language or text, application of the various working actions, characterization and interpretation. For example, two students chose to work with punching and floating. We reminded them that "punching" is "quick" and "floating" is "sustained," and that this should be the guideline for writing each character's dialogue. Character A is a "floating" and B is a "punching."

A: I thought it might be very nice if we went for a walk this evening since it's so mild and pleasant outside.
B: No thanks. Too busy.
A: But you keep promising and promising to go out with me and you never do. Why do you get my hopes up like that and then always disappoint me?
B: Too bad. No time. Maybe later.

The teachers either provided each pair with the opposing actions, or allowed students to select their own. Students naturally created the characters and the context before writing the dialogue. We asked students to rehearse and perform their scripts for the class. After each performance, the student audience was asked to describe the characters, their relationship and the setting. Students then had immediate feedback on the effectiveness of their script and character creation.

Assessment criteria for all exercises involved commitment to performing the working action, ability to sustain the performance of a specific working action and vocal and physical qualities expressed through the working action.

The later exercises involving interpretative choices about character and situation were evaluated in terms of suitability of the working action chosen for the type of character being created, suitability to the context of the situation and overall dramatic effectiveness of the scene (including characters, context, conflict etc.). Students also submitted a brief outline of the "5 W's" (Who, What, When, Where, Why), character descriptions (including occupation, age, relationship etc.) for the last exercise.

The final lesson in this pilot project was used as a summative tool to assess each student's ability to apply Laban's work. The teachers created an extensive list of various stereotypical characters based on employment and/or social status. Students were allowed to choose their stereotypical character with the teacher's guidance. In order to challenge them further, students were again encouraged to select a character that was very different from their own personality and natural tempo.

After selecting their character, students were asked to write a one-minute monologue in the voice of the character, which could easily be presented using the specific working action selected by them for that character. They were also required to write a one-page character biography, which gave some clear indication why that character had chosen that particular career; in turn, this was also their justification for choosing the particular working action or tempo in which they would perform the monologue.

They were asked to use one costume garment in their performance.

Three class periods were devoted to rehearsal. The performances were videotaped in one period. The students were asked to begin their performance by talking extemporaneously on camera as themselves first; they then performed the monologue in character with the selected working action. This allowed them to see a clear contrast between their own usual tempo and that of the character.

The final application of Laban's work would be to work on non-realistic text or any script that is presentational in style (i.e., Brecht, Shakespeare, Theatre of the Absurd, commedia dell'arte, farce).[6] A thorough reading of the script would give important clues to a possible basic tempo (working action) through which, to begin character exploration or where the character's employment, social class or status within the world of the play, suggests a possible working tempo.

Summary

"I think everything you do and the way you speak involves the Laban work. This could help me in lots of ways."
— a drama student after completing the Laban work

We have attempted to illustrate through these lessons that there exists a basic language and methodology which is useful and applicable by both students and teachers. This language provides them with an understanding of their own movement qualities, and allows them to explore and extend their personal boundaries as they work to develop characters for performance. We have worked to create a path which allows for sequential development and mastery of the eight working actions.

The acting experience for both actor and audience is deepened when a character is alive, both physically and vocally. A versatile and skillful actor is obviously one who is able to transform into a variety of characters, giving each a distinct physical and vocal life that, in turn, will create a new and distinct emotional life. In providing a clearly delineated set of actions, Laban's work provides the basis for more precise exploration of a character by selecting a predominant working action, that will form the "core" of the personality of the character.

190

Student responses to this work varied from genuine enthusiasm, to lukewarm appreciation or total negativity. Yet once students have learned and are comfortable with the specific language of Laban, and have broken through the barrier of fear surrounding intense physicalization, the potential for genuine experimentation and exploration in character work is limitless. When students can analyse exactly what they are "doing" as the character, they are free to make discoveries about "why" their characters behave as they do within the context of a script. Laban's work is, in fact, an "outside-to-inside" approach which is beneficial to actors at any age; it is particularly useful with high-school adolescents who have a ready abundance of physical energy on tap. In our opinion, this approach for adolescents is preferable to "method" acting which, in relying on intense emotion, demands a degree of life experience which they simply do not have. It is also much less potentially threatening.

The beauty of Laban's work, particularly at an elementary level, is that it is based on an analysis of movement that each of us, as living human beings, intuitively understands and "knows" from our own life-long use of movement. In effect, we are teaching students the structure or pattern which Laban created to describe all movements which, in turn, provides a precise vocabulary by which specific movements may be recreated, as desired or as required. In other words, we are simply "reawakening" students' inherent knowledge of their own physical movements, allowing them to use those movements to engender and recreate specific emotions for text and/or character exploration.

At the same time, students' preoccupations with their physical appearance and "image" often stands in the way of utilizing the very evident open range of opportunities provided through Laban's work. In our experience of this project, it is unlikely that we converted any student into finding a new level of commitment to character exploration if she did not already possess this initially. In effect, the same students who would most likely have made bold choices in creating character without Laban, did so using the working actions.

In short, this work does not, and cannot, provide a simple solution to inspire the majority of students whose understanding and motivation for in-depth character work is fairly limited. In fact, during later units in which students were asked to use Laban's work in their characterizations, there was a reluctance on the part of many to incorporate it. At the same time, those students who had taken up the challenge of using Laban, made quite remarkable progress in developing exciting, larger-than-life interpretations. They recognized that Laban's work was an entry point into a new level of acting experience. Many of these recognized that having achieved this level of expression, their next task was to work for greater subtlety and variety within the given action chosen. Even a few of those students, who expressed strong resistance to the work, admitted that they had been challenged and that, perhaps, in time, could return to the work with new confidence. Regardless of each student's final assessment of the work, it is clear that within this pilot study, there were many moments when all were engaged in serious risk-taking and discovery; it is doubtful that any educator would dispute that risk-taking and discovery are important learning outcomes in any classroom, and even more essential within the drama classroom.

Endnotes

1. David W. Booth and Charles J. Lundy, *Improvisation: Learning Through Drama*, (Toronto: Academic Press, 1985), p. 17.
2. Rudolf Laban and W.M. Carpenter, Quoted by Yat Malmgren "Movement Psychology," Lecture Series, (London: The Drama Centre, 1978).
3. Jean Newlove, *Laban for Actors and Dancers*, (New York: Routledge Theatre Arts Books, 1993), p. 15.
4. The most extreme "male" action is punching (strong, direct, quick) and the most extreme "female" action is floating (light, flexible, sustained); also use pressing vs. flicking, slashing vs. gliding, wringing vs. dabbing to find extremes of opposite elements within the eight working actions.
5. Harold Pinter's *The Dwarfs and Eight Revue Sketches*, David Mamet's *Short Plays and Monologues* and James Saunders's *After Liverpool* are excellent sources of short minimal scripts.
6. See pp. 81–90; *Theatre for Young People: A Sense of Occasion*.

Acknowledgements

We wish to thank: The students of ADA 3A0, Grade 11, Semester 1 at T.L. Kennedy Secondary School, Mississauga, Ontario; Mr. S. Russell, head of drama, Turner-Fenton Secondary School, Brampton, Ontario; Mr. L. Stern, head of drama, Streetsville Secondary School, Mississauga, Ontario; our workshop participants from the Peel Association of Education through Drama and the Council of Drama in Education.

$\mathcal{T}$he Collective Creation in the Classroom

JEFFREY GOFFIN

Introduction

At Maskwachees College in Hobbema, Alberta a class of native students present a play. In a series of brief scenes, they tell a story about peer pressure and social constraints endured by teenagers and their families as a result of royalty payments paid out by oil companies. As a group, the students have written and produced this play themselves. It is a short presentation, yet it allows them to demonstrate the performance skills they have acquired through a university extension course in drama. It also offers the opportunity to create an original play on a subject important to them.

At a conference on international development held at the Banff School of Fine Arts, a group of professors and scholars kick off the event with a short play. The six performers come from several different disciplines including nursing, sociology, communications and medicine. None boasts theatre training, although all share a common interest in development. *The Pregnant Camel Partnership* deals with an organizational meeting for a fictitious development project focusing on nomadic peoples and their camels. The audience at the conference immediately identify the characters as types familiar to their own work. The problems of obstinancy and self-interest draw laughter as everyone recognizes the situations and the personalities.

Cory's New Year's Resolutions is a play presented in an art gallery in Manila by a group of cultural workers at the end of a short workshop of improvisational theatre. The performers incorporate recent news events, including the attempted coup of the previous week and labour unrest in the Philippines. The small audience viewing the presentation responds to the satire of President Aquino's policies and the growing alienation of her supporters. "In the new year I resolve to speak Filipino more often," she says in English to her Filipino-speaking audience.

These three plays are examples of collective creation. This is a theatre form that has been used effectively around the world as an

193

alternative to commercial means of theatrical production. It has been beneficial in the development of original work, and in the creation of topical, highly-relevant theatre. Derived from political theatre forms of this century, the collective creation is a useful educational tool.

Theatre is a Collective Art

Even in its most solitary form, the one-man or one-woman show, theatre relies on a group of people — a collective. Every individual must provide a specific task in order for the production to work. The lighting crew, the stage crew, the actors, the costume designer, set designer, director, stage manager and props master must all make their own distinctive contribution for the production to be a success.

Commerical theatre has evolved in the West geared towards activity in major centres such as New York and London. This kind of theatre operates much like any other business. It employs a hierarchy allowing for top-down structure. Within the structure, roles are clearly defined regarding the nature of participation in the production. For example, the designer is responsible for the areas of costume, setting and lighting. It is expected that the designer will offer instructions and criticism to the workers in these areas. However, if the designer crosses the boundary to criticize an actor or the director's interpretation of a scene, the result can be devastating to the production. Upsetting the strict roles of the theatre is taboo. Unions protect these responsibilities to the extent that overstepping the boundaries can halt production.

In practice, there is often much overlap in these roles. Only a particularly obtuse or tyrannical director will not encourage or accept suggestions or spontaneous contributions from their company. Yet, on the whole, we operate following a business model with clearly-defined roles.

In a school context, theatre can be less strict in its division of labour. Coping with a limited budget, the whims of student actors and the difficulties of inadequate production facilities can be an organizational nightmare. Relying on the traditional theatre structure can alleviate some of the stress involved in the production of the school play.

The process, while successfully carrying a production from initial conception to the closing night party, can alienate the participants from their creative work. Even the initial step of selecting the script for production can be detrimental. Often in Canadian schools, this involves locating a play that was a success in a foreign country, possibly separated from this school and its audience by culture, generation and language. The process of production can compound the separation or distance between performer and his work.

Of course, there is much to be said for the encouragement of individual talents. Quiet children who show promise as artists can make valuable contributions to the set design of the production. Their work makes them part of the production, and can offer them a strong sense of accomplishment. Were they required to perform in the play, the experience could be an ordeal. What could be an important experience celebrating their talents could be overwhelmed by the trauma of being on public display. Certainly any educational value is negated by such an experience.

The process of collective creation can maximize the benefits of the collective nature of theatre. It incorporates the creativity of the entire company, creates a work with relevance to its audience and develops a strong group dynamic that can outlast the production.

Definition of the Collective

The term "collective creation" refers to both a process and a product. It is an effort to create a play through the aesthetic of collective action. In the simplest form of collective creation, a group of people work together, sharing all of the tasks of production equally, according to their talents and interests. No single individual is identified as the playwright, director or designer. The director ceases to be the centre of production. Many collective creations rely on no single individual as director. Likewise, the script is not the product of one individual's vision; every member of the collective participates in formulating it. All decisions are made by group concensus.

The collective creation relies on a company of performers and theatre craftspeople skilled in many different tasks. Ideally, each member can function in several traditional roles, such as actor, stage carpenter and playwright. The work is extremely demanding for every member of the collective, yet the result is very fulfilling for all involved.

The History of the Collective and its Forms

Collectives experienced their greatest popularity in the twentieth century. Their forerunners are political theatre. While used across Canada in the seventies and early eighties, the collective can be traced back to the workers' theatres during the Depression. The play *Eight Men Speak* produced by Toronto's Workers' Experimental Theatre in 1933, is the best example of this. While not a true collective in that the script credits a group of writers as author, rather than simply the cast as would normally be the case, it was largely the result of a collective effort. It featured a variety of theatrical techniques as is characteristic of collectives. It focused on the arrest of eight leaders of the labour movement and the attempted assassination of the one of them. Other plays from the workers' theatre dealt with strikes, social unrest and economic problems.

In the sixties and seventies, many theatres tried to respond to increasing awareness about social problems with plays addressing those issues. Collective creation offered a method to allow these companies to create a play through improvisation incorporating topical events and even playing off of the spontaneous reactions of their audience.

In Canada, the collective creation marked an important step in the development of a national theatre. During the late sixties, funding agencies and audiences responded favourably to the creation of theatre on Canadian material. The demand quickly overtook the existing body of dramatic literature. The existing companies responded by exploring the collective process.

Initially introduced by theatre companies whose mandate encouraged the use of alternative or non-traditional methods of production such as Toronto Workshop Productions and Theatre Passe Muraille, the collective quickly gained popularity. Through this method, an original play could be created from indigenous material, while allowing for a distinctive contribution from every member of the collective.

Through the collective process, plays could be staged quickly and effectively, focusing on content that had never before been explored in any art form. In the late seventies, Saskatoon's Twenty-Fifth Street House Theatre explored the co-operative movement among farmers in the province of Saskatchewan in *Paper Wheat*. Their play celebrated the settlement of the Prairies, the development of agricultural co-operatives and the spirit of the movement. Presented in Legion halls, churches and community halls across the province, for many of those in its audience, the play offered the first real reflection of their own lives. The same can be said of many plays produced across Canada by companies such as the Mummers' Troupe, Theatre Passe-Muraille, Catalyst Theatre, the Mulgrave Road Co-op, and the Vancouver East Cultural Centre.

Also, the collective process enables the director to incorporate the special talents of each individual actor. According to Paul Thompson of Theatre Passe Muraille, it also offers more control to the actor:

> Part of the concept of doing "collective" plays is saying that the actor has more to give than often is required or demanded of him in traditional plays. I think, you know, he should be more than a puppet. He's got a head, he's got his observations and he's quite as capable of making a statement or passing on observations. In the kind of work we're doing, we like the actor to really put some of himself in the play. We also work through the skills an actor has. If an actor

could yodel, for example, then I'd really like to put his yodel into a play.[1]

Obviously this approach could be taken to extreme, but basically it is a reaction against two very negative aspects of commercial theatre. Firstly, that actors should not think for themselves. Secondly, that indigenous art forms such as yodelling, clog dancing, mumming, square dancing or folk-songs are somehow less important or less valid than the forms of song and dance in theatrical hits from New York and London.

The true collective creation is distinguished by the process of production. As mentioned above, throughout the production, all tasks, from the initial research and workshop of material to the performance of the play, are shared equally by all members depending upon their respective talents. All decisions are made by group concensus. Toronto's Theatre Passe Muraille used this process to create a series of plays in the seventies such as *The Farm Show, Doukhobors* and *I Love You Baby Blue*.

There are many variations on the collective creation which are useful in coping with specific groups of participants and particular subject matter. The "directed collective" and the "scripted collective" are variations on the process of collective creation. Other forms drawn from political theatre indicate a process and a distinctive product such as "agitprop," the "living newspaper," "documentary drama" and the "trial documentary."

DIRECTED COLLECTIVE

The most common version of the collective is one in which some concessions have been made to the structure of traditional theatre. Often a collective will rely upon one individual as their director. This can be a very useful method, enabling the smooth operation of the collective. The director can keep the company from straying from the task at hand. As in traditional theatre, the director's role as informed audience during rehearsal can save a lot of time.

Many collectives have relied upon the participation of a writer to assist in direction. The writer in this context has a very challenging task. Rick Salutin described his participation in the collective creation, *1837: The Farmers' Revolt*, as being the writer "on" not "of" the play.[2] Salutin was one part of a group dedicated to writing the play. The actors used improvisation to contribute to the script. Salutin wrote his material, as well as edited and reworked the actor's offerings. Betty Jane Wylie, playwright on *The Horsburgh Scandal*, claimed that her role was one of overseeing the project, providing a detached or objective perspective as an alternative to the subjective view of the actors. Despite this objectivity, the input of the writer does not take precedence over that of the rest of the company, and can often be overruled.

SCRIPTED COLLECTIVE

The scripted collective relies upon the creation of a script by either the group as a whole or by a playwright working within the group. The collective creation *The Age of Maturity*, produced by Calgary's Mount Royal College Youtheatre Workshop in 1984, is a good example. The play grew out of an improvisation game. Contestants in the game improvised scenarios chosen at random from a collection written by members of the company. Eventually, several of these scenarios, each relating to the effort by teenagers to demonstrate maturity amid pressure from peers and parents, became the structure of the play. Members of the collective wrote individual scenes and submitted them to two playwrights. The two playwrights edited the scenes for length and consistency, composed transitions and added the opening and closing of the play. The play was then rehearsed much like any other new script. The entire company participated in improvising and writing the script, although relying on the two playwrights to provide an overall perspective to the work.

AGITPROP

"Agitprop" comes from "agitational propaganda." It refers to a form of political theatre intended to move the audience to action regarding a specific idea or issue. Particular techniques evolved to attain this goal. According to E. Cecil Smith of the Workers' Experimental Theatre active in Canada during the thirties, there are three different kinds of agitprop techniques. These are the mass recitation, the short agitational-propaganda sketch and "realistic" plays from the "realist school" of theatre.

The first two forms are quite similar. Both are noted for their simplicity. While this is primarily due to budget constraints, it has the advantage of increased mobility, enabling them to be performed on picket lines, in union halls or even in the street.

The mass recitation is a form of choral speech. In it, a small group of actors address the audience individually, and as a chorus, calling for social action. Emphasis is provided by dividing questions and responses between individuals and the group. The play, *Theatre — Our Weapon*, is a good example of this form:

CHORUS: WORKERS OF THE WORLD, UNITE!
1ST: What have we to lose?
CHORUS: OUR CHAINS.
5TH: What can we win?
CHORUS: THE WHOLE WORLD.[3]

The script requires variety in vocal delivery and simple stage movement to create an effective visual component reinforcing the dialogue.

198

The mass recitation is a metaphor for collective endeavour, moving back and forth between the individual and the group. The mass recitation is primarily a morale booster or a crowd warm-up, calling for further action. The performers wear simple, neutral costumes. No special setting or props are required.

The agitprop sketch retains the simplicity of the mass recitation, while including rudimentary characterization and conflict. A wide variety of theatrical techniqes could be used in order to present a short play as quickly and effectively as possible. Caricatures and stereotypes are a prominent part. In the thirties, a typical play might have the evil capitalist and the honest worker engaged in the class struggle. During the Vietnam War, a sadistic general might be confronted by a righteous draft dodger. A uniform costume is supplemented by scarves, skirts, collars, masks or hats to establish characters. Simple props such as boxes, tables and chairs could serve a variety of purposes on stage.

Performing outdoors and at large public meetings dictates that the performances be larger than life to reach a varied, and often inattentive, audience. Content would be topical and support a call for action on the part of the audience.

The realist drama refers to the popular commercial theatre of the 1930s. It required realistic costumes and props and a traditional theatre space for performance. Lighting and set design would be used. During the Depression, this form generally focused on domestic situations. Typically, a family would suffer through the tensions and difficulties arising from a lay off or a strike. It is distinguished by its increased production demands, three-dimensional characters and complex situation. Clifford Odet's *Waiting for Lefty* is a good example of this form. In its day, this play was produced around the world.

The play *Eight Men Speak* from the Workers' Experimental Theatre provides examples of all of these forms of agitprop.

While the mass recitation incorporates the collective aesthetic into its structure, all three of these forms of agitprop were the result of collective effort. Although the sentiments expressed in agitprop plays become dated quickly, the form retains its usefulness. Later, collective creation often shared the same educational or activist intention as these plays; accordingly they repeated many of the same techniques and structure.

LIVING NEWSPAPER

The living newspaper can be traced back to pre-Revolutionary Russia, when workers' theatre groups used theatre to transmit news to the illiterate peasants in remote parts of the country. Relying on a variety of performance techniques including singing, choral speech, dance, gymnastics and tumbling, cultural groups such as the Blue Blouses informed their audiences of the latest current events. They might simply read reports from the Moscow newspapers, or they might act out the stories. Enacting the events allowed for a wide variety of interpretation, and quickly became a popular technique in promoting solidarity with the workers' cause.

During the 1930s, the American government responded to the Depression with a variety of federal initiatives to increase employment. One such effort was the Federal Theatre Project. Hundreds of unemployed theatre professionals worked in this company which popularized the living newspaper. Initially, a response to the need to employ large numbers of actors and writers in a theatrical production, they quickly became a characteristic of the project. The Federal Theatre Project created a series of plays on subjects such as the Italian invasion of Ethiopia, federal programmes for assisting agriculture and the evils of venereal disease.

Each living newspaper used a similar process of production. A group of writers would research a selected topic, providing the company with all manner of information including news reports, statistics, interviews, historical documents and government publications. Collectively, the writers would create a play illuminating the subject. Few of the plays relied upon the traditional elements of protagonist and antagonist. Each had an episodic structure consisting of many short scenes. Each relied on simple setting and technical requirements, allowing for a fast pace and a fluidity of movement from scene to scene. Budget limitations also demanded that minimal technical work be used such as simple lighting and set design. Each presented a multitude of roles, emphasizing the issues of the play over the individual characters. The plays had an immediacy from their use of current events. They also presented an optimistic perspective on these events, which tended to be supportive of government initiatives.

DOCUMENTARY DRAMA

The documentary drama experienced international popularity in the sixties and early seventies. The primary aesthetic of this play, established by Peter Cheeseman at the Victoria Theatre in Stoke-on-Trent, England and German playwright Peter Weiss, demands that all material be derived from documentary sources. Any written document may be used as a source for dialogue. Cheeseman used this form to examine local historical events such as the history of the North Staffordshire Railway in *The Knotty*, and the effort to keep a local steel mill open in *The Fight for Shelton Bar*. Weiss explored the Vietnam War in *Discourse on...Viet Nam*, the colonization of Africa in *Song of the Lusitanian Bogey* and the Holocaust in *The Investigation*. In Canada, documentary drama focused on historical events such as the Riel Rebellion in the 1880s (*The Trial of Louis Riel* by John Coulter), labour movements during the thirties (*Black Powder* by Rex Deverell), the Second World War

(*Gravediggers of 1942* by Tom Hendry) and the coming of socialized medicine (*Medicare* by Rex Deverell).

As in documentary film, the challenge with a documentary play is how to dramatize the facts. The playwright must find creative techniques that will serve the strict confines of history. Perhaps a scene described in a letter or a newspaper can be enacted or presented in mime while accompanied by the account as narration.

Although documentary dramas do not necessarily rely upon the collective process, the aesthetic has influenced many collective creations. Many of the most well-known Canadian collective creations such as *1837: The Farm Show, Paper Wheat* and *Ten Lost Years* incorporate documentary material. While remaining faithful to events, documentary drama employs editing, sequence and perspective to provide an interpretation or a thesis regarding those events.

TRIAL DOCUMENTARY

The trial has been a source for drama since ancient Greece. It has a clear structure, specific roles and a heightened language. The trial transcript provides an outstanding source for the documentary dramatist. Many plays incorporate documents from trials and judicial inquiries. The trial documentary dramatizes a single inflential trial such as *The Trial of Louis Riel*, the Nuremburg trials in *The Investigation* or the security hearing regarding the development of the atomic and hydrogen bombs *In the Matter of J. Robert Oppenheimer*. The playwright must strive to clear away the tedium of the court room to reveal the events of the case. Once again, editing and restructuring are allowed, provided they remain faithful to the original event.

Yet the trial documentary can provide considerable freedom for expression. Toronto Workshop Productions' *Chicago '70* re-enacted the conspiracy trials following the 1968 Democratic National Convention. The trial transcript provided the starting point for the production. The collective nature of the play enabled the company to satire the proceedings by improvising throughout, as well as juxtaposing the trial with that of Alice in *Alice in Wonderland*.

These related forms of collective creation provide a range of responses which allow for use of the form in specific settings. The performance skill, level of awareness regarding their subject and competence with group work will feature in the selection of the appropriate form for a specific group.

The Collective in the Classroom

There are many reasons for the teacher to use the collective creation in the drama class as well as in many other subject areas. To the drama teacher it offers a solution to the problem of finding relevant material suitable for a specific class. For the drama student it offers the opportunity to have control over the creative process. Beyond this, a variety of behavioural and cognitive objectives valuable in both in any area of study can be explored through the collective process. Group facilitation and organization, research methods and simple performance skills are integral to this work.

The collective creation can use any material as its focus. It can be topical, as in the case of the BUGKOS workshop production of *Cory's New Years Resolution*, which explored the status of President Cory Aquino at a time when national attention in the Philippines was focused on that issue. It can address a specific issue, just as *The Pregnant Camel Partnership* examined the difficulties of co-operation within development projects for a conference dealing with that specific issue. Like *Paper Wheat* from Twenty-Fifth Street House Theatre, it can offer a reflection and a celebration of a way of life to those who experienced it. The level of performance skill in the class can also be addressed in the collective form undertaken. Will the class be able to deal with the strict confines of the trial documentary, or will the agitprop sketch be a sufficient challenge? Whatever route is taken, the collective play will offer a unique outlet for originality and experiment.

Even logistical problems can be overcome through the collective process. What play will be suitable for a specific age range? What will fit a class with a certain number of male or female students? How can a handicapped student be incorporated? Relying on the collective process, the play can be tailored to fit the company rather than the company to fit the play.

By far the best reason to use the collective creation in the classroom is the opportunity to offer the students control over the process. It provides a real opportunity for substantial contributions. Their perspective, opinions and ideas are validated. Their work is valued by their fellow students and by their teacher.

Control will likely be the biggest decision in regard to the use of collective creation in any classroom. This control may be unconditional, or may have a few practical limitations placed on it depending upon the teacher. How much control of the process will be delegated to the students? How much control do the students require? How much control does the teacher require? Can discipline be maintained in the classroom if the students have complete control over the process? Obviously, this will vary from class to class.

The collective relies heavily on a strong dynamic within the group to complete the process of production. Accordingly, it offers the opportunity for the class to examine methods of group facilitation and organization. Will the group operate with a leader? Will it rely upon group concensus for decision making and problem solving? Will it find it's own alternate method of operation? The skills learned through the successful production of a collective play can be transfered to other areas of work.

They must be able to work under minimal supervision. They must be able to work effectively and quickly in groups. They must share mutual trust in order to accept and offer ideas regarding the creation.

In addition to skills in group management, any class about to begin collective work will have to be prepared in performance skills. They must be comfortable with elementary vocal and physical technique in order to transfer their knowledge of a specific subject into theatre.

Collective creation is distinguished by its reliance on a variety of theatrical techniques. Improvisational acting is the cornerstone of collective creation. If part of the rationale for using the collective process is returning power to the participants in the dramatic process, then improvisation is the ultimate method of empowering the performer. Acting instructors such as Viola Spolin and Uta Hagen relied upon non-scripted performance to teach acting techniques. Keith Johnstone's work in improvisation has been influential in returning control to the performer. It is essential that performers involved in a collective creation be able to improvise in order to transform raw research into drama.

Popular techniques such as shadow theatre, choral speech, tableaux, dance, creative movement, the use of masks and singing can add excitement to the play. Any or all of these forms can be introduced in the classroom in order for the participants to have a range of methodology at their command.

In the drama class the emphasis may be on the use of these specific theatre conventions. How many different conventions can the students incorporate while maintaining the cohesiveness of the play? How is their execution of elementary skills such as effective vocal technique and movement on stage? Is their play a complete whole with a structure moving logically and smoothly from beginning to end? How appropriate and believable are their characters? How well do they use simple technical effects?

In another subject area, the emphasis may be on the incorporation of other material. In fact, if anything, the collective process, with its emphasis on improvisation, can be a useful method of ensuring that the students understand the subject at hand. The performer must have a very clear understanding of a historical event before they can transform it into drama. Students in social studies, language arts or even science can be introduced to a variety of theatrical conventions quickly and easily. These conventions are then used to dramatize their research. The result may be a smooth, polished performance that can be shared with other students in the class. It may be rough and less than stage-worthy. Yet it is unfair to judge the work on the basis of the product alone. The process is just as important, if not more so, than the final performance. Often students will discover much about a subject through the research that they cannot present in their play.

In December, 1989 I had the privilege of working with the BUGKOS arts group in Manila. Over a few days, we explored several different theatrical techniques moving towards a collective creation at the end of the workshop. The participants divided into two groups and spent several hours working out a play. One group came up with a very polished, entertaining and exciting performance. The other group presented a rough play, inventive yet less smooth and effective than the first collective. In our ensuing discussion, we found that the second group had spent much of their time exchanging information about the events they were dramatizing. Accordingly, they had little time to work out the fine details of performance. For these performers, this was a truly educational experience allowing them to share their own knowledge about human rights in their country, their chosen subject for their play. However, their performance could have been improved by a longer rehearsal period. Aside from their own personal satisfaction at having a better product to offer the group, their work was extremely successful. The collective process allowed them to examine a specific issue of importance and celebrate their findings in a dramatic presentation.

Some difficulties can arise when using the collective creation in the classroom. However, awareness of these problems and sensitivity to them should they arise, can do much to alleviate them.

Clearly the instructor must deal with the question of class management and the extent to which the students are responsible for the work. Even at its best, the collective process has very little formal structure. The company constantly responds to the input and effort of the participants, making it difficult, if not impossible, to establish a firm rehearsal schedule. This absence of structure can sap the enthusiasm of participants accustomed to linear modes of working.

Selection of the subject is also problematic. Whether the instructor chooses the subject or the class arrives at it by concensus, this is a crucial step in the process. The enthusiasm and energy of students can evaporate if confronted with an esoteric, exotic or irrelevant topic.

There is also the difficulty of teaching performance skills if the collective process is introduced to a subject area outside of drama. How much time must be alloted to this work? How knowledgeable must the instructor be about performance in order to do this work confidently?

The instructor will find evaluation of the collective creation a challenge. While most often the final performance is a good indication of the participants' understanding of their subject, there are exceptions to this. As in the BUGKOS workshop, the final performance may not reflect the students' actual cognitive achievement. The focus of evaluation must also consider the process of production. This requires observation tempered with respect for the participants' work. The presence of the instructor will often inhibit students' work, even if only to the extent that they will solicit approval for their decisions. If group harmony is weak, the instructor may become a crutch in decision making. Accordingly, individual and group evaluation must be involved in order to examine the process.

The collective creation is an invaluable tool for educators. It enables the participants to take control over the form and content of their own work. It offers an opportunity to breath life into content areas while creating a dynamic social relationship. The performance of the collective allows for the celebration of that work and may also be beneficial to the audience. It offers an alternative to commercial theatre forms, resulting in original work directly relevant to both the performers and their audience.

Endnotes

1. Robert Wallace, "Paul Thompson at Theatre Passe Muraille," *Open Letter*, 2:7 Winter, 1974:55.
2. Rick Salutin, *1837: The Farmers' Revolt* (Toronto: James Lorimer, 1976), p. 202.
3. "Theatre — Our Weapon," in *Eight Men Speak and Other Plays from the Canadian Workers' Theatre*. Richard Wright and Robin Endres, eds. (Toronto: New Hogtown Press, 1976), p. 1.

Section Four

Developing a Personal Praxis: Making Connections Between Theory and Practice

$\mathcal{R}$eflections on Curriculum

BELARIE HYMAN-ZATZMAN

"Please don't shoot the pianist. He is doing his best."
— *Oscar Wilde, Impressions of America*

Prologue

In the spring of 1987, I sat in my blue chair and stared at the boxes
that were lining the hall outside my office in the Arts Centre. The
bookshelves were empty, my desk looked utterly barren; would there
be any trace of me left here, after seven years of blood and guts teaching? I was nine months pregnant, finally ready to take our Noah, then
two and a half, to meet my husband in Toronto. Halifax was raining
— perpetually as it usually does in March — and night fog obscured
University Avenue. I greeted change with ambivalence: I was ready
for the challenge of Toronto. I had for years dreamed of working on
a Ph.D. with Professor Richard Courtney. But hell, I had just resigned
from Dalhousie's Theatre Department, and I was grateful for its security
and the professional freedom and growth it had afforded me. I stayed
with them a term longer than I should have — ignoring the increasing
urgency to get to Toronto — in order to get my classes through to the
end of the year. And so I got on the plane (hiding my enormous belly
from the stewardesses as best I could) with a full heart. I arrived in
Toronto by the skin of my teeth — four days later I gave birth. Consequently, I began my doctoral programme with a pen in one hand,
and breast-feeding my daughter with the other!

By the time the cradle at the foot of our bed was replaced with
the desk and computer, my research had begun in earnest. I discovered that for the first time in almost 10 years, my classroom empty,
I have the opportunity to reflect on and re-evaluate my own teaching
practice **without** the immediate demands of students or the stuff of
administration looming. With Courtney's guidance, I began to explore
something about the teaching of theatre at the university, opting to
practise what I had preached — "start from where you are."[1] Brian
Way incarnate. I wanted (still do) to know something about what other

209

theatre teachers in university theatre programmes were doing: what they were doing, **how** they were doing it, and why? And so I came face to face with curriculum. Almost smug in my accomplishments at Dalhousie — I had created a strong Developmental Drama programme that had not existed for years, in addition to teaching theatre courses — I began to research university curricula with the certainty that I had been a bloody good teacher. Now, the idea of this opportunity for reflection, it fairly rings of a time replete with luxury; it ain't. Reflection can be dangerous territory, I warn you. This journey has been fraught with a kind of darkness.

The Script: University Curricula

Initially, my analysis of the research began with a marked disdain for the incredible lack of curriculum guidelines and absence of accountability in university teaching. Dewey's legacy teaches us that curriculum resides at the centre of education, and deals with the most fundamental issues about the nature of that which is worthwhile to know and experience.[2] Yet, the design of university programmes, in general, and university drama programmes in particular, are seemingly unaffected by these issues. The universities clearly recognize the problem. And in response, attempts at curriculum design have been made; these range from the superficial "Catalog of Goals of Higher Education,"[3] to those which offer higher education a model that maintains the need for interrelationships and reciprocity between various elements of the curriculum.[4] The best of these harbour a deep concern that the university curriculum should and can be more than an "aggregate of disparate courses and experiences" at the mercy of professors' individual preferences.[5]

In practice, there have been efforts made to remedy the situation. Harvard introduced the concept of a "core curriculum" in 1978, after much debate (the value of their solution is not at issue here).[6] Numerous Canadian universities have also implemented required classes (most commonly, a language or science credit) for undergraduate programmes. Nevertheless, the U.S. National Endowment for the Humanities issued a report stating that the universities have lost a clear sense of purpose and "without purpose, curriculum becomes little better than an 'educational garage sale'."[7] A year later, in 1985, the Association of American Colleges' "Integrity in the College Curriculum" Report, scathingly declared that university curricula were incoherent, in a state of disarray and without vision.[8]

The reality of my own university experience speaks to the truth of these indictments. I wandered through the first two years of my undergraduate programme, picking and choosing classes with no more sense of discrimination than an intuitive idea about what interested me, and timetable scheduling! And in the absence of a curriculum design to guide my educational choices, luck provided what the university could not. For I had schlepped myself to enough drama classes that, by the end of a four year Honours English degree, I found myself planted on the doorstep of the Graduate Drama Centre. And so it is only by happy accident that my educational career began to mirror my other life, outside the university. I suspect that I was more than a little naive, since it never occurred to me to even consider questioning my professors about the "big picture," the curricular vision of my progress through the university system. And my advisor? That was someone who signed the form that had already been validated by five other signatures. So much for vision. The relationship of the secondary school to the university also becomes significant here. For ultimately, I fared no better there. Though I was devoted to my theatre arts classes (as they were then called), my teacher and school productions, that love never got translated into curricular terms broader than the scripts, exercises and productions. I had been accepted into the university of choice, and into one of its "best" colleges. To what end? So I could graduate proudly with merely a "congratulations, dear, much success in your future endeavors?" Was the hope that the university, in its curricular wisdom, would nurture me? From this side of the desk and motherhood, I have come to recognize that not only does each level of education need to be cognizant of the function of its own curriculum, but also its relationship to the succeeding ones, if we are to teach with any sense of vision, at all.

I'd suggest that the absence of a comprehensive curriculum design for universities, generally, is symptomatic of the state of curriculum for drama programmes at the post-secondary level, specifically. Curriculum design for drama programmes is clearly "problematic"; for this discipline is inherently complex, because of the great diversity of orientations which exist in the field itself. For example, these include: production/performance, history, criticism, aesthetic and drama education.[9] My own research in preparation for distributing a questionnaire about university drama/theatre programmes right across Canada, tallied 18 separate subject areas. And while my investigation is still in its preliminary stages, the respondents do appear to have listed at least three new subjects (under a section entitled "other"), for categories I had not included in the survey. This diversity is further complicated because presumably, each specialty is framed by its own particular sets of assumptions and epistemological structures. These discrete courses are generally viewed as the province of the individual instructors, and left to their own recognizance, they can become territorial in an often political climate, vying for administrative focus and budget commitment. Moreover, in drama, the diversity of the structure is an

Aristotelian phenomenon, and it has emerged as a characteristic North American pattern of fragmentation.[10] Under all of these circumstances, one may well argue that no single model of curriculum design can accommodate these historical fragmentations.

These were the results of my academic research. I imagine that it was almost inevitable that I would begin to consider my own relationship to these phenomena. And here is the first hint of reflection's dark side — revealed when the experience gets messy! No longer were these merely statistics, because I recognized myself in the data. Reflection forced me to acknowledge the extent to which I had researched from the outside. Determined to paint an accurate picture of how theatre instructors create curriculum, I researched and wrote about the phenomenon of idiosyncratic curricular decisions. Knowing what I had experienced, I took a perverse kind of pleasure in discovering the prevalence of "piecemeal" university curricula — programmes and courses — which seem to be structured, validated by the whims of its instructors. I considered these issues, without heart, because I had forgotten how one is impelled to teach **this** play or exercise; I had denigrated university theatre teaching practice — without recognizing that my critical analysis was one-dimensional, because I had researched and responded to it from the outside. In the struggle to give form to feeling, I went to my bookshelves. I actually pulled down every play that had ever touched me deeply. The floor was a mess. I spent four days immersed in memories of the first time I had read that scene, or that one — **that** moment! I found myself recalling actual productions, performances, scenes I had witnessed or directed, remembering myself moved to tears, to terror, to anger. On the floor we sat: Ibsen — Ghosts, Hedda, Rosmersholm, Bergman's Doll's House, John Gabriel Borkman; Pirandello, Sartre, Shepard, Brecht; Phaedra, Godot, The Maids, Lear; Bacchae, The Shadow Box, Long Day's Journey Into Night, and on and on. I leafed through them all and was exhausted by the effort. And I remembered student scene work: their triumphs, my triumphs through them. It was an unbelievable journey for me; and I began to feel sympathy and empathy for the impulses of my colleagues:

Instructor B: "I want **this** play on our reading list."
Instructor R: "No. I hate it."
Instructor D: "O.k., I'll do it if you'll give me."

I recognized that my passion to teach theatre is based upon my passionate response to the work of these artists, my gatekeepers. Making use of that passion as a foundation for curriculum, whether tacit or explicit, is not unique to my practice. For I am discovering that questionnaire respondents repeatedly cite passion, or variations on that theme, as a major influence on their teaching: "I want to participate in an art form which I care for deeply"; "passion"; "nothing else interested me as much"; "a love of theatre"; and, "theatre is important." I still believe that in creating curriculum one needs to be grounded by principles that are more than simply a reflection of the vagaries of instructor preference. Nevertheless, I am at least able to understand the motivation behind this teaching practice, appreciate its dimension — both intellectually and from the reality of my own experience — and know it consciously.

There are several implications to the realities of teaching within a system that functions without an established curriculum. At its best, we have the promise of academic freedom, the opportunity to rigourously pursue our areas of specialty, as artists and scholars. Thus, we may share with students the struggle or fruits of our research, enabling them to explore a variety of traditions, techniques and (hopefully) extraordinary insights. Indeed, from the responses to my questionnaire it appears that many theatre instructors chose to teach at the university level precisely because "I wanted the academic freedom of the university"; because of "freedom and expression" or "research opportunities." However, without the limitations implied by a set curriculum, we run the risk of simply perpetuating the legacy of fragmentation. In this context, limitations should be perceived as a positive force, insofar as curriculum can encourage departmental cohesiveness and balance. Embracing academic freedom, however, means that curriculum must not be allowed to homogenize a department; rather, it means valuing individual difference within the context of a curricular vision; it requires articulation of a mandate that embraces diversity, allows students and faculty opportunities for synthesis, but does not demand unity. In visual terms, this is the distinction between balance and symmetry. The former can be dynamic, because aesthetic balance can be achieved by conflicting elements; the latter can reduce a piece to the realm of deadly art.

Thus, my apparently altruistic motivation for examining university theatre/drama programmes — to provide a broad perspective on its post-secondary teaching — is disclosed as much more than that. Why do we look to other teaching models? Because, whether they exist at the primary, secondary or tertiary level, they provide us with a mirror to our own practice. What did I hope to see reflected there? It was a search for curriculum in context. In the language of the theatre, my given circumstances were that I had actually learned to teach in a university milieu, "on the job." How do teachers learn within a professional environment? The "Personal Practical Knowledge" studies[11] emphasize that teacher development happens through inquiry. Donald Schon suggests that it is the process of holding a reflective conversation with "the materials of one's situation and by so doing, remaking a part of [our] practice world."[12] Thus, I wanted to know if I'm doing the best that I can; have I made good choices; are there better ways to create conditions for significant meaning in the classroom — both for myself and my students. As such, this is not just a process of defining curriculum, rather, it is about the discovery of a creative curriculum, the search for artistry.

So, fragmentation is the nature of the beast. But have there been any attempts at curriculum design for university theatre/drama programmes, specifically? Gardner reveals that "there is virtually no material available on approaches to the teaching of drama from Canadian sources with the exception of Courtney's seminal *The Dramatic Curriculum*."[13] My own research updates and confirms this serious lack of curriculum guidelines at the tertiary level, whereas in contrast, excellent guidelines do exist at the primary and secondary levels.

Stalemated by the lack of resource material, I looked to less traditional avenues for research, and my persistence garnered three Canadian documents that at least approximate a look at curriculum issues in theatre/drama programmes. The Canada Council has commissioned two inquiries into selected aspects of theatre training in Canada. The first was submitted under the chairmanship of Malcolm Black, in 1977; the second explored the role and funding of the National Theatre School, and was chaired by Dr. Davidson Dunton in 1980. The most recent report was prepared, last year, for the National Theatre School of Canada by Jean-Louis Roux (with contributions by Robin Phillips) and it, too, focused on the future of N.T.S. And while two of these studies did **some** examination of university theatre programmes, as a part of their research, none have been devoted to a specific, in-depth exploration of university theatre/drama programmes themselves.

In fact, it was my frustration with the lack of literature about university theatre/drama curricula, that prompted me to collect my own data in the form of the qualitative questionnaire. The results of the survey will provide me with the opportunity to address the problem of traditional curriculum "piecemeal procedures" in drama programmes and, as Gardner and Courtney suggest, to point to the way their structure of knowledge has been conceived. Indeed, the research on curriculum theory acknowledges that "we need to recognize that problems in the structure of knowledge ought to be on our agenda when we consider problems of curriculum."[14] I would agree that without the benefit of curriculum guidelines and because of the exigencies of course building, drama departments have failed to see their own curricula as an ontological process.[15] The 1973 U.S. report on "The Arts in Higher Education" also reveals this recurring pattern: "even when they (academic and practical theatre courses) exist side by side, they are not integrated."[16] Thus, the lack of good curriculum design is evidenced by the proliferation of programmes which are "linear and segmented in structure," offering a series of classes that are "valuable in themselves" but are never "brought into some clear relationship."[17]

Scene Study: The Questions and Improvisations

Consequently, as the months passed, I discovered that I had begun to question my own practice. Was I any different than other university instructors? What did I think I was doing in the classroom? What did all those games and exercises really amount to? What were they about? Did it make any difference? Would I ever be able to teach again? Would I ever **want** to teach again? "The best in this kind are but shadows and the worst are no worse, if imagination amend them."[18] God forbid. Nevertheless, what had begun as recollections of triumph in the classroom, became focused upon vivid pictures of those times I **know** I had failed. The fact that there were so few disappointments over the years did nothing to diminish the frequency of replaying those losses. Imagination? Had I ever been the best of any kind? Was I as guilty of neglecting curricular accountability? Did I ever offer any of my students a sense of theatre or developmental drama that was framed by a context broader than my individual course? Kerr suggests that the solution to this problematic is to "keep historians and critics in the colleges of letters and sciences and split off the creators and performers. The two groups do not mix well."[19] Schwab, a father of curriculum theory, would have had a fit. He speaks directly to this problem when he asks:

> What will teachers need to know and...do in order to enable students to discriminate and appropriately connect the insights of artists, the accounts of historians.[20]

Indeed, the phenomenon of academic and practical theatre courses existing "side by side" but not integrated, is fascinating, particularly because instructors repeatedly assert that their practice is grounded by the desire to combine their interest in theory and practice. The teaching of theatre was premised on the "recognition that it draws together several academic disciplines"; "it unites academic and practical work, relates pure research to production and unites vocation and avocation in the most satisfying way"; "I wanted to encourage students to see the connections and interplay among various aspects of theatre and drama," and "to combine my intellectual and practical interests."

Given these acknowledgements, what more do we "need to know," in order to create a context that will ensure that courses and programmes enable students to "discriminate" and make "connections?" How does one assess whether our idiosyncratic choices have been creative ones — at any educational level, within a set curriculum or outside of one. In a paper delivered for the International Symposium on Drama Education Research, at O.I.S.E., in May, 1989, I looked to the body of literature on creativity and giftedness to find some answers. This discipline acknowledges the place of theatre/drama students, by definition, insofar as arts students who have chosen to enroll in, or audition for placement in a theatre/drama programme, will demonstrate a capability for high performance, achievement or potential ability in the "visual or performing arts". further, arts students may also be identified as gifted/talented students insofar as they may reflect an "advanced or accelerated function" through their creative ability.[21] The value of this research is twofold: first, the literature not only provides an extensive analysis of creativity, but it also establishes a revealing portrait of the creative (gifted) individual.[22] The characteristics that emerge repeatedly in these studies, served to confirm my own experience with theatre/drama students, generally, and supported the curricular decisions I had made in the attempt to meet their differentiated needs.

Barbara Clark's work was particularly appealing — and useful — for providing an integrated concept of creativity from which to assess how to "start from where" arts students "are."[23] For not only does her synthesis of the major orientations in creative research make accessible a wide range of approaches, but it complements the holisitc view of education integral to developmental drama. Clark also provided a "creativity circle" model, which focused upon charting the full range of creative orientations. In the attempt to thrust Clark's model into a three-dimensional mode and, implicitly, to account for the essential dynamic between teacher and student, I found it necessary to introduce two additional layers to her paradigm. The first new layer was designed to illustrate the actual characteristics and needs of theatre/drama students, by extrapolation; further, it corresponded directly (both aesthetically and theoretically) to Clark's thinking, feeling, intuitive and sensing functions. Finally, in order to develop a fully integrated, non-linear model, I recorded the attributes of the **teacher**, or the qualities of teaching, that are considered essential to the development of the creative student. This sphere, too, is designed to correspond specifically to the four functions she originally illustrated. Way's circular model of "facets of the person" might be interesting to examine in juxtaposition to this expanded creativity circle, as would a detailed look at Heathcote's thresholds.[24] Thus, I refer you to Clark's categories of creativity (which seem to echo Jungian typology), if only to provide you with a touchstone for reflecting on the responsiveness of your curriculum choices.[25]

One's perspective on a generalized profile of creative theatre/ drama students can be given depth by a recognition of the role of the arts, specifically. As such, Tannenbaum's distinctions of four categories of talent become central. His definition of "surplus talents" has been developed in order to accommodate the place of artists in society. It is a definition which provides one with the ability to view the specific needs and creative work of artists, in a context that helps to define the explorations of a student of theatre/drama, in particular. Consequently, it is essential that the creativity of theatre/drama students be perceived by the instructor (primary, secondary or tertiary) as an expression of their "cravings for ways to enhance the quality of life."[26] For, if their "surplus talent" is viewed as "precious in an intrinsic sense," then their creativity must be understood to acquire value on a wholly existential level. If theatre/drama students are striving to create meaning in order to "sweep away meaninglessness," then the instructor must be cognizant of a responsibility for nurturing their path toward discovering this significant meaning.[27]

It was a crooked path, this journeying. Academic improvisation, as it were. And its momentum was carried forward by my reflections on the body of creativity research. I humoured myself by imagining that, in my search to account for meaningful curricula, I was exhibiting all those attributes of the creative individual delineated in the expanded Clark model. Crooked too, because how was I to know that these reflections on curriculum would translate into such a personal journey of my own practice; crooked again, because I had failed to anticipate where the next bend in the road would take me. For suddenly, Schwabian demands for discrimination and appropriate connections, Clark's integrative perspective, Tannenbaum's emphasis on the creation of meaning, and my own narrative, all conspired to make the notion of integration the first expression of an **explicit** set of criteria for framing curriculum. David Booth describes what is essentially the integrative drama process, and its significance to curriculum:

> The primary aim of drama should be to help children extract new meaning from their experience and to communicate those meanings in the form of efficient, coherent responses. In this sense, drama is both a subject matter and a teaching approach of inherent value to the school curriculum.[28]

Thus, an integrated programme has the capacity to provide the student with the means of re-interpreting curriculum, reframing their experience and discovering meaning. We can — and do — practice this in the confines of individual developmental drama courses; Courtney names the phenomenon, mediation. It is inherent to Heathcote. And in my own experience as a parent, it is what I cherish for my children. I am humbled, and taught, by my children's pre-school classes, which serve as examples of integration lived. Noah and Samahra play it; draw it; paint and cut it; they story it; they learn about mathematics and science because of it; they dance and sing it. It is curriculum where those essential elements of interrelationships and reciprocity are valued; it is curriculum where the relationship of their inner world to their outer world is engaged metaphorically.[29] Thus, we have accessible, precious models of **where** it works. This is the stuff that dreams are made on, indeed. But again, failing to see curriculum as an ontological process, we seem to move through our educational system — from primary to secondary, and finally to the university — abandoning this metaphorical process more and more, with each passing grade.

> Metaphor is important for learning in a variety of ways. There is a genuine need to construct effective classroom techniques that make use of memorable imagery. As root metaphors vary with culture, they can teach us much about our multicultural world. Imagining also relates to the promotion of creativity; contemporary schools are in real need of the power of active metaphor to stimulate innovative and expressive thought.[30]

Thus, when I bring my bias to bear on university theatre/drama programmes, where (with a few exceptions) integration is all but completely dismissed, I must inevitably pose some hard questions. Can you tell me what your programme's second year performance class has to do with the fourth year playwriting class or a third year developmental drama class? Schwab vehemently contends that no programme grounded in "but one subject can possibly be adequate or defensible"; it can "be nothing but incomplete and doctrinaire."[31] My research reveals that part of the problem is the failure of instructors (and by extension, departments) to reflect on their own teaching practice. *The State of the Art Review of Research in Curriculum and Instruction,* reports that it is "somewhat ironical that as academics [at the university level] we advocate a scientific approach to learning...while omitting from scrutiny our own curricular practices."[32] If we fail to provide an interactive curriculum, we simply cannot hope or assume that students will inherit the power to integrate. Rather, I believe that we must accept responsibility for providing strategies for integration; responsibility for giving our students the means with which to engage in metaphorical thought, to synthesize, to nurture their meaning making. Integration could happen at a variety of levels either as a part of the first, second and third years, respectively, and/or at the conclusion of a programme, and it is essential to the dynamic between student and supervisor at the graduate level. Indeed, there is almost something immoral about its absence in our curricula, about our denial of this form of mentoring. However, the need for integration in curriculum does **not** vitiate the students' role in assuming responsibility for their own learning; clearly, that must remain a requisite. But it does direct us to review the significance of the extrapolated version of Clark's "creativity circle"; precisely because it provides an immediate, holisitic, visual paradigm from which to begin to assess what role the instructor can assume in providing the mentorship that, as Bloom suggests, is so essential to students.

The Promptbook: A Record of Practice

Because I am bound to examine the history of my own curricular practice, I find that I must specifically address the "fork in the road": that is how I must describe the distinction between a conception of curriculum for one's own unique classroom, and its extension, a vision of curriculum which is a comprehensive conception of theatre/drama programmes. Yet, these two conceptions are intimately connected; ultimately, one should never be viewed without reference to the other.

Just as Peter Slade distinguished forms of play, by describing "**Personal Play**" (in which the whole person or self is used) and "**Projected Play**" (the internal drama is projected outside the body),[33] I borrow his typology to help frame my experience. Thus, my reflections irrevocably lead down intersecting paths of "**Personal Curriculum**" (curriculum development for an individual course) and "**Projected Curriculum**" (curriculum for the whole of a department). I look back at my own faculty meetings in which, occasionally and briefly, the latter reared its head. But notions of holistic curriculum never stayed on the table very long. There were more pressing issues to solve: R. is going on sabbatical, who can teach his courses; we will have six graduating students who want to take the the fourth year directing class, but, although it is on the books as a requirement, and we must offer it, we have no faculty to teach it, no money in the budget to hire even a part-time instructor for it; we have to decide on our production season — what kinds of scripts do we want to select; but we have only three men to 12 women. It never seems to end, and one can just hear echoes, again, of "drama departments have failed to see their own curricula as an ontological process." Had a curriculum mandate been in place, it would have served to inform all those crises. But, like my colleagues, I was blind to the importance of developing a curriculum that was integrated and visionary. Thus, the value of my journey is evidenced by inquiry that has become an active rather than passive process. For with the opportunity to "re-make a part of (my) practice world" I would now urge a department from a position of advocacy: "we **must** take the time to make choices about our programme's curriculum."

In contrast, its double — my version of the "personal curriculum" — still seems to hold up to scrutiny, despite having been plagued by doubt (another form of the darkness of the journey). The research on creativity and curriculum served to reinforce my belief that my artistic decisions in teaching had intuitively, been good ones. The recollection of gatekeepers and the subsequent collegial negotiations described earlier, had only occurred because I had initiated some sense of accountability in the development of our respective curricula. I persisted in asking that those of us teaching the same course should meet at least once every two weeks. And I continued this practice (though undoubtedly it had originated, in part, because of my own uncertainties as a "novice" university teacher) because of the integrity it gave our choices, until the day I departed — seven years later.

I have also come to believe that when I had failed in the classroom, they were honest failures, borne of risks I willingly took. Paradoxically, it was precisely those risks — and subsequent successes — that led me to discontentment. My praxis had evolved; my curriculum had become obsolete, unbeknownst to me. At that time, the world making I did in the classroom was structured by a dedication to process. Like for so many other teachers, performance/product ends in those days were verboten. I had, after all, spent many pre-Dalhousie years explaining to parents my idea of theatre. Now, it seems almost a cliché, though its truth survives: "no, they were not going to see their 10-year-old in a play; theatre was the art form, yes, but we were exploring the possibilities of theatre to develop their child — the whole child — for living life itself." "Yes, I think your child has talent, but we are more concerned with his imaginative life, his ability to make sense of his world." "No, I can't recommend an acting class, but would you like to see his drawings, the scene she wrote herself, the mask he built?"

In Schon's terms, my movement away from a wholly process-oriented practice, was the result of my own reflection on reflection-in-action (the thinking about the process of remaking our practice world). I was hungry to move beyond the games; to construct and play with "new categories of understanding, strategies of action, and ways of framing problems."[34] I grew frustrated and tired with teachers who came to me with tales of drama classes in which they asked their students to be a tree. I hated "be a tree"; to this day, I cringe when I hear someone preparing this kind of a lesson plan. Albeit that this is a specific response to the attempt to move beyond the inherent limitations of a set curriculum; however, it does not begin to meet the needs of a curriculum which must create conditions for sweeping "away meaninglessness," conditions for creating significant meaning. There is more to the improv or game than that! "Be a tree" is **not** a game; and it is a game; it is about being and becoming — and how do I **teach** that, really teach it? That is to say, **how** do I do it: how do I teach the practical issues of setting up an effective improv in class; and how do I do it to **them**: how do I teach my students to understand the vision that must accompany the game; the gestalt of developmental drama, as it were; the bones and tissues and skeleton of all their choices and subsequent action as teachers.

Somehow, these two different issues are more than the sum of their parts, more urgent than praxis. It is another manifestation of the metaphorical. Consequently, I needed to get at this "be a tree" stuff, this being and becoming from different dimensions — both in practice and in theory. The implications and reverberations don't stop there — into the fire. "Be a tree" is a single medium of an ontological process and it is, at once, an invitation to the ritual of theatre itself. Today, my curriculum choices are different because I recognize explicitly that just as each level of awareness is like the proverbial stripping of the player's mask, so the actual practice of the game can be repeated forever. Because if we are seeking meaning, then each time we approach the work, our context (the changing expressions of the mask, perhaps a new mask, perhaps our face) will allow us the opportunity to discover a new depth, to expose the three-dimensionality of the game. Further, if the contextual delivery of curriculum is paramount, then playing in the territory of performance can also become revealing; both process and product become viable tools for learning in the classroom. I discovered that accommodating "both the uniqueness of the individual and the specificity of the context" was also critical for John McLeod.[35] His assessment of the value of the Arts Propel journal work, corresponds directly to my perspective on the use of theatre forms:

> ...the finished work is placed in the context of an artistic
> process. The debate between process and product
> which has plagued the arts for years, consequently
> ceases to be relevant.[36]

Moreover, exploring the development of a meaningful curriculum from the two counterpoints of "how do I do it" and "how do I do it to them," invests curriculum with a vitality that will not only serve the students' context, but the teachers' as well. It is a treacherous precipice: because creating conditions for significant meaning in the classroom **is** negotiation. A delicate and elemental battle between teacher-as-learner and teacher-as-teacher, as it were; between context and curriculum; between student and teacher; mask and face; eternal I and thou's.

Rehearsal: Professional Development

It was because of these kinds of fundamental and incessant questions, that I began to reframe my explorations in developmental drama and theatre. I knew I couldn't look to any type of in-service programmes that were in place in Halifax; these were in their inception and I felt that my development required more depth and rigour. Consequently, my solution was to aggressively seek professional development in a Theatre milieu — to return to that ritual of theatre itself. Uncertain but determined, I called Equity Showcase Theatre in Toronto to find out about their classes, because they had earned the reputation as "a powerhouse in Canadian Theatre training."[37] I got more than I bargained for: for the first time, Equity Showcase was offering the Canadian theatre community an "International Theatre Congress," with the co-operation of the International Theatre Institute, The Goethe Institute, and Ryerson Polytechnic Institute. It was described by both Canada Council and the Ontario Arts Council as a "cultural event of national character and significance."[38] The intention of the congress was "to bring together 25 great theatre innovators, international master teachers, directors and performing companies" to work with a core group of 42 artists, participating full-time for a period of six weeks. Limited places were made available for part-time participation.[39] In addition, the congress included weekly colloquia and a public component, the presentation of five internationally acclaimed productions (which were Canadian premieres).

I had been warned that Equity Showcase might not want to accept my application because I wasn't a professional. But armed with a c.v. that attested to my commitment to theatre, and letters of recommendations from professionals, I presented what I thought to be a strong case. Dammit, I explained, I am a professional teacher: if I don't have the opportunity to learn alongside the artists, to experience — both academically and in practice — the cutting edge of theatre, how could I function effectively? I had a whole generation of students in my hands — future performers or audience or teachers — and I am the foundation of their learning, the source of my own artistry. They let me enroll. They probably thought that the workshops would kill me and they'd be done with me, and they would have been right! So for six weeks in the summer of 1983, I worked my mind and my body harder than I had ever done in my life; and at the very least, it changed the texture of my classes forever.

It is difficult to give you a taste of that experience, to articulate its impact on my teaching and learning. Perhaps that is one reason why among university faculty, there seems to be a reticence, or an apathy, about sharing the secrets of our practice. May 16, 1983: it began with workshops run by South American, Victoria Santa Cruz. These were daunting, because her demand for precise attention to detail and rhythm, inspired one to try to do the work with utter perfection. From her I learned how rhythm creates an internal and external narrative, rhythm and response, with body and soul wholly integrated; "taste the conflict", she would charge. With MTM (mimoteatromovimento), the *commedia* group from Italy, I not only did vocal work and character exploration — from improvisational to formal representations of the range of stock *commedia* characters — but, woe is me, their training also included a whole series of physical work: somersaults, flips, handstands etc. This may not sound extraordinary, but I had not done a somersault since I was 5 years old, and handstands et al., were completely out of the question. By the end of those two weeks I could somersault backward. Not beautifully, but backwards!

Even the optional daily morning warm-ups led by Ellen Pierce, had something to teach me about use of space, relaxation that was authentic, not contrived, and the creation of group work. Michele George is perhaps one of the greatest treasures living right in our midst; from her I learned something about the power of one's spirit to speak simply in performance, when it is supported by a tacit knowing or truth. Through her text work which focused on the power of words to take you and let go, to the improvisations which create a complete universe in their quiet passion and intensity, to the centrality of song. She and director Steven Kent also introduced me to the practice of the "check-in" and "check-out"; these rituals, which took place (for approximately 10 minutes) immediately before and after the work, not only framed our experience, but it served to make individual reflection a part of the very process of the workshop, and as such, each voice in the class became significant.

But not all of my experience was positive. I was particularly distressed by the action of a leading avant garde Swedish group from the Institute For Stage Art. Unlike the playfulness inherent in the *commedia*'s physical work, what they demanded brought me face to face with the breath of God — it was absolutely threatening to our physical well-being. We all knew who had had the Swedes workshop by the way people willed their legs to negotiate the stairs, descending very slowly and in great pain, even after the first "light" day of work. Ultimately, I believe their work was barren, not because of its physical dangers, but because they made no attempt to connect it to the context of our lives. This entry in my journal was dated June 3, 1983 and was titled *Swedish Thighs*:

> ...response to them immediate and generative. I suddenly realize that with each day, each instructor, a new sense of perception is triggered. These recognitions have not been an act of will; rather, the realization about theatre or teaching will simply occur and subsequently I recognize its presence. Initially, fear, incredible-I-can't-do-that...with the Swedes, it is the doing and the pain. And awareness of danger. But still the doing. And fear. heart rendering. terrified. paralyzing. sobs rising from somewhere I rarely touch. I worked so hard to control it. And I willed myself to return the next day. Tears — why? because I wanted, desperately needed, the release. And I felt so alone; isolated by emotions hidden, discoveries silent. And most importantly, I have learnt the need to be more demanding and at once more gently with my students. To recognize each barrier and the passing through.

And Santa Cruz's exhortation to us came back strong and hard. "Don't do my games. The rhythm is ours; the games mine." Not play the games? I had come to Toronto to find just these kinds of treasures; are you nuts? Only at the end of the congress — with many participants becoming daily casualties (almost always spiritual, tears or anger) — did I recognize why: because of the depth of the touching, the potential for hurt, and the capacity for learning.

Nevertheless, I discovered that I was tempted to break a cardinal rule; another manifestation of the "Heathcote-syndrome." This syndrome is found in that moment when my students, who studied Heathcote's teaching, wanted to rush right out and be Dorothy! It was a testament to her practice, but it don't work that way. I caught myself up short. And so I did not do the games till months later, when they became mine. Santa Cruz, Michele George, and later, John O'Neill's storytelling, Stephen Kent's improvisational artistry, and Joseph Chaikin's delicate and sensitive text/scene work. My journal had recorded hundreds of hours of workshops, that would ultimately yield not merely hours of classes, but rather years of work. Even the two-week workshop with Eugenio Barba (director of the world-famous Odin Teatret), though brutal, I wouldn't have missed for the world. It was said that those of us who took that fourteen-hour-per-day workshop were Barba-qued. Believe it. But I am still learning from his organic work, his particular, context-bound montage theatre — building relationships and marrying them to what he called "serendipity."

Clearly, I devoured the stuff; but I did not embrace everything: I was involved in the workshops with a very particular want. I was searching for ways to create significant meaning in my classes and some of the work left me cold or angry (in fact, the Barba workshop was so distasteful, I abandoned it one day — I needed brief respite — in order to spend the day with Chaikin. The contrast between the ferocity of the one approach and the gentleness of the other was remarkable). Some of the workshops seemed to provide a means of breaking down the work, actor, student, but never focused upon the necessary rebuilding process or transformation. I don't mean to suggest a fairy tale, mind you; transformation doesn't mean we live happily ever after, just that we are empowered to keep working. But even my strong negative reaction was revealing; it helped me to identify what it seemed to me really mattered, that which had integrity and depth; that which intrinsically had the capacity to turn the individual inside out in the search for some kind of truth. And I pursued this want, informed by intuition and a kind of tacit knowing of what I needed for me and what I must endeavor to bring back home to Dalhousie.

I find it extraordinary that it has taken me seven years to truly understand the significance of the congress. I had been emersed in a wholly creative environment; their meaning making exposed me to so many different conceptions and forms of theatre, to the extent that it had exploded my repertoire of skills and experience, my sense of artistic value. Each instructor was a world-class master teacher or director; but further, these disciplined artists had an acute awareness of each other's work and strengths. They would come to see each other's classes; they would refer to each other in the context of their own work. They engaged us in their process of "sweeping away the meaninglessness"; they extended themselves beyond the particulars of their own work and idiosyncratic (though valuable) approaches, to explore and reflect on the significance of artistic action. And they exploded my sense of values by offering a healthy balance to traditional naturalistic theatre and, by providing me with the opportunity to do exactly what Booth named as inherent to curriculum: helping the student to "extract new meaning from their experience."

The artistic coherence of the congress — the integration of workshops, colloquia and productions — allowed me to transcend the map, and **begin** to address the territory![40] I dare say that it provided exactly the kind of curriculum we are lacking at the university. Moreover, the experience of the congress underlines the the importance of bringing professionals into the university. Equity Showcase was clearly aware of this possibility, for their planning report specifically stated that the "new skills" acquired by performers and directors through participation in the congress would allow them to function as "teaching resource(s) to their colleagues in their future work."[41]

Further, university theatre/drama faculty seem to recognize the benefit of inviting the profession into their departments. For, to date, questionnaire respondents express that the motivation for bringing in guest instructors is "to provide students and faculty with opportunity to collaborate with recognized artists presently in the field and to support the artistic community"; "top ranking professional theatre people...can maintain a link between the university and the professional world and provide both quality and variety to the department"; "they have expertise I don't possess"; "they can offer special skills, special insights"; and "to give students the advantage of learning a wide variety of approaches and methods". Indeed, I must agree that their vision and artistry can only serve to enrich the curriculum.

Scene Study: Emergent Philosophy

Clearly, revelation has not come quickly or easily to me. This fundamental understanding of the significance of the congress has been built on a succession of insights. And my reflections on curriculum are, in part, the story of those pieces. "We know more than we can tell"[42] was the process of my discoveries that summer; but the tacit dimension of my knowing had yet to be integrated with my actual experience — my practical knowledge — of teaching in the classroom.

That is why it took me months to make use of the now reinvented games in my courses (and rehearsals). Those discoveries had to be reframed contextually. And that movement was sometimes accomplished with elegance and ease; sometimes by difficult adaptation and redefinition of my exercises and objectives. It was the process of creating a meaningful relationship between theatre and my classes; not only replaying the continuum between theatre and developmental drama (devotion to Slade, Way, Courtney, Heathcote, Spolin, Johnstone intact), but also exploring the relationship between these counterpoints and the specifics of my students' multiple realities. I wanted to develop some kind of a dynamic — so that the relationship itself could evolve into a practice that was collective and which addressed the context of my students' lives. And this journey has proven to be an enduring one.

Thus, the congress served as a touchstone for artistic research that not only informed my practice, but my art. And it was only the first (though the most profound) of numerous workshops I continue to seek out. If I was at all uncertain about the necessity of this kind of professional development, Courtney, Booth, Emerson and Kuzmich point to its significance. The study explains that:

the crux of an arts teacher's practical knowledge lies in two types of skills: skill as a teacher, and skill as an artist. At the secondary level, these skills can only be obtained by the teacher with specialist arts qualifications; when the teacher does not have these skills, then the student does not receive comprehensive arts experiences and, in some cases, appropriate knowledge and/or techniques. At the elementary level, these skills are equally required for a teacher's practical knowledge; if the generalist teacher does not have them, then it is essential to have good resource people who can support and/or implement these programmes.[43]

Although they are addressing themselves primarily to an examination of elementary arts teachers, I believe that their findings about practical knowledge can be applied equally to the teaching of theatre at the university level. However, one of the difficulties here lies in the awareness that there is no "reward" or acknowledgement for "skill as a teacher," per se, in a university milieu. Although I by no means wish to diminish the significance of the university's mandate for research, promotions and tenure are never secured on the basis of "teaching skill" criterion; moreover, nor are these "rewards" denied on the basis of a **lack** of skill in the classroom. Thus, on the one hand, there is no incentive to urge university teachers to engage in professional development, if they, themselves, don't feel the need to do so; and on the other, it again reinforces the notion of bringing artists into universities and schools (for example, the Ontario Arts Council's "Artists in the Schools" programme).

Further, the attempt to create a vital dynamic in my courses was made difficult by my recognition that my curriculum **had** to emerge from issues revealed in the classroom. It was the pedagogy I lived by, though I would have certainly hesitated to name it that. If you had asked me if a philosophy of arts education was being generated in the process of curriculum making, I would have told you, no. In retrospect, and in light of my research on curriculum, and as a reflective practitioner, I do believe that is exactly what was evolving. Indeed, *No One Way of Being* also speaks directly to this tacit theory-building:

These teachers "philosophize" innovatively about arts education, particularly in their own spheres of interest. But they may not necessarily have developed fully-fledged "philosophies." Their practical knowledge gives them the capacity to articulate why arts education is important to them: to speak of the issues that **emerge** from what happens in the classroom. On the other hand, they do not normally operate from a specific theoretical basis. Rather, they "philosophize" from theoretic emergents that arise from their experience and the intuitive mode.[44]

My work was grounded in a concern for the contextual delivery of curriculum — the second explicit criteria I've come to acknowledge — and a fundamental belief in a design which holds, at its heart, creative questioning and problem-solving. In this way, **everything** I did in the classroom became particular. Curriculum was, in essence, designed by virtue of a dialogue between me (my experience, practical knowledge, and thresholds) and my students (laden with all the luggage they must inevitably carry with them). Blood and guts teaching, I called it. And that it was: wholly "on-call," willingly subject to the interest and expertise of every student who entered my class.

Significantly, I am not a renaissance woman. As such, the invitation to integrate curriculum and their lives, meant that there were many times when I had to respond by saying "I don't know, but if that is what you want to explore, let's find out." Together, we would generate an armful of ideas for research, and when the meeting concluded, I would set about marshalling my contacts and resources and my own capacity for facing that Deweyian "problematic." And, in part, this is the source of the vitality and risk of teaching: the adventure would always begin anew because each student is particular.

I recognize that this approach to curriculum building is not necessarily ideal, because of the possibility of (and the politics of) creating a completely fragmented class. However, insofar as each student was confronted with the demands of responding to a experiential curriculum by preparing contextual workshops, maskwork, storytelling, scene work and a "symphony" (my title for a multiarts assignment), and we were all witness to it, the specificity became community; the individual focus became a kind of cultural literacy in which we all shared. Teacher-as-learner: I had to consciously work at flexibility and at once, to allow myself to function as master teacher; strict yet open; allowing dissent and seeking compromise; personal, yet maintaining distance. It was a constant game of craps, I suppose.

> If pupils are to grasp concepts, understand complex issues, solve problems and work creatively and co-operatively in drama, they will be helped by a clearly established context and a strong but flexible framework to support and extend the meaning of the work.[45]

My students, especially in the later years (I did it better, I hope), seemed to make extraordinary gains. But they did not do so easily. While the problems I set for them were always rigourous in their structure, they were completely open in content. Initially, I think I was shocked by student response: "tell me what you want; how do I solve this?" Clearly, this was not curriculum delivered in a transmission mode.[46] That familiar territory — of mirroring one's instructor — was a useless strategy here; they could not read me, because what I wanted was something only **they** could provide. "But I won't get it right"; there was no wrong. They, too, needed to learn to risk, and as such, mentorship and modelling again become significant. The classroom, in essence, became a ritual space in which contextual curriculum allowed the students the opportunity to "mediate forms that have specific relations to meanings," to experience transforming and reconstructing reality.[47]

But I must confess that I am no teacher-saint. There was such a thing as mistakes — I couldn't abide laziness, superficiality or lack of commitment. And I let them know it. And so their initial response to a contextual curriculum was similar to the initial reaction to the classic puzzle in which one is asked to draw four straight lines through nine dots without retracing and without lifting pen from paper. How do we (**both** teachers and students) creatively approach problems? How do we handle limitations? How do we avoid inventing restrictions that don't exist? How do we work through imposing too many fictitious boundaries, limitations and constraints and hence fail to find solutions? To this day, former students will call to ask about "those games we played that March; I want to use them with my class." I simply cannot answer them. For while my own journals are full of the games, exercises and scene work compiled over the years, I cannot re-create the context for them. I don't know how we used that exercise in November 1986, what it was about (for that individual or group), or where I was trying to move them. And in any case, my recollection of its power may be totally different from theirs. This was the consequence of neglecting to do the journal work, an essential but ungraded component of my curriculum. Consequently, we would have to deal directly with the given circumstances of this class, if I would be able to function as a resource for them.

Thus, I can only trust that my courses reflected the philosophic approach that "drama is the dramatic process in life as a whole, and theatre is the art form of that process."[48] With this basic tenet, Courtney calls for the establishment of university theatre/drama curricula in which the "student can explore his own dramatic nature", both as self and other, as "process-actor and as art-actor."[49] Thus, the creation of meaning implicit in Tannenbaum's assessment of the intrinsic value of "surplus talent" is given primacy by Courtney's insistence that instructors can establish "knowledge in" dramatic action. Clearly, I am compelled to agree that this "whole form of knowledge," knowledge which is intuitive and hands-on, is essential for structuring a curriculum which provides creative opportunities for experiencing significant meaning.

Ironically, as I continued my inquiry, I recognized that — now buried in academia — I was starved for precisely this kind of hands-on expression. And the absurdity of my dilemma rests in the awareness that even my own graduate programme neglects "whole forms of knowledge" in its practice. I discovered balance in the decision to build a mask. This action served as a milestone, for while I had taught mask making for almost 18 years, been midwife to hundreds of masks for my students, or for productions, I had not built a single mask for myself in all that time — not since I myself had been a student. Teacher-as-learner, she whispered.

Figure 1: This series of masks was built as an artistic response to the academic struggle to find a strong theatre curriculum.

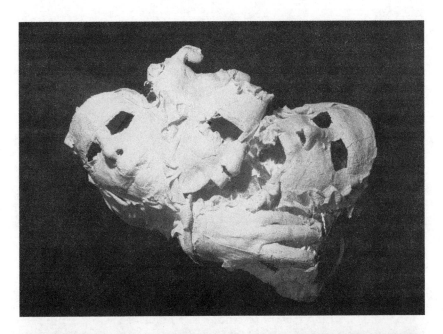

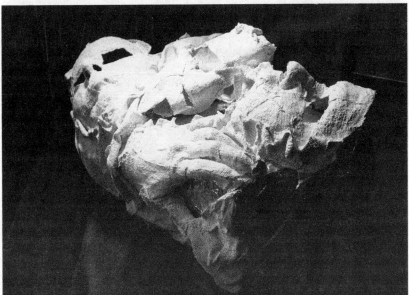

Figure 2: These masks serve as an alternate method of research of negotiating meaning through Courtney's "whole forms of knowledge."

That single mask subsequently evolved into a series of masks, manifestations (again) of transformation and mediation, integration and metaphorical world making. They served as a form of substitution, research in another medium; an alternate method of negotiating the search for curriculum, for meaning in my own work.

Roleplay: The Function of the University

Ultimately, the creation of the masks functioned to direct my research toward a specific analysis of the relationship between artistry and academia. My own experience at Dalhousie taught me that the place of arts in a university is somewhat controversial. The annual ordeal of filing out the "boast sheets" (as they were fondly called) made the issue patently obvious. These forms were the university's accounting system, used to assess its faculty's accomplishments. And to that end, we were asked to list our current research, published papers or books, contributions to conferences and the like.

This criteria is largely inappropriate because, as artists, our research is undertaken in the theatre or studio; our published work is the performance for director, actor, technical director, stage manager, critic and playwright alike. And in my questionnaire respondents are making certain that I am aware of it. Thus, the recognition of the uniqueness of artistry in an academic milieu does not preclude research responsibilities; rather, it simply translates the notion of research differently. As such, the university should ideally serve as a kind of sacred ground for theatre/drama programmes (not unlike the ritual space of my classroom). If theatre is to function in a university, it must demand the same privileges as a laboratory scientist or literary researcher. Alternately, it is the responsibility of the programme — acting, technical, general or educational streams — to explore, to experiment, to develop new techniques, to rediscover neglected work — in short, to perform the theatrical equivalent to basic research. Yale's Robert Brustein suggests that "the practical applications of this research might not be immediately apparent, but it was the university's responsibility to provide the facilities, tools and tolerant atmosphere to permit such work to proceed".[50]

The need to inform the mind and the imagination in order to create curricula that provides an organic relationship between artistry and academia, speaks directly to the necessity of bringing artists into the university, once again — as sources for primary research. The Equity Showcase Congress was an extraordinary event, not only in my life, but for Canadian theatre as a whole. In practice, its impact may have been revealed by the number of graduate students that entered our universities, subsequent to the congress. Yet, no new productions or companies sprung up in response to it; in the commercially vital theatre of Toronto, this congress found no home. Thus, in order to nurture remarkable research, we **must** look to the sacred ground of the university theatre/drama programmes. We also needs to recognize that its mandate must include a commitment to provide a synthesis between past and future, between tradition and experiment, text and performance, process and product. As such, those "piecemeal" programmes are bound to fail. Teaching academic theatre courses without approaching its relationship to theatre practice is not only little better than the "educational garage sale" described earlier, but it has the potential to create curriculum that is invulnerable to new ideas and therefore in danger of becoming a "museum"; and further, Brustein (reminiscent of Schwab) believes that developing theatre courses that "pull themselves out of history" could result in classes becoming "insular, narcissistic, self-absorbed."[51] Consequently, once again I am bound to question how a university department can function effectively without cohesiveness and a well-articulated aesthetic — a contextual, creative curriculum.

Essentially, I am confronted here with the most basic of questions: how do university theatre/drama departments define themselves? Without definition, what hope do we have of initiating contextual curriculum? The *Black Report* stated that many university theatre departments do not declare "the intent of their programmes," and that many seemed uncertain — even confused — about their own mandate (e.g., whether they were actually a professional training programme or not).[52] If one juxtaposed this conclusion against Jean-Louis Roux's statement, 11 years later, that "the number of theatre departments in colleges and universities has increased spectacularly,"[53] one senses a profound need to question. By implication, I would suggest that Roux would urge these departments to re-examine and redefine their role, in light of the National Theatre School's quest to do so. Particularly, to explore how they differ from these departments National Theatre School, given that, unlike NTS, they are housed in a university. Finally, this re-examination should also be undertaken "in light of the need to respond to changes in the theatre community and the general public."[54]

Definition was also the focus of a commentary in the *Globe and Mail* entitled "One Last Curtain Call."[55] In its presentation of the arts at the close of the decade, the article suggested that if Canada does not learn "to protect and nurture its indigenous arts and culture, we'd soon be Americans, or worse."[56] In part, Fawcett believes that this is a consequence of the "curatorial senility that has been growing in our universities since the mid-seventies."[57] Further, he cries out for Canadian artists to face the "public and private reality" of doing much more than providing faint echoes of the status quo. Cannot the same sentiment be addressed to our entire educational system in Theatre and Drama? For it is a call to arms for vision. Precisely what we lack at the post-secondary level. If — as Fawcett provocatively suggests — the arts and artists exist so that we can all reflect "without the lies made necessary by expedience" on exactly who we are, what we are and what we are up against, then the need for contextual, integrated curriculum becomes urgent. We need to hold up that mirror with "a lot more vigor — and daring." He admonishes us to make choices: the challenge is to choose (like Brustein) between:

> those elements that remain active and valuable, and those that, with regrets, we can consign to the museums. We made no choices at all. Another decade of protecting the past and resisting change will land both the arts and the artists permanently in the museum's back room, with the milk pails and the butter churns.[58]

So what are theatre/drama departments — and individual instructors — supposed to do about it? I am beginning to understand what works for me, but to date, I am at a loss to provide a definitive answer. Indeed, that may be the point: there may **not** be a curriculum design that fits each of the 27 theatre/drama programmes in Canadian universities. But at the very least, begin the inquiry. My journey returns me again and again to the notions of context, integration and vision. These reflections have served to redefine the very notion of "bloody good teacher." Thus, for all our theatre/drama classrooms, at the primary, secondary or tertiary level, reflection-in-action might be replayed as curriculum-in-action, as it were. Fawcett addresses himself specifically to the arts and individual artists, but his commentary here, is also dead right for us:

> There is no easy answer... We can begin by raising our eyes from the ragged formalist lily-pads we're fighting over, and looking beyond the pond.[59]

Endnotes

1. Brian Way, *Development Through Drama* (New York: Humanities Press, 1967), p. 8.
2. W.H. Schubert, "Educationally Recovering Dewey in Curriculum," paper presented at the Annual AERA Meeting. sponsored by the John Dewey Society, Washington, D.C., April 1987, p. 27.
3. H. Bowen, "A Catalog of Goals of Higher Education," in *Missions of the College Curriculum* (San Francisco: Jossey-Bass Publishers, 1978).
4. R. Axelrod, in C. Conrad, *The Undergraduate Curriculum: A Guide o Innovation and Reform* (Boulder: Westview Press, Inc., 1978).
5. C. Conrad, *The Undergraduate Curriculum: A Guide to Innovation and Reform* (Boulder: Westview Press, Inc., 1978), p. 77.

6. M.P. Maxwell, "The Arts Curriculum and University Reform," in Shere, W. & Duhamel, R. (eds.), *Academic Futures: Prospects for Post-Secondary Education* (Toronto: OISE Press, 1987), p. 95.
7. Ibid.
8. Ibid., p. 96.
9. M.C. Wittrock (ed.), *Handbook on Research on Teaching* (New York: McMillan Publishing Co., 3rd edition, 1986), p. 912.
10. R. Courtney, *The Dramatic Curriculum* (New York: Drama Book Specialists, 1980), p. 100.
11. D.J. Clandinin, "The Reflective Practitioner and Practitioners Narrative Unities," in *Canadian Journal of Education*, 11(2), 1986, and F.M. Connelly & D.J. Clandinin, "On Narrative Method, Personal Philosophy, and Narrative Unities in the Story of Teaching," in *Journal of Research in Science Teaching*, 23(4), 1986.
12. Donald Schon, *Educating the Reflective Practitioner* (San Francisco: Jossey-Bass Publishers, 1987), p. 36.
13. R. Gardner, *The Dramatic Script and Procedural Knowledge: A Key to Understanding of Dramatic Structure and a Foundation for the Development of Effective Curriculum Design in Dramatic Instruction at the Tertiary Level*, Ph.D. Thesis, University of Toronto, OISE, 1983, p. 16.
14. L. Stenhouse, *An Introduction to Curriculum Research and Development* (London: Heinemann Educational Books, 1975), p. 20.
15. Gardner, op. cit., 1983, p. 19.
16. J.S. Ackerman, "The Arts in Higher Education," in C. Kaysen (ed.) *Content and Context: Essays on College Education* (New York: McGraw Hill Book Company, 1973), p. 225.
17. Gardner, op. cit., 1983.
18. W. Shakespeare, *A Midsummer Night's Dream*, Act III, scene ii, line 4–7 (New York: Penguin Books Ltd.).
19. C. Kerr, "Introduction" in Morrison, *The Maturing of the Arts on the American Campus* (Lanham: University Press of America, 1985), p. x.
20. J.J. Schwab, "The Practical 3: Translation into Curriculum," in *School Review*, Vol. 81, 1973, p. 317.
21. Barbara Clark, *Growing Up Gifted* (Columbus: Charles E. Merrill Publishing Co., 1979), p. 5.
22. Abraham J. Tannenbaum, *Gifted Children* (New York: McMillan Publishing Co., 1983).
23. Clark, op. cit., 1979.
24. Betty Jane Wagner, *Dorothy Heathcote: Drama as a Learning Medium* (Washington: National Educational Association of the U.S., 1976), p. 32.
25. For a discussion of the extrapolated Clark model, see B. Hyman-Zatzman, "Full Circle: Nurturing a Creative Curriculum," in On-Site Proceedings of the International Symposium for Drama Education Research, OISE, May 1989.
26. Abraham J. Tannenbaum, "Giftedness: A Psycho-Social Approach," in Sternberg and Davidson (eds.), *Conceptions of Giftedness* (New York: Cambridge University Press, 1986), p. 23.
27. Ibid., p. 24.
28. David Booth, "Talking in Role, Thinking for Life," reprinted from *Drama Contact*, in the On-Site Proceedings of the International Symposium for Drama Education Research, OISE, May 1989, p. 11.

29. Richard Courtney, *Play, Drama and Thought*, 4th edition, revised (Toronto: Simon & Pierre, 1989), p. 185.
30. Ibid.
31. Schwab, op. cit., 1973, p. 306.
32. G. Tompkins, F.M. Connelly, & J.J. Bernier, "State of the Art Review of Research in Curriculum and Instruction," *SSHRC*, September 1981, p. 37.
33. Peter Slade, *Child Drama* (London: University of London Press. 1954), pp. 29–30.
34. Schon, op. cit., 1987, p. 39.
35. John McLeod, "Change and Development", in the On-Site Proceedings of the International Symposium for Drama Education Research, OISE, May 1989.
36. Ibid., p. 14. Note: The italics are mine.
37. Equity Showcase Theatre, *History and Purpose*, from an in-house document, 1982, p. 1. (Reprinted from a series of articles on Equity Showcase Theatre in the *Toronto Star*, 1982.)
38. Equity Showcase Theatre, *Project Description*, from an in-house document, 1982, p. 2.
39. Equity Showcase Theatre, *Project Description II*, from an in-house document, p. 3.
40. A. Korzybski, in Courtney, op. cit. 1989, p. 50.
41. Equity Showcase Theatre, *History and Purpose*, op. cit., 1989, p. 2.
42. M. Polyani, *The Tacit Dimension* (London: Routledge and Kegan Paul Ltd., 1966).
43. R. Courtney, D. Booth, J. Emerson, N. Kuzmich, *No One Way of Being: The Practical Knowledge of Elementary Arts Teachers in Ontario*, Research Report (Toronto: Ministry of Education, Government of Ontario, 1988), p. 26.
44. Ibid., p. 75.
45. Cecily O'Neill & Alan Lambert, *Drama Structures* (London: Century Hutchinson Ltd., 1982), p. 9.
46. J. MIller & W. Seller, *Curriculum Perspectives and Practice* (New York: Longman Inc., 1985).
47. Courtney, op. cit., 1980, p. 142.
48. Courtney, op. cit., 1980, p. 101.
49. Ibid.
50. Robert Brustein, *Making Scenes* (New York: Random House, 1981), p. 29.
51. Ibid., p. 27.
52. Canada Council, *The Report of the Committee of Inquiry into Theatre Training in Canada*, Malcolm Black, Chair, 1978, p. 38.
53. Department of Communications, Ottawa, *The Future of the National Theatre School of Canada*, Jean-Louis Roux, Chair, 1988, p. 8.
54. Ibid., pp. 8–9.
55. Brian Fawcett, "One Last Curtain Call," in *The Globe & Mail*, Arts Documentary, December 30, 1989, p. C1.
56. Ibid., p. C4.
57. Ibid.
58. Ibid.
59. Ibid.

"Liberation Now — Education Later": How Political Context Affects Curriculum Development

LYNN DALRYMPLE

Preface

At the time of writing this preface (21 April 1994) to an article originally written in 1989, South Africans are breathing more easily again. The miracle has moved on and the Inkatha Freedom Party (IFP) have decided at the eleventh hour, to join the election planned for 27–28 April 1994. Looking at the broad view at where we might have been, at the apocalyptic race war, violent extremist revolutions, vicious overthrow of the fascist state (things we once thought the future would almost inevitably contain) the tale of modern South Africa is one of miracle.

It has not been without cost but a process has been started again which should lead to the steady cooling of conflicts that have brought education in many regions in this country to a standstill. Schools have become a site of political struggle and many have stood empty in spite of the constant clamour for more and better education.

Now without doubt the system of education in South Africa will be extensively restructured and those of us who believe in the fundamental importance of the arts in education have been lobbying for their inclusion in the syllabus as general formative disciplines. The development of creativity and critical thinking will take priority over arts appreciation, and the methodology used for arts education will reflect those priorities. As set out below, the emphasis for drama will be on a pedagogy committed to building an open society, and the play making process will be a key feature of the drama syllabus. We are also lobbying intensively for all teachers to have some understanding of the use of drama as an educational tool.

237

Introduction:
"Liberation Now — Education Later?"

The catch phrase "liberation now and education later," expressive of the determination of black students in the last decade to spearhead political change in South Africa, needs to be placed in historical context. In 1953 patterns of inequality in the South African system of education were entrenched and "Bantu Education" was established for black South Africans as one of the cornerstones of apartheid. In the words of one of the architects of apartheid, Dr. Henrik Verwoed, Minister of Bantu Administration (1950–1958) and later Prime Minister (1958–1966), "there was no place for blacks in the European community above the level of certain forms of labour."[1] His government proposed to plan for more education for "blacks" than any previous government had done, but to offer "blacks" the same education as "whites," he argued, would "mislead them by showing them the green pastures of European society in which they were not allowed to graze."[2]

Running parallel to "Bantu Education" has been "Christian National Education," established for "whites" in order to prepare them for their role of running the economy and government. Hence appeared a legal entrenchment of a social phenomenon, noted in other countries, where certain schools reinforce the class and racial divisions in the society. It was out of step with the world trend — and yet, in the 1950s not so far out of step, not so strongly rejected, as it came to be when other trends emerged in the 1960s, such as the American Civil Rights Movement and the winds of change that blew away colonies in Africa.

Verwoerd's aims in establishing "Bantu Education" have, in the gradual reforming of policy, been refuted. While much of the thrust of the attempt to reform the system has been in response to a growing shortage of skilled labour, there has also been much industrial and school "unrest" and internal and external condemnation of apartheid. However, South African education retains the apartheid structures which set up the system. At the time of writing this chapter (January 1990) there are some 15 different departments of education in this country, some based in the quasi-federal states but most based in the notorious inequalities provided for different "groups" of South Africans. And, not surprisingly, the protests which have occurred since its inception, culminating in an explosion of resistance in 1976 and nationwide boycotts during the first half of the 1980s are far from over.

"Native Education" was offered prior to 1953, albeit to a small number, and was based on the premise that the acquisition of knowledge trains the mind. Then, at least, black students received enough stimulation to apply themselves to their studies and continue with self-education. While "Bantu Education" has increased the numbers of pupils dramatically, it has served to strengthen the premise that a major function of education is to perpetuate the status quo. It has provided fertile ground for radical thinkers to argue that it is impossible to change apartheid education without a revolution that will carry away the entire social system. Hence the call for "liberation before education."

Clearly, no system of education can be neutral; it must be an integral part of the social system that initiates and supports it. In South Africa the state has attempted to devise a schooling system that will maintain the power and control of a settler group over a conquered indigenous population. The Nationalist government has stressed its history of successful conquest and the superiority of a technological civilisation. When it came to power it suppressed the processes of integration taking place between different "groups" that could be seen in the arts and in languages and, indeed, in some education. Perhaps it has not been sufficiently machiavellian in its debasing of education, but the state has discovered over 40 years that it does not have the power to impose any policy without reference to what is possible in a given context. It has had to offer a recognizable system of education, achieving literacy and numeracy. Inherent in a command of a global language such as English and access to scientific concepts, is a basic "liberation" through modernization. The provision of schooling aimed at preparing young people for various kinds of labour also provides skills that give workers greater bargaining power vis-à-vis capital. The contradiction of suppression by education or education without liberation has always been recognised by black South Africans whose attitudes to schooling remain ambiguous. Clearly, schooling has not simply preserved the status quo. In addition to providing jobs and upward mobility, it has provided a means of resistance to state policies no matter how inferior it has been. Thus education is a site of struggle and is an important part of the process of change in a crisis-ridden society. As Caliban said "You taught me language and my profit is now I know how to curse you."

It is therefore not surprising as we turn the pages of contemporary history, that there are some signs that out of the crisis in education a liberatory solution may be seen to be emerging from the community itself. Although apartheid policy had attempted to undermine the status and power of students, they took it with a vengeance and in the great urban areas like Soweto, almost brought schooling, though not education, to a standstill. The 1984–85 school boycotts horrified parents, ruined the morale of teachers, and showed what the slogan "liberation now and education later" might bring about. As a result the National Education Crisis Committee (NEEC) was formed at a conference hosted by the Soweto Parent's Crisis Committee on December 28 and 29, 1985 in Johannesburg. The NECC came up with a new slogan: People's Education for People's Power.

Although the committee was effectively immobilized by the detention of many of its leaders and the subsequent forcing of others into hiding, the seeds of a mass-based education programme inseparable from a non-racial democracy in South Africa were sown. This alternative system of education seeks to empower oppressed South Africans while instilling the principles of democracy. Alternative schools were out of the question but an alternative course content was not. It was with this in mind that the National Education Crisis Committee sent out a "back to school" call and resolved to implement people's education programmes wherever possible. The 1985 student slogan "liberation before education" was replaced with "education for liberation." This change signalled a shift in emphasis from a suspension of education in the midst of open warfare to a strategy of emancipatory education.

This chapter explores the potential of drama to make a contribution to the changes that are needed in education in South Africa. After a brief historical survey of drama teaching in South Africa, the impact of political changes on the development of a drama curriculum over 10 years at the University of Zululand, is examined.

Drama Teaching in South Africa

The reasons for the introduction of a particular approach to drama studies at the University of Zululand, with the designation "Speech and Drama," become apparent when drama teaching is related to a wider social and educational context. "Speech and Drama" was established in South Africa as an extramural subject in the 1920s in Cape Town, Durban and Johannesburg. It began in the white English-speaking community, as it did abroad, as "elocution," or the teaching of an English accent that was prized because it was the approved accent of the upper-middle classes in England. It expanded to include a study of oral communication skills and theatre arts under the auspices of the Trinity College of London. As in the case of music and ballet, children were encouraged to take "Speech and Drama" lessons after school and the work was examined each year by examiners who came out from England. Drama teaching was South Africanized to some extent when the University of South Africa (UNISA), a correspondence university, working in conjunction with the South African Guild of Speech and Drama Teachers, offered their own series of diplomas for expressive and public speaking. This meant that "Spraak en Drama" offered in Afrikaans now runs parallel to "Speech and Drama" offered in English.

240

"Speech and Drama" was introduced as a university discipline at the University of Natal (Durban) and the University of Cape Town during the 1940s. The curriculum that was introduced met the requirements of the established philosophy of English-language universities, which was in broad terms the "emancipation of humanity" through the acquisition of knowledge. The dominant tradition of liberal humanism that focuses on personal growth and development, the nurturing of independent thought, the ability to make decisions and the cultivation of heightened sensitivity and awareness is the rationale of these universities. However, in a way that seems entirely South African, it was possible to overlook the contradiction of offering a liberal education under circumstances of domination and subordination incompatible with the liberal spirit.

Drama was introduced into the Afrikaans-language universities during the 1960s and Afrikaans drama departments have successfully promoted Afrikaans theatre as a counter to the dominant role of the English language in film and television. The ethos of these universities is derived from German models: knowledge first finds legitimacy within itself, after which it becomes speculative or philosophical. In this paradigm the great function to be fulfilled by universities is to lay open the whole body of learning and expound both the principles and foundations of all knowledge. Schools are seen to be functional and universities speculative. The University of Zululand, which will be discussed later in more detail, wavers between these two schools of thought, tending more towards conservative versions of "knowledge for its own sake" than liberal humanism. This provides a rationale for academics to pursue research that has no immediate relation to their undergraduate teaching, or the needs and interests of the vast majority of the community for whom the university was established. (An example of such a research topic is: "the influence of some German dialects on the development of the Afrikaans language.") When taken to extremes this paradigm allows for the needs of the local community to be ignored and for the university to indeed become an ivory tower.

When "Speech and Drama" was established in the 1940s, a central premise was that through exposure to "art" the individual would achieve personal growth and development, an understanding of "civilization," heightened creativity, communication skills and aesthetic judgement. A predominate concern of Elizabeth Sneddon, who played a major role in establishing "Speech and Drama" in this country, was the self-realization of the individual through her exposure to art. "Drama" as an art form is described as "conveying a vision of what constitutes a civilized world."[3]

Not all activities that might be loosely described as drama fall into this capital letter category. Drama as defined in "Speech and Drama" refers to a body of work or a category of plays that have been carefully selected as the masterpieces of the Western tradition. These plays are thought to have an intrinsic value of their own and the emphasis on them is as valuable objects rather than on the way they are embedded in the contingencies of history. This allows for an analysis of their universal values with very little reference to the wider area of social practice in which they gained significance. The rationale for establishing departments of speech and drama was that great works of drama should be performed and not only read as literature. Thus the production of masterpieces became an important function of departments of speech and drama.

Despite the emphasis on productions, the early proponents of "Speech and Drama" did not stress a professional training for theatre practitioners. Rather, it stressed the education of the mind and a general ability to communicate for as many as wished to choose the course, although it was essentially available only to arts faculty students. Significantly this general education was achieved through a large practical component in the course which included public and verse speaking, movement and acting. Sneddon claimed that "Speech and Drama" is a central human study and argued that, "As a discipline, Speech and Drama is the source from which all other disciplines derive."[4] She never ceased to argue for the general formative powers of "Speech and Drama," and sought to establish the discipline in areas other than the arts, such as commerce and medicine.

During the 1960s, the concept of a general formative education was challenged by increasing demands for universities to prepare students for a profession. At the University of Cape Town a three-year diploma course which offered a professional actor's training for students selected by audition, was introduced. A general course in the study and analysis of plays, that does not have a practical component, runs parallel to this course. Although these departments developed a different emphasis in the discipline, there was common ground in that an engagement of the mind with great works of art of an established canon was considered to be of profound educational value.

Generally, "Speech and Drama" is not part of the formal school curriculum. With other activities that could be considered to be "drama," including "the school play," concerts, debates and public-speaking competitions, it takes place after school hours in some schools as part of the informal curriculum. The more affluent the area the more likely the school is to have this informal curriculum. This is somewhat surprising because drama studies are well established in universities, technikons and teacher's training colleges that cater predominantly for white students. But the fact remains that nearly all the various departments of education in this country have, until recently, ignored drama as a school subject and excluded it from their formal curricula. In the 1980s, drama was recognised as a subject for the matriculation examination and introduced into some "white" and "Indian" schools in Natal by the two relevant departments of education. Drama has not been established as a curriculum subject in any black South African schooling systems. Furthermore, drama is not yet offered at the teacher's training colleges for "black" teachers.

When drama was eventually introduced in Natal into "white" and "Indian" schools as a matriculation subject, variations of the original Natal University syllabus formed the basis of the school courses. There are four strands to this syllabus — theatre history, theatre arts, movement and speech communication. The concern of the theatre history and theatre arts courses is to teach an appreciation and love of the masterpieces of Western theatre, and the emphasis in the movement and speech courses is on the development of the individual's physical, emotional and intellectual abilities through an engagement with realised art. For "Indian" schools, Eastern classical drama and dance appear on the syllabus.

Other Approaches to Drama Teaching

South African systems of education are deeply conservative in methodology. As mentioned earlier they also uphold the view that blacks and whites have different traditions and that these different "cultures" should be preserved. The emphasis on memorizing knowledge for examination purposes means that the system is product-orientated, very often at the expense of the development of creative or critical thinking. However, running counter to this dominant view, there have been efforts to incorporate progressivist trends in education into the system. This has been the particular concern of some drama teachers, made possible by the marginalized position of most drama teaching.

There is a reversal in priorities in the progressive approach to drama teaching from the approach inherent in the discipline "Speech and Drama," with its focus on realized art. In the drama-in-education approach, children are not taught to interpret poetry, prose or selections from plays but to engage in acting-out in order to construct their own representations of the world. The work is learner-centred, based on the premise that active involvement in symbolization develops a basic process of understanding, which is the capacity to see the world through symbols. Drama as a methodology helps to focus an area of study and refine questions that will reveal that area more thoroughly. The D.I.E. (Drama-in-Education) movement is by no means uniform in its approach and a significant debate about the nature, purpose and future of drama in education has been taking place in the United Kingdom for some time. In brief, this involves a challenge to the work of pioneers in the field, such as Dorothy Heathcote and Gavin Bolton, from teachers who seek a more contextualised and politicized approach that has the potential to change society. Running parallel to the D.I.E. movement is T.I.E. (Theatre-in-Education) with its focus on devising challenging theatre programmes that are taken on a tour of schools by companies of actor/teachers.

In South Africa, the 1950s and 1960s were not a period for innovative experimentation in education, but a time for consolidating apartheid, and the arts, when taught, where perceived as a way of "preserving civilisation." Not surprisingly, the proponents of Christian National Education and Bantu Education have no truck with progressivist movements, although the idea of learner-centred education is called on to support mother-tongue instruction and "separate education for separate cultures." However, some universities responded to the progressivist movement in spite of the scarcity of opportunities for drama teachers trained in D.I.E. and T.I.E. The University of Cape Town is notable for its work in this area, and in the 1980s, Rhodes University and the universities of Natal (Pietermaritzburg), Durban-Westville and Zululand have focused their attention on D.I.E. and T.I.E. In 1979, the Southern African Association of Drama and Youth Theatre (SAADYT) was formed in an attempt to bring together all teachers involved in progressive drama teaching. In contrast to the South African Guild of Speech and Drama Teachers, these teachers do not centre their attention on training individuals for diploma examinations, public-speaking competitions and drama festivals. Their concerns are using drama and theatre for group work to focus on problems, as a methodology for teaching English and other subjects and as a way of developing self-confidence through integrating indigenous performance skills with Westernized dance and drama forms.

It is within this context that the potential of educational drama and theatre methodologies to contribute towards an alternative approach to education in South Africa can be examined.

The University of Zululand

The rest of this chapter will explore education as a site of change and struggle at the University of Zululand. The focus will be on drama education and how political context has influenced the development of the drama department and its curriculum. The University of Zululand did not develop in the Ongoye hills out of any existing tradition of learning established either by the indigenous population or the missionaries who, until 1953, provided most of the formal education available for black South Africans. In 1960, a university college academically affiliated to the University of South Africa was built at KwaDlangezwa by the state, with the express purpose of implementing its apartheid policy. Apartheid policies deepened the distinctions between rural and urban sections of the labour force and created a pecking order in terms of access to urban employment. Education has played an important role in separating unskilled, semi-skilled, technical and clerical workers into different segments of the working class. The homeland policy necessitated the fostering of a black élite and a supporting middle class, hence the establishment of a high proportion of South Africa's "black" secondary, and nearly all its "black" tertiary education in the homelands by the mid-60s.

In 1970, the college was granted autonomous status. It ceased to be affiliated to the University of South Africa and in 1979 black students from any ethnic group in South Africa were accepted. In the 1987 university calendar there is a statement that the university is a fully autonomous educational institution and, therefore, free to makes its own decisions about educational policy. There is also a conscience clause which reads:

> It is the university's avowed policy not to discriminate
> on the grounds of race, religion, colour or creed.

It appears, on the surface, that in 25 years the university has made remarkable progress from a tribal college to a fully autonomous university. Despite a pervasive sense of crisis, student enrolment has continued to increase, as has the size and splendour of the facilities. However, there is a constant threat of student boycotts. In 1984 the university was closed for the second semester and in 1989, boycotts brought the university to a close for several weeks; a total closure for the year was narrowly avoided. Clearly, the success of the university in quantitative terms is not an indication of its success in formulating an academic programme that students regard as "education for liberation." The lack of an acceptable legitimizing rationale to support the acquisition of knowledge, other than getting a degree in order to get a job, allows the balance to sometimes swing in favour of those who call for boycotts for political ends, despite the considerable hardship that results from a closure.

About 70 per cent of the students speak Zulu as a first language and the remainder speak other South African indigenous languages. The courses are offered in English. Students arrive at the university from schools lacking even the most basic facilities, set in socially unstable and economically impoverished environments. At the beginning of 1990 it is difficult to assess the extent to which alternative course structures urged by the NECC have been introduced in schools, but a powerful spirit of resistance to change among all those in authoritative positions within the system of education cannot be underestimated. The difficulties of changing are exacerbated by a lack of books, of training in more learner-centred teaching and by uncertainty and ambiguity about what is to change. Moreover, there are entrenched mind sets to change: authoritarian state practices, formulaistic modes of teaching, rote learning, teacher dependency and subservience to established codes and practices, especially to the examination system which dominates schooling from the junior primary level to the tertiary level.

Among blacks a deliberately inculcated sense of inferiority and inadequacy does not generate attitudes either willing or ready to engage in the radically new. The present mark-orientated and exam-dominated system forces students into the mould of conformity, unquestioning obedience and information regurgitation. The teacher is likewise in bondage to the system and to a curriculum which emphasizes information that will be examined and then simply forgotten. At the university the prevailing attitude is that education is a means of getting a certificate and a job. The school system does not encourage a love of learning or develop critical and enquiring minds. The ambiguous nature of education which promises liberation through advancement on the one hand and threatens brainwashing on the other, means that many students actively or passively resist what they consider to be "white man's" knowledge. In any case, much of the learning that goes on at the university does not take place in the classrooms and for most students there are strong pressures towards political commitment from within the student body. The university administration requires "neutrality" and students who are earmarked as being politically active are simply not "invited" to return at the beginning of each academic year. The university council has absolute power in this matter and excluded students have no redress even to a disciplinary committee. Students therefore walk a daily tightrope in their attempts to get a degree, respond to political pressures of fellow students and avoid the attention of the university administration. The undercurrents of political life on the campus are comparable to those which are tearing society apart and making fear and funerals a way of life in Natal black suburbs (and slums).

The Department of Drama: Drama and Theatre Studies

"Speech and Drama" was introduced as a discipline at the University of Zululand in 1979. The first syllabus was closely related to the courses offered at other universities with a focus on the history of Western drama and the development of individual communication skills through movement and public speaking. The history of theatre was taught chronologically beginning with the Ancient Greek theatre and continuing with Medieval, Elizabethan, 19th Century and modern theatre. There were immediate difficulties with the presentation of "masterpieces" and the department attempted to solve the problem with adapted versions of Shakespeare and classical dramatists. Students were also required to speak English prose, poetry and play extracts for practical examinations. It soon became apparent that far from achieving personal growth, an understanding of "civilisation" and aesthetic judgement, the emphasis on the power and values of Western culture was either reinforcing a sense of inferiority among our students or building a strong resistance to this kind of learning.

Problems Encountered with this Syllabus

Arguments about the value of understanding and preserving "civilisation" through an education in the arts, (defined as Western masterpieces) founder in a colonial context. In Africa, and especially South Africa, the legacy of colonial education has meant a crisis of identity. The common-sense knowledge of an indigenous and rural people was negated by colonizers driven by the industrial and cities revolution, thus reinforcing a self-image of ignorance and incompetence. Those who received a formal education were encouraged to despise their own culture and traditions and Western Christian education became a focal point of hope for social status and integration into white colonial society. A petite bourgeoisie was formed that was tempted to see European culture as its own, but which was destined never to be accepted by its white counterpart — a group in Fanon's words, with "black skins and white masks." The rise of black consciousness in the 1970s to counter the sense of inferiority instilled in blacks has meant an increasing pride in being black but a difficulty remains in finding a modern version of an African identity. The emergence of urban, popular and contemporary performing arts is an indication of a search for this identity.

White South Africans, in their turn, receive a Eurocentric education which reinforces their sense of belonging to a different and superior culture. This supports a self-image of superiority encouraging arrogance and a lack of understanding and humanity when dealing with fellow countrymen. The result of this legacy is the ambivalent and contradictory attitude of South Africans to their sense of identity. White South Africans determinedly attempt to preserve their "civilized identity" by relating to European culture, and yet have ended up as the "white tribe of Africa." Ironically, far from going down in history as having preserved Christian values and "civilization," the "white tribe" will probably be remembered as a group of brutal oppressors that retarded the advancement of the country. The system of education has systematically denied white South Africans any understanding of the heritage of black South Africans and it is only in recent years that some indigenous languages have appeared on the school syllabus for "whites." For those of us working in the department of drama it became clear that an approach to the arts that emphasizes the cherishing of a heritage that was myopically defined, was not achieving its educational aims.

Attempts to adapt plays from the Western heritage by focussing on their "universal themes" and devising an African setting, were largely unsuccessful. Two of the plays we attempted were *Macbeth* and *Peer Gynt*. They were adapted by selecting key scenes, linking these with narration, and using costumes, sets and dance sequences inspired by African designs, motifs and rhythms. The plays foundered on the artificial setting and the "language problem," because Shakespeare and Ibsen's poetry does not transplant into Africa, and, short of rewriting the entire script, the exercise was rather futile. In addition to the unsatisfactory setting of the plays the structured language presented second-language speakers of English with problems of observing rhythmic and intonation patterns which they found totally unfamiliar. This difficulty resulted in rather wooden or completely inaudible performances. It began to seem increasingly inappropriate to focus on the "great tradition" just for the sake of it.

The concept of universal values that can be discovered in plays and taught to students is fraught with difficulty. The notion that we can largely ignore the social conditions inherent in an individual consciousness gives, rise to a number of serious educational problems. Such a view implicitly presents men and women as passive receivers because it refuses to take into account the social creation of the individual. The drama course that we inherited tended to stress that we are all autonomous individuals and disregard our nature as social beings. The course was planned on the premise that students will "develop universal values" or that lecturers can help them to develop these values through hard work, extensive reading, taking part in productions and from background information. This assumption of a specious universality or commonness at the core of all human cognition means that failure is ascribed to either teachers or students — usually students. We began to recognise the potential of a learner-centred approach which would pay attention to the social creation of consciousness and encourage students to make their own knowledge and culture.

In Search of New Directions

The political context in which educational changes are taking place in South Africa is complex and fluid. In broad terms two major challenges to apartheid have found expression in the Africanist and charterist movements. The struggle for an authentic national culture and national liberation is underpinned in the case of Africanist groupings by analyses based on race, whereas the charterist movements favour class-based analyses. The black-consciousness tradition stresses black cultural pride and political self-reliance. Psychological liberation and re-evaluation of South African history are consequences of these interests. Whites are excluded from black-consciousness organisations until the attainment of a socialist democracy. A desire to build an authentic national culture is also the declared aim of charterist groupings that favour integration and the forging of a new non-racial democratic South Africa. The Africanisation or rather "South Africanisation" of education is a major concern of these and more "moderate" groupings in spite of differences about an appropriate economy for South Africa.

The Contribution of Drama to a South Africa-Based Curriculum

One of the results of Bantu Education is that students are not only ignorant of their own cultural history, but also of the works of contemporary novelists, poets and playwrights. When I first began working at the University of Zululand in the early 1970s many students considered the study of Shakespeare far more worthwhile than a study of, for example, the poetry of Pascal Gwala or Oswald Mtshali. This is because the popular performing arts are viewed with suspicion by conservative educationalists and the loss of traditional culture is posited as a process of disintegration that must be resisted. In a conservative approach, the development of aesthetic judgement depends on the ability to recognise "great works" of drama and popular forms are ignored. This meant that emerging South African theatre was largely ignored as an appropriate area of study in schools and universities.

The black consciousness movement has, however, made considerable gains in stressing the value of an anti-élitist stance and of relevance and direct communication in literature and performance. The South African Students Organisation (SASO) set up a cultural committee with the aim of "awakening and heightening cultural awareness and involving black people in their struggle for identity, self-respect and liberation."[5] One of the functions of literature and art that is consistently drawn on by this movement, is that of changing perceptions and raising the level of political awareness of black people. The black consciousness perception of the function of performance is that it should be politically relevant and contribute to the liberation struggle.

The emergence of urban, popular and contemporary performing arts in South Africa is a significant way to bring about psychocultural change in performers and audiences. The structured symbolism of the arts provides a way of understanding the rapidly changing environment and developing a new sense of identity. People in situations of urban change use performance metaphors as instruments of social movement, order and self-transformation. The forging of a new culture requires symbols that will actualize changes in status and help to bring order out of the chaos of diverse and conflicting images. In addition to the work inspired by the black-consciousness movement, a number of non-racial theatre groups and organisations have made a significant contribution to the development of South African theatre. The Market Theatre in Johannesburg is perhaps the best known in this respect. Encouraged by the constant reassessment of courses undertaken in some of the drama departments in English-language universities, we set out at the University of Zululand, to forge a new and relevant course for our students. We began with research into developments in the popular performing arts and African theatre in general.

A change of focus from Western masterpieces to indigenous South African performance forms and popular theatre was strengthened by new approaches to drama and theatre studies abroad. The dominant idea of drama as "Art" was being challenged as the concept of performance took root. Attention is paid to performance forms world-wide and in South Africa there is a growing interest among scholars both within the discipline and outside it in indigenous South African theatre. New research in the field stressed the interaction between text and context rather than "universal values" in isolated texts. The importance of learner-centred approaches in the search for new directions is that they erode the idea that the primary function of drama in education is to engage the mind with the works of "distinguished playwrights." This is especially the case when those being educated are constantly reminded that they have a different heritage which is by implication inferior.

Attempts to develop a South African base for the drama syllabus began with the inclusion of a section on African and South African plays at third-year level, while the remainder of the theatre history course focused on the Western heritage. It soon became apparent that this was a "cosmetic change" and an analysis of the philosophy underpinning the entire course was required.

A Pedagogy Committed to Building an Open Society

Within the peculiar circumstances of South African history and society, many of the claims of a liberal education have been undermined. Under the pressure of "preserving civilization" the emphasis on a European heritage greatly prejudiced an understanding of South African culture. An emphasis on the individual achieving a free, enriched, autonomous identity tended to breed a myopic vision rather than a sense of justice — the prime claim of liberalism. This distorted version of a liberal education that became entrenched in some disciplines in South Africa, notably "Speech and Drama," has been challenged by the proponents of a participatory, learner-centred approach to drama studies. In other words, for education to be meaningful, public traditions of thought must connect with the actual thinking of particular people.

This crisis of legitimacy generated an increasing interest in "critical" theory in the English-language universities. Critical theory, based on principles of dialectic tension, and wary of unquestioned assumptions, provides a tool to analyze entrenched methodologies. This emergent paradigm postulates that society is socially constructed, sustained and changed through the ongoing interaction of men and women. The emphasis on culture as a received body of experience handed down from generation to generation shifts to a concept that culture is constantly being made by men and women. People, including students, are recognised as actively participating in reconstructing, maintaining and changing the social reality in which they live. This new perspective challenges the concept of knowledge as a product disconnected from the processes which have produced it. Instead knowledge is seen as a social construction legitimated by those in positions of power and control.

It is characteristic of any critical theory that the starting point of its argument must be people's everyday view of the world. In South African systems of education where knowledge is defined by departments of education and entrenched through the examination system, there is little or no grasp of students' or pupils' viewpoints. An impression is given that knowledge is "absolute" and that no further development, correction or change in a way of thinking is possible. In the Department of Drama we actively set out to discover some of the views, concepts and values that students would bring to bear on a situation. We became committed to finding a pedagogy that allows young people to consciously make their own knowledge and culture and become aware of alternative ways of knowing and seeing.

In line with progressivist trends in education, the proponents of D.I.E. emphasize the central importance of subjectivity in learning. They claim that as the process of dramatization exploits the impulse to make sense of, express and communicate from the inner world of subjective experience, it is an ideal learning medium. In some drama teaching the tendency to emphasize self-realisation and the fear of stifling spontaneity has set up a false dichotomy between learning through drama and an engagement with realized art. In the Department of Drama we sought a methodology that would make connections between all the educational functions of drama and theatre. We focused on playmaking in order to set up opportunities for understanding the point of view of our students and of examining drama as a way of communicating ideas. The playmaking process taken through to the production and presentation of a play allows for connections to be made between drama and theatre and for the educational process to go beyond private experiences into public realms of knowledge.

Ken Robinson has suggested three ways of focussing on the process of dramatization as whole.[6] The three major educational functions of drama are identified as heuristic, communicative and receptive. When the emphasis is on the initiation and construction of ideas through processes of improvisation and the exploration of issues, themes and events, then the general function of these activities is heuristic (learning through self-discovery). From improvisations and workshops, teachers can draw on the conceptual tools and the habits of thinking used by students in order to negotiate meanings. This is not to argue that any conception of reality is as good as any other. It is up to the teacher to point out strict logical limits and provide students with a framework in which they can reason and present their points of view.

When the emphasis is on the broad processes of staging a play, then the emphasis shifts from the initiation of ideas to their communication. Robinson refers to the intermediary between the original creative act and the audience as the animator. The director, the actors and the theatre technicians are all animators because they realize a drama for an audience. Here the educational potential is focused on acquiring appropriate skills for successful communication to take place.

The third process in dramatization is the receptive activity of the audience. According to Robinson this is both interpretative and appreciative. The schematic symbolism of performance demands a complex effort at understanding and responding to its signifying systems. The process of making a play, scripting and rehearsing it and then presenting it to an audience has the advantage of taking students through all three processes of dramatisation.

The Playmaking Process

The playmaking process is multifaceted. For those involved in the project, learning takes place on a number of levels; self-exploration, social interaction, the use of body, voice and language for self-expression, the refinement and extension of conceptual frameworks and a grasp of publicly developed traditions of thought. The learning process engages all the faculties and unlike most modern educational practices, in drama classes, there is no divorce between learning with the body and learning with the mind. Playmaking becomes a focal point in the drama syllabus, with two distinctive teaching methods utilized in this playmaking process: improvisation and workshopping.

The playmaking process can be considered in three phases that correspond to the heuristic, communicative and receptive functions of drama — workshopping, rehearsing and performing.

Workshops — The Heuristic Function

In the playmaking process, workshopping has the most potential for developing critical thinking. It is in this phase that common sense perceptions can be deconstructed. As accepted ways of using the body and accepted attitudes and relationships are shown spontaneously they can be "frozen" and discussed. Most workshops begin with "warm-ups" of various kinds designed to induce relaxation and confidence in the group and build up trust. I have a collection of children's rhymes and games in Zulu that I use with groups that are unfamiliar with improvisation. Action rhymes that are usually sung and performed by young children, ease the tension and are helpful in getting adults to move confidently. Students are invited to contribute rhymes that they remember and teach them to each other; this phase of the workshop usually breaks the ice. I have also used this technique successfully with "mixed" groups of adults. It is nearly always helpful to put white South Africans on the spot by encouraging them to sing in Zulu and attempt unfamiliar rhythmic movements, because this equalizes the group dynamic.

The rhymes are one of many ways of providing a point of departure for improvising. In a recent workshop, a rhyme was used to initiate improvisation and an exchange of ideas around the relationships between men and women. Students told me that the rhyme stressed the important role that women play in rural communities as providers of food, and that the work is organized as a group activity. The function of the rhyme is to discourage laziness by disparaging those who want to eat without having done the work. I thought it significant that it was one of the women rather than a man who was being criticized and in response to my comment, a student from a rural area earnestly explained that women do all the work:

> They do everything. Everything. They work in the fields, planting and hoeing and reaping the vegetables or whatever they have planted. They fetch water every day and sometimes it is very far to walk and they fetch firewood. There are a lot of children to look after and if the men are at home everything must be nice for them. They sweep around the homestead and some make baskets and do beadwork so that they can get a little bit of extra money.

Following on these initial ideas I asked the students to improvise around the idea of women's work and after a lengthy discussion they came up with an improvisation in which the women were working in the fields and then went to fetch water when a group of men abducted one of the girls. They wrapped her in an overcoat and dragged her off in order to force her to marry against her will. I was rather surprised by this improvisation because I did not think that forced marriage was a source of concern, until I discovered that one of the students had recently read a short story called *Nokulunga's Wedding* by Gcina Mhlope, and that the improvisation was an enactment of this story. I realized after further discussion that the majority of the students were not on particularly familiar ground when it came to rural practices and that enacting a published story that one of them had read gave them confidence that what they were doing was "right." I suggested that we read the story together during the next class and research rural attitudes to women. I asked the students to make some connections between the story they used as a basis for improvisation and the situation on campus regarding the relations between the men and the women. They acted out the following sequence of events:

Everyone was watching a film in the student centre. The men and women were not sitting together but in two groups. The women were sitting very close to each other and there was a sense of intimacy and friendliness about the way they held onto each other. After the film was over everyone left and one of the men grabbed one of the girls and pulled her aside. The girl cried out in anguish most convincingly and everyone, except for one couple who were deeply engaged in conversation, went to her aid. There was a quarrel between the men and the women. The women accused the men of being brutal and violent and of only wanting sex from them and the men retaliated by telling the women that they were too proud and only interested in money. The scene ended with some jeering between the two groups while the courting couple remained engrossed in each other.

Subsequent discussion centered around the sense of inferiority experienced by black women. Male domination was related to men's physical strength and many of the students (both men and women) said that they believed that men are innately superior to women. Some women rejected this view saying that women are not necessarily even physically weaker than men and they cited an example of a group of women, on another campus, banding together and physically attacking a man who had been bullying them. Some members of the group felt that men resort to physical violence far too easily and the men retorted that they were driven to using force because the women did not respond to anything else. It now seemed to me that the choice of *Nokulunga's Wedding* was more pertinent than I had first thought. There was a deep concern in the group about sexual violence and ways of dealing with it.

This work continued in a series of workshops until a group of seven men and seven women made a play called *Lolo Bambo Lolo* (*That Extra Rib*). The play deals with the relationships between men and women in three different historical contexts and all the dialogue was created through processes of improvisation in workshops. An important aspect of these workshops was a consideration not only of the way in which women are dominated and oppressed by the cultural system into which they are born, but ways in which they might discover new relationships. This was difficult work because the image of the "new women" was not yet formulated — it had to be discovered from within and manifested in action and interaction with others. In the workshops there were moments when the participants really surprised themselves as if there was a sense of discovery of latent thoughts during the experience. When working on devising one of the episodes of the play, the group spontaneously formed a scene with a train where a rural woman left her family and travelled to Johannesburg to find her husband. This may seem like a fairly clichéd response, but in this context where rural women remain perpetual minors and may not leave home without permission, it was a breakthrough.

A basic component of most improvisational work is that it is done through social interaction. The negotiation of meaning takes place on two different levels — the level of actual negotiation within the group as the participants find roles and interact with each other, and the level of selecting symbolic systems in order to produce patterns of meaning. The work also offers opportunities in language development. When the emphasis is on fluency rather than accuracy of speech, and the inhibitions of speaking up in front of the class are removed, many students are forthcoming. As a first-year student wryly remarked "I soon realised that if I did not speak out and make a role for myself I would be left out and that would be boring."

A major benefit of group work is that it provides an opportunity to move away from the cult of individualism fostered in an examination-orientated system of education and the pressure of individual competition. The negotiations that go on within the group are for an end result that is not an individual achievement but a collective one. As one student commented in a diary that all students are required to keep:

> It is essential to bear in mind that a group making a play is a team, what effects you, effects the group. The whole process needs patience, dedication and understanding. These have got to be our food. Tolerance is

the gateway to success. Group work needs a tremendous amount of self-discipline.

In the making of *Lolo Bambo Lolo* the interaction between the participants within the group reflected some of the difficulties experienced in the wider society. The struggle for equality and a sense of identity experienced by black women was evident in the way the group worked together. Many of the ructions that were experienced were as a result of the women being unable to assert themselves and resorting instead to disruptive tactics such as sulking, refusing to help with technical work and absenting themselves from workshops and rehearsals. Several of the workshops dissolved into heated quarrels which the leader of the group was unable to control, or often promoted because he felt the group was not working properly. My attempt to persuade one of the women to take on one of the leadership roles was unsuccessful. There was, however, a genuine desire to overcome these difficulties and the group stuck together, discovering that some of their attitudes were not "natural" or "common sense." In some cases good sense prevailed and there were perceptible changes of attitude among the participants about alternative and possibly more appropriate ways of behaving between genders. As one woman remarked:

> We became so close that sometimes when we bumped into one of the men at the Student Centre he would come up and hug us. Nobody felt embarrassed. But should this be done by any other male student you would assume a sexual advance and scream heaven and hell.

Although this group worked together for several months the men remained firmly in control. However, they became resentful because the women generally refused to take any responsibility and also were unhelpful in practical ways like carrying sets, painting the floor cloth and so on. The production was successfully performed at a student's drama festival on campus, smoothing over some of the difficulties. However, it seemed that although the group became aware of some of its internal dynamics, they were unable to easily resolve problems or change entrenched attitudes.

The important difference between this kind of work and the presentation of plays with the intention of promoting "stars" and "lead roles" is that the emphasis is on collective achievement through working together and not on reinforcing a sense of hierarchy. When used in this way the playmaking process has the potential to become a testing ground for democratic processes and for discovering areas of difficulty.

For the women who took part in *Lolo Bambo Lolo* there was the realization that unless they were prepared to take responsibility, they could not expect to command respect as equals. The difficulty of how to assume responsibility remained, but a first step was taken in recognizing some of the dilemmas inherent in establishing democratic processes.

Communication Skills — Rehearsals

The teaching of communication skills remains central to the drama course. However, the class offered at the University of Zululand as one course within the B.A. degree cannot claim that its students will master any conventionalized art form. What can be mastered are the basic skills required to present a play (or any formal type of communication) to an audience within its own environment. In the playmaking process there comes a time when workshopping changes to rehearsal. The script is written down and for the most part becomes fixed and attention shifts to the projection of voice, character and story line to an audience. There may be adjustments to the script to facilitate this purpose, but the emphasis has moved from making a play to presenting the play. The work undertaken in tutorials and movement classes helps to develop these skills while providing a broad educational base. In "Speech and Drama" there is a clear distinction between training professional actors for the theatre and working through drama and theatre as a way of educating the mind and developing oral communication skills. The approach that we have adopted takes this concept one step further. In our view the best way of achieving this kind of education is not through an engagement with selected literary works. We have posited instead a learner-centred approach that begins with identifying the learner's own experience of life and then providing ways in which this experience may be understood, modified and even changed.

Receptive Function

Watching our own and other plays and writing a critical appreciation is a significant feature of the course and, because of the isolated nature of the campus, we take our students to other universities and larger centres. However, it is beyond the scope of this chapter to discuss audience responses to plays and the analysis of performance. Suffice it to say that we have not abandoned the study of texts both written and performed. Also, while attempting to respond to our student's needs, we have been mindful of maintaining a university course with a theoretical and practical base. The course has become South African, with an emphasis on learning through the processes of drama. The study of theatre history still remains, however, beginning with an analysis of South African ritual, theatre and dance. The study continues with Western theatre history and its profound impact on modern ideas of the theatre.

The students are introduced to theatre studies through a critique of plays that they are familiar with. There is no need to give some "background" lectures on apartheid in order to discuss *Woza Albert, Asinamali or Sarafina* with South African students. The symbols are accessible and connections can be made between text and context. But the course would be limited if it were to stop at the point of learning though personal experience. Personal experience must be mediated through conceptual categories and the introduction of new ideas, and this means there is a need for theory and analytical tools. Theory is of necessity imported — but new theories related to new ways of seeing and knowing can constantly be developed.

Teachers and Facilitators

There is no easy path for teachers who genuinely attempt progressive and democratic approaches to education. There is a fine line to tread between encouraging and setting up situations where genuine participation between all those who are involved occurs, and anarchy. Drama classes can very easily degenerate into pointless exercises in self-expression. I was dismayed to watch a newly fledged drama teacher ask his class to cry and then to laugh for no reason except that they were "doing drama." I wondered if the impression that he had received after taking a four-year course was that this is what drama classes are about — simply expressing emotion for no reason except as a kind of exercise. Of course the class responded very well to the command to laugh — the situation was so grotesquely funny that there was good reason to indulge in hoots of laughter which they did at length. As for the command to cry! Suffice it to say that this drama teacher responded and wept inwardly.

The aims of drama teaching are often so diverse that teachers find themselves in the awkward position of being a figure of authority one minute and a nuisance for imposing unwanted ideas the next. The difficulty is usually a matter of timing, of knowing when to step in and when to keep out, and it is impossible always to get this right. I have sometimes handed work over to students only to find it handed back to me when they have found leadership roles difficult to maintain. I have also resorted to completely authoritarian practices when things have seemed on the point of collapse, and yet tried to encourage a sense of equality in the groups that I work with. For me the advantage in this work is that most of the time I am on very unfamiliar ground as far as direct experience of the students' lives is concerned and this forces me into a tentative and enquiring position. Some students find this reversal of usual roles very disconcerting. In the early stage of workshopping a play, a student commented:

> What we did today worried me. I thought that when we are preparing to present a performance that the lecturers would come with everything — material, and parts which one would perform. But I find that the students come with ideas, improvise them and try and improve them.

Comments from students have indicated that they have found working together to make and put on a play a worthwhile educational experience and one that is liberating:

> We develop from within ourselves the potential to make a play. This makes us aware of our ability and we realize that when something has to be done it is not only the few deemed clever who do the work. Everyone has potential and we were excited when this was actualized. When we were making the play everyone was equally important. Our discussions were often long and hot. Everyone contributed. Those who wanted to remain passive were encouraged to voice out their ideas. But some people do rest on their laurels and let others do all the work. They gain nothing from that approach.

When a learner-centred approach is adopted, and active problem solving substituted for traditional passiveness, the emphasis is on the learning process rather than on gaining knowledge of "things." The learning process is relevant to the students' experience of life and becomes an integral part of their being and not an alienating and distancing experience that reinforces a sense of inferiority. This is because the experiences of the individual are considered to be valid and valuable by the teacher.

However, there is a danger of students becoming "experience-bound" and unable to see issues in a broader perspective. As an aspect of the receptive function of drama, students must be provided with tools for critical self-exploration and an exploration of the context in which they are making the play. These moments of reflexivity should ideally become part of the play itself. My contribution to the workshopping process is usually in this area. A conscious effort must be made to move beyond superficial portrayals of events and relationships. Thus the role of the teacher or facilitator is to ask key questions

259

that will lead the group into deepening their perceptions. Students also need to be introduced to different styles of presentation. For example, the influence of film, radio and television is pervasive; new students inevitably choose modern realism as the "natural" way of portraying their ideas through drama. The work of Bertolt Brecht is an important antidote to this perception and I constantly ask students to consider other ways of expressing their ideas; we work on building images and on songs, dances and direct address to the audience.

Practical Changes to the Curriculum

In broad terms, I have considered a change in emphasis in a university course from a curriculum based on socially prepared knowledge, external to the knower and there to be mastered (curriculum as fact), to a curriculum that explores the way in which a society collectively attempts to order its world, and in the process produces knowledge, (curriculum as practice).[7] The "curriculum as fact" abstracts knowledge from those who have selected and given legitimacy to what should be taught and learned. Knowledge becomes a "thing" and the teachers and pupils are denied possibilities except within its own framework and definitions. The "curriculum as practice" is concerned with recognizing teachers and pupils as conscious agents of change, as theorists in their own right and to emphasize the human possibilities in all situations. Its success is dependent on the teachers' classroom practice, and herein lies a paradox. In South Africa most educationalists are steeped in the dominant view of "curriculum as fact" and in the sense of hierarchy that it supports. While universities have a measure of autonomy and are able to change course structures, teachers in schools work within narrow and closely defined parameters. Those who attempt to introduce progressive ways of teaching are up against a system of examinations, inspectors and entrenched positions as well as their own common sense assumptions about the nature of teaching and learning. In order for extensive curriculum change to occur, existing hierarchies within schools themselves need to be challenged and this means the involvement of the wider community.

It is only when the political and economic aspects of education are generally grasped and clarified that it becomes possible to bring about practical changes in the curriculum. We cannot continue to support the myth that education is neutral. If the present system is properly critiqued, political questions will inevitably rise for teachers and for everyone involved in education. Also, we cannot overlook the idea of technical rationality and efficiency as a modern "saviour." This idea is becoming entrenched, and in some economic systems such concepts as liberty and free choice become subservient to the establishment of modern technology. The cry "liberation now and education later" reflects the fine balance between education and a form of indoctrination into an existing system. There is a need to constantly define what is required from education, not only in universities and colleges but in offices, classrooms and communities. It is imperative that the whole society becomes educated about education so that we understand what can be achieved and devise a system that does not set up false expectations, remove initiative and offer no opportunities for problem solving. The crisis in education in South Africa at present is a source of much debate and discussion and hopefully the beginning of some comprehensive changes.

Pupil Power

The political character of education must be made explicit to young people, as well as its potential. The present system of education is a disaster because it promises all, while offering virtually nothing. Education should not be understood as a one-way ticket to the stars, to a higher standard of living or from the country to the town, as many young people and their parents believe today. When these ambitions are not realized, the result is frustration and unrealistic demands from young people from the wider society. There is, for example, a slogan "pass one, pass all" reflecting a deep mistrust of the whole matriculation examination system. At present "pupil power" tends to operate as a destructive force and opportunities to harness the energy and commitment of young people are lost or exploited.

Although "pupil power" might worry some teachers and administrators, there are valuable gains to be made from the participation of young people in the decision-making processes relating to their education. Much can be achieved by finding out their views and building their confidence in their schools. This might help to break down the sense of "them" and "us." When children are given more responsibility, and feel their opinions count, they tend to behave in a more concerned and responsible way. "Pupil power" is a way for young people to achieve their liberation through education.

To conclude, however draconian and inhibiting the attempts are to prevent change, I contend that there is most clearly a contribution which drama and drama educators can make towards developing a system of education as a means towards a just and democratic society. There is a flexibility inherent in some contemporary approaches to educational drama and theatre which could lead the way in making the kind of changes needed. Those who work in educational drama are thoroughly attuned to process orientated approaches. Drama has the potential to be a central methodological, as well as conceptual, influence upon the processes implicit in a system of education for emancipation.

Endnotes

1. Peter Kallaway, (ed.) *Apartheid and Education* (Johannesburg: Ravan Press, 1984), p. 92.
2. Ibid., p. 93.
3. Elizabeth Sneddon, *The Power of the Spoken Word* (Natal Education Department, Bulletin 28, 1981), p. 18.
4. Ibid.
5. *Black Review*, Durban, 1973.
6. Ken Robinson, (ed.). *Exploring Theatre and Education* (London: Heinemann Educational Books Ltd., 1980), pp. 167–175.
7. Roger Dale, Geoff Esland and Madeleine MacDonald, (eds.). *Schooling and Capitalism* (London: Henley Routledge and Kegan Paul, 1976), p. 185.

Seeking the Faces of Buddha in "The Last Forest": A Quest for Enlightenment in Educational Drama

RON RICHARD

Introduction

A group of young adults, aged 20 to 29, are gathered in a large desk-free classroom at the Loyola campus of Montreal's Concordia University for the first class of a unique course.[1] Many of them have eagerly anticipated the beginning of this course, or at least the beginning of the project that makes up this course. Students accepted into this course are often envied by those first-year drama in education students who do not yet qualify for the course, and even some of those who took it before and are thus denied the opportunity to take it again.

Despite this anticipation, many of the registered students arrive late. This is not a good sign. The course instructor,[2] also the programme co-ordinator, is not impressed. He communicates this to the group, yet he nonetheless engages the group in interesting and humorous (if generally insubstantial) talk for a few more minutes, hoping the tardy will soon arrive before beginning the session proper. He then explains what he thinks the group can expect over the next 13 weeks. He goes over the course syllabus he has handed out, introduces the production crew for the project, introduces the intended environmental theme of the show, breaks the class down into initial research groups, and fields a variety of questions. Finally, he does what he does with all his classes: he begins by inviting the class to play.

Most of what I do on this project, at least at first, is to observe and take notes. I observe the group; I observe their participation in the activities and discussions the instructor engages them in. Later I would design and organize the development of an educational package

263

for the teachers of the elementary students who would come to see the performances. But mostly, I found myself observing an experienced drama teacher in action.

While this chapter, like the course itself, is mostly about the creation of a theatrical experience, underpinning all of it is the question about what makes a drama teacher a "good" drama teacher, because without it, this project would never have succeeded.[3] "It" is an attitude, a calling; the Buddhist might call it "a condition of enlightenment." Whatever it is, it accounts for the sometimes overtaxed metaphysical metaphor used throughout this chapter.[4] As a novice, I go in search of whatever "it" is, and like all such metaphysical endeavors, I can never be sure when I've found it.

Seeking A Rationale: A Novice Drama Teacher Asks "Why Do I Exist?"

Educational drama, when studied as an academic discipline, seems to me to be as much akin to philosophy as it is to education or theatre arts. There seems to be a constant struggle to define in concrete terms what is essentially an abstract preoccupation — the nature of human growth, development and learning. While undoubtedly vague and idealistic, the pursuit seems nevertheless an important step. It is an attempt to identify the processes through which, collectively, all educators seek to create, mould or inspire an amorphous product: the intelligent, fully developed human being.

Of course, this is hardly a new endeavour; it is as old as the ancient who first asked "What am I?" But in this particular intellectual guise educational drama hardly goes back half a century, and in that time it has spawned its own particular breed of experts, people who have established themselves through their ideas and teaching, as veritable experts to a growing number of followers and practitioners of their ideas and methods.

Consulting the Sages

It seems logical, then, to seek the wisdom of one of these sages in helping me define what educational drama is, or should be. Richard Courtney has written what has become almost an educational drama bible, *Play, Drama and Thought*. This is an invaluable reference guide in which is painstakingly charted the historical background, evolution and development of educational drama, as well as a conspectus of each of the multitude of intellectual and methodological canons that have directly or indirectly influenced and contributed to the field.

According to Courtney, educational drama "is the use of dramatization for the purposes of students' learning."[5] Learning is a personal improvement, and he goes on to describe four distinct types of learning:

1) *Intrinsic Learning*: improvement of perception, awareness, concentration, creativity, motivation, problem identification and problem solving etc.;
2) *Extrinsic Learning*: improvement of understanding of subjects, such as history, literature and so on;
3) *Aesthetic Learning*: improvement of the quality of feeling, (that is, response to outside stimulus) and thus the tacit level of insight and intuition;
4) *Artistic Learning*: improvement of older students' skills in creating theatre.

For the purposes of this chapter, and in the course of my pursuit, I have chosen to switch the focus of these categories from things learned to things taught, and so to the art of teaching. In an article entitled "The Liminal Servant and the Ritual Roots of Critical Pedagogy," Peter McLaren presents a fascinating metaphor for the effective, authentic teacher: the liminal servant.

When students responded with a sense of immediacy or purpose, either verbally or gesturally, to the teacher's performance — when, for instance, they became the primary actors within the ritual of instruction — then they engaged in an authentic pedagogical rite: the surroundings were sanctified, and the students became co-celebrants in the learning process which was characterized by intense involvement and participation. In this case, the teacher achieved the role of liminal servant.[6]

The liminal servant is a guide, a facilitator, a partner in the student's journey from one stage or level of understanding (knowledge, development, whatever) to the next. It is this space in between that Victor Turner (from whom McLaren borrows the term) describes as liminality. Similarly, in describing how actors situate their sense of self in their characters, Richard Schechner calls this space "between not and not not" (i.e., between not being you in role and not not being you in role). What the liminal servant does is teach in the realm of critical pedagogy. His pedagogical interventions are intentional and purposeful: it is a social function committed to engaging and critically reconstructing "the possibilities of human life and freedom," and incubating that natural inclination in the student.

There is, to me, a very critical connection between this metaphor and what I believe I am trying to capture in my pursuit of whatever it is that makes a good drama teacher. Again, I found that others have tread this path before me. In *Dialogue and Drama: The Transformation of Events*,

Ideas and Teachers, Cecily O'Neill describes the key concepts of drama in education, and parallels these concepts to the works of Ira Shor, Paulo Friere and, most notably, Peter McLaren. In particular, she compares McLaren's liminal servant to Dorothy Heathcote's "authentic" teacher.

Heathcote, of course, is another educational drama sage. She has been very influential in the development of role-play in the classroom, and is perhaps best known for developing the "**teacher-in-role**" approach (where the teacher joins the students in their role-play as an equal and non-dominant character) and the "**mantle of the expert**" (where the teacher, in role, allows the student, also in role, to assume a higher status than the teacher, usually in a situation in which the teacher's character needs the guidance or expertise of the student's character to accomplish a given task). The authentic teacher is one who is a teacher first, and a teacher of drama second. And this authentic teacher, for all intents and purposes, is also a liminal servant.

The Three Faces of the Educational Drama Buddha

Heathcote, McLaren and O'Neill all describe the process of teaching, and the role of the teacher, in ways that suggest that there are different kinds of teaching, and different roles that the teacher might play. I believe the drama teacher is such a unique creature that we need to seek out new terms and metaphors to try to describe what a good drama teacher does. The instructor, Warren, for example, himself a good drama teacher, believes educational drama teachers can teach three things: skills, students, and subjects.

These, then, I will identify as three faces of the educational drama Buddha, the three areas or styles under which the drama teacher generally operates. One can easily see that these faces do not differ significantly from Courtney's kinds of learning (you don't get to be a sage for nothing). It does, however, help us concentrate for the moment on the teacher, rather than the student. It should also be understood that, by and large, none of these faces exist in a vacuum, that most effective teaching will involve some combination of the three. But for our purposes of trying to identify aspects of good teaching, we will separate them, and place them on three corners of a triangle, with the actual teacher standing somewhere within that triangle, probably leaning towards one corner or another according to her personal skills and tastes, and the needs of the specific task at hand.

THE FIRST FACE: THE TEACHER OF SKILLS

The first face, the teacher of skills, is perhaps the easiest to define. This is the teacher as craftsman, tactician, coach, the teacher who seeks to have the student discover the larger picture through the acquisition of particular abilities or skills. My doctoral thesis supervisor is such a teacher. As a director of plays (of which I have been in two) he teaches his actors precisely how he wants a part to be played; every movement and utterance is taught a piece at a time, as if the actor/ student were a mannequin or robot being programmed. The effectiveness of this kind of teaching rests on both the ability of the teacher to draw from the actor a suitable representation of the director's vision, and on the actor's ability to both trust the director and to see this vision come to life as the pieces come together. This particular director/ teacher comes from a very traditional, classical school of directing and choreography, wherein the director/choreographer has the power to dictate the performer's every move.

But my supervisor also comes from a background of teaching special populations — young persons with physical, mental and emotional disabilities — and in this capacity has given many young people with special needs and abilities the opportunity to recognize within themselves skills and talents they may never have otherwise known they possessed. He has drawn from them skills that elevate them above the norm for perhaps the first time in their lives, that empower them to take some control over their lives and environment, and ultimately give them the confidence they need to overcome some of the obstacles that society places before them. It is in this, that I see the true value of the teacher of skills.

The teacher of skills can easily be confused with the teacher of facts, for in many ways they are similar. The teacher of facts, the one who insists on the student learning things by rote, to memorize multiplications tables and poems, the one who pines for a return to the three R's, demands, like the teacher of skills, complete dedication and commitment from the student. Unlike the teacher of skills, however, the teacher of facts rarely gets that dedication and commitment from today's student, and thus actually teaches less and less. The underlying reasons for this are many and much discussed, but what must be recognized is that these reasons are more often than not directly related to what is happening to the student outside the school. The teacher of facts, even a "good" one, does not seem to address this as effectively as the "good" teacher of skills. The latter can help the student develop an ability to do something, to enact and empower herself in social situations both inside and outside the classroom, life skills that once were the responsibility of parents.

THE SECOND FACE: THE TEACHER OF STUDENT

The second face is probably the most difficult to see. While with the other two faces one can more or less define the thing being taught, a subject or a skill, the second face must try to define the person being taught, the student. This teacher is largely the product of the revolutionary ideas of Jean-Jacques Rousseau. In Rousseau many of the notions came together that would later serve as the foundation for progressive educationalists, from Pestalozzi and Froebels, through Montessori, Dewey, Cook and Bruner. These ideas include:

- Children learn naturally by playing and pretending;
- Emotions influence understanding and learning;
- How children learn is as important as what children learn;
- Children think, learn, and experience things differently than adults;
- Education should focus on the individual needs of the child.

What these educators developed was a movement towards child-centred learning, one which viewed the child as a flowering seed which the teacher was supposed to nurture, as opposed to an empty vessel into which the teacher was to pour society's knowledge.[7] In the field of drama in education there appeared a progression of influential educators such as Slade, Way, Ward, Heathcote and a multitude of others (including the contributors to this book) that have inherited and modified these ideas. This work began in the 1940s and 50s when Peter Slade attempted to recognize the significance of children's natural play, dramatic play, and the interconnected relationship of these to growth and development. Brian Way in the 1960s inspired and influenced an entire generation of drama teachers in designing specific exercises to implement Slade's philosophy of using drama (as opposed to theatre) to encourage the growth and development of the "whole" person, and in particular, a slant towards the creative individuality of the student. As Way himself states:

> Education is concerned with individuals: drama is concerned with the individuality of individuals, with the uniqueness of each human essence.... Individuality is also concerned with originality and deeply personal aspirations; drama encourages originality...and this is important to the full development of personality...[8]

Slade and Way's legacy in the field of educational drama lies primarily in shifting the focus of attention away from what was being taught to who and how teachers were teaching.

THE THIRD FACE: THE TEACHER OF SUBJECTS

The third face of the Educational Drama Buddha, the teacher of subjects, is the one that the mainstream educational system both needs and perhaps fears the most. This is because, almost by definition, the effective use of this kind of teaching requires a radical overhaul of the existing structures of education. These teachers are not so much in opposition to Slade or Way or their pedagogical descendants, as much as they espouse a logical extension of their ideas. The teacher of subject sees drama as an avenue towards the acquisition of knowledge and understanding in any field, regardless of it's apparent relationship to the arts, especially theatre. Drama, and in particular role-playing, provides a framework for the student to work out and discover solutions and approaches to real problems, situations and relationships in real time, all under the protective blanket of the suspension of disbelief.

I believe it is this teacher that Dorothy Heathcote refers to when she speaks of the "authentic" teacher. The authentic teacher recognizes that education (like art) is process, rather than product-oriented, and that teaching this way means: learning to present problems differently to students; discovering more subtle means of induction and communication; encouraging student interaction and decision-making processes; giving more leeway to students to discover other ways of tackling situations; imagining and carrying into action a greater variety of tasks; engineering a greater variety of feedback techniques; taking more risks with materials; tolerating more ambiguity in classroom set-ups because people may choose a variety of speeds to work at the same tasks. It means apportioning time differently, not necessarily slicing minutes in an orderly chronological sequence.... Process orientation means devising programs and tasks which induct through first intriguing, then engaging and interesting (the) pupils.[9]

Setting Out: Walking With My Eyes Open

The faces of the teacher of skills, the teacher of subject, and the teacher of student are the faces I have peered upon, read or heard about in my years as an educational drama novice. It has only been recently that I have known what to look for; indeed I have always looked at one face or another throughout my studies and never really recognized it for what it was. It has not been until my involvement with *The Last Forest*, in my capacity as an observer and assistant to a "good" drama teacher, that I have been able to recognize and appreciate the relative properties and values of each face within a single project, separately and in conjunction each with the other.

It should be noted here that from an educational point of view this project catered to two distinct sets of students: the undergraduate students in the show itself, and the much younger elementary students that came to see it. Most of the material written about educational drama (with the notable exception of Heathcote) is almost exclusively dedicated to approaches and applications with children in classrooms.

This project was equally concerned with the needs and development of the students in this university course, people who may well become teachers of the not-too-distant future. Naturally the course instructor had to choose activities and exercises that challenged the group's ability to collaborate, improvise and extrapolate within the workshop atmosphere. And because this course was also about creating a presentable piece of theatre, some of the sessions, particularly as the show's opening approached, bore scant resemblance to any of the faces I've described. Indeed, they most often involved little more than the all-too-necessary process of line readings and repetitions, blocking or other "rehearsal" activities.

What is important is that in the development of this project, which lasted almost four months, all three faces, as I have attempted to identify them, were indeed present, and that while the skills and experience of the students on stage may have been different than those of the students in the audience, the approaches of any of the forms of teaching are equally viable to each group; only the applications will be different.

Phase One: Drawing Up the Map

The initial stage of this project involved deciding upon and finding the material that would be the basis for the play. The director/teacher had already decided that it would revolve around an environmental/ecological, or "green" theme, and suggested a presentational style that incorporated elements of folklore and mythology with particular focus on animals as a common, linking vehicle between style and theme. Another element he wished to include was a movement style based roughly on the "soft" martial arts, particularly t'ai chi ch'uan.

With this in mind, the students were paired up and assigned specific assignments based on their particular interests, first in the form of a bibliography of relevant books and articles on their subject, and later in the form of fact-sheets of pertinent and/or interesting information concerning it. They were given a number of weeks to prepare this information.

The First Face

The skills face of educational drama appeared early, and varied according to factors not directly related to its goals. A common denominator in virtually all the cases of skills teaching was for the instructor to demonstrate and explain, and then have the group copy and repeat. What differed was in the way or ways the leader or teacher chose to encourage and motivate the group into active participation in an exercise that would presumably lead to skills acquisition.

For the first few weeks of the course, in-class activity centred on two areas: a) movement style, with respect to the martial arts, and b) development of archetypical or generic character types through ani-

mal imagery. The first of these groups of activities, developing a movement "vocabulary," involved primarily the first type of teaching, the
teaching of skills. However, I discovered that this face could wear a
variety of masks. Most sessions were led by the course instructor, but
others were conducted by the students themselves in a special peer-
teaching exercise, and then later by a t'ai chi expert.

What follows are excerpts from the notes I kept during the development of *The Last Forest*. They represent three examples of the
teaching of skills, three different glimpses into this face of the Buddha.

FROM 12–09–90: THE INSTRUCTOR LEADING GROUP

The instructor's style of teaching in this guise is fairly
consistent: unless in pairs or playing a game, most exercises are done with the group in a circle, allowing
everyone visual access to everyone else, including the
instructor. He speaks to the group as they mimic his
actions of whatever task he wants them to do. He can
then move about the group as they continue the task
to give individual attention.

FROM 25–09–90: THE INSTRUCTOR LEADING GROUP

In all of these exercises tried this day there is a critical
need for control, even more than balance (which is, I
suppose another way of looking at control); too many
members of this group exhibit very short concentration
spans and are very prone to losing sight of the point
of the exercise, especially evident when movements
were moved into the tag game where it very quickly
became a frenetic free-for-all until the instructor used
the basic elementary school "okay, everybody get in
a circle" technique to focus their attention to the connection between the point of the movement and the
game — even then a few opted for a kind of silliness
that the instructor often chooses not to stifle or rebuke
for the sake of retaining a spirit of spontaneity and
freedom of expression within the group.

FROM 25–09–90: PEER TEACHING

In this first of a series of peer-teaching sessions, J and
KP alternate explaining and demonstrating the exercises they have been asked to pull directly from the
text. Both seem relaxed and confident, J inserting characteristic humour while being quite intense during
the exercises themselves. It appears obvious to me
that both have worked together in preparing this

assignment, and are very familiar with the material. The class seems to have no problem following their instructions. Both observe the progress of the group and offer general pointers when they see irregularities, rather than pointing out individual mistakes. Also, both quickly and clearly address any questions anyone has about an exercise.

FROM 10–10–90: CLASS LED BY A GUEST INSTRUCTOR

KB, an experienced t'ai chi instructor, demonstrates in it's entirety the first stage of a t'ai chi movement set, known as T'ai Chi Tao: The Mountain Crane... She demonstrates and teaches the group the t'ai chi walk, which is the basic movement style for the specific elements of the Crane sequence. She then proceeds to teach the first four sections of the Mountain Crane. She does so in clearly delineated segments which she first slowly demonstrates and then has the group copy and repeat several times as she moves about the group, tending to individual posture and positioning. She seems to be adjusting well to what I presume is a larger group than she is used to.

She closes the session with a discussion about the philosophy of t'ai chi, and her particular affinity with the crane, including some wonderful photos of Japanese Snow Cranes. In classical Oriental mythology, the crane represents several things, including longevity and loyalty. It also represents the ideal balance between the yin and yang, the masculine and feminine, the hard and soft, the aggressive and the yielding. There is also a healthy dose of what I would call humanism from a feminist perspective in her approach: femininity is not considered in terms of refuting negative aspects of masculinity, but rather in positive terms that make both genders equal yet interdependent parts of the whole.

OBSERVATIONS ON NOTES

The course instructor, perhaps because he had the long-term interests of the project in mind, seemed most conscious of group dynamics; while leading by example, he actively pursued a friendly and playful atmosphere in the group. Sometimes this approach led to a lapse in focus and concentration, at which point he would invariably bring the group back on track by switching to a new exercise, changing his tone, or some combination of the two. It was the ability to gauge and adapt, to be able to read the group and its needs and then have a wealth of alternative exercises and approaches at his disposal, that thus determined the effectiveness of his sessions.

The objectives of the peer-teachers more often appeared to be to simply complete the assignment rather than teach the material. As such, they usually committed themselves exclusively to their preconceived lesson plans, to what they were supposed to teach as opposed to how they taught it. This tack, of course, is understandable given their own lack of familiarity with the material; it nonetheless marked the relative success of their lessons.

The effectiveness of the t'ai chi instructor's sessions, whose objectives were not so different from those of the peer-teachers (that is, to teach a series of t'ai chi steps and movements), was determined by factors that the peer-teachers did not really have available to them. The first was an obvious mastery of the material; there was none of the self-doubt that was evident with the peer-teachers. Related to this is a confidence that comes from having successfully taught other less talented students the basics of t'ai chi. Another, perhaps less obvious factor was the respect she generated for the passive and holistic philosophy that underlies all the soft martial arts. No one felt the urge to fool around in her classes, and most people worked very hard in trying to master and memorize the sequences of movements she presented to them. I have to admit that I was very impressed by how well some of the people in this group learned her lessons, or were able to use and adapt some of these movements elsewhere in the project many weeks after she had taught them.

Phase Two: Finding Other Faces Through Improvisation

The other faces of the Educational Drama Buddha, at least as they appeared to me, only emerged after the routine and tone for the course had been set in the first phase through the teaching of skills. The second phase of the project involved play and improvisation. Combining the skills acquired through the martial arts sessions already described, as well as other sessions dealing with clowning and tumbling, the instructor attempted to develop a common movement vocabulary, a common "language" that the group could incorporate in their improvisational exercises. Most of these improvisations initially took the form of games and play which the instructor would incorporate into the warming-up phase of each session. As the term progressed these games took on more importance as vehicles for developing both a healthy group dynamic (i.e., the ability to feel comfortable working and playing together as a group), as well as building a confidence in each member of the group to express and create individually, and to establish the freedom to contribute to the group.

The form and complexity of these games varied considerably: simple tag and other childhood games; co-ordination and timing exercises such as *The Odin Circle*; concentration and focus exercises such as *Ninja Walk*; vocalization and projection exercises and games such as *Throw The Sound*; inner awareness and visualization exercises such as *Imaginary Journeys*; and finally more improvisational exercises such as *Excuse Me, I Must Be Leaving*. Much of the focus when playing these games was on stretching levels of imagination and creativity, of self-awareness and awareness of others. These exercises helped the students learn to contribute individually to a group effort, to work and play together. In this sense, simply learning and using these games and exercises as part of the regular class routine fell squarely within the realm of the teaching of student, the second face of the Educational Drama Buddha.

As the complexity of these games and exercises increased and began to shift toward dramatic role-play, they were modified to include the information that was accumulating from the research assignments on animals, ecology and the environment. These exercises were intended to lead to the development of interesting characters and situations which the instructor could use as a basis for a play. This process of combining dramatic play with the subject of academic research is in essence the third face of the Educational Drama Buddha, the teaching of subject.

A fairly early example of this kind of learning was through an assignment where each student was asked to do a simple character study of a fantastic and imaginary animal which included where and how it lived, its relationship to its environment, and, if any, its mythological significance. While the style of the presentation of this assignment was left fairly open, most students chose to present their creations either in character as their animal, or in a different character who was an authority on the animal. This exercise proved to be very successful. Not only did it provide a unique perspective on understanding basic, if sometimes fanciful relationships between animals and their environment, it resulted in the creation of at least two characters that were strong enough to make it into the final show.

As a process, this exercise is not very far removed from Heathcote's "mantle of the expert" technique, wherein the roles of the teacher and student are reversed, and the student in role becomes an authority on a particular subject. The prime difference here is that the teacher did not actively assume the role of the student. He was simply being a passive observer.

Other more complex improvisation games and exercises were developed as the term progressed, structured to produce usable material in the development of the script. The process began with developing characters that combined both animal and human characteristics and personalities. This then evolved into improvised scenes with the use of flash cards under different categories, such as the human/animal characters, archetypes (i.e., the Traveller, the Warrior, or the Wise Fool) and place (in the forest, on a mountain etc.). Scenes were then improvised wherein random combinations of characters in assumed archetypical roles would meet in a particular place.

This phase of the project continued for several weeks, with interesting scenes being re-worked and refined, and the less interesting ones eliminated. The scenes evolved, becoming less improvisational as characters and situations gelled in both the actors' and the director's minds. The instructor finally began working out ways in which these scenes and characters might be pieced together, eventually producing a simple story line that included most of the best that had been developed in this improvisational phase of the project.

By this point, all three faces of the Educational Drama Buddha had shown themselves. The teacher of skills, introduced early and present throughout, presented the group with the necessary language and tools for this project's development. From this work emerged the face of the teacher of student, in the form of the games and exercises through which the students could become comfortable working and playing together. The teacher of subject was then introduced to focus the group's attention on the methodology involved in the theatrical development of the production, as well as explore the material on mythology and the environment that would be the theme of the production.

Phase Three: From Playing to The Play

The final phase of this project moved quickly away from the development of specific skills and the evolution of a script through improvisation and play, to the more conventional routine of preparing a theatrical production. The three faces, however, were present to the end. The characters and scenes the instructor had chosen to be part of the story were further refined and reworked. Using the same processes as before, new scenes and characters were developed to fill in gaps that were discovered in the story. The working script was finally decided upon, most of it coming directly from the actors as they finalized their improvised scenes. The bulk of this phase, however, was dedicated primarily to sorting out and memorizing lines and blocking, and to completing work on the more technical aspects of the production.

Significantly, a new character, the storyteller, was introduced near the end of this phase to provide a narrative voice which might to tie the scenes together. She was "invented" at the last moment to try to fix an apparent problem. I thought it was interesting to note that this new character had many problems fitting into the play, indeed into the ensemble as a whole. I believe this stems from the fact that she was the only character that did not evolve, as did the others, from the animal improvisations in phase two. In a sense, she did not arise out of the teachings of the three faces, but came from outside these processes.

The Educational Package: Old Faces in Other Guises

The educational package which I supervised to accompany the production, was interesting because it attempted to make a connection between the learning of the older students involved in the presentation of the play and the younger students who came to see it. For the undergraduate students, the package was a way of reflecting on the role and purpose of their learning, of focusing on the other set of students, the ones who they were ultimately taking this course to help. Their work in developing this educational package itself allowed them to get a glimpse of the three faces of the Buddha themselves.[10]

In the package was a play synopsis, as well as fact-sheets and a bibliography about mythology and the environment (i.e., teaching of subject). It also contained puzzles and drawing, and descriptions of many of the drama games and exercises that the students could try in their own classes (i.e., teaching of student). Finally, in conceiving the package components, I asked the undergraduate students exactly what it was they hoped the elementary students should learn from our production. In focusing on how and why these things might be transferred to the elementary students, the undergraduate students got a taste of the teaching process itself. They were forced to reflect on the skills needed to develop a simple curriculum and suggest ways of teaching this material to their much younger peers (i.e., the teaching of skills).

Another important aspect of the educational package was the notion that I impressed upon the undergraduates that the package would not be effective unless it helped the student audience make the connections between the mythological allegory they saw on stage and the serious issues that it contained and motivated its making. It was a conscious decision on our part to create a play that was in essence an extended metaphor. The actors used the power of drama to draw these young people into the metaphor, and so make it a part of themselves. To re-enforce this the actors came up to the lobby after each performance, to greet the audience as they left and to answer any questions about the show or the displays. Whether on-stage or off, the actors encouraged the students to explore the metaphor with them, and so take into themselves the sense of responsibility and empowerment for actions that can affect their lives and their world. In this the actors were embodying the spirit of all three faces: the teaching of skills, subject and student.

Conclusion

Despite all this reflection, I am still not quite sure what it is that makes a "good" educational drama teacher. I can say that I have seen the three faces of the Educational Drama Buddha, and I think I can attribute to them the resounding success of *The Last Forest* and the course that led to its realization. The show played to over 1,500 students and teachers, and their response was very positive.

While understandably exhausted after the final performance, the students involved in this production had obviously come to appreciate the work, mental and physical, that goes into this sort of creation. Some, like myself, may have recognized the effectiveness of a teaching strategy that encompasses all three kinds of teaching: Skills (to learn the "language" and "tools" of a given medium); Student (to learn how to work, play and learn effectively together); and Subject (to learn to access, synthesize and disseminate the target material).

Perhaps like these students, as well as the elementary students and teachers who came to see our production, I should look upon this experience as a signpost, a mileage marker along a road of learning and growing. This project, culminating in these reflections, is the first of many journeys I will take along this road, and it has been a profitable trip. Like these young learners, I can hardly expect to become fully enlightened all at once; few people ever are. At best we can try to appreciate the few revelations that come our way, and through these revelations, have a slightly clearer vision.

Endnotes

1. Participation in the project described in this chapter constituted the requirements of DINE 413/2, "Theatre Production for Young Audiences", a course offered within the Drama in Education program of the Theatre Department of Concordia University in Montreal, Canada. In this course, the students produced and presented a collectively created theatre piece specifically designed for young audiences. This play, presented at the D.B. Clark Theatre of Concordia University on December 11–15, 1990, was entitled *The Last Forest*.
2. Dr. Bernie Warren.
3. I should note at this point that my use of "good" is not necessarily, or at least exclusively, synonymous with moral or decent, but rather a term I will use to mean conscious of objective goals, sympathetic to student needs, competent in preparing and handling of relevant material, and effective in the execution of the teacher's role: to facilitate the intellectual and developmental growth of the student.

4. While the use of Buddha imagery in the development of this paper sprang largely from the East Asian and martial arts philosophies that informed much of *The Last Forest* project, its continued use is not taken lightly, nor is it meant to show any disrespect toward believers in the Buddha. As I learned more about the Buddhist philosophy, I recognized the cogency of the metaphors, and so sought to use them more directly in my exploration, for a common interpretation of the term "Buddha" is "an enlightened life condition."

5. Richard Courtney, (1989) p. 13.

6. Peter McLaren, (1988, Feb.) p. 165.

7. Paulo Friere, whose ideas on critical thinking and liberatory education have influenced McLaren's writings among others, uses yet another metaphor to describe this traditional approach to education: education as banking. Teachers are owners of a thing called knowledge, and they deposit this knowledge into their students, much as a banker would deposit a client's money into an empty account. When it is full, the account is closed, and the student graduates; the student is now full of knowledge and can now go out into the world and deposit their acquired knowledge into other people's empty accounts. For a more extensive discussion of this metaphor, see Friere, (1984).

8. Brian Way, (1967) p. 3-4.

9. Dorothy Heathcote, (1984) p. 179.

10. A Buddhist friend of mine suggested that the real Buddha resides in the rehearsal, not the performance. But I digress....

The Use of Drama in Teacher Education: A Call for Embodied Learning

JOE NORRIS

Voices that Haunt Me

I am challenged by the books I read and the people to whom I talk. They encourage me to discover and create a better self so that I can become a better gift to others. They challenge me to create classrooms where publicly accepted meanings are negotiated with the personal meaning of those who participate. They warn me of bifurcating knowledge into digestible bits which are easy to swallow but lack connection and relevance. Like the wisdom behind Heathcote's statement about drama, they remind me that life in classrooms concerns "Man (people) in a mess."[1]

This chapter will look at my voyage in the creation and the teaching of a graduate education course which employed creative drama as its primary mode of instruction. To tell it fully would require a series of novels as there have been many ports of call which have made provisions available for this latest voyage. I have chosen to summarize some of the influential voices using a dramatic, rather than a literary form, as this form demonstrates one I have often used in order to summarize course readings. By employing a **voice collage**[2] in class, I can provide an opportunity for individuals to focus some of the many voices which influence and haunt their daily practice. In this literary form, they serve as a backdrop, or as reference points, from which a course is charted. These particular ones have supplied me with a friendly nudge to take the next challenge in my pilgrimage in becoming a teacher. I have deliberately chosen voices outside of the educational drama field to demonstrate that a) there may be more kindred spirits than we realize and b) that they are calling if not begging for an increased use of drama in education. Let us set the stage by listening to some of the voices that haunt me:

> It is commonplace for writers to point out that we live in a time of deep division, in which mind is separated from body and spirituality is at odds with materialism. But how do we get out of that split? We can't just "think" ourselves through it, because thinking itself is part of the problem. What we need is a way out of our dualistic attitudes (Moore[3]).

> The unity of consciousness and the interrelation of all psychological functions were, it is true, accepted by all; the single functions were assumed to operate inseparably, in an uninterrupted connection with one another. But this unity of consciousness was usually taken as a postulate, rather than as a subject of study (Vygotsky[4]).

> Interfunctional relations in general have not yet received the attention they merit (Vygotsky[4]).

> ...it was quite hopeless for a European to penetrate into this realm of spiritual life — perhaps the strangest which the Far East has to offer — unless he began by learning one of the Japanese **arts** (bold mine) (Herrigel[5]).

> Before we learn how to teach in such a way, we must learn how to learn in such a way (Pinar[6]).

These and other voices beckon me to teach in a way which goes beyond knowing and doing to a sense of **being** which is reverent and significant. They challenge me to develop activities which, by their very nature, demand integration and relevance, and they ask me to ask the same things of my students. Using creative drama activities to explore issues and fashioning these ideas into a play makes pedagogical sense to me. The process responds to the voices which ask me to teach in an integrated way.

The Beginnings

During my 12 years of teaching in junior high schools, I had employed creative drama to teach literature interpretation, historical understanding, theatrical conventions and decision-making skills. In *blind walks*, the students and I examined the lives of Tito and Pierre, blind characters from two short stories in their anthology. These helped us to develop a partial understanding of how these people went about their daily tasks. In the history class, students developed characters to re-enact signing of the "Doomsday Book." In the discussions preceding and following the enactment, we explored the significance of mandatory compliance, the consequences of refusal and emotional impact on the people of that time. In another exercise, the role-playing of team members who would decide who would remain in, and who would be excluded from, a fall-out shelter, assisted us in examining our own values and the decisions we make based upon these values. Further, the exercise enhanced our understanding of the people in Britain who lived with the constant threat of a Saxon invasion as we explored the universal concept of impending doom. In the drama club we discussed and role-played the difficulties of being an adolescent. In our attempt to translate our insights into performance vignettes we came to better understand both the content and medium as we deliberated on what dramatic form would best get each message across.

During these sessions, my students and I (teacher) became partners in learning as we explored and shared our thoughts and ideas. We negotiated new directions which drew on our collective inner resources. Through each other's eyes we examined and re-examined the world as we looked from each other's vantage point. We were engaged with our bodies as we explored various ways of packing our bags during a collage of leaving-home scenes. This could not be separated from the affective domain as we examined the emotions of joy, sadness, hope and fear during the packing. Through the discussions which followed the scenes, we came to understand more fully the concepts of goodbye, independence and adventure, through the universal dimension of "leaving home." For our play we focused on the partings between parents and offspring and structured a series of family vignettes representing four generations. In these, and other activities, the learning from both the **doing** and the **reflecting on the doing** enhanced our understanding and commitment to the topics under investigation as well as creating a greater commitment to each another. Friendship was a concomitant result of our playing together.

In our work we were able to blend and **integrate the cognitive, affective and psychomotor elements** of Bloom's *Taxonomy*.[7] This widely accepted educational taxonomy, although it has been in existence for a number of years, has not been fully utilized as there seems to have been little movement on the part of academia to embrace it fully. In practice, the cognitive domain has been hegemonic[8] leaving the affective and psychomotor domains to take seats at the back of the classroom, if they were allowed into the classroom at all. The use of creative drama in curricular areas places greater emphasis on integrated knowing with the mind, body and soul and Vygotsky's plea for the interrelation of functions, is addressed there. What we know is connected with what we feel and what we live. The integration of theory and practice is encouraged in these classrooms by the way creative drama unites the participants thoughts, with their bodies and with their feelings in role-playing situations. Learning in the creative drama classroom is "**embodied learning**."

A Challenge

With the completion of a doctoral programme and employment in the university system, I entered the realm of teacher education. Here my chief responsibility was the teaching of drama methodology courses to drama major and minor education students. Through the use of creative drama, group drama and "**teacher-in-role**," I introduced my students to **drama as a learning medium**. In a peer-teaching lab environment, they taught each other. Through discussions of these in-common experiences, they and I came to a better understanding of the tacit subtleties of drama education. In so doing, the bachelor of education students began to understand, not through lecture but through direct involvement, the value of creative drama in teaching and learning. For me, however, this wasn't enough. "Something's lacking," often rang through my head and ever so slowly emerged the question, "If I truly believe in what I am professing, why can't I teach this way in the generic education courses I am asked to teach?" Following closely behind this question was the challenge to implement. So I began devising a graduate course for teachers, not actors, which would employ creative drama rather than lectures and seminars to teach and embody current curriculum theory.

The Proposal

Employment opportunities kept me in the province of my doctoral studies which is approximately 3,000 miles away from my place of upbringing. During one of my trips home I visited Saint Mary's University in Halifax, my first alma mater, and explored the possibility of teaching a graduate summer course there. A proposal was submitted and adapted to suit the needs of the institution. This course would focus on using drama as a methodology to teach content in the public school system. It was not exactly what I had hoped for, but it was a stepping stone. It touched upon using role-play and metaphor as a vehicle to expand our understanding of our lives as teachers but most of the course focused upon how to use drama to deliver the curriculum to my students' students.

The course was very well received and requests from students and faculty for a sequel were made. With credibility established, I proposed a course in curriculum theory in which teachers would explore their own personal and professional life worlds through creative drama. We would read stories and theories which would serve as triggers to our own memories and from these we would create scenes for discussion and a "possible" performance.

The Announcement

The proposal was slightly modified but accepted and I returned a second year to offer the course which appeared in the summer calendar as:

EDU642.OTR:[9] UNDERSTANDING TEACHING THROUGH DRAMATIC EXPLORATIONS

Course participants experience and analyse the potential of role-play as a means of investigating educational issues and reshaping their pedagogical ideas and behaviours. The process is collaborative ("collective creation"), based upon a willingness to "play" with individual and public knowledge systems concerning education in order to discover alternatives to, as well as confirmation of, previous stances.

The course would be offered from Monday through Friday, July 5 to July 30, 1993 from 9:00am to 12:30pm. As with many summer courses, its delivery was dependent upon a satisfactory enrolment but fortunately 19 of the possible 20 places were taken and the course was offered.

The Planning

The role of a teacher/director in planning a collective creation is a complex one. "Our task is to develop a context in which process and content reflect each other, without imposing our own agenda in terms of content or analysis (Moon[10]). I needed to develop a structure loose enough to encourage my students' personal understandings to emerge but fixed enough to enable us to have over 70 hours of meaningful experiences together. Adapting a elementary school unit plan I devised an extensive list of possibilities (Figure 1).

My deliberations were fourfold. First, from my work with various teacher groups over the years, I was aware that many, if not all students, would have little or no theatre or creative drama background. I could expect that they were unaccustomed to exploring ideas through planned and spontaneous improvisations. Their repertoire of voice and movement work would be minimal and they would consider that any presentation would be judged as a polished piece rather than a **work in progress**. I subscribed to Alberta Education's elementary drama curriculum guide[11] which claimed that anyone doing drama for the first time, or was working with a new group or topic, needed an **orientation**. Consequently, I was prepared to do many activities

TOPIC

What is Education/Schooling?
Who is a teacher?
Who is a student?
What is knowledge?
What is worth knowing?
Who am I as teacher?

Objectives

recognize the being behind the doing
to reconceptualize
unpack/repack
question role in education process
conscientization
uncover personal metaphors
discover and articulate belief system
turn cacophony to polyphony
accept multiple points of view

Scene Ideas

Brainstorming
Word Collage
Tug of War
Devil or Angel
Trial
Debate
Talk Show
Narrator/Mime
Awards Committee
Legend
When student/now teacher
Styles (Western, Soap opera etc.)
Experts
Dramatic Forms
Convention Charts
Job Interview
Meet the Expert
Hot Seats
Parable (Story Theatre)
War/Scary stories
Imaginary Friends

Possible Issues/Themes

Classroom management
Buzz Words
External Special Interest Groups
What is Advised?
Servant of Many
Mainstreaming
Accountability/Trust
Ambiguity/Intentionality
Honesty/Tact
Consistency/Flexibility
Inclusion/Exclusion
Freedom/Control
Work/Play
Curricular/Co-curricular/Extra
Methods (Being/Doing/Knowing)
I-Thou
Lived/Planned
Standards/Success/Excellence
Teacher Effectiveness
Models of Teaching
Integration
Teacher needs—perceived/actual
Student needs—perceived/actual
Job Security/Surplus
Leadership
Social Context
Administration/Learning Styles
Motivation
Change
Censorship
Hegemony
Myths
Gangs
Bloom
Ethics/Morals
Trust
Caring
Hope
Evaluation
Norm/Criterion (discrimination)
Curriculum Theory
Four Commonplaces (tetrahedron)
Technical/Interpretive/Critical
Theory & Practice
Reflective Practice
Reconceptualists
Emancipatory Pedagogy
Producers/Consumers
Zone of Tensionality
Thresholds

Research/Theory

Popular Education
Popular Theatre—Boal, etc.
Life world
Psychodrama/Sociodrama
Narrative/Story/Autobiography
Journal
Collective Creation
Data Collection
Participant/Observation
Interviews
Brainstorming
Imagery
• Progoff materials
Parallel Play
Games
Memory
• Humorous
• Sad
• Management
• When student/Now that teacher
Triggers
Readings
Stories
Songs
Movies/T.V.
Artifacts
Textbooks
Comic Strips
Journal Articles
Parables/Fables
Write to Meaning
...Letters to...
Conversations with...
Qualitative Research
Ethnography
Phenomenology
Action Research
Changes (from where)
Celebrate the Mundane
Icons

Collective Creation

Collage
Thesis/antithesis
Don't preach
Fusion of horizon
Unity of Form and Content
Exploration

Mining
Berry and Reinbold's Stages
Norris' Stages
Trust to Voice
Diamond Shape
Process/product

Focus of Speech/Sound

As if's
Choral Speech
Videotapes
Readers' Theatre
Word Collage
Music

Instruments
Make a song/poem/rap/opera

Personal Curriculum

Face of the Other/Juxtaposition
Resonance
Life's Learning
Autobiography
Catharsis/Synthesis/Epiphanies
Personal Metaphors (life is a...)

Change
Evolution
Get out what you put in
What do teachers do?
What is a good teacher?
Everything I Needed to Know...

Orientation/Creative Dramatics

5 things —
4 true/1 lie
Name cards
• phone
• programme
• teaching history
Say name "as if..."

Colours
"My name is..." (belief)
Being/Doing
Mirror
Word Sorts

Focus of Movement

Laban
Creative Movement
Puppets
Mime

Sticks
Music/Tapes
Dance

Professional Curriculum

List names of teachers
Conversations with
• former teachers
• former students
• Artifacts

Last year's teaching experiences
Professional Metaphors (teaching is a)
Self as Student
Stories of Teaching

Performance

Publicity
Costumes
Set
Lighting
Recording/scripting
Stage Management

Scene Collection
File Cards/Charts (Titles)

Stories of:

Evaluation
Discipline
Staff Room
Yard Duty
School Assemblies

Parent/Teacher Relationships
Magic Moments
Tragic Moments

Self As Artist/Creativity

Free Play & Zen in *the Art of Archery*
Authentic Voice
Collaborative Voice

Road Blocks
Fear
Neatness
Willis Harman

Figure 1: Unit Plan for Understanding Teaching Through Dramatic Explorations

to loosen us up physically, vocally, imaginatively, spiritually and artistically. By listening and responding to my students daily, I would chart the following day's activities. But first, each person would have to trust himself, and later each other.

Secondly, I could expect some students to be beginning or in the process of going through a personal paradigm shift. They would be moving from a fixed universe to a hermeneutic or constructivist one.[12] I was familiar with their graduate program and knew that some would have taken courses in critical theory and action research but that others would be just beginning their program. For some, the only valid knowledge would be that which could be verified by acceptable statistical designs. Personal knowledge and narrative would be suspect, if accepted at all. Pinar's concept of "**currere**"[13] or personal curriculum may be viewed as irrelevant to "schooling."

In a pre-course assignment I asked my students to prepare for our work together by completing a non-graded assignment. They were to read a book of fiction or non-fiction which focused specifically on one person's life. The book could be biographical or autobiographical but the focus had to be on one person's journey. *Siddhartha* was given as one example of a fictional piece and *The Diary of Virginia Woolf*, as a non-fictional piece. As they read their books they were asked to make three lists. In the first, they would list the epiphanies or influential turning points in the character's life. In the second, they would list their own personal epiphanies as triggered by the characters. For the third, they would write the personal metaphors used by the character to provide meaning to his/her life.

This assignment was designed to prepare the students for personal disclosure which is the foundation upon which this course is constructed. By doing the assignment it was hoped that the students would begin to re-examine their lives and be prepared to continue this process publicly in class, as much or as little as they preferred. This assignment was also the beginning of an informal class contract. Those who may have felt uncomfortable with this process were given a strong indication of what this course was about. They were provided with ample time to withdraw and take another course. I assumed that those who remained were willing to give the process a try and we discussed this more fully during the first few days of the course.

Thirdly, I did not want to neglect curriculum theory itself. I wanted to create a comfortable place for the examination of practice but I wanted that practice to be informed by current educational theory. A list of possible issues and themes was created and an extensive bibliography was generated. These readings would lend a critical eye to practice by providing various frameworks from which the lives of teachers and students could be examined.

Fourthly, and in some ways the most important, was the examination of self as artist. We would be working metaphorically and creatively, therefore we would need to look at our collective work under that frame. The book (text) *Free Play: The Power of Improvisation in Life and the Arts* would become our source of inspiration. The book focuses on the ability to listen to and trust one's inner voice in the ever-changing dance of responding to the inner and outer worlds of being. The tension of technique and freedom from technique is discussed problematically and one leaves the book being called to **remove fear**, the major obstacle to creativity, and to act "with the assurance and spontaneity of the child, knowing that my self-balancing sense of quality will keep me on course."[14]

This unit plan was non-linear but it enabled me to have many diverse directions at my fingertips so that I could meet the various emergent needs of my students. I was prepared, yet the structure was broad enough to be responsive to my students as we came to know and understand each other.

The Process

To provide a synopsis of the entire course would be well beyond the scope of this chapter, therefore, I have chosen a few activities from various segments of the course to highlight some chief aspects of the process of creating a theatre in our classroom.

ICE-BREAKERS

We started with some common ice-breakers. There are two criteria needed in order for personal knowledge to be articulated. First, the participants must have something they feel they need to say and secondly, that they **trust** one another enough to say it.[15] Ice-breakers which are challenging and meaningful initiate a trusting atmosphere. However trust is a fragile state and exists at different levels for various people. It needs to be constantly nurtured in order to spiral upward and permit personal stories to be publicly examined.

The first ice-breaker was a name game. I had the chairs arranged in a circle and started off by saying my name and a word that begins with the same letter as my name. "Joe jellybean" is my usual choice. I then pass a signaling/focusing object such as a set of keys to my left or right and ask the person to say my name and word and add her name and word. This builds cumulatively so that by the end, the last person is saying every name and every word. In the name of fairness, I usually go around one and a half times and as an extension, I have people rearrange themselves and ask a few to volunteer to try everyone's name. I participate in the activity with the students, **modeling my own risk taking** and vulnerability.

There is certain to be much **laughter** as comical words are associated with names. There is certain to be **collaboration** as we give hints
to one another. There is certain to be increased **familiarity** as we establish eye contact to look for clues to help us remember each other's
names. We begin to know each other through the **safety of play**. We
begin to create an atmosphere of trust so that we can all share in the
joyful labour of co-authoring each other's thoughts and ideas.

In another name game, students were placed in groups of two with
me taking part in one group due to the odd number of participants. We
would carry on a natural discussion giving each other factual information about ourselves. When we reconvened, rather than introducing
ourselves, we would introduce our partners. In the introduction we
would present five pieces of factual information, four of which would
be true and one would be a lie. The audience would then discuss what
information they thought was a lie.

This exercise would fulfill three aims. First of all, the lie would
heighten the audience's attention and encourage involvement in the
discussion after each presentation. Secondly, by speaking about another, rather than oneself, the **spotlight was dimmed** on the presenter.
The eyes of the audience were as much on the person being spoken
about as on the person speaking. Since this would be the first spotlight,
it would gently lead the class into becoming comfortable presenting
to each other. Thirdly, it lead to a discussion regarding **belief**. If we
were to convince an audience, we would have to convince ourselves.
Understanding the degree of belief needed in the telling of a "lie"
would heighten our understanding of the belief needed in **expressing
our convictions.**

These and other ice-breakers recognize that the cognitive and affective domains cannot be bifurcated and that **serious discussion can
only result in probing thoughts and questions when a playful trusting
atmosphere exists**. Students will begin to take risks when the consequences of failing are minimal. If we were to reach a point in our
working together where we would honestly and critically examine our
own practices in each other's company, we needed to feel each other's
comfort and support.

ROLE-PLAY

From these and other activities we moved into an educational role-
playing exercise. Here, small groups were assigned the task of creating
an educational journal/magazine/newspaper based upon cards which
were passed to them. Each card gave the name of a journal and a
series of questions, the answers to which would determine the nature
of the journal. The students could change the title but they had to
keep the intent of the original title such as "The Educational Watch
Dog" and "Teachers' Digest." They were also given character devel-

opment sheets and in addition to coming up with the journal, they had to create their own personal histories and current role on the journal staff. We met as an entire group and described the journals and the characters involved.

When this was completed they were told that they were to interview an instructor who was teaching a new experimental course and that we would use my course outline as the instructor's "press release." They were, as a team, to create a series of interview questions which I would answer. Again they broke into small groups to create some questions and then met in role to interview me.

The purpose of the assignment was fourfold. First, in the creation of their journals, they were **brainstorming** educational issues. Secondly, they would be **addressing specific concerns** they may have about the course. Third, I would be **modeling risk taking** as I entered the "spotlight" or "hot seat," as I called it. Finally, and most importantly, all of this would be done **in role**. The class brainstormed, developed questions and interviewed me in role. Since their **real** lives and their **fictional** ones were not that different, the overlapping of the two would help bridge the gap for those who weren't used to being in role. I was also aware that the role would **provide a distance** for them, enabling them to ask questions of me that they normally wouldn't in their real roles as students.

In my own practice I have experienced this phenomenon quite often. The involvement in role tends to de-center and re-center the participants so that new meanings are found in the juxtaposition of the two simultaneous selves. An example which highlights this, happened in the course offered the previous summer.

One student, in role, asked with a Southern drawl, "How come we need someone from Alberta to come all the way to Nova Scotia to teach a course in drama? Don't we have any of our own experts here?"

In my response I told them that I was originally from Nova Scotia and that, in actuality, Alberta needed to import the expert.

We laughed.

During the break the student came up to me quite apologetically and said that she didn't mean to be rude, that she was just "playing the part." I agreed but asked her who made up the question? Of course it was still her but through the role. It seems that in this particular case the "fiction" allowed this student to ask a genuine question which she would not have been as comfortable asking within the protocol of classroom decorum. The question did exist for both the student and the character she was portraying but the fictional form afforded it expression. The role, in a "real" (?) sense, freed her from **reality** and enabled her to ask a question which, in reality, she wanted to ask, but couldn't. The role (**fantasy**) allowed her to come closer to her "real" self. The ability to participate in such a dramatic activity and the intellectual skills necessary to accept the ambiguity created by the blending of fantasy and reality, indicates an awareness of both the medium and the message and how the two interrelate.

Courtney may argue that this "provides a split reference that in usage indicates an advanced form of intelligence."[16]

ORIENTATION

During the first few days many such orientation exercises were conducted to limber up our voices, our bodies and our imaginations as we became comfortable playing together. We stretched our bodies as we did physical relaxation exercises and moved creatively to music.[17] We explored our vocal ranges as we said our names, words and phrases with **subtext**;[18] we practiced precision skills through mirror exercises and precision walks; and we expanded our imaginations with guided imagery exercises. We started with the **emotionally safer** imagery exercises such as listening to the sounds in and out of the room and then we focused on the feeling of things touching the body such as various articles of clothing and our weight on the floor. Later I planned to move to a potentially more intense exercise of having the students imagine some old school memories, both as a student and as a teacher.

The orientation exercises introduced the students to the realm of creative drama. The senses of sight, hearing and touch were emphasized as ways to decode the world around us and as methods of communication. Every exercise was followed by a discussion or **debriefing** in order to a) check if any of the participants were having difficulty[19] and b) extend the exercise by permitting the participants to voice, discuss and understand what they had just experienced. Debriefing creates classrooms in which the students' thoughts and feelings of what they do are legitimized and sets the stage for them to become co-authors of the curriculum, in this case, a play based on their own beliefs and experiences.

Recently in my work I have separated the teaching of drama into three major areas. I find that most lessons have a **context**, a **process** and **content** which needs to be taught.

CHART 1

	Example #1	Example #2
PROCESS	Brainstorming, Small Groups, Presentations	Individual, Parallel Action
CONTEXT (FORM)	Choral Speech	Tableau
CONTENT	The Shooting of Dan McGrew	Bear Story

I label the dramatic forms (puppetry, mime, choral speech etc.) the context, the classroom conventions (brainstorming, parallel action, debriefing, side-coaching etc.) the process, and the topic under investigation (Three Little Pigs, History of the Black Empire Loyalists, Teaching Experiences etc.) the content. In most lessons all three dimensions need to be taught in an integrated way and if one of the three is missing, the lesson may fall flat. In our case, although all three were present, the orientation focused primarily on context and process skills as many of the participants had little experience with these. Once these were established, a balance among all three could be achieved.

TOPIC INVESTIGATION

Interspersed with orientation exercises were discussions on the pre-course assignment, the theory of drama education, journal writing, course evaluation and reading assignments. One of the texts was *Stories of Teaching*, a compilation of many short narratives by teachers who focused upon specific events, experiences or issues in their own teaching. The book was selected to serve as a trigger to the students' own stories. The first story chosen for exploration was *On Losing My Copycard*,[20] a short story which depicts a teacher's angst over loosing hers. It is a humorous tale but the undertones highlight the enormous pressure placed upon teachers' lives, all under the banner of "accountability." I asked them to get into small groups to a) tell their own stories about the photocopy room and b) translate these into a presentation. Before sending them off, I gave one of my few lectures.

The danger I find with giving such an assignment to a novice group is that many students do not have a repertoire of scene possibilities and usually come back with a realistic scene which does not translate well to the stage. I provide them with a table of possibilities using the theatrical conventions, light/darkness, movement/stillness and sound/silence.

Chart 2, with my accompanying comments, indicates that in order to communicate the intent of a scene, one must choose a form which complements it. I explain that realistic **dramatic action** may not be the best way to get the message across. For example, a scene may have one person **miming** the marking of tests while another person uses an **off-stage voice** to provide an inner dialogue to portray the frustration of the character. Chart 2 offers a number of beginning variations from which a scene can be built.

The photocopy scenes were accurate and poignant. They encapsulated many dimensions which make up a teacher's **life-world** and provided each of us with a glimpse of the powers which structure a teacher's life. They were humorous but like the story which triggered them they told powerful messages.

One scene had the cast backlit by an overhead projector and all that could be seen was the silhouette of one teacher at a time as he or she confessed to a "sin" regarding the photocopier. One teacher had access to another teacher's code and used it to run off extra copies while another "stole" paper. In the discussion which followed, many resonated with the scene. One question which arose was, "Why do we feel guilty when we are doing things which we believe are for our students' benefit?" and an equally compelling one was, "Do we want to live this way?"

CHART 2

	LT	DK	MV	ST	SD	SL
DRAMATIC ACTION	X		X			
MIME	X		X			X
NARRATION	X			X	X	
PICTURE TABLEAU	X			X		X
STEREO RADIO		X	X		X	
BLACK OUT (time)		X	X			X
MONO RADIO		X		X	X	
BLACK OUT (no time)		X		X		X

LT = light; DK = darkness; MV = movement;
ST = stillness; SD = sound; SL = silence

Other scenes dealt with favouritism, temperamental machines (with the machine's own inner dialogue), ecology and paper waste, and the paranoia created by watching over each other's shoulders. Each scene highlighted an aspect of human existence and demonstrated the class's understanding of how to meld content with an appropriate dramatic form. Some confessed that they were skeptical of the exercise at first but were amazed at how we a) were able to analyse significant teacher experiences though the lens of a photocopy room and b) were able to present our analyses in a dramatic form. They were beginning to learn that drama is a powerful research tool in the collection, analysis and presentation of data. With this initial success behind us, we were ready to delve into a collective creation project.

COLLECTIVE CREATION

Berry and Reinbold define a collective creation as "a play researched and written by a group of actor-writers."[21] They propose a set of stages that a group goes through in order to move from the

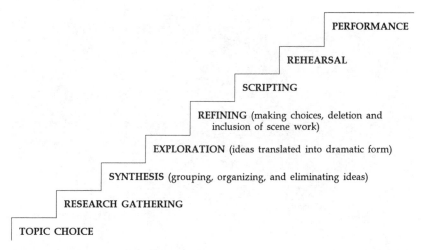

Figure 2:   Process of Collective Creation (after Berry and Reinbold)

topic to a performance piece. Although they claim that it is not as linear as it looks on paper they believe that there are distinct sections which overlap (See Figure 2).

For our class, the topic choice was omitted as the nature of the course imposed it. We would co-author a play on "Our Lives as Teachers and Students." The next four stages were not disconnected but were merged. We **researched** many of our own personal experiences both as teachers and students and interviewed others outside the class to obtain a distant perspective. We **explored** our findings through creative drama activities, drew conclusions (**synthesis**) from our discussions and made suggestions and notes to **refine** scenes for future use. In our case, the research, synthesis, exploration and refining stages worked as a spiral with much movement back and forth among the four.

As one who has been through the process many times, I have found that making scripting decisions too early can prematurely drive the play into a false structure and that only when enough data is collected, can a play take shape. I prefer to wait to the last moment to structure the play and am comfortable with this process. However, this is not the experience shared by many first-time participants. Although the class trusted me, by the time we came to the scripting and rehearsal stages, a few were anxious as they saw no play in sight. I was prepared for this, as this had previously occurred in a class in which I was a participant/observer.[22]

In that class the students trusted the teacher, based upon her previous reputation, but had no idea where they were going. She could

Figure 3: Class Photograph Using Tableau

see the play taking shape as she knew how to read the emerging signs but since the process was foreign to the students, they could not. It was a great surprise to her when they informed her that they felt completely lost until a script was laid before them. With this knowledge, I expected that a certain degree of uncertainty would exist with some members in the class and that this could produce some anxiety. I was prepared to respond to their concerns with patience, as this would be their natural reaction to a foreign situation. Jokingly, I would say to a few, "Do you see it yet?" and their responses were, "Noooooo!"

The scripting and rehearsal stages were also merged. During the other stages we had kept a record of each scene on file cards. Each card had a creative title which would help us to quickly remember the scene, a list of the initial players/co-authors, and sometimes, a few notes. We began the scripting/rehearsal stage by reviewing the cards and listing all of the scenes we had worked on. We deliberated on where to begin and once the first scene was chosen and presented we asked, "What scene makes sense next?" Earlier we had done a few improvisation scenes to prepare us for this stage. In one exercise, a student would go to the center of the room and freeze. Another student would enter, take a complementary position and freeze. This continued until the entire class was frozen. We repeated this a few times and discussed why we chose the positions we did. Later, our class picture was constructed in a similar fashion (Figure 3).

During one improvisation exercise, after the scene was rolling, I would say "freeze" and have one of the players leave and another take the body position of the person to be replaced. Taking suggestions from the body position, the person would have to find a new but natural direction for the scene. This continued with the students themselves initiating the freeze and entering a scene. Both exercises helped the students to a) recognize that scenes and our work together were offers[23] to the class and that others could adapt and change them, b) obtain a sense of picturization and c) understand how scenes could either complement or blend into one another.

The play was scripted and rehearsed in a similar manner. Once a scene was finished, we would find the next scene that would fit. This procedure was done on the second last day of the class and only then did we make the decision to perform. Many in the class had a few tentative audience members in mind and they were invited to the performance which would take place during the last half of the last class after we had another dress rehearsal. Even after these structured rehearsals, one student still claimed that she could not see the play. It was only after performing in front of an audience that it took shape for her.

There were some guidelines that we used in the creation of scenes and scripting which helped us to structure the play. One which is ever so basic to drama is "**show; don't tell.**" Lectures themselves can be deadly, but nothing is more deadly than a play that begins to preach. During our working and playing together we became comfortable in critiquing each other's scenes as we recognized them as offers. So whenever a vignette or character moved into the preaching mode, we were quick to point that out.

But this does not mean that the play had no messages. An alternative approach to preaching is **to provide both thesis and antithesis and allow the audience to synthesize.** Either within a scene itself or by juxtaposing a scene with another scene with a different point of view, we made certain that more than one perspective was brought forth. Even among ourselves we agreed to disagree and this natural and playful tug of war kept the play **in balance.** We aimed to provide multiple perspectives on teaching and utilized the differences of the cast to do just that.

The Content

However, the performance was not the major focus of the class. In fact, some of the scenes which best helped us to understand our lives as teachers did not make it to the final play. Only one of the photocopier scenes was included and it grieved us deeply to leave the remaining photocopier scenes, as well as others, out of the final performance.

They were good vignettes but they did not fit the emergent structure of the play. The major purpose of the course was to employ drama as a tool to help us better understand the life world of teachers and these scenes fulfilled a greater purpose. As Barone[24] puts it, "Aesthetic content opens up the text to the multiplicities of experience, conditions it, plants it specifically in virtual space and time, and provides a term of reference for the sense of the text." The play was indeed a focal point but its major function was to provide an open platform upon which educational experiences and concepts could be examined, recognizing that any examination brings with it a particular point of view. The learning about and the understanding of teachers lives was our aim and the use of drama in our classroom was for self-enlightenment. We placed greater emphasis on the research and explorations stages than on the scripting, rehearsal and performance stages.

To put the research and exploration stages in context with both the course and with the scripting, rehearsal and performance stages, the issue of **self-indulgence** needs to be examined. Many collective performances have been accused of being self-indulgent and the initial temptation is to become overly cautious and avoid any trace of personal knowledge. I disagree. I have found that **if the participants are not transformed in some way through the process, they have nothing significant to say to an audience**. So rather than avoiding personal knowledge, I aim for it. As teacher/director, I search for dramatic activities which can lead the participants to new understandings about an event or issue. I help them to examine how they perceive and react to things, so rather than avoiding the self, I aim to have my students/actors to become **centred-in-self**. In our dramatic playing we are continually in a process of de-centring and re-centring our points of view and all perspectives are held as **placeholders until the next insight**.

But being centred-in-self is not the same as being self-centred. They are similar, but have different ways of being in the world. An individual who is self-centred perceives oneself in an "I-It"[25] relationship with the world. Self is at the centre and the function of the world it to serve the self. The centred-in-self individual has an "I-Thou" relationship with the world. This person recognizes that the world is mediated by his own interpretation and that it is difficult to get beyond one's own skin. For this person, the universe is centred or focused by the lens of self but all other aspects of creation are also acknowledged as having their own centred selves. We recognized that we needed each other to go beyond our own skins, beyond our own point of view. In our collective performances, we bring our own perspectives forward but we make them problematic. In this way we go beyond self-indulgence as we continually question ourselves. Buber[26] claims that the

14) Focus

13) Belief PUBLIC KNOWLEDGE

12) Ownership/Co-ownership

11) Ideas Accepted (co-authorship)

10) Responsibility

9) Commitment

8) Purpose

7) Challenged

6) Engaged

5) Interested

4) Articulation

3) Trust COLLECTIVE KNOWLEDGE

2) Personal Meaning

1) Stimulation PERSONAL KNOWLEDGE

Figure 4: Stages of Interpersonal Development

function of an artist is to make herself the best that she can be so that she can be a better gift for others. Our play is for ourselves but we are also aware that ourselves are gifts to others.

In our exploration and research the self is ever present but is also ever questioned. We grow from the challenges we present one another and are grateful for the learning which transpires. However, we must go beyond this stage if we are to present our new understanding to an audience. As a complementary set of stages to those of Berry and Reinbold (Figure 2), I have devised an interpersonal set of stages which move the process from personal knowledge through collective knowledge to public knowledge or performance (Figure 4).

As discussed earlier, the purpose of an orientation is to help the participants to begin to trust one another. Once this starts, they are freer to express what they think and feel. It is my responsibility as teacher/director to provide the stimuli or triggers to help them recover personal memories and beliefs. When this occurs, and trust is present, personal meanings are explored, examined, debated and tested through dramatic activities. The individuals and the group become interested and engaged in the activities and a commitment to the project is achieved. Through the research and explorations stages, our awarenesses, attitudes, and perhaps even our behaviors were reconceptualized.[27] Together we created new meanings from old understandings and were excited in the ways we became co-partners in learning. I also label the collective knowledge stage, an emergent curriculum.

However, if it is left in this stage and presented to an audience, it may well be perceived as self-indulgent. In our playing together, we have created a mini-culture with our own set of signals, conventions and understandings. In order to perform for the public, we must translate our collective knowledge into a publicly understandable medium. Leaving it at the this stage makes pedagogical sense, taking it to the third, makes theatrical sense.

However, these stages must not be seen as hierarchical. Each stage is important and valuable in its own right. The point worth noting is that **depending upon the purpose, it is vital to know what stage you are in**. In fact, I find that the collective process has the potential of shutting down the **creative drama versus theatre debate**. In a collective creation, creative drama and theatre are complementary as they greatly influence one another. Both personal and collective knowledge inform the artistic (form and content) decisions of the theatrical presentation and the act of translating these into a theatrical medium provides another lens through which to examine personal and collective knowledge. They are not mutually exclusive but vital for each other's survival.

Our class did many dramatic explorations which helped us to understand pedagogical practices, far too many to explain in depth here. We planned and taught "how to" lessons using Aoki's three curriculum orientations[28] to tease out how the theory may look in practice. We did a voice collage using quotes from *Free Play* to summarize the book. Students taught "mock" lessons in which we heard the inner dialogue of students. Together we brainstormed a list of issues we would like to examine. This list included gender issues, power/control, standardized testing, work experience programmes, magic moments in our teaching experiences and opening day in September. Each of these were given to small groups to explore. They presented the scenes to the entire class and the discussions, which followed, focused on both theatrical and pedagogical issues. A workshop using sound and image was given during a visit to another graduate education class at Mount Saint Vincent University. This day exemplifies much of our work.

THE VISIT

Early in the course, just after our success with the photocopier scenes, we went on a field trip to another university approximately 100 kilometers away. In the previous year I had taken my former class there in order to team-teach with Allan Neilsen who was teaching a course on teacher narratives. Allan and I had met at a conference, found similarities in our work and looked for an opportunity to work together.

In the first year, we merged our two classes. Allan described his process, had his class share some of their writings, and we discussed both the process and content of the pieces shared. Later, I conducted a metaphor workshop using colour and sound and we met at the end of the day to share small group work based upon the workshop. It was an enjoyable learning experience for us all and Allan and I decided to repeat the workshop the following year, if I returned.

Needless to say, this class was a little nervous about going to a foreign place, especially with the possiblility of presenting some of our photocopier scenes. However, we contracted that they had the right to decline[29] and that the workshop alone would suffice. The decision "to perform or not to perform" would be made there. We did end up performing them all.

Since there were many new people who did not know one another, we started with some ice-breakers. Just because each group had good internal working relationships, it did not mean that the two groups would or could work together. A few short orientation exercises started our day. First, they were given a short lesson in concrete poetry which is basically defined as "the way the word is written encapsulates some of its meaning." I used the word:

> DRI
> P

as one example and drew my name:

explaining that the top of the "J" represents a smile, indicating that I believe in the value of play. The "O" was drawn in a Zen-like fashion as I slightly dabble in the Zen notions of artistry. The "E" drawn from one focal point represents that I like to look at things from multiple perspectives.

Individuals were asked to write their names on name tags using concrete poetry and after ample time was given for most to finish, they were divided into small groups and were asked to explain their name tags to one another. Since there were over 45 participants and we would only be working together for that day, I decided that we did not have enough time to introduce ourselves to the entire group. Each group had a mixture of students from each class.

Allan, then gave a brief history of his class to date and one of his students read her written story of an experience she had. This led to much discussion and both groups were actively engaged in sharing and analysing stories of teaching experiences. As a transition, I explained that we, too, were examining teacher narratives but in a collaborative way. I informed them that we were taking stories, ana-lysing them using creative drama activities and co-authoring scenes for possible inclusion in a final production. I then introduced the pho-tocopier scenes and all groups had decided to present. Again much discussion was generated and we continued our discussion over lunch.

After lunch, I emptied a duffel bag full of an assortment of per-cussion instruments before them and explained that in the next exercise we would use metaphors to help us to find and understand some other teaching stories. I further explained that the exercise was new for both groups and neither one was at an advantage. There were tambourines, clavicles, triangles, spoons, wooden sticks, agogo bells, a gwiro and a casaba, to name a few.

I asked the participants to recall a few students they had either taught or had as a peer in classes they were in. Further, they were asked to remember at least three or four people. Some would be the "good" ones, some the "bad" and others, various forms of neutral. Each person was asked to choose one from his list and an instrument upon which they could play the rhythm of that person. They weren't to play it aloud but were to think about playing it for the next part of the exercise.

When everyone was ready, they were instructed to enter a mock classroom, one at a time, playing that student on the instrument. Once a person sat down, it was a signal for the next person to begin. No decision was made on order of entry as they were asked to listen and find a moment when they thought it was appropriate for their character to enter. As the exercise emerged there were smiles, frowns and laugh-ter as we recognized people we knew via the rhythms of the sounds.

When we were all assembled, I brought the collage alive with all of the sounds being played at once and initiated a short discussion with the question. "How can we meet the need of this diverse group of students?" We could have discussed this one for hours but this exercise was used more as a warm-up rather than for in-depth explo-ration. The next activity focused on epiphanies or major turning points in one's life. Both Allan's and my classes had discussed the pedagogical nature of epiphanies and new small groups were formed to a) tell each other a turning point in her life and b) to choose one to tell, using the musical instruments.

The presentations were thoughtful and moving. Without words, the audience was able to understand the scenes and connect the emotional intent with similar life experiences. By this time the day had ended and we left discussing informally the power of the presentations remorseful that we had no videotape record of the magic we had experienced.

The scenes touched us deeply and reminded us that teaching is a human activity. Our conversations focused on creating classrooms which are cognizant about teaching in a caring manner, recognizing that the affective side of learning must not be ignored. We saw pain, misunderstanding, fear, confusion and hope. These scenes requested and challenged us to make classrooms more humane places for us all. The stories themselves, not the intellectual theory behind them, informed our thoughts, and in turn would influence our practice.

After our visit to Mount Saint Vincent University, our work was far more focused and relaxed. We knew that what we were doing was valued by others and that it was significant educational research. We knew that we could uncover many implicit aspects of school life through dramatic exploration which are difficult to access through other research forms. We knew that what we would find would be relevant and informative for ourselves, even if our work never resulted in a performance. And we were having fun doing it. When we arrived back in Truro we went into high gear.

Evaluation

The final item worth noting about the course, is the method of evaluation employed. The collective was not an extracurricular activity nor was it a community theatre event. It was situated in the context of a graduate education course with the typical internal and external expectations. Students were concerned about "the grade" and how it would be determined and I had obligations to the university as well. Yet **typical evaluation procedures did not seem appropriate**. 1) We were working as a team and, as such, how could individual marks be assigned? 2) Since we were primarily using dramatic forms it seemed inappropriate to use the written medium as the chief evaluation tool and 3) since most were newcomers to this way of learning, assessing the drama also itself seemed inappropriate.

The major focus of the course was to use drama as a reconceptualization tool and who would know better about what they learned than the students themselves? I proposed the following criteria to the class:

1) Each student would keep a daily journal which would
   a) have listed the events of the class; and
   b) contain a reflective entry focusing on one or more aspects of that day.
2) At the end of the course each student would pass in a 10 to 20 page paper highlighting what they had learned about themselves, about teaching/schooling/education, and about drama in education.
3) They would aim for a performance but that would be renegotiated near the end of the course.

4) All students would receive an "A" but each student must write a short essay explaining why he felt that he deserved one.

These criteria were discussed and approved. However, it was made clear that I would not neglect my responsibilities as an evaluator. I would still respond to each assignment with formative feedback and provide questions for further thinking.

My rationale for such a system is twofold. 1) This system made each student accountable to herself, to each other and to me. Since the course was a collective creation in which we would collaboratively assist each other in a re-examination of educational issues, the assignments chosen met our aims and complemented our work together. 2) Nachmanovitch claims, and I agree, that the spectre of the judge and the fear of failure can inhibit the creative spirit. Grading these students would run counter to my educational aims, as whatever scheme I employed would have them second-guessing my intent. Was I the coach encouraging them to do better or was I a reminder that their marks were going down? The contract of the "A" removed this fear and enabled them to do "A" quality work.

The content of the final papers was as diverse as the students. One student reread the *Tao of Pooh* and compared the philosophy of the book with the process that our class went through. Others wrote a few stories, similar to those in *Stories of Teaching* and a few, like the collage format used in the final performance, focused upon a few classroom experiences which touched them. Some wrote poems, one did a quote collage with a few reflective lines under each one. Each paper documented the struggles they went through and insights they found while creating a play in our classroom.

An analysis of these papers is a chapter in itself as each demonstrates the depth to which the students went to in order to "play with individual and public knowledge systems concerning education in order to discover alternatives to, as well as confirmation of, previous stances," as the course description states. Each found new voices within them and each recognized that drama is a highly underestimated teaching tool. Through the drama we all experienced a classroom in which learning could be relevant with all aspects of self. As we examined our own classrooms with our bodies, thoughts, and feelings we began to study and portray education in an integrated fashion and recognized that it is a human endeavour. We came to understand that an emergent collaborative curriculum, in which all participants are co-partners, is built on a strong sense of community. We saw that such communities must appreciate differences and celebrate them as gifts for the benefit of all. We rejected the polarization of roles and advocated classrooms in which teachers and students have separate but complementary responsibilities. One student, Eva Taylor, summed this up quite nicely in her final paper. She reflected on how her understanding of the pedagogical stance of a teacher changed as a result of being in this course.

> I watched as
> a solitary figure
> made his way
> along the street.
> Barely noticing
> the people,
> objects
> that he passed,
> Apparently
> lost in thought....
> alone.
>
> I watched as
> the solitary figure
> made his way
> about the classroom
> the same way....
> alone
> Not lost in thought,
> but separate
> from the exchange, the stories, laughter
> his students
>
> Apart yet....alone
>
> the teacher
>
> on the outside....but
> more connected than the rest!

Upon rereading my initial quote collage and the last line of her poem, I now find the common thread upon which the course was based: **connections**. In the process of creating a play we became connected with the material, connected with our pasts, connected with our audience, connected with ourselves and connected with each other. We learned that a **playful community can transcend the "people in a mess"** and that an embodied curriculum can be achieved.

Endnotes

1. Dorothy Heathcote, *Three Looms Waiting*, a BBC Omnibus programme (Ipswich England: Concord Films, 1972).
2. In a voice collage, the participants focus on words or phrases which relate to a specific topic. They then recite these one at a time by listening to what has been previously said. For example, I had a group of junior high students reflect on things that are said on Christmas morning. Then, they articulated their thoughts. This led to a stronger discussion about the meaning of Christmas and eventually this collage opened the play.
3. Thomas Moore, *Care of the Soul* (New York: Harper Collins Publishers Inc., 1992), p. xiii.
4. Lev Vygotsky, *Thought and Language* (Cambridge: MIT Press, 1986), p. 1.
5. Eugen Herrigel, *Zen in the Art of Archery* (New York: Vintage Books, 1981), p. 15.
6. William Pinar, "Curerre: Toward Reconceptualization" in W. Pinar (ed.), *Curriculum Theorizing* (Berkeley: McCutchan Publishing Corporation, 1975), p. 412.
7. Benjamin Bloom, *Taxonomy of Educational Objectives Handbook I: Cognitive Domain* (New York: David McKay Company, Inc., 1956); and Benjamin Bloom, *Taxonomy of Educational Objectives Handbook II: Affective Domain* (New York: David McKay Company, Inc., 1964).
8. Hegemonic refers to the ruling class or domain. For example, the certain subjects are privileged in a school curriculum while others are perceived as secondary. We could say that the core subjects are hegemonic.
9. Although the course was taught through Saint Mary's University, this was an extension course taught in Truro, Nova Scotia at the Nova Scotia Teachers' College.
10. Celia Moon, "Addressing Social Issues in the Drama Classroom" in E. Errington (ed.), *Arts Education* (Victoria: Deakin University Press, 1993), p. 137.
11. Alberta Education, *Elementary Drama Curriculum Guide* (Edmonton: Alberta Education, 1985).
12. Hermeneutics can be considered a theory of interpretation and constructivist knowledge recognizes that much of our knowledge is not fixed but constructed through of a frame of reference. Both ascertain that reality is a construction not a given.
13. **Currere** is a term that William Pinar uses to expand our notion of education beyond that of schooling to the curriculum of life. It recognizes that our personal histories have a large part to play in our understanding of life and our behavior in it.
14. Stephen Nachmanovitch, *Free Play: The Power of Improvisation in Life and the Arts* (Los Angeles: Jeremy P. Tarcher Inc., 1990), p. 171.
15. Joe Norris, *Some Authorities as Co-authors in a Collective Creation Production* (Doctoral Dissertation, University of Alberta, 1989).
16. Richard Courtney, *The Dramatic Curriculum* (New York: Drama Book Specialists, 1980), p. 68.
17. Grocery shopping to *March of the Cue Balls* by Henry Mancini with side-coaching was a great success.
18. Vocal exercises with a context are useful for beginners. Exercises such as "Count to 10 as if...counting pennies, counting a boxer out" etc., were done.

19. My rule of thumb is NOTHING IS NEUTRAL. In drama, the slightest suggestion may trigger an unpleasant memory. It is vital that this be articulated and reconciled before we move on. In my practice, debriefing falls under the rubric of emotional safety.

20. Carol Fay, "On Losing My Copycard" in J. Parsons and L. Beauchamp (eds.), *Stories of Teaching* (Richmond Hill: Scholastic Press, 1989), pp. 11–12.

21. Glenys Berry and Joanne Reinbold, *Collective Creation* (Edmonton: Alberta Alcohol and Drug Abuse Commission, 1984), p. 5.

22. Ibid.

23. I have found that when actors work alone and later bring their artistic visions to the group, a battle for ownership can result which interferes with the emergent collective consciousness. I ask my actors to bring in their ideas as placeholders or tentative "offers" which will be changed and reshaped by us all. Nothing belongs to an individual: once an idea is articulated, it becomes ours. In this way we can play with one another without becoming offensive or defensive.

24. Thomas Barone, "Using the Narrative Text as an Occasion for Conspiracy" in E. Eisner and A. Peshkin (eds.), *Qualitative Inquiry in Education* (New York: Teachers' College Press, 1990), p. 309.

25. Martin Buber, *I-Thou* (New York: Charles Scribner's Sons, 1958).

26. Martin Buber, *Between Man and Man* (London: Kegan, Paul, Trench, Trubner and Company Limited, 1947).

27. Pinar defines educational reconceptualization as the study of curriculum from an historical, political, cultural, and gender perspective. Reconceptualists do not see curriculum as merely content and management but focus on the power systems embedded in the content and its delivery. I extend this concept to whenever an individual recognizes her perspectives and changes as a result. This form of reconceptualization looks at power from an individual/small group perspective rather than at a societal level.

    William Pinar, "Introduction" in W. Pinar (ed.), *Contemporary Curriculum Discourses* (Scottsdale: Gorsuch Scarisbrick Publishers, 1988).

28. Ted Aoki, *Toward Curriculum Inquiry in a New Key* (Edmonton: Department of Secondary Education Occasional Paper Series, 1989).

29. Another rule I adhere to in ALL of my drama work is the right to dissent. My rule is, "You don't have to do anything you feel uncomfortable doing." Its complementary rule is, "...but try."

Report from Baghdad: A Hunt for MORINs in a Culturally Diverse Drama Classroom[†]

Anton Frank

A Nest of MORINs

During the week of the meeting of the British Association for the Advancement of Science in Birmingham, a panel of eminent scientists and educators (all of them men) were gathered in a BBC Radio studio. The central topic for discussion was the status of science and the lamentably low take up of science places in further and higher education. When pressed by the presenter on the reasons for students' lack of interest in science, one panel member wryly commented that he was afraid that there seemed to be a case for the existence of our old friend the MORIN. His colleagues chuckled in appreciation of his sense of irony. I was mystified: what is a MORIN? Yes, he went on after the chortles had subsided. This was an area where **MO**re **R**esearch **Is** **N**eeded. The picture came to my mind of a small inquisitive rodent-like animal, a MORIN, an elusive creature that scuttles at high speed across the floor, a creature that one glimpses only at the periphery of one's field of vision. Once sighted, they are bound to breed at an exponential rate, until a whole nest of the little creatures infest the place.

Every field generates its families of MORINs, and drama in education is no exception. The purpose of this exploration is to get to grips with the nature of the particular family of MORINs which we in drama education can name as our own. In common with many drama

---

† The first version of this article was prepared for a publication following an International Research Conference on Drama and Learning (Institute of Education, University of London, 8–11 September, 1993) organized by Sue Hubbert (University of London, Institute of Education) and Pam Bowell (Kingston University).

teachers, I feel, I have been looking to find a cohesive way of looking at drama in the classroom, a "flexible web" of theory that might allow an adequate description of the nature of learning **in and through dramatic activity**. To extend my MORINs analogy, the net by which we try to capture our particular nest of MORINs seems to have gaps through which the little creatures escape. This is not to ignore the likelihood of any such net or web developing holes; indeed nets and webs are full of them. But, like our scientific colleagues, I am looking to construct a framework that would hold the MORINs long enough for them to be transformed from their perceived status as vermin, into the objects of study and experimentation.

The difficulties of this enterprise, however, are numerous. In the first place, as an ephemeral form, dramatic activity is marked by its particular location in time and space. Of all media, it is the one which most closely resembles the everyday flow of social life, communicating through speech, act, gesture, posture, spatial relationship and so on — that is, the media of everyday communication and activity.[1] Any attempt at recording the entirety of the process causes problems. A transcript of audio or video recording can offer, at best, only a partial description and, therefore, a kind of fiction or story. The ear of the tape recorder or the single eye of the video camera are bound to frame only part of an active drama session. These devices frame and distort the depth and perspective in ways that will mean the activity will not be perceived and interpreted in the same way as live action. Describing only parts of the processes and products associated with learning through drama is to miss the key to the learning process itself, the ways in which these elements combine and interact to form the wholeness of the learning process.

In order to describe learning in and through drama, and in common with most educational theory, we have always had to draw threads from a wide variety of disciplines. The work of Heathcote and Bolton, for instance, focuses on dramatic activity and learning processes, drawing from many disciplines. What I would wish to add is an emphasis on drama as a learning process within a wider sphere of diverse social and cultural practices. Through locating dramatic activity in schools within wider social and cultural frames, we can, perhaps, develop a consistency of approach which might account for learning in and about the discipline of drama.

I want to start by offering you the story of a classroom drama to ground the discussion. After the story of the drama, I shall be confining myself to three broad areas (namely: **the body, and the construction of personhood; the nature of dramatic languages and the creation of texts; and mind, body and learning processes in drama**) from which I wish to draw the main threads of my web of theory for drama in education.

A Report from Baghdad

This lesson happened in early January, 1991 with a group of 13- and 14-year-old boys in a school in Hackney, East London. I was expecting a student teacher to arrive the following week, and did not want to launch into a series of lessons without meeting him and finding out about his interests. Every so often, with each of my classes, I would operate a "one-off" lesson structure in which I would ask them to prepare a news broadcast. I would then record their work on videotape and end the lesson by viewing their work. It was fast and furious work which I thought would allow them to feel a sense of completion, would stimulate them to explore, consider and frame their perception of news events and, for my own purposes, allow me an insight on their developing awareness of world events and the ways in which these are mediated to them. As I had taught this group for over two years, they were familiar with the format of the lesson, and could operate within it with little intervention from me.[2]

This week, early in 1991, the Gulf War had started. When I put the idea for the lesson to them, one of the students, a fairly dominant personality within the group, asked if they could "do" the Gulf War. Under the circumstances of history, I was not about to refuse his request. Without any further instruction, the class divided into groups of four and five and began to work on their "reports" from the Gulf. At times, this class was capable of behaving in difficult, dissenting and disruptive ways, but on this occasion there was an atmosphere of concentrated effort. I left them to it and prepared the video camera. After 20 minutes or so, they were ready to record.

Out of the four groups which recorded their reports, there is one group's presentation which stands out in my memory. Their names were Olu, Gem, Nazim, Osgur and Ali. From these names alone you get some idea of the nature of the school intake. In this class, there were students whose families came from various parts of Nigeria, Bangladesh, India, Turkey, Vietnam, the Caribbean, Cyprus, Ireland and so on. This particular group comprised of boys who would have spoken Yoruba, Turkish and Kurdish at home, but here, their presentation was in English.

Gem, a Cypriot Turkish speaker, was sitting behind a table stage right, and behind him on a room-dividing screen, a hastily penned logo for news network was pinned (I cannot remember what it said exactly, but this was an accepted convention in this lesson structure). Centre stage, Olu, from a Yoruba background, was waiting, clutching a felt pen as a "microphone" (another convention of style in this structure) and wearing a pair of mirrored sun-glasses. Stage left, Nazim, Osgur and Ali (two Turkish speakers from different parts of Turkey and a Kurdish speaker) were arranged in a line of descending height, with Ali at front, kneeling down. Nazim had taken off his grey uniform sweater and had it draped over his head.

I counted them down to start, signalled to them when the tape was rolling and brought up the studio lights to focus on the stage area. They were used to dividing the stage area into various locations, and they would brief the camera operator (usually me) with their outline scenario so that the action could be followed. I focused on Gem, hands clasped on the desk in front of him, smiling into the camera and welcoming the audience to the evening's special report in smooth and reassuring tones. He said that within the past hour, the "Allies" had launched an air attack on Baghdad, and that we were going over to our reporter on the spot (Olu), who was now on the streets of Iraq's capital. With this verbal cue, I panned to Olu, down-stage centre, and closed up on his head and shoulders. He was grinning expansively into the camera, wearing his mirrored sun-glasses and welcoming his viewers to the centre of "sunny Baghdad." In the background, Gem was making voiced sound effects — muffled thuds, explosions and whistles — to enhance the evocation of the city under siege. The incongruity of Olu's smiling face and effervescent manner against this both "real-time" and fictionalized account of horrific events, made me feel somewhat uneasy (what if the head-teacher was to walk in?).

By now, I was following Olu as he walked stage left, still smiling and talking to the camera in a forced Anglo-American accent, saying that he was about to talk to an ordinary family on the streets to find out how they felt. He approached Nazim and, clearly enunciating each word (in the way that we might talk to speakers of other languages), he greeted this "mother" and asked what she thought about the bombing. In the viewfinder, I saw Nazim's covered head, his arm around Osgur who rested his hand on Ali's head; as Ali's knees were not in frame, the illusion of the mother with her family was perfectly evoked, an image of quiet anger, fear, despair and disorientation. After a pause, Nazim simply asked, "Why are they doing this to us? Why are they doing this to my family? We are innocent people." The sudden contrast between the ebullient and heroic reporter and the quiet understatement of the "mother" on the streets of Baghdad was startling. Olu "signed off" from the streets of Baghdad, handing us back to the studio where Gem ended the report, promising more to come soon. The whole thing probably took less than three minutes.

The story I have told, the dramatic event that I have focused on, the evaluative phrases that I have chosen to describe what happened, all of these have combined, I hope, to set a context for the action and give impressions of what took place. For all its apparent cohesiveness, it has gaps which I must seek to fill with other kinds of narrative, if we are to begin to describe and analyse the relationship between the dramatic action and learning processes. So much is going on in this example, that if we ask how we can describe the process and what is its relationship to learning processes, we would come up with a range of different perspectives and analyses. On the face of it, the pluralistic and interdisciplinary approach would seem to be the most appropriate strategy. But if, as Gavin Bolton suggested in a recent panel discussion, we tell the anthropological story in role as anthropologists, or the psychological, the literary, the televisual and so on, in role as specialists in each of the disciplines, there is a danger of a lack of cohesiveness in our overall approach —a danger of fracture and fragmentation which, although it might truly reflect a certain state of things, is not helpful in making analyses of the wholeness of the dramatic event.

The Body, the Person and the Subject in Place and Time

Because dramatic action only happens when socially organized persons meet and act out at particular points in history and in particular locations, I want to place the person at the centre of my web.[3] By this I mean real persons, with histories of their own, with identities constructed through family, social life and schooling. They have bodies which act, they have minds which feel and think, and these act in an undivided way. They make sense of the world through these actions and they generate meanings.

The boys whom I introduced you to, "doing" their "Report from Baghdad," came to that lesson in that school with their own individual histories, identities and bodies. I indicated from what kind of home culture they came and what languages they spoke at home so that you could place them in historical and geographical terms. They did not just materialize at a secondary school in Hackney, they came from homes, they met in school, they combined in a class and chose their own working group in the lesson. Importantly, even though I suggested the format to them, they chose their own content. They, as social bodies with thinking and feeling minds, expressed desire, a desire to explore a battleground, some thousands of miles away, framed within a "news" format. As students caught in a particular space (school/drama studio), at a particular time (school-day/wartime) they expressed a desire to be other than themselves (news reporters, Iraqi woman and children) and to place themselves in another space (Baghdad, imagined for them, mediated to them through television, but in real space and time).

So they were bodies acting in space and time, they were persons who had a sense of identity and personhood from their histories and from their social interactions which combine through experience.[4] The way that we in drama education are used to identifying the facets of personhood we adopt and project through the dramatic medium, is held in the concept of role. It is through the adoption of role that we are able to transform ourselves into "other." But another way of approaching the projected facets of self is through the concept of **subject position** — that is, subjectivity as it is defined by class, race, gender and through whole sets of relationships.[5]

A few of the important relationships I need to consider in analysing this "Report from Baghdad," are those within the family, between their peers, between themselves as students and myself as teacher, between their roles as viewers of the news and others who are the makers and transmitters of the news and so on. All of these might be expressed in terms of unequal relations of power. This notion of subjectivity spirals outwards from particular relations within the school environment, through their status as subject or immigrant to the realm of the United Kingdom, to their positions as subjects within a global context. As receivers of international news, the Cable News Network reports from the streets of Baghdad, their bodies, their personhoods and their subjectivities combine in direct relationship to the events in Iraq. They are Moslem, they are/are not English, they are of home cultures which have actual and metaphoric borders with Iraq. They are positioned differently in relation to these world events and they value them in different ways. They are inexorably caught within relations of power and powerlessness.[6] The status of English/not-English holds them in place, their social geographic situation as residents of Hackney in the Eastend of London subjects them as "disadvantaged" relative to residents of more prosperous areas. As students, they are subject to the will of the education system at large, and the specific hierarchies of the particular school and its staff. Between themselves, they are at various shifting points powerful or not in their peer group. Nonetheless, they combine in action to generate a multilayered, but cohesive, text through which a fabric of combined value is woven.

As bodies and persons, they have been involved in cultural action;[7] this is to say they are agents who have made something, a piece of drama, and through this medium, they have generated meanings which express values. One of the means of expressing these values is through the transformations from boy-subject in school, to newscaster, reporter with mirrored sun-glasses and woman-child-family subject in Baghdad. They want to know about being a media personality, they also want to know about the lives (and deaths) of ordinary people in Baghdad. As subjects, they have negotiated away some of the power invested in me as teacher to dictate the content of their learning. In their form of presentation, they have weighed and expressed values, challenged, parodied and explored issues, but only with my tacit consent for one aspect of their presentation was designed to directly challenge myself as teacher and agent of the educational system. It is because I want a framework that accounts for persons acting through social and cultural practices that I choose to start with bodies, persons and subjects. Without socially organized persons, and without there being relational differences between these persons, there would be no drama at all, there would be nothing to say and nothing to act out.

Dramatic Languages and the Nature of Dramatic Texts

One of the major difficulties in analysing the dramatic medium is that, of all media, it most closely resembles the action and communicative processes of everyday life. It is not everyday action in the real world. It is action on the "semiosic plane";[8] it might closely resemble real action, but it is purely symbolic action. Again, this is nothing new for drama in education; we have often talked of signs, symbols and texts in drama.[9] Not only do these signs and symbols articulate to communicate and express meanings, they are also material evidence of learning processes.

If we look again at the "Report from Baghdad" and ask about how it was constructed, we are immediately confronted by the densely-textured fabric of dramatic languages the boys deployed in order to create this text. Each form of mediation needs its specific form of description.[10]

On the linguistic level there are, for instance, the stories of Gem and Olu, of how they came into the lesson speaking in the voices of the peer group; the classmate, the friend, the rival, the adversary and so on, each with their own generic qualities of speech. They then became the voices of Gem, the calm news presenter and Olu, the intrepid reporter, complete with the "standard" mid-Atlantic accents and syntax appropriate for the purposes and audience of an international news network.

They used their bodies as signifiers, both as individuals and in the spatial relationships between themselves — Gem calmly composed at a "news desk," his hands clasped in front of him; Olu bouncing and grinning into the camera, clutching his "microphone" and wearing his mirrored sun-glasses; Nazim, the "mother," his head covered with a pullover, her "headscarf"; The "mother" with the two "children" in carefully-arranged postures and group composition. Each of the five performers were grouped and arranged in significant relation to each other, the news desk mid-stage right, the reporter down-stage centre and the family group mid-stage left. There was minimal but effective use of costume (the "headscarf" and the sun-glasses), of props (the felt-pen "microphone") and of setting (the newsdesk and station "logo" behind it).

The spatial arrangement bore a direct relation to the way in which the report was constructed in time. The report followed a symmetrical pattern of time: the opening and closure of the whole report started stage right with the reassuring tones of the presenter. Sandwiched between these items was the energetic presence of the on-the-spot reporter. In sequence of time, the family "shot" and interview with the "mother" was the central pivot of the piece.

The absence of certain features and the deletions were also significant. There was no interview with military personnel or with studio experts in their news report; both were common features of other such presentations. Besides their play with representations of media personalities, it was the ordinary family that captured their interest. In a heavily militarized state; in a state of war, males are more than likely to be absent from civilian and family life. Hence, there was no husband/father in the family interviewed on the streets of Baghdad.

In my brief analysis of this example, through describing some of the ingredients of this text, I have made moves towards an analysis of the meaning of this performance. In order to reach a deeper analysis of meaning, one has to examine the performance text as a whole. As a dramatic text and event, it can only have any meaning when set beside other texts already in the world. It gathers its full sense only when set against the context of special news reports, and a "theatre of war," beamed via satellite into people's homes. This group's report from Iraq was set as if in answer to the real reports they saw on television, probably just before they came to school that morning. They were able to take on the form of the news report, and through constructing it in their own terms, they could offer comment not only on the events of this war, but also the way in which it was mediated to them. In the combination of Gem's plausible media persona, Olu's outrageous news reporter (with his shades of the "rap artist") and Nazim's tragic archetypal family, the boys were playing with the signifying functions and "syntax" of dramatic roles.

Signs and symbols are never neutral. They are constructed and traded within structures of power. In the "Report from Baghdad," the boys had selected a powerful form — the television news report — to present (or "re-present") a military and ideological confrontation which had a real and immediate meaning for them. Although they could not directly intervene in the conflict (they could not fight there; their report would not be beamed from satellites), they could offer a commentary, from their very particular perspective.

But if we are to begin to uncover the range of meanings generated through the production of such classroom dramas, we have also to look for other levels of semiotic activity alongside the explicitly performed texts. Of central importance is the semiotic activity that takes place in the group-devising process. There are two significant levels to look out for in this process: the social and the individual. At a social level we can look out for the ways that signs and symbols are traded, selected and shaped by the members of the group. For the individual person, we could speculate about how the process of internalizing these socially-generated signs connects with processes of thought — that is, in the relationship between the inner and the outer performances. The outer performance text, the "Report from Baghdad," can be seen as a socially-negotiated metaphor or paradigm of the performers' inner performances, the individual understandings and evaluations of the "Gulf War." It is through an exploration of the internalization of meaning through social practice that we might be led towards accounts of learning.

Mind, Body and Learning Processes in Drama

How can we give an account of the learning that took place in this lesson? There are several ways that one could come at the problem. One measure of learning, for instance, could be found by reference to (Britain's) national curriculum criteria in the attainment targets for English: understanding and using different kinds of language, standard English and non-standard varieties, and participation in group presentations under speaking and listening; recognizing whether subject matter is presented as opinion or fact in non-literary and media texts under reading; writing (and performing) texts in a variety of forms under writing.[11]

However, although these schema might give some sort of framework for the classification, assessment and evaluation of **what** has been learned, we have to investigate other frameworks if we want to illuminate **how** learning happens. For example:

- What is the nature of the motivation, or desire to learn in and through drama?
- How do dramatic languages and texts relate to the way the mind works and develops?
- How can we label, or conceptualize the structures of development or processes of learning in and through dramatic activity?

The boys about whom I have been writing wanted to make a "Report from Baghdad"; these frequently recalcitrant individuals got through a whole lesson without being shepherded or driven by teacherly instruction. What accounts for this? Even against the backdrop of an increasingly-prescribed and narrowing curriculum, subject areas like drama and English retain a certain "protected zone" in which the content of lessons can be defined in response to the interests and perceived needs of the student group.[12] As teachers, we know that each student group has its specific interests and demands, but these have to be balanced against the institutional demands of the education system.

I chose the news; Olu modified that to include the immediate interests of the group. The specific world they wished to inhabit was one that had presented itself to them over their television screens. To understand the events that may reasonably be construed as the start of a world war, complete with multinational offensives and the threat of nuclear or chemical warfare, this must have been a compelling motivation to these young people. To boys of African, Turkish and Kurdish backgrounds, the battle over Kuwait must have impinged strongly on their thoughts and feelings. If the desire to know and understand these events was there at general or other levels, so was the specific desire to emulate and to parody the events and their form of presentation, as well as the desire to know what it might be like for the ordinary woman and her family on the streets of Baghdad. The desire for pleasure was there, but also the need to reflect on serious issues. They had the opportunity in this drama lesson to put these desires into constructing something through action, to produce a videotape, which they could look at, reflect on and laugh at. Part of the motivation to learn in drama lessons must have something to do with the medium of drama. It is a medium in which attainment in literacy and numeracy, the conventional indices of attainment in schools, are subsumed and embedded within the processes of **"dramacy"** — that is, expression through the complex medium of dramatic action.

So for me, the desire, the motivation to learn, is of primary importance. There are accounts of play and desire available to us in drama and education.[13] But these are complex and difficult arguments, and I shall not try to reduce them here. I would, however, still like to emphasize that we still need to look very carefully at what motivates our students in drama, and to speculate about why they desire to engage with certain contents and particular forms.

This leads to the next set of questions about how the languages of the dramatic medium relate to the ways in which our minds think and develop. How did the "Report from Baghdad" relate to the ways in which the boys thought and felt about the Gulf War? It is safe to assume that they traded words, gestures and actions in the vernacular language of the peer group to sort and shape the finished product, switching into different, more public modes of speech, gesture and action for the performance. As I have already pointed out, these words, gestures and actions were combined into a specific text — a television text, a news item, an on-the-spot report — anchored to a studio presenter. To ask if television affects thoughts and deeds is not to ask an unusual question these days. How much were these boys affected, then, by the news from Baghdad? The only way we can answer this is to look at the text they produced and speculate how they came to it. But what is evident is that they were able to hold the morning reports from the war zone **in mind** and then to re-present them **in body**.

The term **negotiation** holds a concept central to the way in which we speak about drama in education. We talk of negotiating contracts with the group, negotiating contents and forms. I want to take it a step further into the realm of learning by suggesting that what is negotiated is thought. In all kinds of drama in many classrooms, we can see the way that ideas are traded, negotiated and from this, artefacts are produced; this is to point towards the social nature of thought. In order for thought to develop in the social arena, thoughts need to be expressed in signs. A Russian thinker, Volsinov, in developing a social theory of language in the early part of this century writes, "consciousness itself can arise and become viable only in the material embodiment of signs."[14] In the "Report from Baghdad" the signs were words, gestures and actions. They were, indeed, materially-embodied signs which articulated together to create a multilayered text.

Pedagogic theory emphasizes the importance of **word** in the development of "higher orders" of thought,[15] but in drama, word is only one of the communicative and expressive media available for expression. The description of my "Report from Baghdad" emphasizes the importance of time, space and televisual framing in the construction of its meaning. To produce the "Report from Baghdad," the boys worked a lesson structure for themselves that I had established in previous lessons. Within this structure, they selected and shaped their own presentation operating the wider generic structure of television news reports while employing the specific discursive structures that marked the reporting of the Gulf War. They not only increased their capability of manipulating these forms and the particular languages of the genre, they also demonstrated, through action and the construction of their text, that they had thought about the issues at a conceptual level, exploring values embedded in the reports from the war zone, weighing them up against their own sets of values.[16]

The paths of learning are to be traced in the ways in which the boys received and processed the news from the Gulf, then carried them to school and negotiated with others to produce the finished texts. They used processes of internalization (viewing, reading and thinking) and externalization (negotiating, planning and performing). They both ingested texts and produced a text — an embodied text. All of this is transformational activity.[17] They had come into the drama room as fairly normal school students of diverse backgrounds, but with common interests, and they had transformed themselves. In adopting roles, they positioned themselves in television studios and on the streets of a besieged city. A new story had been presented to them in a familiar format — the television news item — and they had transformed the text, sustaining its credibility and integrity by sticking more or less to the rules of producing a news report.

Gavin Bolton took the concept of **metaxis** from the theatre work of Augusto Boal;[18] it is defined as the ability for the actor to hold both the real and the fictional worlds in mind when performing. Bolton suggests that the pivot between the real and the fictional — this metaxis — is essential to the learning process in improvised classroom drama. In my account of learning from the "Report from Baghdad," the suggestion is that this notion of metaxis is expanded to include moving through a variety of worlds, both lived and received, on the "mimetic" and the "semiosic" planes. They shifted between their everyday lives of home, street and school; they shifted towards texts that represent other places and other lives.

For Olu, Gem, Nazim, Osgur and Ali, the most important audience was themselves. They are not privileged performers and producers — their piece would have little currency in the real world of events and mass media reports, and they know this — but they are producers nonetheless. This is not only a process of learning, it is also a process of cultural making, of cultural action. It is through this action, and in the interactions between themselves as members of a particular group, that they enter into dialogue not just with other people, but with events in history, and the ways these events are represented or mediated to us.[19]

The Hunt for MORINs

I began this piece with the intention of hunting out the genus of MORINs that lives in our territory of drama in education. It was, as you will remember, a mission to sketch out a web of theory which, as a drama teacher, I could clamber around on and look at dramatic activity in my classroom from different angles, looking for the places where more research is needed and trying to tell different kinds of stories about what is going on. These might be the stories of the student, the teacher or the researcher — perhaps the stories of all three.

In domains around bodies and personhoods in history was where I began; people, school students with different stories to tell. They possessed a certain expertise in deploying a range of different resources to enact these stories and to produce a cohesive text. Next, through an account of social and cultural action in the context of schooling, the "Report from Baghdad," there was a brief speculation on the nature of the learning processes integral to this activity.

317

The pattern of the web that has held these speculations together might best be characterized as a view of classroom drama as **cultural activity**.[20] The French sociologist Pierre Bourdieu suggests that:

> Culture is not merely a common code or even a catalogue of answers to recurring problems; it is a common set of previously-assimilated master patterns from which, by an "act of invention" similar to that of writing music, an infinite number of individual patterns directly applicable to specific situations are generated.[21]

He goes on to suggest that these patterns have become so much like second nature, we can comprehend them "only through a reflexive turning back."[22] The "master pattern" of world history, transmitted over the global network of satellite television, was represented in the "Report from Baghdad." The "act of invention" is more similar in this case to making drama than music. I suggested earlier that we should perhaps talk of "dramacy" alongside literacy and numeracy. This quality of dramacy, as enacted by these Hackney school students for instance, represents an attempt at comprehension, a "reflexive turning back" towards real events happening on a global stage.

It has to be admitted, however, that the particular species of MOR-INs I have trapped here for a while are quite specific to a history, a geography and a social setting. They might not be found outside of Hackney in the Eastend of London in other parts of the world. This notion of the specificity of circumstances is another central strand to my argument. It is the escape clause which allows me to address the reader directly and say: you have to find your own species of MORINs, the ones that live in your drama room with your particular sets of students. I would be interested to hear about them.

In order that we may develop a flexible web of theory, we need to think quite deeply about the unexpected, disturbing or downright boring bits of drama our students produce. Many times over the years, I have heard drama teachers talk about "real drama" as opposed to "not quite drama," or to speak of "bad drama" as opposed to "good drama." What is it to make these kinds of judgements? Has "our kind of drama" become too much like second nature? Do we need to stand back and ask, "What's going on here? What are they thinking? What is being learned? What are they teaching the teachers as well as teaching each other?"

I have turned the "Report from Baghdad" drama around in my mind for some time now, as you have seen. MORINs still scuttle around on the periphery despite my having captured a few here. The more drama in schools I see, the more it occurs to me that we drama teachers live among plagues of the little creatures. They need hunting out.

Endnotes

1. Here I owe a debt to Tim Crusius, who, in applying the philosophical work of Kenneth Burke to dramatic action, allowed me to formulate the difficulty of description in this way. Ideas were discussed at an International Research Conference on Drama and Learning, held at the Institute of Education, University of London, 8–11 September, 1993.
2. I operated within a "spiral" model of curriculum in my schemes of work.
3. This is an expansion of a reference from Volosinov (1986), p. 12: "Signs can arise only on interindividual territory..."
4. I was helped here by Helen Nicholson's presentation at the International Research Conference on Drama and Learning (Institute of Education, University of London, 8–11 September, 1993). She developed ideas on the construction of self through "performative acts," which she worked towards drama in education from the ideas of the American feminist philosopher, Judith Butler. There are also ideas floating around "personhood" derived from a keynote speech delivered by Brian Street at the "Domains of Literacy" conference, at the Institute of Education, University of London, 9 September 1992.
5. The reference to ideas of body and subjectivity, subject as an alternative expression of role, is worked towards drama education from ideas I am beginning to gather from the work of feminist and "poststructuralist" thinkers, such as the early writings of Julia Kristeva, *The Kristeva Reader* in T. Moi, (ed.), (Oxford: Blackwell).
6. This proceeds from the base of a Marxist analysis and post-structuralist elaboration of Marxist theory that can be found in the work of Michel Foucault and Julia Kristeva, for instance.
7. "Cultural action" is a concept I take and develop from the work of Paulo Freire, *Cultural Action for Freedom*, (Cambridge, Mass.: Harvard Educational Review, 1970); and Augusto Boal, *Theatre of the Oppressed*, (London: Pluto Press, 1979).
8. Robert Hodge and Gunther Kress, *Social Semiotics*, (Ithaca, N.Y.: Polity, 1988), p. 5.
9. Heathcote and Bolton have written extensively about sign and symbol in drama. See especially Heathcote's "Signs and Portents" in Dorothy Heathcote, *Collected Writings on Education and Drama*, (London: Hutchinson, 1984), pp. 160–69. There are also Aston and Savona (1991), Elam (1980), and Esslin (1987), for examples of semiotic approaches to theatre and drama, mostly derived from the structuralist perspective.
10. This refers again to Kristeva, "The System and the Speaking Subject" in T. Moi, (ed.), (1986), p. 26.
11. Key Stage 3, Programmes of Study and Statements of Attainment, English for Ages 5–16 (Cox Report), HMSO, 1989; Chapters 15–17.
12. The Cox Report placed emphasis on not wishing to prescribe or proscribe the content area of English in the national curriculum, but rather, to provide a framework for individual practice.
13. Gavin Bolton, *Drama as Eduction*, (London: Longman, 1984), draws on Vygotsky's article, "The Role of Play in Development" and Richard Courtney, *Play, Drama and Thought*, (London: Cassell, 1968) uses Piaget and Freud in analysing the connections between drama, desire and thought.

14. V.N. Volosinov, *Marxism and the Philosophy of Language* in L. Matejka and I.R. Titunik, (trans.), (Cambridge, Mass.: Harvard University Press, 1973), p. 11.
15. See, for instance, Lev Vygotsky, *Thought and Language*, in Kozulin, (ed. & trans.), (The MIT Press, 1989).
16. The work of Carol Fox on children as storytellers shows how children transform the form and content of stories for instance. See Carol Fox, "Children Thinking Through Story" in *English in Education*, vol. 23, no. 2, Summer 1989; and "Poppies Will Make Them Grant" in M. Meek and C. Mills, (eds.), *Language and Literacy in the Primary School*, (Falmer Press, 1988). Also, Steedman, C., *The Tidy House*, (Virago, 1987), is a fascinating account and analysis of a group of girls in primary school constructing a fictionalized and metaphoric account of their experience, drawing on romantic fiction and televisual sources.
17. See Hodge and Kress (1989), Chapters 6 & 7, for social semiotic accounts of transformational processes.
18. Augusto Boal (1979), and Bolton (1984), pp. 141–42.
19. I refer here to the ideas around "dialogism" developed by the Russian thinker, Mikhail Bakhtin, in *The Dialogic Imagination*, Holquist, M., (ed.), Emerson, C. and Holquist, M., (trans.), (Texas: University of Texas Press, 1990). See especially "From the Prehistory of Novelistic Discourse" in this volume.
20. The particular cultural approach adopted here is derived from the work of the English, media and drama department at the University of London Institute of Education. I acknowledge here the support of the teachings of predecessors such as James Britton, Harold Rosen and Margaret Meek. But pre-eminently the influence of current colleagues Tony Burgess, Jane Miller, Anne Turvey, Gunther Kress, John Hardcastle, Sue Hubbert and other teachers, writers and researchers associated with the department.
21. Pierre Bourdieu, "Systems of Education and Systems of Thought" in *Schooling and Capitalism*, R. Dale, (ed.), (Routledge and Open University Press, 1978), pp. 194–95.
22. Ibid.

Risinghill Revisited: Reflections on Returning to Classroom Drama

KEITH YON

Introduction

PREFACE

In May of 1989, as a guest of the Department of Theatre at Concordia University in Montreal, Canada, and as part of their involvement in the local community, I taught a programme of drama with several groups of children, students and staff at a number of elementary and high schools in the Montreal area. As my teaching schedules usually cover the range of the educational spectrum from theatre training to therapy, I welcomed this return to the classroom. It provides the norm with which periodically I need to engage in order to centre myself, to regain the balance between my personal development and educational commitment. Hanging over my head, as must be with other teachers, was the question, "...but will it work with (normal) children?"

The groups that I encountered differed from British children basically in their appearing more articulate, or, more accurately, more verbal. Some of them were familiar with up to six languages, and I was always tempted to ask, "in which language do you cry?" Their behaviour ranged from placid to disruptive, encompassing varying degrees of activity and passivity, all producing interesting responses to drama. Twenty-five years fell away and I was back in similar, if more extreme, classroom situations at Risinghill. This was a school of some notoriety in North London in the '60s, from which my present praxis may be said to derive.

Risinghill Comprehensive School had a short life, 1960–65. It was a brave but ill-fated experiment in introducing liberal practice and attitude into the state educational system, brave because of the enormity of the task facing the headmaster, a man of vision and commitment, in running this school in an underprivileged inner-city area, and ill-fated because it fell scapegoat to a change in local government.

A QUESTION OF LANGUAGE

My appointment as music teacher covered 3½ years, excluding the initial year horrors such as milk bottle fights between the ethnic groups and the fatal final year (during which I was away, seconded to a drama course), when unfavourable press caused the school to be shut down. My first year of teaching was disastrous. Having worked some years as a professional musician, I was out of touch with the children. I attempted teaching music as conventionally as I had been taught, namely as a means to musicianship, rather than a discipline to meet life. Frustrated and exhausted, but committed to this notion of learning life discipline through art, I realized that a radical reappraisal was called for. Could I morally teach music to children who would not, or, as was more likely, could not talk with each other? How could I communicate with children for whose most expressive means, their musical language, I had as little respect as they had for mine? Compromise had worked up to a point, but in the long run, it would only dilute what we, in our different ways, held dear.

Ironically, the change came through realizing that my exhaustion was partly the result of the number of stories and songs which I had to improvise; they were the only things which seemed to interest them. A glance down at the written page or the piano keyboard was time enough for one or more of the children to disappear through a window. How could they themselves create these songs and stories? How were they to listen to each other's songs if they could not bring themselves to converse? How might they be put in a position in which they could be with the others without confrontation?

The answers lay in engaging them in structures and forms which were common to both our needs. They wanted to create music as much as I did, but we had to begin at sympathetic levels, simpler and deeper than the complexities of our respective musical languages. They would provide, indeed they would **be**, the content, and I would provide the forms to contain and contextualize their expression. "Forms" is perhaps not the correct term for our starting points. Rather, I had to begin with those elements which were common to us, and are indeed common to all forms of expression: time (in our case, rhythm), space (i.e., melody and/or harmony), and texture (the actual sound itself). Concentrating on one element at a time was like having only one thing to worry about, while realizing that the other two elements would freely come into play.

For me, creativity became a matter of identifying these elements, and either rearranging, emphasizing or distorting them, thus affecting the balance of the other two. The challenge to my skills of composition, in which I had been traditionally trained, became a great excitement. A multiethnic Christmas epic developed from classroom activities in the form of stories (one word per child), songs (one note per child), and action sequences (one minute per child) were organized by a group of teachers, whose naive ambition was to unite the school by showing off the individualities of the different ethnic groups. We little realized the impact that this would have on the school, the parents, the governors and the community generally. Having thus shown the differences, we then created a music drama for the whole school of 1,000 students on an Easter theme, to demonstrate how often conflicting cultural forms may be fused without losing or denying their individualities. These epics were in fact exercises in communication; the different ethnic communities within the school "state" identified and expressed their individualities in interaction with the others. The classroom became like a testing ground for society, where the models for creativity could be tried out.

THE COMMUNITY OF THE CLASSROOM

The classroom, seen as society's testing ground, is like a theatre. I provide an allotted space and time in which individual aspiration and potential may be framed, treasured and even challenged, in interaction with the peer group. This dynamic between the freedom of the individual and the moral sense of the community member is the essence of play. It is the property of theatre, education and therapy alike.

The epics were the "theatre of presentation"; the classroom had to be the "theatre of interaction." The aim of both theatre and classroom is to understand and use the present. The children had used models from the past, and concern for their future was paramount, but certainly it was the children's use of the present, (also the aim of the artist), which became my objective; how to use their actual presence in the classroom. Ironically, not only was the material there in their bodies and voices, but also in their aspirations and respect for each other. They responded profoundly to the music we created together, and thrilled eleven- to eighteen-year-olds, English, Turkish, Greek, West Indian, Indian, Chinese and others, to the epics which showed them at their best, at once expressing their cultural identities while communicating through interaction with others. The drama lessons became occasions where (after a long period of experimentation) they could be centred and still in the constant turmoil of school life.

Theatre in the classroom seems to me to range from theatre to therapy. In theatre, time and space veers toward objective play, whereas therapy veers towards subjective play. Therapy provides the content; theatre is the form. In the praxis with which I am concerned, the emphasis is on the theatre, a most objective aim. The teacher (admittedly as in any lesson) sets the parameters, but by becoming more of an observer and involving the peer group as audience, there is a shift in the teacher's role. The objective is individual centring, going beyond drama and exploring how to become a social member, or therapy and the remedial situation. The likelihood is that 99.99% of the children will not want to become performers, and for those who have aspirations of stardom, an effective classroom process will have worked the "stage-glitter" out of their systems. The very few who would want to pursue theatre will have come to gain some inkling of the craft it is. But whatever the intentions of the children, education in theatre, i.e., the experience of being between the ordinary and the extraordinary, is invaluable as a life skill, in the struggle between the humdrum and the vital.

OBJECTIVES

The objective of the classroom is the education of the effective social actor, and this entails a paradox. Most people are effective social performers because they are passive performers; they are centred in life, attuned in self — and other — awareness. The peer group is therefore an active audience. The classroom has to consider the essential element of passivity through exercising active performance in the classroom. At Risinghill, at least some of the children began to develop competence in perception, observation and, above all, listening as the basis of the skills of interaction and intervention. Watching is as important as doing; the ability to be **still** is as creative as acting out another character or aspect of oneself. This internal/external interaction is vital. Externally, one works through one's mask to "become" another person; internally, one moves inward through oneself as if to meet another person. Thus may one develop space with and within oneself. The challenge of the teacher is to provide stimulus and parameters so that those in their charge may go inward only so far as they have the means to come back out.

The children themselves are the material. Internally they hold the essence which may be triggered in performance through drama and dance. At Risinghill, the classroom became a theatre. The means, or form (whether by use of sound, words, or movement) was "music," (a term which has been respectably on timetables since schooling began, and which was less likely to encourage license than would the new-fangled subject of "drama"), but the methodology had to draw on drama. Though my discipline is music, I worked in drama to understand creativity. At the end of a lesson, I had to feel that I, and through me the children, had undergone a musical experience. The exercise of a lesson, for me, is keeping the various strands alive and interactive, an exercise which parallels my musical education of 16th century counterpoint.

THE ROLE OF THE TEACHER

Theatre defines the parameters of madness, and the teacher personifies this authority. Some years after Risinghill, a fifteen-year-old boy, in another school, having improvised quite the most brilliant sequence of movement and voice ever to come out of my classes, paused, and in the stunned silence, looked around and saw from the amazed looks on the faces of his peer audience, how far he had moved beyond the pale of their comprehension. Feeling isolated, he turned on me and said, "**You** are a bloody fool!" Thus he placed total responsibility for his "madness" onto me. In other situations, the responsibility for the "madness" had to be established at the beginning of every lesson, a ritual argument which had to be gone through about why they had to do this work, what use was it to getting a job etc., until they reached the point of saying "It's madness." Only then, having released the responsibility from themselves, could they give themselves to the theatre event, and work with vivid imagination. It must be noticed that they said "It's madness" and not "It's silly." The teacher sets up the rituals into and out of this madness, a transition from the ordinary to the extraordinary, and back again.

The Elements of Theatre and Classroom

The timetabled drama session encapsulates the essence of theatre: an allotted **space** and a period of **time** during which the **physical means** (i.e., participants, in the presence of others) may create **forms**. The process is a journey from the known to the unknown, and then return enriched. In other words, it is an experience during which the child's ordinary behaviour can be transformed into the extraordinary, and then returned to the norm, reassured with a greater dimension of themselves, or a greater expectation of their potential. In the classroom the actual bodies, the allocated space and time, are the basic material and the means for creating forms, the order of which I will soon consider in some detail. Ultimately, I consider the theatre lesson to be concerned fundamentally with developing the management of these strictures of time and space. This is life and art experience at its most rudimentary.

PHYSICAL MEANS

In performance, social or theatrical, the body may be represented by the voice; sometimes they work together, sometimes separately, sometimes in opposition. Drama is concerned that what happens internally, (i.e., the individual's feelings and ideas), may be made manifest externally in action, translated into spontaneous actions and considered forms. Feeling may be perceived as internal movement which, when suspended, becomes thought. The external parallel to this is the free flow of spontaneous action which, when suspended, creates, or is supported by, forms. (The voice, in which I am particularly concerned, may be perceived as "movement-in-sound"). The alignment of external and internal concerns is central to education, for which reason movement should be considered central to the timetable, particularly in adolescence, when there is greatest need for the child's growing feelings, thoughts and spirituality to be integrated, balanced and aligned with their instrument, the developing body.

Performance is here practised less as expressing **at**, but rather **with** others. The performer aims to be **at one** with the audience. The audience, as a physical extension of the performer's physicality, is the crux of this praxis. The dynamic between being a group member and an individual determines whether and when the group is secure enough in choric movement and sound to be gradually provided with space to explore individual "cadenzas." The lessons become more than drama by the fact that the teacher (and at times the group) operates as audience, while stimulating the exercise and setting the response in context.

Self-consciousness, the bane of performance, is a crucial element. Self-consciousness is excessive self concern for the external monitoring that is being concentrated on the performer. When this audience consciousness can be internalized (i.e., the performer is at one with the audience, expressing to herself through them, and the adrenalin raised is centred in the body), then the performer becomes self-centred, which is the basis of self-awareness, and one of the objectives of the drama lesson.

SPACE

Regarding the potential of the allocated space, a rectangular room is, in my experience, the most effective in allowing children some choice of control. Lengthwise suits those who cannot manage the expansiveness of feeling (which width implies), and who need to be "tunnel-visioned" and more in control. The narrow crossing of the room is also helpful for those who are very self-conscious. Expressing lengthwise in this way encourages confrontation, which needs to be countered by working with one's back to the long wall and feeling the lateral embrace of the room, which is the physical basis of interaction.

A couple of benches or a circle of chairs are helpful for defining a smaller space for those who cannot manage the whole room. Much of the exercise for such children might involve venturing out into the vast spaces of the floor and returning "home." Those children who cannot manage the space of the floor may play in the smaller dimension of the tabletop, through manipulation of objects and writing. Conversely, children whose skills are reflective and in writing may begin on the tabletop and have their expression expanded out from their chairs and onto the larger "script" of the floor.

In one comprehensive school, I was made aware of how important the identity of the room was. It was virtually impossible to discipline the group of children I was working with in the hall where we did movement. Their rationale was that it was not a "disco." I asked them what they normally did in the hall. They ate sandwiches. Where did they work? In the classroom. We called a truce. We would do movement in the hall, the only large space where we could do so, but would always rush back into their classroom for the last ten minutes of the lesson to "work," which meant encapsulating what they had done in the hall on paper. Writing, being a "proper" activity, gave approval to what we did. The security of text manifests itself in so many situations, at every level of competence!

Specialness of space is crucial. When one has, for example, a double period in the hall, and at the changeover of lessons passers-by catch the group at an exposed moment (i.e., the usually chaotic middle of the exploration), a lesson ploy I use is to gather the class at that moment for a group discussion of something similarly normal, until the "intruders" have passed, and the children may return to their "madness." The work remains secret and special. When space proves to be scarce, and a corridor has to be utilized, it, too, has to be "sanctified." This can be done by placing the chairs in a semi-circle facing the wall, within which is the performing space, and by returning to normal behaviour in the presence of passers-by.

I have found that some city children possess skills which are mostly verbal. Perhaps because the crowded streets allow little freedom of movement, their play is on their tongues. Their movement on the floor is often insecure and they take refuge against walls or in the corners, or play havoc. It is necessary, in these cases, to base the exercises on verbal exercises which allow the elements of silence and listening to enter. In one group, for example, the children were each asked to make up sequences of sentences which, in groups of twos, threes and fours, were "larded" into each other, making for some absurd dialogue. In the silences thus allowed into their work, they could substitute physical for verbal gesture, first in the arms and legs, for very controlled movement and usage of space. Or, in pairs, children could talk to and with each other from opposite sides of the room, the increasing distance causing them to increase the space between their words or syllable. They are thus forced to lengthen the vowel, the spatial element of voice.

Conversely, working with country children (who were perhaps used to vast horizons), I found their movement was more fluent, possessing a quality of great stillness. Their verbal language, however, was comparatively dull, and it was playful to inhibit their travelling so that they had to cover the distance in sounds and verbal images.

327

TIME

The basic pattern of a lesson follows a narrative structure which (using "pulp" romantic literature as a model of satisfaction) may be accepted as natural. In this structure, characteristic of popular fiction, there are two peaks or climaxes. The first, near the beginning, is a moment of quiet resultant upon the warm-up, which will have mapped out the area of physicality and feeling to be explored in the lesson, and is the ritual of transition from the ordinary to the extraordinary. This transition is helpful in transporting the participants into, and secure them in, this play area, where normal social rules do not apply. This moment of pause leads into the period of exploration culminating in the climax of the sharing of the work. The work is then placed in context in the postclimactic stage of reflection and repose, or the transition or transference back to the norm.

The 45- or 90-minute weekly lesson, (as opposed to a rehearsal), should be seen as special, but not overspecial. My sympathies are with Nadine Senior, now director of the Northern Dance Company in England, who, as a teacher in a North of England Middle School, produced marvellous dance with all her multicultural pupils. She was pressed by an avid admirer who commented that if she had more time than the single weekly lesson with her pupils, then they could achieve even greater results. She replied that it was the fact that there was but the one lesson per week that made it special to the children and urged them to come prepared and toned up to make the most of every moment. Those who wanted to pursue dance professionally could do so in extra time out of school.

Children should have equal performance opportunity in the classroom. How easy it is in difficult situations to concentrate on the extremes — that is, the brightest or the most disruptive children — and ignore the middle bulk. This need for equality of attention gave rise to a successful ruse which the Risinghill children readily accepted. I told them that we had 45 minutes together, and since there are 35 students, each was entitled to one minute of my undivided attention. Clearly, this is morally a suspect point, but it worked. By rationalizing the situation in this way, I was allowed to exclude those who preoccupied more than the allotted time. That was the negative side. Positively, certain very creative situations resulted.

During their one minute, children could perform however they wanted to in movement and sound, given certain structures and provided it was socially acceptable. Of course, watching 35 individual performances would prove a daunting experience, and time was needed at the beginning of the lesson for preparation, and at the end for reflection. It was therefore demonstrably necessary for the pieces to be presented in groups of twos, threes and fours. This practice, apart from helping those who would feel very exposed if performing singly on the floor, set up very imaginative counterpoints with the potential for interaction, and which extended their preconceptions of communication and performance.

FORMS

Some teachers like to set up themes from which the children may work. My preference is to present forms or elements and allow content or themes to emerge. The exercises, models or structures which are set up to stimulate the participants have been, because of my interest in history, based on art forms. Forms are presented through which the participants may reveal their individual content in action, feeling and thought. Whether content is given first and forms then explored, or vice versa (forms given and content explored), the material and means of its exploration are present in the actual elements of the sessions: the bodies, the allotted space and the period of time, which, given play, trigger ideas and images.

At the extreme situation of dealing with children who are incompetent in the classroom, one might find it necessary to permit only the minimum of freedom, and surround the most insecure child with the maximum elements of the narrative situation: **who** is involved, **what** is happening, **how** it is done, **where** and **when** it is done, and **why**? In other words, tell them all the details of the story and let them reproduce them. Gradually you can eliminate the provision of these elements, thus releasing more responsibility and initiative to the child until only the "skeleton" of the material is provided, allowing the child the maximum of imaginative play.

The stages of this process of elimination of initial information the children are given, may be seen as follows:

1) supply the whole situation, both words and actions, of the **who**, **what**, **when** and **where**, leaving them to explore the **why**;
2) provide only the **who**, **where** and **when** elements, having them find out **what** happens, and **why**;
3) supply only the "skeleton" of the situation, (i.e., an abstraction), leaving the children to flesh out the **who**, **what**, **how**, **when**, **where** and **why** themselves;
4) only the dimensions of physicality, space and time are provided (i.e., themselves, the room and whatever time the lesson allows), and they are allowed total freedom to explore creative possibilities.

At the extreme situation, when only the "skeleton" or the dimensions of the situation are given, the children may be so well adjusted that they need only an idea to start. Appropriate stimulation is crucial, and it is more effective to work from thought in order to find feeling;

the reverse approach can become bogged down in very murky work. In the ideal situation, I see the teacher's role reduced to providing a contained ambience, to drawing the children's attention to the further development of their strengths, and to remedying cliches, done by adjustment or rearrangement of physicality, space and time. Finally, and most importantly, the teacher is responsible for placing what the children offer in context.

To summarize, at one extreme, the form and content are wide open; at the other they are both constricted. Midway is the transition which distinguishes between children being **given** form and content and their **finding** them. Structures, even constrictions, need not be seen negatively. The most imaginative and competent children respond well to the discipline of concentrating on one element (e.g., a change in direction, limitation to one word etc.), or when exercises are devised to develop technical skills (e.g., concentration, flexibility etc.).

The creations which are presented to the group are shown in the context of art — that is, between participants of theatre and other practitioners — rather than between members of society and other people. Whatever a child offers, particularly if it is very clichéd, has to be accepted and developed by changing the space. Accept a piece of work, but ask the student to recreate it in a larger or smaller space, with more or fewer objects involved — at a higher or lower level, in a nearer or farther relationship etc. If the classroom is the testing ground of society, it is to be expected that clichés (of television drama, for example) will crop up. The teacher's task is to accept them and expand the potential of the principal by questioning the language. Accept a clichéd fight scene, then ask the performers to repeat it, with one element altered (e.g., increase the space between the combatants, forcing words to substitute for the physical action of touching; change the time frame, placing the piece in the past, or having it happen over a much longer period of time; or alter the physicality, so that instead of using fists, bows and arrows, or even words, must be used.).

So, with a background of teaching strategies developed from meeting the needs of Risinghill and other situations, I went into the Montreal schools. Examples of these experiences in Canada provide the basis of the following writing.

The Groups

GROUP 1: (Twenty-five 16- to 17-year-old high-school students; one 1½ hour lesson)

To begin, the group showed me pieces that they had created and performed to great effect and success in a competition. They were extremely competent, very verbal and very finished. From my British and restrained perspective, I found them slick and overprojective (i.e., performing **at** the audience for effect). To this end, the pieces were light-hearted. The teacher expressed a concern about tackling serious work, or tackling the serious element in work. I asked myself and the students why did I find some of their situations which got laughs so moving?

My analysis of the situation was that these children had over-worked one dimension of performance — timing — to the detriment of others — physicality, space and action. We explored, through short exercises, the interrelated nature of these elements, and of the dangers of losing the balance between them. For example, physicality (the sensuality or texture of character) can show a tendency towards indulgence; action can result in busy attention to peripherals with little sense of focus or stillness; and space, whether the external relationship with the audience or the internal spaces of feeling, can result in narcissism. Timing (in this case language and articulation) tends towards slickness.

I asked them to repeat some of the situations, altering one of these elements, or switching focus to an element which was undernourished in their original performance (e.g., actually **seeing** the landscape, questioning the intention of the actions, examining the quality of the physicality of the character and its effect on the voice etc.). This switch, or "distortion," challenges the safety of the piece, and places the performer in a greater state of vulnerability and unknowing. It forces communication at levels deeper than words, the articulation of which are very time-geared.

GROUP 2: (Twenty-five 16- to 17-year-olds; one 1½ hour lesson, timetabled as English rather than Drama)

This was an excessively polite high-school class, calm and inscrutable. They were respectfully and utterly silent when I introduced myself, as I usually do to a new group, by allowing them three minutes to form whatever impression they have formed of me, followed by another three minutes where they could ask any question of me that I could answer "yes," "no," or "maybe." (I find that by transforming cultural characteristics which might be impediments to communications, e.g., colour, voice tone, age, class etc., into playthings, the group is able to show how they handle first impressions.) Their silence suggested that they considered it improper to make personal remarks directly (though some did secretly pass notes), which meant that I could not ask them directly about themselves. Performance is concerned with behaviour, and so far they showed that they needed some indirect or alternative expressive approach.

The consideration of alternatives of expression arises in situations where the voice has to be the main means of expression, perhaps because the children are not used to moving, or because there is no space to move. The movement must therefore go into the words, in "movement-in-sound." In situations dealing with communications skills at remedial levels, one cannot always concentrate directly on spoken words, because that is the very area which needs examination. In such cases I often turn to writing exercises, for it can provide a level of security and privacy they cannot feel in an open verbal exercise or game, while feeling they are still actively participating in it. With this particular group of intellectually very able students, I felt that writing would not be a problem, as witnessed by the note passing in the introduction to the class.

I asked the class to write an impression of themselves individually on slips of paper which they would allow me to take away with me. Nobody would know who wrote what. These were handed in, unsigned and folded up. With a flourish I threw them into the air of this (to me) excessively tidy room, and, injecting a little action into the session, had the children get out of their seats to retrieve one. They were then told that they would read the note they had retrieved out loud to the class as a character. This being a drama lesson, whose object is the building, detonation, sustaining and release of suspense, I wished the class to go beyond a simple reading in character. I also wanted them to focus their excitement towards the performance moment. I therefore asked them to rehearse their piece while speaking it in as many different ways as possible, choosing various qualities of expression (e.g., fast/slow, high/low, smooth/rough, heavy/light, sustained/percussive). What does, for example, a slow, high, rough, light, sustained voice signify? Who is such a character? To further suspend their expectation, they were asked to explore voices with qualities opposite to their original choices. They had to make decisions about their characters. Who might speak in this way? And where, when, and why might they do so? They spoke their pieces, and, while vocal impersonations were impressive, none of the children dared (in this first lesson) to change their body physicality. There was only a little time to extend their performances to what may have happened before or after their little moments, which may have involved including another person, thus beginning a narrative and a dialogue. The listening audience were given a chance to respond, and questions of focus, alignment, and breathing were raised.

Because of the limited time of any single session I had to use a minimum amount of material to maximum effect. Aware of this class's verbal facility from the beginning, it was necessary, in this case, to develop their skills in depth, exploring a point before extending it in action, to concentrate on creating an internal image before externalizing it.

Another parallel strand in this process was to help them develop their skills as audience members, in their ability to respond objectively and attentively to new situations without giggling. We discussed giggling and decided that it was uncontrolled energy rising from the pit of the stomach, where it is generated and, if focused, may be controlled. Energy rising to the top of the torsal chamber blocks in the chest and becomes confused with the muscle tension preparatory to the making of sound at the vocal cords. This confusion often results in a giggle. Understanding this physical mechanism opened the way to using arm gesture to press feeling downward in reaction to sound rising, and massaging the neck tendons downward to the sternum to counter blockage of feeling at the vocal cords. These gestural movements extended to elaborate arm movement, and to the exploration of the healthy build up and release of energy, as seen when we yawn. This naturally led into singing, which may be experienced as the ecstatic build up of energy, not released suddenly, but rather sustained in full-gutted sound.

The students had progressed far in this lesson, from muteness to a bravura of physical and vocal gesture. This development, I suggest, was based on the security of knowing that at any moment they could have stood apart from this "madness" and rationalized their behaviour in socially-acceptable terms; they were immersed in concentrating themselves and sustaining communication. They were able to relate to dropping into gravity, to earthing themselves, before suspending their sound into the air — for this is a similar process to many sporting events, either as participant or spectator — and gave them a rationale for their otherwise nonsensical behaviour. They were making interesting sound and movement patterns which could be viewed as being incidental to, or the means towards achieving, a central goal when, in fact, the enjoyment of this experience (an enjoyment which is difficult to acknowledge in task-rewarding cultures) was, I believe, unconsciously and umembarassingly the core of the experience.

GROUP 3:   (Twenty+ 16- to 17-year-olds; one 1½ hour lesson)

Compared to Group 2, this group was an abrupt shift to the other extreme of classroom co-operation. After some confusion, I found myself sharing the class with a substitute teacher, another stranger to a disturbed group. The room provided had been (at least by Risinghill standards) vandalized. In order to instigate a common activity and establish the specialness of the place (particularly since the time element of the class had been so confused), to transform it into a little "theatre," we — or more accurately, I — set about ordering the tables and chairs along the walls, straightening the bent blinds and cleaning the blackboard of graffiti. When the group saw that I was meaning business, some gradually joined in, with the others at least keeping out of the way. The cleaning of the floor, picking up papers etc., became more deliberate, conscious and formalized, a ritual to remove the menial nature of the activity, to establish something of the "sacredness" of the space, to slow down the pace at which the group seemed to be functioning and to transform the antagonistic attitude of most of the group into a shared seriousness.

Rituals for beginning and ending a session are crucial, particularly for children in remedial or maladjusted situations, for whom distinguishing the normal from the playful, the ordinary from the extraordinary, is no easy matter. That the classroom is to be the focal point of society touches on social drama or social therapy. These elements should be at the core of any performance situation. As teachers, however, we should ultimately be concerned with making theatre that takes the children beyond their expectations, not simply in a "free-expression" way, but taken to the point where expression is formalized.

With this group, this did not mean taking them outside themselves. Indeed, I felt that they were already outside themselves, that is, maladjusted and overexpressive, and to suggest having them extend their powers of expression would be an anomaly. On the contrary, they needed to be contained and to learn containment (and here, containment must not be confused with constriction). Just as overexpressiveness becomes maladjustment, conversely overcontainment becomes inhibition. There must be a moment of transfer along the spectrum from containment (inward functioning) to expression (outward release) and vice versa; this is the awareness of oneself and one's resources, and the crux of drama.

This class ranged from clearly disturbed students, their voices attention-seeking and noisy, through the core of dissatisfied "mutterers," to those dumb and apparently disengaged with what was going on around. As a focus in the room, I used myself as an example of a still centre with a vocal quality cutting under (not adding to) the general level of noise. (The use of the voice to speak **with** or **at** a class has to be clearly differentiated; both have their effectiveness and place). I could not trust having them move around the room, so most of the activity, at least initially, was on the spot, seated on the floor. The excuse (for me) and rationale (for them) would be exercising observation of character and gesture: creative watching and listening. Those who might usually submit to their more extroverted peers for attention might this way find a space for a moment of self-statement.

I asked the group to sit in a semi-circle bounded (i.e., contained) by a corner of the room, in which I sat facing them, to be observed in silence for two minutes, commented upon, and then questioned. Their inability to focus and sustain interest or comment in this exercise provided fodder for the session; this was a drama lesson, and performers had to know how to focus and be interesting! One of the students changed places with me and posed like a model. The class observed, trying to get "inside" his thoughts from the details of his posture. How was he sitting? Where was his weight placed? Consideration of physical weight led to the "weight" of feeling and thinking.

Then another student stood in the semi-circle as "neutrally" as possible. Three members of the class came up to her in turn and altered one of her features (e.g., the position of the head, an arm or a leg, creating a frozen character making a gesture). The audience discussed what the gesture might mean, with particular attention to whether it was a character or caricature: how much of a person can one gauge from a first impression. The model then picked up some of the class's observations, verbalizing the impression she thought she was putting across. Once again she was asked to pose, and the audience was now asked to provide her with dialogue. What might she be saying, audibly or in silence, externally or internally? They were asked to provide information about what came before and after this "pose," in response to which the model, now a character, came to life and moved.

This exercise of accruing a mass of information as a group from which individual members could select their individual story had proved effective in raising self-esteem with similar low achievers. A person is put on the spot, i.e., facing a group and feeling self-conscious. They listen to the comments of the group, thus transforming their external concerns to internal concerns; self-consciousness becomes self-awareness, the basis of confidence. The listener then selects from what they have heard spoken about them and creates a statement or poem.

With this particular group of maladjusted children, the learning was less in the activities — they were after all quite competent in putting on plays — than in keeping still and managing the stringent demands of coping with the "creepy" sensation of suspense. The experience has, as it were, to be "sold" to them by the quality of my voice and actions, suspending them through each part of the lesson, and then the lesson as a whole, much as through the narrative of a story. Afterwards, we discussed the management of suspense as an essential element of theatre. As protagonists and antagonists in this lesson, they had to provide it themselves through their actual reacting against the structures of the classroom. But rather than demolishing the situation, they were encouraged to enjoy meeting and challenging the rules up to (but not including) the point of breaking them: in fact, they were playing. In order to relieve the tension of sitting, reasons were provided for moving purposefully around. For example, three pairs of characters stood around the room like *tableaux vivants*, while the others walked around them, as in a museum, following the usual rules of speaking low and not touching the exhibits, observing and commenting among themselves. The models had to be very still! The silence was, for those who usually found themselves having to be silent, a chance to listen and take from the scene, rather than having it imposed or impressed on them. They were centring themselves in, and making sense of "noise." Interaction can take many forms, and confrontation need not lead to aggression. In my early days of teaching, I would use an excuse such as exercising concentration in order to play with silence. Half the group stood around the room trying to maintain a silence, a sound, a sequence of numbers or a thread of a story, while the others, without touching them, tried to distract them using gestures and sound.

The rituals for closing the lesson had to be strictly adhered to. The room, being a classroom, had to be rearranged before the next class arrived. This left time for a few moments of reflection to recall the "narrative" of the session, extolling the good points and offering remedial suggestions. Above all, they had to leave that space knowing individually the experience of being valued. Fortunately, the attendant substitute teacher was also a poet, who took some of their words which had come up and improvised them into poems — something momentous for students of such low self-esteem.

GROUP 4: (Twenty 16- to 17-year-olds; one 1½ hour lesson)

The work of this group was excellent. The pieces they presented from their repertoire were very sensitive in all four performance elements: physicality was clearly etched, action was economical, space sensitive and timing engaging. I was interested to see how they would function at the most fundamental of levels: simply enjoying the elements, the "skeleton" of their pieces for themselves, their input being as neutral as possible. I believe that great performance transcends the "trappings" — which by their very precision allows this transcendence to happen — to the abstraction of the form which, touching such universals, sparks the imagination beyond the immediate.

I asked the class to analyse their pieces at their most fundamental level of action, to show each story in a single action, like a climax with movement. Asked what they saw, the audience responded with answers such as "I saw three people meet one person"; "Three people are together, one stays and two leave"; or "There were two pairs and in each one person had a higher status." In other words, the pieces were stripped of as much information, suggestion and movement as possible. These "skeletal actions" were listed on the blackboard. After changing their groupings, the new groups strung these actions together in an arbitrary order. This new piece would show a sequence of frozen moments, little climaxes, with movement between each being as neutral as possible, a simple changing of position. The students may have felt this experience nearer to dance than theatre. It was like presenting a series of "nouns," inarticulate things, and the question became how to vitalize them, to introduce the "verb." ("Nouns" becoming "verbs" is not just an intellectual exercise. The act of the inanimate becoming animate is the grammar of creativity, of life itself.)

Thus, the next stage was to explore how to move from one "climax" to the next. Individuals chose different qualities of movement (e.g., direct/indirect, fast/slow, heavy/light etc.), and a particular story began to emerge. Considerable imaginative demand was being made, particularly as individuals were likely to be arriving at the "climaxes" of each stage at different times. The give and take required here among the performers challenged their clichés of performance.

In this session there was time enough only to begin to allow dialogue to emerge, so instead, words were imposed. Each person chose a different nursery rhyme, the lines of which were spoken to accompany the moves, either before, during or after the movement, as the student wished. This surrealistic or nonsensical putting together of material really stretched their imaginations further, not least because they could not resort to logical sequencing, but, as in a dance, they had to stick by their commitment to the performance moment, an intuitive sense of "rightness." In their original presentations they had shown themselves to be very competent (perhaps too competent) in the drama end of the spectrum. This exercise allowed them to give themselves over to the hazards of creativity, and I was immensely impressed by the manner in which they managed it.

GROUP 5: (Twenty high-school students; two 1½ hour sessions)

Another excellent group! It is always impressive when a class enters the room ready to begin, that is, aligned with the confidence of knowing their worth and "toned up" for something to happen. After the introduction, in a circle, I asked them to give one word each to describe me. As they gave them, I played with their words, repeating and grouping them in sequences and patterns, while pointing to the author of the word, presumably trying to commit them to memory. Ostensibly the game was about memory, but I was utilizing the exercise to centre myself in the group. My movements of body and arms, exaggeratedly indicating the memory aids, sustaining pauses with sustained gestures, produced an interesting dance in a chair. Members of the class then performed similar dances. Because they knew each other, the "dancer" would select or be given a theme (e.g., "on graduation," "deciding between friends" etc.). Thus different vocabularies were presented, and what was essentially a memory game produced often poignant "poemes concretes et vivantes."

Having become used to being the centres of attention (i.e., self-consciousness transformed into self-awareness), and to sustaining a performance (i.e., being competent in their space and time, improvising on ready-to-hand material), the students were now in the position of the storyteller. An important aspect of this exercise was for each person to experience being **with** the group at the same time as speaking **to** them. They sat in a circle and individuals took turns telling a story, the details of which were tendered by the group and fused together by a "storyteller." The students were encouraged to regard their initial moment of presence, the "fright" and rise in adrenalin, as the building up of "weight," as the "substance of feeling" which would form the basic material of the story. This energy would be expended in the telling of the story. They were to feel themselves as enormous spheres, balloons of feeling which could engulf the audience, but as if caught in a net of articulation. The agent of the balloon (and of feeling) is the vowels, and that of the net (and articulation) the consonants. In this way, the students would learn to distinguish prattle from incision, using only as many words as were necessary.

In telling the story in a circle, it would become apparent that focusing on one person changed the circle, with those on the side of the storyteller either drawing away to become part of the audience, or joining up and becoming adjuncts of the storyteller. Those that drew away aligned themselves with the others in a semi-circle, focusing on the storyteller for whom they were providing memory aids for the story. More important were the students who joined the storyteller understanding that the audience continued to be a part of their "circle," but at a distance. It is better to use the term sphere, which is three-dimensional; the audience hemisphere is seen as a physical extension of the performer's hemisphere. Those flanking the storyteller became part of the story by offering comments, helping build excitement and mood in words, sound and movement, drawing attention to details, providing metaphors and clarifying the situation. They served the role of the Greek chorus, heightening the scene with miniature lyric passages. Gradually, others in the audience joined the storyteller's numbers until a substantial chorus emerged behind the storyteller, offering material individually, and picking up from each other, until they found they were beginning to move spontaneously as a group. Seeing the class as an embryonic Greek chorus leads the way to exploring the evolution of Greek drama as a practical classroom exercise.

While continuing to relate the action of the story, the storyteller moves to the next stage. A character — the protagonist — is introduced in the form of somebody stepping forward from the chorus and speaking the words of the characters described by the storyteller, using their hands as a mask to identify different characters. After this, another character — the antagonist — is introduced, in opposition to the first, and with whom confrontation and friction occurs. Finally, a third

338

character — the *deus ex machina* — is introduced to mediate and resolve the situation. The storyteller, by now simply the chorus leader, gradually fades with the rest of the chorus into oblivion.

Even though this sequence covered two lessons, the stages had to be rushed. The students were not familiar with Greek drama, but it gave rise to an interesting discussion with the class teacher on how other developments in drama (e.g., the proscenium arch, theatre in the round etc.) could be the basis of other classroom activity.

GROUP 6: (Six 16- to 19-year-olds; one 1½ hour evening session)

This was an evening group performing at their reception centre for adolescents at risk. Relationships between members of this group were generally volatile; on this occasion, they were more so having their teachers involved with them in the session. They normally studied individually or in pairs, singing, acting or painting, and had been brought together with their teachers for this session. Their response to the introductory exercise of observing, commenting on and questioning me was very uninhibited. It is characteristic of this type of child that their direct response to this introductory situation — confrontation and drama in actuality — provides a strong, if difficult, basis to the lesson. When too confrontational, it is difficult to allow space for ideas to grow. Clearly, these students wanted to create strong, selfish — as opposed to self-centred — statements. The notion of self-centredness has to be distinguished from selfishness; the aim of the drama lesson seems to be to develop self-centredness, which is the ability to create one's own universe, to have a focused centre from which to radiate outward, allowing others to be self-centred in the hope of interaction. Selfishness is all give or all take; self-centredness is the balance of give and take, the ability to be at one with oneself and finding the stillness in the midst of noise. It is the basis of all communication.

I asked the students to present themselves through a short piece of work. They presented pieces derived from their work at the centre, songs, self-appraisals etc. They were then asked to pair up and teach their own piece to their partner, dictating the exact movement, words, intonation etc. The ability to share not only means releasing something from oneself, but working at getting something out of others, not just accommodation, demands coming to terms with oneself at a certain level.

A further feature to demonstrate their handling of the situation was the placing of the audience; each performer arranged the rest on the group as extravagantly as they wished, where their piece would be seen to greatest advantage. Thus, though they were apparently having a session about working with others, the students were, in fact, learning to be sensitive to others by asking them to be sensitive to themselves. These students, being maladjusted, were expert at expressing and projecting, but not receiving; they were very adept at using the spatial element of performance, to using and manipulating social and audience space.

Their works were generally very linear, a clear narrative which they drove through relentlessly, allowing no lateral element of resonance or question; competent, but devoid of warmth. We worked on developing a sense of presence, another aspect of give and take. It is the ability to pick up on the generalized energy of an audience, energy which becomes feeling through the specific intention of the actor, the thing that he wants to express. We explored the most appropriate channel of release of this energy from the torso, the feeling chamber: arms, legs, genitals and head.

This class had to be encouraged to comment positively on others' performances, but instead of "armchair criticizing," they had to get up and actually perform their "correction" or development (a technique drawn from Forum Theatre). They were consciously exposing themselves to self-consciousness, a state they often found themselves in and which may be said to be a major contention of performance. The question for the performer, social or dramatic, is how to be the centre of attention without collapsing, becoming embarrassed, indulgent or selfish. The lives of these students, so mucked and mixed up, had forced them to become so defensive, giving out to prevent taking in (allowing no means for the listener to "get inside," they could be seen as "noise" instruments), that the job of their performance teachers would seem limited to supplying them with techniques for helping them get started in life. These techniques, which one hopes would not degenerate into tricks, contain the principles and means of self-generation.

GROUP 7: (Twenty-five 10- to 11-year-olds; one 1½ hour lesson)

This was an elementary school group with little experience in drama, hence their use of themselves in the space was limited. Remembering a situation some years earlier of how very articulate city children had needed to have their space made more manageable by being constricted — that is, divided into smaller units — I divided the room into four parts, one for each season of the year. The ploy was to get the children to show me, a stranger, what they did year long. They were grouped and asked to undertake a journey through the seasons, beginning with the one in which they were placed. Thus was created the structures for certain dynamics to take place, such as between freedom within each stage or season, and the cohesion of the collective, or year; between individual exploits and group decision concerns, which would distinguish those inclined to wander off on their own and those taking initiatives with the group; between wanting to

340

get underway and wanting to linger sensorially in the moment. This last dynamic between linear and lateral concern is central to narrative and story, and is crucial to personal development.

When children got underway on their stories, their concern naturally tends toward the narrative, through which they would rush headlong. Thus, it was necessary to have a moment of preparation to attune their bodies to new possibilities beyond their clichés and preconceptions in the narrative details, and also to be more alert to what was going on around them, to what I call these linear-lateral concerns. It was also a ploy to delay the journey and build the level of excitement towards it, which would provide them with more material — in the form of feelings — to manage. We considered ways of travelling, giving the narrative formula of **who, what, when, where, how** and **why**. Eventually we concentrated on the **how** element, which allowed us to rehearse, using very rudimentary movements of walking, rolling etc., and various movement qualities, such as direct/indirect, fast/slow, heavy/light, symmetrical/asymmetrical, upper/lower body use etc. The **how** element, of course, implies the other elements, but more important was the concentration of the children in the movement for its own sake — to trigger unpremeditated action.

The "warm-up" complete, the journey began, a story revealed in action. Afterwards we sat and recounted the stories, including the preparation, significant moments of which were described as anecdotes, transformed into improvised verse or jingles. This stage of reflection at the end of the lesson was crucial, for it attempts to recapture, or intellectualize, the rhythm of the warm-up, presentation and reflection: in short, the process of creativity.

GROUP 8:　(Twenty-five 10- to 11-year-olds; one 1½ hour session)

This elementary class was clearly competent in drama, by which I mean that they entered the hall in which we were working with a "special" attitude. One could feel the scales of structure and the norm peeling away as they removed their shoes, and feel their bodies expanding to the space and the potential of the imagination as they went through unsupervised preliminary stretching. After the observation and questioning introduction, I set up the "seasons" exercise.

Their sense of balance between expression (i.e., individual striving and communication, creating and working with the others' spaces), was remarkable. Their improvisational skills were well developed and, unlike many of their seniors, they did not settle for the slick and sensational. They built on those elements of place and time, the **where** and **when**, which are too easily neglected in narratives. I felt that I could work at a deep level with this class in the area of stillness, that is, being in a state of balanced response and action, or inward and outward alignment, in which images and ideas are spawned.

The children, after having undertaken their journeys and discussing them, were asked individually to improvise another journey, watched by the class audience, who gave certain starting points, such as being slow, indirect, top-heavy, unbalanced to the left etc. The traveller would begin the journey, allowing these qualities of **how** to suggest the **where**, **when** etc. The audience described what they were picking up, without disturbing the flow of the traveller. At certain moments I would interject changes, changing the quality of movement. The traveller was forced to pause a moment to assimilate this physical change, which would trigger a new situation, a change of direction, impelling the performer on their way.

Of course, as in all these classroom exercises, the education is two-sided, for the class is being challenged both as performer and audience. Thus in this last exercise, much consideration was given to helping the audience to sustain their passivity by acute observation and sensitive reaction.

GROUP 9: (Twenty-five 6- to 8-year-olds; one 1½ hour lesson)

This was a very lively group. With this age group I am interested to see how they might work as a unit with the same uninterruptible concentration that they often achieve working individually in their own space and times. It is a challenge to me as a creator, with my interest in linear-lateral processes, of creating a story in action, to stimulate and support ideas with children working at different levels and abilities. It is important that the teacher finishes a lesson with a sense of achievement, that the discipline has allowed the student to conceive an idea and to work it through. Most of the problem in the classroom is organizational, the spreading of material in time and ordering it in space. Ideally, one has to trigger exactly the right stimulus, not so powerful that the child's involvement is at the expense of individual responsibility, but not too weak that it needs overexplaining.

I began the lesson with a warm-up: sitting on the floor, checking body parts, touching parts of the body, slapping the resonant parts for sound, in patterned movements and improvised jingles. This very structured movement developed into the freer play of rolling and movement to stimulate both tension and release. The improvisation concentrated on playing with choices of qualities of movement, e.g., fast/slow etc. They thus arrived at the core of the lesson: "a river crossing."

The room was defined as an imaginary river, across which children had to cross with the aid of stepping stones (pieces of paper). The stepping stones were arranged as the children wished, basically either to meet the need of getting across with urgency or information, or the desire to linger, enjoying and "becoming" the sights and sounds around. The pieces of paper then had vowels written on them, which travellers sang out as they stepped on them. (This is the basis of reading exercises in which children travel along a runner of words, articulated into syllables, i.e., the vowel contained in syllables, so that they can experience dipping into the vowel or syllable with their whole body.). Then, as individual children travelled across, they chose the length of time to stay on each vowel. The remainder of the class watched and as a chorus sang the vowel for as long as the traveller stayed on it. The travellers were encouraged to be daring with their lengths of stopping, ostensibly to test the audience, but which created interesting musical phrases.

An important transition can be seen in this exercise. In the first part of it, the reward comes in the satisfaction of having completed a task, in getting through the journey. In the latter part of the exercise the reward is actually in doing it, being for the moment lost in the note or syllable (an experience nearer poetry than prose), supported by the sound of the chorus. Another development in this exercise was to use the steps as notation for music. The steps were placed in a straight line as regular beats, and then some of them were halved, so that the children could equate their timing with the step. They arranged these whole and half pulses into interesting, often asymmetrical rhythms. Though a concentrated class, even these children had to be helped to watch and to avoid giggling.

The children are finding and using their actual physical weight, and if one accepts that physicality is the means by which a person understands and manifests their feelings and thoughts, and that intelligence is a fusion of physicality, feeling and thought in action, then clearly what is being educated is finding a way into using the "weight" of feeling and thought spontaneously. The integrated person is, I believe, the objective of the theatrical experience, whether in the theatre or in a classroom.

This session, like the other elementary classes, was observed and videotaped by members of the staff. Many commented on how long the children could be kept engaged within certain stages of the lesson. I think this touches on the rhythmic skills of the teacher, where rhythm is seen as the dynamic between the overall phrase or gesture and the underlying pulses or stresses. An unsatisfactory story and lesson jumps, as interest in each segment fades, from action to action, stage to stage, activity to activity, creating this kind of repetitive rhythm:　⌢⌣⌢⌣⌢ . The result may have a certain linear logic, but the overall experience is very nervous, overstructured, with little room for freedom of expression. A more organic rhythm is, having reached the end of a period of interest or bout of energy, to go back into itself, picking up on an earlier point, a moment of repose to gain momentum before leaping into the next phrase: ⌢ ⌢ ⌣ ➤ . This way, the children would be using their own rhythms as a basis for working with others. Ultimately, I believe that we are concerned with educating "weight," whether physical, emotional, mental or spiritual, and individual rhythms of working; these are the resources for meeting and managing the structures of everyday life.

Summary

Meeting up with fellow practitioners, particularly across cultures, and articulating ideas is always exciting, provided that it is accepted that the transaction is two way. The principles and strategies outlined in this writing, coming from the praxes of myself and others, represents my side of the engagement. In encountering staff doing interesting work, meeting the particular needs of their students, and drawing on their creativity to the maximum, it is usual to find those who can and those who cannot talk about it. The inability to talk about one's work in this field is usually the reluctance to acknowledge the individuality of one's creativity and its worth. Dependence on others to interpret what is being done might produce satisfying, if safe work, but the quality loses its particularity. Sharing from strength extends the context and confidence of the teacher.

When we can reveal that we have both ideas to initiate practice and (the most difficult aspect of teaching), knowledge within which to place both our and our students' work in context, then they provide a parameter of confidence beyond which the praxis can develop. We are like a performer doing what comes naturally and the act of distancing ourselves from our work is, as every performer knows, difficult. Extending parameters is the task of the artist. As a performer, we must have our act together, our feelings and mind focused in the exactness of our physical response, like an animal, equal to the situation, intuitive and intelligent. In order for the intuitive skills to develop, space has to be provided with oneself. The mind takes over and intelligence becomes intellect, practice becomes praxis. Again this translation is not easy, particularly for teachers trained to put ideas into practice.

Although we know the objective of the lesson, we should not be close ended about the result. Having set up the idea or form to be worked at, the teacher should become like the audience — naive, appreciative — while unknowing of the outcome, even of a familiar play or situation. The director is the audience's eyes and ears in the rehearsal stage, the objectifier of the practice, the intellect questioning and shaping the intelligence being explored in front of them. In the classroom, the teacher's eyes and ears should serve a similar purpose.

344

The teacher is at base a storyteller, the facilitator of play, imagined or actual. Our concern is for a balanced linear-lateral event. We strive to sustain the event overall while allowing the student/audience freedom **within** structures, challenging them to the point of, but not actually breaking those structures. Perhaps the most difficult balance to achieve is that between projecting and receiving; the effective actor and storyteller can both act and listen, both give and take. Sustaining the narrative line through the overall objective is like managing a great musical phrase, divided into activities which for variety need contrasting or enhancing pulses; the storyteller/teacher is the embodiment of rhythm. This dynamic between phrase and pulse produces the internal patterning, little incidents or moments which are the vitality of rhythm. These individual "patterns" may happen within the overall phrase of individual lessons, or constitute single lessons in a programme. Each lesson has to be an entity. For some children, it is the time in the week when they are allowed to be "all of a piece," the body, feeling and mind integrated — in other words, intelligent.

This notion has bearing on the fact that, with the exception of one class, all of my lessons in Montreal were "one-off's," like a series of "first nights." These kinds of sessions generally succeed on a combination of novelty and adrenalin: a time to introduce but not pursue ideas. For this reason, students generally perform better, apparently, for the visitor than the teacher. The "second night," is when the real work begins; the tables are turned and the material, interest, adrenalin and other elements which go towards the making of a good performance have to come from the student/audience. They reveal what has been most relevant to them, which often is not what the teacher expected. The "first night" is more concerned with linear concerns, and the "second night" with lateral ones; both concerns need to be in interaction in the single "one off" session.

The question, "In which language do you cry?," posed tacitly at the beginning of these writings as if to the verbally facile students I first met, is a fundamental one. In extremis, when you are at your most "at-oneness" with yourself, and feeling is not enough, in which language do you survive? In which language do you contain and understand that moment of crisis, listening to yourself, so that it speaks at least to an audience of one: yourself. Among all the noises, the voices inside and outside your head, which one, in the final analysis, truly speaks for you? Drama is mostly about expressing, projecting. Theatre requires an audience. How good an audience you are to yourself is the measure of your responses and reactions to others.

The classroom is essentially a place for interactional theatre, or drama. But in developing the sense of performance, of presence, the element of presentation is addressed, and the classroom becomes more than a testing ground of society: it becomes the crucible of human experience.

Epilogue

A Lifetime's Work
in Educational
Drama/Theatre

Over Fifty Years of Drama

BERT AMIES

Introduction

I have been actively involved with drama and the arts all my life. Since my first experiences as a young child in 1924, I have been constantly involved in doing or teaching drama and theatre. During the course of my career I have taught drama to all ages, ranging from young children to mature adults, in the community, in schools and in universities.

What follows is a chronicle of my life's work in Drama In Education in England. It is intended not only as a personal social history, but also a reflection on some of the changes and developments that have occurred in the field during my lifetime.

The Beginnings of Drama in Education in England: A Brief Overview

Of the earliest educational practices we know very little, other than it was made available to some children by means of private tutors and the Church. By the early Renaissance, children of the Chapel Royal were receiving instruction in music, particularly singing, and in Latin. This education was only for boys who, at times, also took part in plays. When the great public schools were founded (Harrow, Eton, Winchester and Shrewsbury to name a few, and again only for boys), a tradition for performing plays was established. Eton was particularly advanced in this practice. The Public School of Shrewsbury, in an area where I would later work, was founded in the 16th century and it laid down that "the boys shall perform one act of a play before they go to their half-holiday games."

By the middle of the 17th century, Dame Schools began to appear in villages and towns.[1] Both boys and girls could attend these schools, but most families were too poor to pay the necessary fees. The teachers were untrained and often coarse; one might say that they were "playing

349

at school"; all they tried to instill was a rudimentary knowledge of the Three R's. This situation continued throughout the 18th century.

Throughout the 19th century great strides were made in reorganizing education with the avowed intention of ensuring free education for all children. Many schools were built to what seemed a universal plan. Classroom ceilings were high, as were the windows, so that children could not be tempted to waste their time gazing out them, and there was only rudimentary lighting and heating. It was to a school building of this type that I was to go in 1924.

School Log books from the latter part of the 19th century indicate that emphasis was still on the Three R's, but that other subjects were beginning to creep in. Geography seems to have been first, then history, and finally basic science, whose inclusion seemed dependant on whether or not the headmaster saw himself as a man of science. Music was not taught in school, but there was some hymn singing, and occasionally some community singing. Drama was never included as a subject.

Yet the children were not altogether ignorant of drama, or at least live entertainment, because during the winter months Penny readings were held in many of the schools. These were for parents and other adults in the neighbourhood of the school, and consisted of recitations, solo singing, piano playing, and a short lecture on some topical subject. Seldom, if ever, was a play by an ensemble included in these Penny readings, but little plays did sometimes appear in the schools, put on by travelling groups in the evening, often sponsored by the local squire.

This is how things were up until the time that I began going to school. So it is in my lifetime that drama in the classroom became established for the first time in our history, and like all new subjects, it has suffered its ups and downs.

Early Life

During the early 1920s, my father farmed the Perry farm, Kyre Magna, Worcestershire, England. Mine was a happy family, sheltered from the harsher world which was developing in urban areas. I realize with hindsight that our world had remained fixed in the previous century. My mother and father had first met in a church choir and they both sang as they went about their work. My mother was also very fond of ballroom dancing, and she encouraged me to dance from an early age. My sister took piano lessons and she sang and played well; it was she who taught me to read, which I suspect was the reason I was accepted at the early age of four into the Infant Class at Kyre School in 1924.

The school had been built in late Victorian days and consisted of one very long room for most classes, with a separate room for infants.

Water was laid on for washing facilities, but the toilets were earth closets, and there was no electricity or gas.

I had, by now, grown old enough to become excited at the thought of Christmas, and as the holiday season approached, all talk was of the school party and — a new departure — an entertainment to be given by some children to their parents in the evening. As much as I enjoyed the party that afternoon, with the cakes, lemonade, and crackers, and especially the visit of Father Christmas (who we could all see was Mr. Chippington), I was longing for the evening to come. I didn't know what I expected; perhaps I had some instinct that something would happen which would impress me for life.

Arriving at the school after dark, my first impression was of the warm golden light, and that particularly homely smell associated with paraffin lanterns. The paper chains which the children had made took on a new life as they swayed in the hot updraughts of air. A space for the action had been cleared by the heating stove, which glowed more brightly than it seemed to do in the daytime, and improvised seating was provided for the audience, with us few infants placed high on chairs on solid tables.

I suppose that similar events took place in many schools throughout the country: a short speech by the principal, some carol singing and then a recitation. Some of the younger girls performed the first play, which had a fairyland theme. I held my breath when a few fairies came in dancing to the music of a gramophone recording. I had never seen such beauty. They were wearing snow-white dresses which rustled as they moved, and they had wings attached to their shoulders. I didn't wonder at the time how the wings were made; to me they were real. They remained in position as the girls danced, and they glistened with sequins and tinsel. I was stage-struck.

At home, my brother and I and our visiting cousins had plenty of places to play in, and our games were often related to farming. My new desire to introduce fairies and fantasy creatures into our games was not received very well. A few months after that Christmas my father collected me from school class to go with him to see a circus at Tenbury Wells. I didn't know what a circus was, but I could see that my father wanted to give me a treat. Small, family-operated circus companies often toured smaller towns as soon as winter was over, so this must have been one of those. I enjoyed the performance of the bareback riders jumping through paper hoops, and the way they were dressed reminded me of the fairies in the play. I also enjoyed the tightrope walker, but I remember being rather scared of the clowns. At the climax of the performance a man dressed in army uniform rode into the ring on a huge horse. They mounted a small rostrum and fireworks cascaded round them as the band played. Now I was circus-struck. Back at home I wanted to include circus in our games, an idea which was greeted more favourably, particularly as my brother had a small grey pony of his own.

My family moved from the Perry farm, in Worcestershire, to Whittington House farm, Kinver, Staffordshire. My father was persuaded to make this move for, like many others, he foresaw hard times for the country, with rising unemployment and poverty. Hence he chose to re-establish his farm nearer to the larger populations of the industrial Midlands of England.

This move affected me a great deal, young as I was, and was beneficial to my theatre aspirations. I now had many playmates, although, as I was already becoming aware, they were divided into two sections by class. There were the boys my own age who came from poor families, with whom I enjoyed the rough and tumble of gang and den play, and then there were the children from the neighbouring farm, and one girl from the Dick Whittington Inn. I played with the first group at any time by day or night; play with the latter group was at very set times by invitation. It was with this second group, however, that I pushed forward my interest in drama.

At my home there was an exceptionally large upper room over the kitchen which had its own separate staircase. Its one window was remarkably small for a room of such size; I suppose that it was the part of the house intended for the servants. My mother used the room to store trunks of old bedspreads and blankets and boxes of unpacked artifacts which accumulated after the move. It became a playroom for my brother and I, and a place where we could store our toys. As my brother was a very out-of-doors kind of boy, I had the room mainly to myself. I can never truly explain the effect this room had on me. It was an escape from absolute reality to my kind of reality. I was reminded of it recently when Peter Brook spoke of a similar attic room where he spent most of his childhood. I feel the atmosphere of my room even as I write.

One day about this time, my mother took my brother and me along to attend a morning business appointment in Worcester. In the early afternoon we walked into the city square and stopped outside a building with a glass awning over the entrance: the Worcester Theatre Royal. My mother said she wanted to bring us to see a pantomime. I listened anxiously as she spoke with the box-office attendant, who was saying that all the seats were sold out. After some discussion, they agreed that the three of us could sit on extra chairs at the back of the circle.

These seats were at a great height above a slope crowded with excited people. Way down below was the stage where the pantomime was going to take place, but all I could see were deep red curtains. Then the fire curtain, covered with colorful advertisements, came hurtling down, and my mother explained how it had to be raised and lowered twice every performance. Finally it rose, the house lights were dimmed and the orchestra began to play. The red curtains were raised to reveal a painted landscape scene, and an old man, Father Tyme, dressed in long white robes and a scythe over his shoulder came to the front of the stage. He was followed by the Demon King, and soon the Good Fairy came on to argue with him. I was straightaway back at school where I had so liked the dancing fairies.

So much happened in this first pantomime, so much which I still remember. Now I was certain that the stage was where I wanted to be. I regarded these performers as charmed people; I did not yet connect them in any way with school, and had no knowledge of any need for any training in the art of theatre illusion. Back at home I sang the comic song over and over again and practiced high kicks. I pushed a small flashlight into a soft toy to in an attempt to get a special effect which had actually been achieved by means of a UV light on stage. It was this UV scene which had overwhelmed me as I watched giant geese laying large red balloons, and life-size teddy bears gamboling.

I now saw a special purpose for my room upstairs: it was to become a theatre. The walls of the room were cream, distempered plaster. I rigged up front curtains by stretching a strong wire from wall to wall at one end of the room, sewed curtain rings onto the edges of two old patchwork quilts, and strung them up. I tacked a blanket over the small window and kept the room in permanent blackout. There was no electricity at the farm, so I lit the room, when required, with candles in jam jars. I staged all sorts of entertainments in this room, from magic lantern shows to live entertainment shows with my friends and myself as the cast.

I suppose that my mother was becoming anxious about my plans for my theatre. At any event, she said she needed the room for other purposes. My little company held a meeting and we decided to set up our theatre in the farm granary. We could only use it when it was empty of corn, and it was a very dusty place, but we managed to stage a few pantomimes, and we had a bigger audience of curious neighbours.

In 1931, at 11 years of age, I was enrolled as a day boy at a minor public school, Sebright School, in Wolverley. My lifestyle changed, and for some reason which I can never remember, my theatre company changed. I had made friends with the children at Whittington Hall, and we formed a new company. There was a very impressive entrance hall where we could perform our plays, and a spacious play room which we totally converted into a pantomime theatre. We had the use of a gramophone, a piano and an exotic range of furniture and props. This is where I staged plays, both indoors and outdoors, until I left this school in 1936.

Schooling

I have already referred to the Christmas concert at Kyre School, which was the only drama I knew there. There was no drama in school at Kinver, which I attended between 1927–31, although in the higher classes, Friday afternoons were devoted to memorizing poems, singing and — very occasionally — playing charades. The latter was obviously meant to increase word power, but I revelled in the dramatic nature of it. At Sebright, although there were no drama lessons as such, there were occasional performances on the school stage. During English lessons in the first and second year, we were allowed to read plays in front of the class, and on very rare occasions we performed short scenes in Latin. It would, in fact, have been surprising to have found drama in the curriculum at this time, as such a development did not begin to take place throughout the British school system until 1939, when local education authorities began appointing drama advisers to the schools, whose main task was to help with the annual school play.

During the war years of 1939–45, drama in schools increased. It became an evening activity for thousands of children who were sent from their homes to live in safer areas of the country. I was called in to help produce a concert with pupils from Clacton-on-Sea High School, which had been evacuated to my home area of Kidderminster. I formed a drama group for a youth club and staged quite ambitious pantomimes and concerts which we presented in a village hall to raise funds for war charities.

After World War II, I began to consider seriously my own drama training. I enrolled at the Birmingham Repertory Theatre Evening School (now defunct), and then full-time at the Birmingham School of Speech Training and Dramatic Art. There I earned the Teacher's Diploma in Speech and Drama, L.G.S.M., and soon after began work as a lecturer and play director in the Birmingham area. I felt, however, the need for further qualification so, while still lecturing and directing, I attended the full-time teacher's course at the Birmingham School of Music, from which I graduated in 1952.

Soon after I started drama studies in Birmingham I became aware that drama was now appearing on school curriculums. The City of Birmingham Drama Adviser at the time, Peter Slade, gave lectures at my college, and I began to shift my attention towards community drama and drama in education. I visited the Educational Drama Association headquarters in Birmingham and passed a test which enabled me to be accepted as an evening class lecturer.

I took up my first full-time teaching appointment at Halesowen, Hill & Cakemore Secondary Modern Boys' School in 1952,[2] where my responsibility was to teach English, drama and music. I now had to put all my theories of drama teaching in schools to the test. The school was not in a wealthy area and, though the boys could be rough, if not tough, the younger ones seemed to revel in drama. I enjoyed the classroom drama, but the principal was a stickler for tradition; he wanted plays presented on the school's poorly equipped stage. He also insisted on scripted plays, having little liking for improvisation.

After two years I moved to a primary school in the same area, to gain experience in working with as wide an age range as possible. I had now made up my mind that my main career should be that of drama adviser or consultant with a local education authority. My days at Halesowen C of E Primary School were very happy ones. I knew that my skills in teaching drama were increasing, and my knowledge of theatre was widening as I directed amateur drama groups throughout the Midlands, and undertook drama adjudication for various youth festivals. This was a good time for drama in England; there was a surge of interest throughout the country.

Drama Adviser

In 1958 the drama adviser's post for the county of Shropshire was advertised and, to my surprise, my application was accepted. My duties included organizing drama courses for teachers, youth, and adult education schemes, and I also had a large county store of stage lighting equipment, stage rostra and scenic units and a costume store to administer. The post was a very full-time one, including much evening work and weekend sessions throughout the year, but I enjoyed every minute of it. It was over a period of 22 years at this post that I really came to understand Drama in Education, helped by the fact that my position required me to attend many national conferences and seminars in the field, as well as opportunities to observe Drama in Education abroad.

Almost at once, after beginning this job in 1958, I was thrown into the business of visiting schools to estimate needs, and in running courses on classroom drama. I ran many of these courses myself, but on occasion could bring in other experts in the field. My predecessor had done much work with secondary schools, and I found that primary school teachers were crying out for help. It seemed to me that if drama could be properly established at the primary level, the chances were good for it to develop well at the secondary stage. I had come into the work just at that time when schools were accepting classroom drama as a distinct subject from theatre art. Most primary school teachers were well aware of this, although some still clung to the idea of staged productions. I had always adhered to Peter Slade's idea that putting young people on stage in front of a massed audience was not necessarily a beneficial experience; only the more extroverted of these children might remain unscathed.

355

The dichotomy between classroom drama and staged drama in the adult style, had to be argued about at great length. A majority of the primary school teachers had come independently to my view. Music and movement and creative dance were also being developed at the time, and together with creative drama, they appeared more and more in class time as a valuable experience for the children. There was a surge of drama work in primary schools throughout the county, and this was helped by the co-operative work of the primary school advisers, who had worked some time to encourage a child-centred ethos in education, rather than a disciplinarian one.

The situation in the secondary schools was not so encouraging. Grammar and high schools staged an annual school play, usually Shakespeare or Sheriden, not so much as an exploration of drama and dramatic literature, but as an exercise to highlight the school's prestigious status. The hope was, in bringing the parents to the school for a pleasant evening, they might endeavour to raise a few extra funds for the school. While these plays were often adequately directed by a member of the faculty, a major problem remained in that the cast had had no rudimentary drama training. Many of them, the head boy or girl for example, were appearing for the honour of the school and not the honour of the play. It was my duty to attend most of these school efforts, some of which were good, while others fell into the category which Peter Brook has called "the deadly theatre."

Some of the secondary modern schools also fell into the tradition of the annual school play, but their choice of plays was wider, and often more child-centred. The acting varied but the sets were often so over-elaborate that they swamped the actors; new schools were often equipped with a large traditional proscenium stage at one end of a spacious assembly hall, and the arts and woodwork teachers would have a field-day constructing huge sets to fill the space.

Because classroom drama and drama workshops had become respectable in educational circles I felt that it was my duty to encourage this move in Shropshire. When I arrived in the county only two secondary schools had drama specialists. These were both girl's schools, and the teachers in question had been appointed as English teachers with an interest in drama. My first task was to support those teachers in particular secondary schools who showed some sign of further developing the subject of drama. As a first move I invited all secondary school principals to an evening meeting at which I hoped to put forward plans for achieving this. I had yet to learn that secondary school principals only attended county meetings on important policy decisions; they did not want to dwell on an isolated curriculum subject. As a result, only five principals attended this meeting, and I believe they came more out of curiosity about who I was, drama still being suspect, than to learn anything about the subject.

This rather depressing situation did not occur when I called meetings of primary school teachers and principals; enthusiasm in this section was boundless. My task in most Shropshire primary schools was a pleasant and easy one, while in the secondary schools it was very difficult. The inroads that were made there, however, were all the more rewarding. The reader must understand that there was a great division between these two types of schools; the whole attitude as to what defined education was at variance. To simplify with a generalization, primary schools, while not lacking in basic discipline, were aiming at self-discipline in the child; the secondary school relied heavily on imposed discipline. It was against this background that I began my work in the county.

I decided to consolidate the teaching of drama in the primary schools first, giving a basis upon which the teachers of first-year secondary school children could build. I had begun to feel that the needs of the primary section were a bottomless pit; so great was their enthusiasm that I could have spent all my time with them. However, I had no brief to exclude the secondary schools. It was not a time for confrontation with this latter section, but rather a time to do some winning over. The best way to do that seemed to be to begin at the level where they were working. I attended all the school plays, staying behind to encourage the teachers and cast. I visited the schools again as soon as possible after the play and positioned myself in the staff room where enthusiasm for drama work could be encouraged.

Part of my contract as drama adviser was to direct at least one play a year with the Shrewsbury Theatre Guild. This was not an amateur dramatic society, but an community organization which existed to supply four plays of literary worth and merit in each season for its members. Since each director could select his own cast for any chosen play, I began to invite the more hopeful teachers to take part in the more experimental plays. In this way I gradually gained their confidence. When my predecessor began work in Shropshire he presented excellent work but a dwindling theatre-going habit resulted in small audiences. (It is worth noting here that from the Renaissance up until the Restoration, Shrewsbury had been second in importance only to Oxford as a venue for touring companies.) The Theatre Guild had been set up in my predecessor's time to ensure that he got audiences for his plays, filling the gap which the subsequent lack of professional theatre in the area created.

After what seemed an interminable wait, three secondary schools appointed specialist drama teachers to their staff, and I was well aware that principals throughout the county were watching for results;

everything would now depend on the impression these three teachers made. And a good one they did. Shropshire is large in area, some of it being very remote, but teachers in the various schools keep in professional contact. Principals began to make serious inquiries about setting up a drama specialization in their schools. (It is possible that some of them had a mercenary incentive, as I had a block grant with which to support drama initiative in all schools and organizations.) By the time secondary education was reorganized into the comprehensive system in the 1960s, many of the principals in Shropshire were seriously considering drama provisions for their students.

During this period much reconstruction of schools was being planned by the county architects. Together with other specialist advisors, I was called in to discuss these architectural plans from time to time. The architects foresaw how many subjects were developing and they intended to make adequate provisions in the new schools. The idea of a large assembly hall with a proscenium arch stage at one end was being discredited; such halls had been used primarily for morning assemblies, and these assemblies were now giving way to classroom-based assemblies. The architects suggested drama studios, some of which were flat, open areas about the size of two classrooms, others incorporating a small raked auditorium. With these drama studios in their new schools, some principals realized that they would have to employ a drama specialist. Some, however, continued to resist the idea, finding other uses for these spaces, such as examination accommodation, or storage of bulky equipment.

During all this time, drama had continued to flourish in primary schools, so that children moving into the secondary schools were ready for further studies in the subject, preparing for first and second grade examinations in theatre studies. By the late 1970s a pattern was well established in Shropshire. Enthusiasm for drama was very high in most primary schools, and about two-thirds of the comprehensive schools were taking the subject seriously.

Yet some problems did persist. The great majority of pupils in secondary schools did not intend to take up theatre arts as a profession. Most teachers realized that general drama training was beneficial to all students and adapted their work accordingly. The subject could be a confidence builder, encourage self-awareness and an understanding of inter-personal relationships. It gave opportunity for development of oral and written language, and general creativity improved. It was also discovered that drama was a dynamic force in the learning process and that it could be used to support other subjects. This was misunderstood by some teachers who seemed unwilling to let the drama exploration move to the logical conclusion of performance in front of another group or audience. I came to call this aberration "de-dramatisation of drama." Nonetheless, every year the teachers of Shropshire were called together for one- or two-day conference and in-service training and drama consistently began to appear as an important discussion area.

New Directions

In adult education, there were many changes as the years went by. My work required me to visit evening classes in drama, and to visit amateur drama groups to appreciate their plays and give advice when they requested it. There was a surge of new playwriting in the 1960s, and I encouraged the groups to break new ground with the plays that they chose. I reinforced this by staging plays which were regarded as avant-garde with the Shrewsbury Theatre Guild and the Shropshire County Drama Group, and continued to cast these productions with many teachers. Those were good times for drama; interest in the country was widespread, greater than in our present age, where materialism is rampant and the arts have suffered some demotion.

Every year, in June, a weekend course entitled "The Amateur Drama Conference" was held at Attingham Park, then Shropshire's adult education college. This course was always fully booked, the participants being members of amateur drama societies, schools and other interested people. I managed to invite to the course a series of very distinguished lecturers, including Litz Pisk, the remarkable movement teacher, Dr. Kosta Spaic, principal of the Zagreb Academy of Yugoslavia, Dr. Yury Zavadsky, director of the Moscow Art Theatre, (and a former student of Stanislavsky), Martin Esslin, then head of BBC drama, Charles Marowitz, founder and director of the Open Space Theatre in London, Keith Johnstone and many others.

While the influence of these speakers began to show here and there in the work produced in Shropshire, it was another group of lecturers from the universities which opened a new vein of thought for me. It was a new method of using drama teaching techniques to develop and educate those who might never otherwise respond to traditional drama teaching. Clive Barker, then of Birmingham University, conducted a weekend drama course during which he introduced the idea of motivation through theatre games. He was enthusiastically supported by Albert Hunt, who was at the time university area tutor for South and East Shropshire. Hunt began conducting experimental drama sessions with students of Shrewsbury School of Art, and found that theatre games were an excellent preparation for performance. Teachers from both primary and secondary schools were invited to a weekend in-service workshop where they were introduced to these theatre games. They responded very favorably to this games-playing method, and saw that the end result was not frivolity but personal development.

When Albert Hunt left Shropshire to take up an appointment in Bradford, I was invited to continue the work he was doing with the art school students. This was something I came to look forward to every Wednesday afternoon, but because of my commitments, I could not go on with it indefinitely. Bill Morris, a tutor from the Shrewsbury Technical College, continued with the work, but now technical students joined the art students, and the venue was changed to my rehearsal room, a large upper room in a vacated Victorian school. As it was also a storeroom for my drama groups, it resembled a prop room in a theatre, with old scenic flats, broken furniture, old carpets on the floor and a collection of what most people would regard as rubbish. The students loved this room and never played truant. I attended these sessions, which took on the name "social drama," as often as I could.

In the 1970s, Bill Morris invited Bernie Warren and Rob Watling to look in on these sessions to enable them to identify teenagers who might help with charitable projects. Both Bernie and Rob took to social drama and became part of the regular team. They made an immense contribution and their enthusiasm led me to ask them if they had time to visit some schools with me, to offer social drama where I thought it would be appropriate. We became a travelling team of three, and our work made some impact in those secondary schools where drama work was minimal or absent.

Retirement

I retired from the post of drama adviser for Shropshire County Council at the end of 1980, at the age of sixty, not for any reasons of disenchantment with the work (for I had in fact enjoyed every moment of it), but rather because I wanted to branch out into other areas of drama. A bonus for my efforts at this job came to me in 1981 when I was awarded the MBE for services to education and drama.

At about this time I was approached by the principal of faculty for art and science at Shrewsbury College of Art and Technology to see if I would be willing to organize an evening class in drama. I designed a pre-diploma class catering to those with some experience in drama who wished to test their abilities through examination. The class was quickly filled, and I found myself not only preparing an enthusiastic group for examination, but was joined by younger students who wanted to use the class as a preparation for auditioning for drama colleges. This class has continued to the present, with some students either gaining their L.S.G.M. Acting Diploma, or gaining places in colleges and universities.

360

In the same year as this class started, the principal of humanities at Oswestry Tertiary College suggested to me that I might assist the principal of drama at the college in setting up an "A"-level theatre studies course. This struck me as an aspect of fate. I took up the work, and this, too, is continuing, bringing me into contact with eager young students and leading me personally to further reading and revision of ideas.

In addition to these activities, I continued to offer one-day or week-end drama courses, as well as sessions of social drama with residential courses set up for social services staff. Much as I enjoyed the work as county drama adviser, I enjoyed these new activities even more because they had no administrative duties; I was able to deal directly with drama development. My more recent appointment as honorary drama adviser for the County of Shropshire has allowed me to keep in touch with theatrical activities in the area. Retirement for me has been a very busy and happy time in my life. In it I have been able to further develop my love of theatre and drama.

Conclusion

The aphorism, "To study drama is to study life," is a self-evident truth. Through the practice of drama and the art of theatre, an individual can gain insight into the human condition. It unlocks the essence of the personality, and in some cases, takes off the blinkers.

When still a young man I was told by a psychiatrist friend that an actor is in a privileged position; to take part in a great work of dramatic literature was to absorb some of the playwright's unique way of thinking and viewing the world. He pointed to Shakespeare as having influenced the thinking of people over several centuries. Shakespeare, in turn, had been conditioned by his contemporary literature, from the Roman playwrights to the great Greek thinkers.

Drama is a very potent force in education. With young children it can be a rehearsal for adult life. It will, in certain cases, lead to an early understanding of self-knowledge and the effect of interpersonal relationships. Its powerful educating benefits are ensured by the fact that most children enjoy play-acting and have, for a time, a total belief in make-believe. This natural play requires an intuitive understanding of language, movement, imagination and creativity. It is not wise to impose an adult concept of "theatre" on these young people, but rather allow their natural, instinctive dramatic abilities to come into play.

In early adolescence, this built-in drama ability will still be present, but it is at this juncture that, for some, drama can begin to merge into theatre. It would be foolish to think that all people who enjoy drama as children will have the ability to practice the art of theatre as adults. Stanislavsky was aware of this, and would take on as students only those who sincerely believed that acting was their main means of expression. The acting of children and adolescents does not indicate certain success as an actor.

A large number of people set out to become professional actors, but the theatre is an overcrowded profession — some succeed, yet more will fail. Even more people stand on the brink and only dream of becoming actors; the amateur theatre movement caters to many of these people. It makes possible a release of inner acting drives and gives further opportunity for individuals to challenge themselves. A few of these people will eventually go on to enter the professional theatre.

Drama in the 20th century has become enveloped in jargon. This is a great pity because drama is in fact a very simple process, and a naturally expressive one for a majority of people. Those who indulge in jargon are often trying to crack the secret of successful, adult acting. They are almost bound to fail if they think they can find the answer through intellectual reasoning; a born actor *knows* by instinct.

Another development in modern drama has been its use as therapy. We can say that traditional acting has always been a sort of therapy for the performer, although less has been said on this than on the cathartic, or therapeutic, effect on the audience. The acting instinct which is natural to us all can be used to develop or give comfort to people who are at some risk in our society. Psychiatrists came to realize this early in this century, and such practitioners as Jacob Moreno used drama techniques to build up a positive therapeutic atmosphere, an approach which has since led to a properly organized dramatherapy movement.

Drama in Education has come a long way, and is now used to teach a range of subjects outside the arts: sociology, history, geography, English and religious studies. At the present time no parent is surprised if drama is included in the syllabus of their child's school, but I must admit that they are not surprised if it is not included. Drama is still optional in schools, and is present or absent at the whim of the principal. With the coming of the core curriculum in Britain I suspect that it could get squeezed out where it but tenaciously exists, and have no hope of starting where it is lacking.

We might be at a point where drama will revert to the annual school play. This tendency is very hard to counter. It has a different goal, namely as a fund-raising venture, or a chance to lend prestige to a school, much like a collegiate sporting event. This is a dangerous regression, for while one must not make over-extravagant claims for the value of classroom drama, it is true that the subject has been with us long enough to show that most children enjoy it. Through their enjoyment comes not only a very basic general knowledge, but also an enrichment and development of each individual's personality.

362

Endnotes

1. Dame Schools were schools that were independently set up and run by a woman of the village. It is from these school mistresses that the British tradition of the "Pantomime Dame" stems.

2. At this time, education at the secondary level was organised into a three-tiered system on the basis of ability. There were three types of secondary school one could attend after finishing primary school, and the placement of students in one or the other of these levels was decided on the result of examinations taken at about age 11 — the dreaded "11+." Grammar and high school (for boys and girls respectively), were designed for those students hoping to go on to university. Technical schools targeted students pursuing careers in skilled labour trades. The secondary modern school provided a general education for those students who did not pass the examination. Educational reform in the 1960s abolished these examinations and students of all abilities went to one "comprehensive" secondary school.

Reference Section

Bibliography

Allen, J.P.B. "Some Basic Concepts in Linguistics." In *The Edinburgh Course in Applied Linguistics*, Vol. 2. Oxford: Oxford University Press, 1975.

Amies, Bert, Warren, Bernie and Watling, Rob. *Social Drama*. London: John Clare, 1986.

Apple, M. *Ideology and Curriculum*. London: Routledge, 1979.

———. *Education and Power*. London: Routledge and Kegan Paul, 1982.

Aoki, Ted. *Toward Curriculum Inquiry in a New Key*. Edmonton: Department of Secondary Education Occasional Paper Series, 1989.

Aston, E. and Savona, S. *Theatre as Sign-System*. London: Routledge, 1991.

Baird, E. "Language through Drama: The Choice of Goals and Controls." In *World Language English*, Vol. 4, No. 1, 1984.

Bakhtin, M.M. *The Dialogic Imagination*. M. Holquist (ed.), C. Emerson and M. Holquist (trans.). Texas: University of Texas Press, 1981.

———. *Speech Genres and Other Late Essays*. V.W. McGee (trans.). Austin: University of Texas Press, 1986.

Barker, Clive. *Theatre Games*. London: Methuen, 1977.

Barone, Thomas. "Using the Narrative Text as an Occasion for Conspiracy." In E. Eisner and A. Peshkin (eds.), *Qualitative Inquiry in Education*. New York: Teachers' College Press, 1990.

Barrs, M. "Voice and Role in Reading and Writing." In *London Drama Magazine*, Vol. 7, No. 6, Jan. 1989.

Barton, John. *Playing Shakespeare*. London: Methuen, 1984.

Bazalgette, C. (ed.). *Primary Media Education*. London: British Film Institute, 1989.

Beckerman, Bernard. "Theatrical Perception." In *Theatre Research International*, Vol. 4, No. 3, 1979.

Bennedetti, Robert. "Notes To An Actor." In Richard P. Brown (ed.), *Actor Training: Vol. I*. New York: Drama Books Specialists, 1972.

Berry, Glenys and Reinbold, Joanne. *Collective Creation*. Edmonton: Alberta Alcohol and Drug Abuse Commission, 1984.

Best, David. *Philosophy and Human Movement*. London: Allen and Unwin, 1978.

Biber, D. *Variation Across Speech and Writing*. Cambridge: Cambridge University Press, 1988.

Blatner, Adam and Blatner, Allee. *The Art of Play*. New York: Human Sciences Press, 1988.

Boal, A. *Theatre of the Oppressed*. London: Pluto Press, 1979.

——. *Games for Actors and Non-Actors*. London: Routledge, 1992.

Bois-Simon, L. *The Use of Dramatic Techniques in the Teaching of English as a Foreign Language*. Université de Saint-Étienne, Centre Interdisciplinaire d'Études et de Recherche sur l'Expression Contemporaineates, 1978.

Bolton, Gavin. *Towards a Theory of Drama in Education*. London: Longman, 1979.

——. *Drama as Education*. London: Longman, 1984.

——. "Changes in Thinking About Drama in Education." In *Theory Into Practice*, Vol. 24, No. 3, 1985.

——. *Selected Writings on Drama in Education*. David Davis and Chris Lawrence (eds.). New York: Longman, 1986.

——. *New Perspectives on Classroom Drama*. Hemel Hempstead: Simon & Schuster Education, 1992.

Booth, David. *Interpretation*. Toronto: Harcourt, Brace Jovanovich, 1983.

——. *Drama Words*. Toronto: Toronto Board of Education, 1987.

——. "Talking in Role, Thinking for Life." Reprinted from *Drama Contact*, in the On-Site Proceedings of the International Symposium for Drama Education Research, OISE, May 1989.

Booth, David and Lundy, Charles. *Improvisation*. Toronto: Harcourt, Brace Jovanovich, 1985.

Booth, David and Martin-Smith, Alistair (eds.). *Re-Cognizing Richard Courtney*. Markham, Ont.: Pembroke Publishing, 1988.

Bourdieu, P. "Systems of Education and Systems of Thought." In R. Dale (ed.), *Schooling and Capitalism*. London: Routledge and Open University Press, 1978.

Bowen, H. "A Catalog of Goals of Higher Education." In *Missions of the College Curriculum*. San Francisco: Jossey-Bass Publishers, 1978.

Bowker, J. (ed.). *Secondary Media Education: A Curriculum Statement*. London: British Film Institute, 1991.

Breland, H.M. et al. *Assessing Writing Skill*. New York: College Entrance Examination Board, 1987.

Britton, J. *The Development of Writing Abilities (11–18)*. Schools Council Research Studies, London: Macmillan Education Ltd., 1975.

——. *Language and Learning*. London: The Penguin Press, 1992.

Brook, Peter. *The Empty Space*. Harmondsworth: Penguin, 1972.

Broudy, Harry. "The Arts as Basic Education." In *Journal of Aesthetic Education*, Vol. 12, No. 4, 1978.

Bruner, Jerome. *On Knowing: Essays for the Left Hand*. London: Atheneum Press, 1962.

Brustein, Robert. *Making Scenes*. New York: Random House, 1981.

Buber, Martin. *Between Man and Man*. London: Kegan, Paul, Trench, Trubner and Co. Ltd., 1947.

——. *I-Thou*. New York: Charles Scribner's Sons, 1958.

Campbell, Joseph. *Myths to Live By*. New York: Bantam, 1972.

Canada Council. *The Report of the Committee of Inquiry into Theatre Training in Canada*, Malcolm Black, (Chair), 1978.

Chatwin, Bruce. *Songlines*. Middlesex: Penguin, 1988.

Clandinin, D.J. "The Reflective Practitioner and Practitioner's Narrative Unities." In *Canadian Journal of Education*, Vol. 11, No. 2, 1986.

Clark, Barbara. *Growing Up Gifted*. Columbus: Charles E. Merrill Publishing Co., 1979.

Clark, K. and Holquist, M. *Mikhail Bakhtin*. Cambridge, MA: The Belknap Press of Harvard University Press, 1984.

Cohen, David. *The Development of Play*. London: Croom Helm, 1987.

Cohen, P. "Against the New Vocatonalism." In I. Bates, J. Clarke et al. (eds.), *Schooling for the Dole*. Basingstoke: Macmillan, 1984.

Cole, David. *The Theatrical Event*. Connecticut: Wesleyan University Press, 1975.

Connelly, F.M. and Clandinin, D.J. "On Narrative Method, Personal Philosophy, and Narrative Unities in the Story of Teaching" in *Journal of Research in Science Teaching*, Vol. 23, No. 4, 1986.

Conrad, C. *The Undergraduate Curriculum: A Guide to Innovation and Reform*. Boulder: Westview Press Inc., 1978.

Courtney, Richard. *The Dramatic Curriculum*. New York: Drama Book Specialists, 1980.

――. *Re-Play: Studies in Human Drama in Education*. Toronto: Ontario Institute for Studies in Education Press, 1982.

――. *The Quest: Research and Inquiry in Arts Education*. Lanham: University Press of America, 1987.

――. *Play, Drama and Thought*, 4th ed. Toronto: Simon and Pierre, 1989.

――. *Drama and Intelligence*. Montreal: McGill-Queen's University Press, 1990.

Courtney, Richard, Booth, D., Emerson, J. and Kuzmich, N. *No One Way of Being: The Practical Knowledge of Elementary Arts Teachers in Ontario*, Research Report. Toronto: Ministry of Education, Government of Ontario, 1988.

Craggs, C. *Media Education in the Primary School*. London: Routledge, 1992.

Crinson, J. and Westgate, D. "Drama Techniques in Modern Language Learning," *The British Journal of Language Teaching*, Vol. 24, No. 1 Spring, 1986.

Dale, Roger, Esland, Geoff, and MacDonald, Madeleine (eds.). *Schooling and Capitalism*. London: Henley Routledge & Kegan Paul, 1976.

Dawson, Anthony. *Watching Shakespeare*. Basingstroke: Macmillan, 1988.

Department of Communications (Ottawa), *The Future of the National Theatre School of Canada*, Jean-Louis Roux, (Chair), 1988.

De Rohan, Pierre (ed.). *Federal Theatre Plays*. New York: Da Capo Press, 1973.

Dewey, John. *Art as Experience*. London: Allen and Unwin, 1934.

Eisner, Elliott. *The Educational Imagination*. New York: Macmillan, 1979.

――. *Learning and Teaching the Ways of Knowing*, 84th Yearbook of the NSSE, Part II. Chicago: University of Chicago Press, 1985.

Elam, K. *The Semiotics of Theatre and Drama*. London: Routledge, 1991.

Errington, Edward. "Researching Drama Classsrooms in the Nineties: Towards a Critical Perspective," paper presented at the World Congress of Drama Education, Oporto, Portugal, 1992.

369

ELT Documents 129. *Academic Writing — Process and Product*. Modern English Publications in association with The British Council, 1988.

Esslin, M. *The Field of Drama*. London: Methuen, 1987.

Ferguson, B. "Practical Work and Pedagogy," *Screen Education*, Vol. 38, Spring, 1981.

Filewood, Alan. *Collective Encounters: Documentary Theatre in English Canada*. Toronto: University of Toronto Press, 1987.

Foucoult, M. *The Archaeology of Knowledge*. London: Tavistock, 1978.

Freire, P. *Cultural Action for Freedom*. Cambridge, MA: Harvard Educational Review, 1970.

————. *Pedagogy of the Oppressed*. New York: Continuum Press, 1984.

Fulgham, Robert. *All I Really Need to Know I Learned in Kindergarten*. New York: Villard, 1989.

Garbarino, James, Guttman, Edna, and Seeley, Janice Wilson. *The Psychologically Battered Child*. San Francisco: Jossey-Bass, 1987.

Gardner, Howard. *Frames of Mind: The Theory of Multiple Intelligences*. New York: Basic Books, 1983.

Gardner, R. *The Dramatic Script and Procedural Knowledge: A Key to Understanding of Dramatic Structure and a Foundation for the Development of Effective Curriculum Design in Dramatic Instruction at the Tertiary Level*, Ph.D. Thesis, University of Toronto. OISE, 1983.

Glasgow Koste, Virginia. *Dramatic Play in Childhood: Rehearsal for Life*. New Orleans: Anchorage Press, 1978.

Grahame, J. *The English Curriculum: Media 1. Years 7–9*. London: English and Media Centre, 1991.

Green, L.R. and Sawywr, H.M. *Write Your Own Storyboard*. New York: Macmillan, 1985.

Grundy, S. *Curriculum: Product or Praxis*. Basingstoke: Falmer, 1987.

Halliday, M.A.K. *Language as Social Semiotic*. London: Edward Arnold, 1987.

————. *Spoken and Written Language*. Oxford: Oxford University Press, 1990.

Halliday, M.A.K. and Hasan, R. *Language, Context and Text*. Oxford: Oxford University Press, 1985.

Heathcote, Dorothy. *Three Looms Waiting*. A BBC *Omnibus* programme, Ipswitch England: Concord Films, 1972.

————. *Collected Writings on Education and Drama*. Liz Johnstone and Cecily O'Neill (eds.). London: Hutchinson, 1984.

Heathcote, Dorothy, and Herbert, Phyl. "A Drama of Learning: The Mantle of the Expert," *Theory into Practice*, Vol. 24, No. 3, 1985.

Herrigel, Eugen. *Zen in the Art of Archery*. New York: Vintage Books, 1981.

Hodge, R. and Kress, G.R. *Social Semiotics*. Ithaca, N.Y.: Polity Press, 1989.

Hodge and Tripp. *Children and Television*. London: Polity, 1986.

Hunt, Albert. *Hopes for Great Happenings*. London: Methuen, 1976.

Illich, Ivan and Sanders, Barry. *ABC: The Alphabetization of the Popular Mind*. New York: Vintage Books, 1989.

Jennings, Sue. *Remedial Drama*. London: Adam and Charles Black, 1984.

Johnstone, Keith. *Impro: Improvisation and the Theatre*. London: Faber & Faber, 1979.

Kallaway, Peter (ed.). *Apartheid and Education*. Johannesburg: Ravan Press, 1984.

Kase-Polisini, Judith (ed.). *Creative Drama in a Developmental Context*. Lanham: University of America Press, 1985.

Kaysen, C. (ed). *Content and Context: Essays on College Education*. New York: McGraw Hill Book Company, 1973.

Kelly, Elizabeth Flory. "Curriculum Drama." In Nellie McCaslin (ed.), *Children and Drama*, 2nd ed. New York: Longman, 1981.

Kress, G.R. *Linguistic Processes in Socio-cultural Practice*. Geelong: Deakin University Press, 1985.

———. *Learning to Write*. London: Routledge & Kegan Paul, 1982.

Kristeva, J. *The Kristeva Reader*. T. Moi (ed.). Oxford: Blackwell, 1986.

Laban, Rudolf. *A Life for Dance*. Lisa Ullmann (trans.). London: MacDonald & Evans Ltd., 1975.

———. *Modern Educational Dance*. Revised and enlarged by Lisa Ullmann. London: MacDonald & Evans Ltd., 1975.

———. *The Mastery of Movement*. Revised and enlarged by Lisa Ullmann. London: MacDonald & Evans Ltd., 1980.

Levete, Gina. *No Handicap to Dance*. London: Souvenir Press, 1982.

Lewis, R. *The Videomaker's Handbook*. London: Pan, 1987.

Mackie, Robert (ed.). *Literacy and Revolution: The Pedagogy of Paulo Freire*. London: Pluto Press, 1988.

Madeja, S. (ed.). *Arts and Aesthetics: An Agenda for the Future*. St. Louis, MI: CEMREL Inc., 1977.

Marowitz, Charles. *Act of Being*. New York: Taplinger, 1978.

Masterman, L. *Teaching the Media*. New York: Macmillan, 1985.

Maxwell, M.P. "The Arts Curriculum and University Reform" in W. Shere and R. Duhamel (eds.), *Academic Futures: Prospects for Post-Secondary Education*. Toronto: OISE Press, 1983.

McCaslin, Nellie (ed.). *Children and Drama*. New York: Longman Inc., 1981.

McLaren, Peter. *Schooling as a Ritual Performance: Towards a Political Economy of Educational Symbols and Gestures*. London: Routledge and Kegan Paul, 1986.

———. "The Liminal Servant and the Ritual Roots of Critical Pedagogy," *Language Arts*, 65, 1988.

———. *Life in Schools: An Introduction to Critical Pedagogy in the Foundations of Education*. New York: Longman, 1989.

McLaren, P. and Silva, T.T.D. "Decentering Pedagogy: Critical Literacy, Resistance and the Politics of Memory." In P. McLaren and P. Leonard (eds.), *Paulo Freire: A Critical Encounter*. London: Routledge, 1993.

McLeod, John. "Change and Development,", in the On-Site Proceedings of the International Symposium for Drama Education Research, OISE, May 1989.

———. *Drama is Real Pretending*. Victoria, Australia: Ministry of Education, 1989.

Miller, J. and Seller, W. *Curriculum: Perpsectives and Practice*. New York: Longman, 1985.

Millerson, G. *Video Production Handbook*. London: Focal Press, 1987.

Moon, Celia. "Addressing Social Issues in the Drama Classroom." In E. Errington (ed.), *Arts Education*. Victoria: Deakin University Press, 1993.

Moore, Thomas. *Care of the Soul*. New York: Harper Collins Publishers Inc., 1992.

Morgan, Norah and Saxton, Juliana. *Teaching Drama: A Mind of Many Wonders*. London: Hutchinson, 1987.

Morrison, J. *The Maturing of the Arts on the American Campus*. Lanham: University Press of America, 1985.

Morrow, Gertrude. *The Compassionate School*. Englewood Cliffs, N.J.: Prentice Hall, 1987.

Nachmanovitch, Stephen. *Free Play: The Power of Improvisation in Life and the Arts*. Los Angeles: Jeremy P. Tarcher Inc., 1990.

Neelands, J. *Making Sense of Drama: A Guide to Classroom Practice*. London: Heinemann, 1984.

——. *Structuring Drama Work*. Cambridge: Cambridge University Press, 1992.

——. "The Starry Messanger." In C. Lawrence (ed.), *Voices for Change*. Gosforth: National Drama Publications, 1993.

Neelands, J., Booth, D. and Ziegler, S. *Writing in Imagined Contexts: Research into Drama-influenced Writing*, No. 202. Toronto: Toronto Board of Education, 1993.

Newlove, Jean. *Laban for Actors and Dancers*. New York: Routledge Theatre Arts Books, 1993.

Norris, Joe. *Some Authorities as Co-authors in a Collective Creation Production*, doctoral dissertation, University of Alberta, 1989.

O'Neill, Cecily. "Dialogue and Drama: The Transformation of Teachers, Ideas and Events," *Language Arts*, Vol. 66, No. 2, 1989.

O'Neill, Cecily and Lambert, Alan. *Drama Structures*. London: Hutchinson, 1982.

O'Neill, Cecily, Lambert, Alan, Linnell, Rosemary, and Warr-Wood, Janet. *Drama Guidelines*. London: Heinemann Education Books in association with London Drama, 1987.

Opie, Iona and Opie, Peter. *The Lore and Language of Schoolchildren*. London: Oxford University Press, 1959.

——. *The Singing Game*. London: Oxford University Press, 1985.

O'Sullivan et al. *Key Concepts in Communication*. London: Methuen, 1983.

Parsons, Jim and Beauchamp, Larry (eds.). *Stories of Teaching*. Richmond Hill, Ont.: Scholastic Press, 1989.

Perera, K. *Children's Writing and Reading — Analysing Classroom Language*. London: Basil Blackwell, 1984.

Pinar, William (ed.). "Curerre: Toward Reconceptualization." In *Curriculum Theorizing*. Berkeley: McCutchan Publishing Corporation, 1975.

——. *Contemporary Curriculum Discourses*. Scottsdale: Gorsuch Scarisbrick Publishers, 1988.

Polyani, Michael. *Science, Faith & Society*. Chicago: University of Chicago Press, 1964.

——. *The Tacit Dimension*. New York: Anchor Books, 1967.

——. *The Study of Man*. Chicago: University of Chicago Press, 1972.

Polyani, Michael and Prosch, Harry. *Meaning*. Chicago: University of Chicago Press, 1975.

Pring, Richard. *Knowledge and Schooling*. London: Open Books, 1976.

Redington, C. *Can Theatre Teach?* Oxford: Pergamon Press, 1983.

Reid, Howard. *The Way of Harmony.* New York: Simon & Schuster, 1988.

Richards, C. "Teaching Popular Culture." In K. Jones (ed.), *English and the National Curriculum.* London: Kogan Page, Institute of Education, University of London, 1992.

Robinson, Ken (ed.). *Exploring Theatre and Education.* Heinemann Educational Books, 1980.

Rosenberg, Harold. *The Tradition of the New.* London: Paladin, 1962.

Rosenberg, Helene S. *Creative Drama and Imagination: Transforming Ideas into Action.* New York: Holt, Rinehart and Winston, 1987.

Rosenberg, Helene S. and Prendergast, Christine. *Theatre for Young People: A Sense of Occasion.* New York: Harcourt, Brace, Jovanovich, 1983.

Salutin, Rick. *1837: The Farmers' Revolt.* Toronto: James Lorimer, 1976.

Sawyer, Ruth. *The Way of the Storyteller.* Middlesex: Penguin, 1970.

Schechner, R. *Performance Theory.* London: Routledge, 1988.

———. *Between Theater and Anthropology.* Philadelphia: University of Pennsylvania Press, 1989.

Schon, Donald. *Educating the Reflective Practitioner.* San Francisco: Jossey-Bass Publishers, 1987.

Schubert, W.H. "Educationally Recovering Dewey in Curriculum," paper presented at the Annual AERA Meeting, sponsored by the John Dewey Society, Washington, D.C., April 1987.

Schwab, J.J. "The Practical 3: Translation into Curriculum" in *School Review,* Vol. 81, 1973.

Shere, W. and Duhamel, R. (eds.). *Academic Futures: Prospects for Post-Secondary Education.* Toronto: OISE Press, 1987.

Shklovsky, Victor. "Art as Technique." In Lemon and Reis (eds.), *Russian Formalist Criticism.* Omaha: University of Nebraska Press, 1965.

Slade, Peter. *Child Drama.* London: University of London Press, 1954.

———. *An Introduction to Child Drama.* 7th ed. London: Hodder and Atoughton, 1976.

Sneddon, Elizabeth. *The Power of the Spoken Word,* Bulletin 28. Natal, South Africa: Natal Education Department, 1981.

Spolin, Viola. *Improvisation for the Theatre.* Evanston: Northwestern University Press, 1983.

Stafford, R. "Redefining Creativity: Extended Project Work in GCSE Media Studies." In D. Buckingham (ed.), *Watching Media Learning.* Brighton: Falmer, 1990.

Stenhouse, L. *An Introduction to Curriculum Research and Development.* London: Heinemann Educational Books, 1975.

Tannenbaum, Abraham J. *Gifted Children.* New York: Macmillan, 1983.

Tchudi, Stephen N. (ed.). *English Teachers at Work: Ideas and Strategies from Five Countries.* New Jersey: Boynton/Cook Publishers, 1986.

Threadgold, T. "Performing Genre: Violence, the Making of Protected Subjects, and the Discourses of Critical Literacy and Radical Pedagogy," *Changing English,* Vol. 1, No. 1. Department of English, Media and Drama, Institute of Education, University of London, 1993.

Tompkins, G., Connelly, F.M. and Bernier, J.J. "State of the Art Review of Research in Curriculum and Instruction," *SSHRC*, September 1981.

Toole, J. *The Process of Drama*. London: Routledge & Kegan Paul, 1992.

Turner, Victor. *From Ritual to Theatre: The Human Seriousness of Play*. New York: Performing Arts Journal Publications, 1982.

Volosinov, V.N. *Marxism and the Philosophy of Language*. L. Matejka and I.R. Titunik (trans.). Cambridge, MA: Harvard University Press, 1973.

Vygotsky L.S. *Thought and Language*. New York: Wiley, 1962.

———. *Mind in Society*. M. Cole, V. John-Steiner, S. Scribner and E. Souberman (eds.). Cambridge, MA: Harvard University Press, 1978.

Wagner, Betty Jane. *Dorothy Heathcote: Drama as a Learning Medium*. Washington: National Educational Association of the U.S., 1976.

Wallace, Robert. "Paul Thompson at Theatre Passe Muraille," *Open Letter*, 2:7 Winter, 1974.

Warren, Bernie (ed.). *Using the Creative Arts in Therapy*. Cambridge, MA: Brookline Books, 1984.

———. *Disability & Social Performance*. Cambridge, MA: Brookline Books, 1988.

Warren, Bernie and Dunne, Tim. *Drama Games*. North York, Ont.: Captus Press, 1989.

Way, Brian. *Development Through Drama*. New York: Humanities Press, 1967.

Wertsch, J. *Voices of the Mind, A Sociocultural Approach to Mediated Action*. London and New York: Harvester Wheatsheaf, 1991.

Williams, R. *Drama in Performance*. London: Penguin Books, 1968.

———. *Marxism and Literature*. Oxford: Oxford University Press, 1977.

Witkin, Robert. *The Intelligence of Feeling*. London: Heinemann, 1974.

Wittrock, M.C. (ed). *Handbook on Research on Teaching*, 3rd ed. New York: McMillan Publishing Co., 1986.

Contributors

The late **Bert Amies MBE** was county advisor for drama and the arts in Shropshire until his retirement in 1978. From that time until his death in 1992 he continued to work as a freelance theatre director and lecturer. In 1981 he received the MBE in recognition of his work in Drama and Education.

Louise Chalmers teaches drama at John Rennie High School in Pointe Claire, Quebec. She recently completed an M.Ed. at the Ontario Institute for Studies in Education, specializing in curriculum development for arts education.

Charles E. Combs is Chair of the General Education Department at Berklee College of Music, Boston, MA. He has served as editor of the *Children's Theatre Review* and was until recently Editor of the *New England Theatre Journal*.

Richard Courtney was, until his recent retirement, a Professor in Arts Education at the Ontario Institute for Studies in Education, a post he held for over 20 years. He is the author of more than 200 publications, including over 30 books.

Lynn Dalrymple is Professor and Head of the Department of Drama at the University of Zululand, South Africa. She conducted and published extensive research in the potential of educational drama and theatre in South Africa, as well as curriculum development in relation to educational drama and theatre and arts advocacy.

Anton Franks taught drama for 10 years in inner London schools. Currently, he is a part-time lecturer in Drama and English in Education at the University of London Institute of Education, while also working as a researcher and lecturer in Drama Education at the Central School of Speech and Drama in London. He is studying for his Ph.D. at the London Institute of Education, researching into Drama Education and Cultural Theory.

Jeffrey Goffin teaches Drama at the University of Calgary and is also a playwright and freelance journalist. He recently conducted research into collective creations in the Phillipines as part of a programme sponsored by the Canada-Asia Partnership.

Belarie Hyman-Zatzman is an Assistant Professor in Department of Fine Arts at Atkinson College, York University. She teaches courses in Drama in Education and improvisation and does Arts Education consulting in Toronto.

Sandra Katz is head of the Drama department at Thomas L. Kennedy Secondary School in Mississauga, Ontario. She has an M.Ed. from the Ontario Institute of Studies in Education at the University of Toronto and is currently a doctoral candidate specializing in Drama in Education.

Yuriko Kobayashi has a M.Ed. in Early Childhood Education (Tokyo Gakugei University), MA in Theatre (EMU) and M.F.A. in Drama/ Theatre for the Young(EMU). She now teaches courses in drama for Early Childhood Education at Kawamura Gakuen Woman's University, Japan.

Barbara Mackay is Associate Vice-Rector (Academic) at Concordia University and an Associate Professor in the Department of Theatre, in which she taught for nearly 20 years. She has researched the published several articles on storytelling and face painting in dramatherapy and is on the editorial board of *The Arts in Psychotherapy*.

George Mager C.M. is a Professor of Educational Psychology at McGill University. He is co-artistic director (with Bernie Warren) of *50/50 Theatre Company*. He has written extensively on the arts and integration and recently received the Order of Canada in recognition of his work on the integration and education of persons with a disability through dance and drama.

Alistair Martin-Smith is an Assistant Professor at the School of Dramatic Art of the University of Windsor. Trained initially as an actor at Canada's National Theatre School, he later trained with Dorothy Heathcote in England, and subsequently taught extensively in Toronto's public school system.

John McLeod is a freelance research and evaluation consultant in the youth, disability services and health fields in Victoria, Australia. Formerly a Senior Lecturer in Drama at the University of Melbourne, he has published extensively in the fields of drama and arts education, and curriculum development.

Joe Norris is an Associate Professor with the Department of Secondary Education at the University of Alberta. He is presently president of the Alberta Fine Arts Council of Alliance for Theatre and Education. He was also a founding member and president of the Educational Drama Association of Nova Scotia.

Cecily O'Neill is an Associate Professor in Speech/Theatre at Ohio State University. Previously, she was Drama Warden of the Inner London Education authority. She is co-author of *Drama Guidelines and Drama Structures* and co-editor of *Dorothy Heathcote: Collected Writings on Education and Drama.*

Ron Richard has recently completed his doctoral studies at McGill University in Montreal, Quebec, where his research and teaching focused on Educational Drama and the integration of students with disabilities into the regular school. He has been a professional actor, director and playwright in a number of theatre companies dedicated to theatre for young audiences, as well as theatre for persons with disabilities.

Sheila Robbie is currently Lecturer in English at the Universidade do Algarve in Faro, Portugal, where her work involves language and didactics. An Honours graduate in Hispanic Studies with Drama, she is now working on a doctorate at the Institute of Education, University of London, which examines the use of drama for the improvement of writing abilities.

Lorelei Rogers was, until recently, academic co-ordinator of the in-service program in The Faculty of Education at the University of Calgary. Prior to this, she worked for over twenty years in public schools in Saskatchewan and Alberta as a teacher, librarian and media specialist. She has written numerous articles on the use of computers in education and on professional development for teachers.

Terrence Slater has an Honours BA in English Literature from York University, Toronto and an MA in Drama from the University of Toronto. He trained in the work of Rudolf Laban at Drama Centre London, London, England from which he graduated in the three-year programme in acting. He has been a professional actor in stage, television and film for over fifteen years.

Bernie Warren is a Professor of Dramatic Art at the University of Windsor. He was co-founder of *50/50 Theatre Company* in Montreal and is currently Artistic Director of *Prospero's Fools* in Windsor. He has written extensively on drama and theatre as art forms and as vehicles for social and personal change.

Rob Watling is a part-time Lecturer in Media Studies at The Nottigham Trent University. Previously he taught at West Glamorgan Institute of Higher Education. He is currently completing a Ph.D. in Media Studies at the University of Nottingham. He is a co-author of *Social Drama*.

Keith Yon was, until his recent retirement, a Senior Lecturer in the Department of Theatre at the Dartington College Campus of the University of Plymouth. He has researched and published extensively on vocal education and on the arts and disability. In addition, he has lectured and conducted master classes throughout the world.

*I*ndex